Universal Meta Data Models

Universal Meta Data Models

David Marco
Michael Jennings

Wiley Publishing, Inc.

Vice President and Executive Group Publisher: Richard Swadley
Vice President and Executive Publisher: Bob Ipsen
Vice President and Publisher: Joseph B. Wikert
Executive Editorial Director: Mary Bednarek
Executive Editor: Robert M. Elliott
Editorial Manager: Kathryn A. Malm
Senior Production Manager: Fred Bernardi
Senior Development Editor: Emilie Herman
Production Editor: Felicia Robinson
Media Development Specialist: Travis Silvers
Permissions Editor: Laura Moss
Text Design & Composition: Wiley Composition Services

Library of Congress Cataloging-in-Publication Data: Available from Publisher.

ISBN: 0-471-08177-9

Printed in the United States of America

10 9 8 7 6 5 4 3 2 1

I thank Melinda for being the best partner a man could ask for and I thank God for blessing me in every way a person can be.

David Marco

With determination and focus, you can achieve anything; with uncertainty and doubt, you will never begin.

Michael Jennings

Contents

Acknowledgments

As the authors of this book, both David Marco of EWSolutions and Michael Jennings of Hewitt Associates feel very fortunate to have had a great deal of assistance in this major undertaking. First, we would like to thank Allstate and RBC Financial Group for agreeing to share their world-class MME implementations with the rest of the industry. Second, there are a number of people who deserve many thanks for all of their hard work in making this book a possibility. Following is a list of the people who have helped in making this book a reality:

- Art D'Silva, RBC Financial Group
- John Faulkenberry, EWSolutions
- Linda Hall, Allstate
- Steve Hoberman, Mars Candy
- Min Wichelhaus-Hsu, EWSolutions
- Bill Lewis, EWSolutions
- Bill Loggins, EWSolutions
- Todd Moore, RBC Financial Group
- Mike Reed, EWSolutions
- Piera Riemersma, Covansys
- Mohammad Rifaie, RBC Financial Group
- Doug Stacey, Allstate
- Debbi Walsh, EWSolutions
- Ethan Kayes, Ingrid Nuber, Robin Salk, Hewitt Associates

Any time a book this size and scope is written there are several special people that deserve appreciation. We were fortunate to have an outstanding group of contributing authors working with us on this effort.

- Attila Finta, A & M Consulting
- Mark Riggle, EWSolutions
- Dan Roth, Bookspan

Attila Finta did an outstanding job on Chapter 6, "Universal Meta Model for IT Portfolio ." Attila is a longtime meta data practitioner, and his knowledge on the subject and professionalism were invaluable to this project.

Mark Riggle had one of the most difficult tasks of this book project, working on Chapter 5 "Universal Meta Model for XML, Messaging, and Business Transactions." Mark's knowledge of object-oriented modeling techniques, XML, and CWM were critical to ensuring the highest standards possible in Chapter 6.

Last, but certainly not least, Dan Roth performed yeoman's work on Chapter 7, "Universal Meta Model for Business Rules, Business Meta Data, and Data Stewardship." Dan did a very good job on this chapter, and his work and dedication were greatly appreciated.

We would like to sincerely thank Bob Elliott and Emilie Herman of Wiley Publishing, Inc. for their belief in this book and their tremendous work helping make this project a reality. Quite simply, they are the very best book publishers in the industry.

Finally, we would like to thank our families (Melinda, Janette, Leslie, Jay), loved ones, friends, and colleagues who have always supported and loved us through the good times and the less than good times.

David Marco
Michael Jennings

About the Authors

David Marco

Mr. Marco is an internationally recognized expert in the fields of data warehousing, enterprise architecture, and business intelligence, and is the world's foremost authority on meta data. He is the author of the widely acclaimed book *Building and Managing the Meta Data Repository* (John Wiley & Sons, 2000). This groundbreaking book has been broadly endorsed by many of the largest software companies in the industry and by several major magazines. In addition, he is a coauthor of *Impossible Data Warehouse Situations and Solutions From The Experts* (Addison-Wesley, 2002 and *Data Resource Management* (DAMA International, 2000. Mr. Marco also serves as the executive editor of *Real-World Decision Support*, a widely read electronic newsletter focusing on business intelligence, enterprise architecture, and meta data management topics (www.EWSolutions.com/newsletter.asp). Mr. Marco has published over 110 articles and is a regular columnist for several technology magazines. Mr. Marco has been selected as a judge in the 1998–2003 *DM Review* World-Class Solutions, 2002 TDWI Pioneering Solutions and 1999–2002 Microsoft Industry Solutions awards. In addition, Mr. Marco was nominated for Crain's Chicago Business 2003 Top 40, Under 40 List, and was a finalist for the 2000 DAMA Individual IT Achievement award.

Mr. Marco is a highly sought after speaker and has given over 120 keynote addresses and courses at the major data warehousing and meta data repository conferences throughout the world. Mr. Marco has taught at the University of Chicago's Graham School and DePaul University, and is the founder and President of Enterprise Warehousing Solutions, Inc. (EWSolutions), a GSA schedule and Chicago-headquartered strategic partner and systems integrator dedicated to providing companies and large government agencies with best-in-class business intelligence solutions using data warehousing and meta data repository technologies (866) EWS-1100 or visit www.EWSolutions.com. At EWSolutions he serves clients as an architect, project manager, and meta data manager, and has provided the vision and strategy across multiple project teams for numerous successful data warehousing projects. He may be reached via email at DMarco@EWSolutions.com

Michael Jennings

Michael Jennings is a recognized industry expert in data warehousing, enterprise architecture, and meta data. He is an enterprise architect and global data warehousing strategist in the human resources outsourcing (HRO) technology architecture practice at Hewitt Associates. Michael has more than 20 years of information technology experience in the manufacturing, telecommunications, insurance, and human resources industries. He has published over 50 industry articles and is a monthly columnist for *DM Review Magazine*, writing the "Enterprise Architecture View" column, and is a panel member for the magazine's online column "Ask the Experts." Michael has been a judge for the 2002 & 2003 *DM Review* World-Class Solutions Awards and 2003 Wilshire Award for Best Practices in Meta Data Management. He speaks frequently on business intelligence/architecture issues at major industry conferences and has been an instructor of information technology at the University of Chicago's Graham School. Michael is a contributing author to the book *Building and Managing the Meta Data Repository*. He can be reached at (847) 295-5000, email at mike.jennings@hewitt.com. Hewitt Associates (www.hewitt.com) is a global human resources outsourcing and consulting firm. It provides services from offices in 38 countries.

Attila Finta

Attila Finta is an independent IT consultant with extensive hands-on experience in information management, specializing in data architecture, data analysis, database design, and data management, with a focus on meta data repository, data warehousing/business intelligence, and XML. His career has also included applications development, IT training, technology management, systems planning, business process reengineering, and project management.

Mr. Finta's niche is the end-to-end planning and implementation of decision support solutions, including business requirements analysis, technical architecture, design, specification, testing, and validation of data warehouses, marts, and operational data stores and their end-user analysis/reporting mechanisms and meta data infrastructure. He has worked on these types of systems in the manufacturing, retail, telecommunications, financial services, insurance, pharmaceutical, petroleum, media, e-commerce, and airline industries and for the federal government.

He is a past officer in DAMA (Data Management Association) at the local and international levels, and has presented at numerous conferences and training seminars on the topics of business intelligence implementation and pragmatic enterprise data management.

Mark Riggle

Mark Riggle has done software research and development for more than 20 years. He has published and taught in the fields of software design, artificial intelligence, programming language design, business intelligence, and data warehousing. He has a BSEE from the University of Maryland and a graduate degree in Computer Science from Rice University.

Dan Roth

Daniel Roth is an information architect with experience in health insurance, warehouse/distribution, banking, and manufacturing. He has many years of data processing experience as an application programmer, a technical support specialist, a DBA, and most recently a data architect. He has been the lead architect on large OLTP and OLAP projects.

Introduction

Corporations and government agencies spend billions of dollars annually on information technology (IT) applications, hardware, software, and middleware, and the personnel that build and use these applications. All of these IT "touch points" generate meta data, which these organizations need to effectively manage in order to optimize and efficiently manage this multi-billion-dollar investment. These corporations are implementing managed meta data environments (MME) to provide a systematic enterprise solution for meta data management.

This book is a follow up to *Building and Managing the Meta Data Repository* (Wiley, 2000). All too often, the meta data repository is mistaken for the *complete* meta data management solution; however, this is not the case. The MME is the complete enterprise meta data management solution, of which a meta data repository is one six MME components.

The first part of this book examines the genesis of the MME, the reasons why it is so vital to all enterprises, and the return on investment (ROI) that it provides. Chapter 3 offers a series of MME use examples, across several industries, and presents two corporations that have successfully built world-class MME implementations. The second part of this book presents physical meta data models that tackle the most common meta model implementations and illustrate the fundamental meta modeling techniques, tools, and concepts that are a must for any data modeler. The final chapter combines all of the meta data subject area models into one encompassing enterprise meta model.

How This Book Is Organized

This book is broken into two parts. Part One illustrates the specific value that an MME can provide to your organization (Chapter 1), then gives an overview of the architectural components of the MME (Chapter 2). Various MME use cases—across several industries—along with two corporations that have world-class MME solutions are presented in Chapter 3.

Part Two presents physical meta models for the MME meta data repository. Here you will learn how to model a meta data repository for the following meta data subjects:

- Enterprise systems (Chapter 4)

- XML, messaging, and business transactions (Chapter 5)

- IT portfolio management (Chapter 6)

- Business rules, business meta data, and data stewardship (Chapter 7)

- Complete universal meta model with all meta data subject areas (Chapter 8), which merges the meta models in Chapters 4 to 7 into one meta model

At the end of the book, we've included a list of helpful resources as well as a glossary of meta data terminology. There is an old saying that real life is funnier than any fictional comedy. In this spirit, we share "war" stories from the field throughout the book. Some of these stories will simply entertain, while others may seem strangely familiar. We hope that you find all of them useful in determining what to do . . . and sometimes what not to do.

Who Should Read This Book

MMEs, meta data, and meta data management solutions are "must have" applications for any large corporation or government agency. As a result, a variety of people will need to understand this topic, including:

Business users.   The MME makes the information in operational applications and data warehousing systems much more valuable to the business because meta data provides the semantic layer between these IT systems and their business users.

IT managers.   The IT manager can use a MME to deliver significant value to the business units that the manager supports. In addition, an MME can make this person's development staff much more productive and cut the development costs for the department.

IT developers.   The developer will learn the fundamental architectural components of an MME. In addition, the IT developer will learn the necessary techniques and strategies for modeling a meta data repository.

Project sponsors.   Solving business problems is at the heart of the MME. The project sponsor(s) needs to be aware of this to allow gains to be made.

We assume that you are already familiar with basic meta data concepts and terminology. If not, we recommend checking out www.EWSolutions.com for more information. We also strongly recommend that you read *Building and Managing the Meta Data Repository* first, because this book builds on the fundamentals found there and often references chapters that offer more information on the topics discussed.

Tools You Will Need

The data models presented in Part Two of the book were created using Computer Associate's ERwin data-modeling product version 3.5. If you wish to explore or modify these models you will need to obtain this software (www.ca.com). The data quality meta data mart presented in Chapter 8 was created using Cognos Powerplay Transformer version 7.0, and the screen shots of the reports were created using Cognos Powerplay version 7.0. Readers wishing to analyze the design of the cube or generate additional reports from the sample data should obtain this software (www.cognos.com).

What's on the CD-ROM and Web Site

The CD-ROM accompanying the book contains the data models and meta data mart files described in Part Two of the book. The data model files are available on the CD-ROM in both Adobe Portable Document Format (PDF), for easy review and printing, and in Computer Associate's Erwin file format for analysis and modification. The files used to design and create the data quality meta data mart presented in Chapter 8 are also on the CD-ROM. The Cognos Powerplay files used to design and create the Online Application Programming (OLAP cube plus the source data files in comma separated format (CSV) are provided.

A 30-day trial version of Computer Associate's AllFusion ERwin Data Modeler product for use with the data model files (.ER1) and a shareware version of Adobe Reader for use with the PDF files (.pdf) is provided for your use.

Please refer to Appendix B for more information on the CD-ROM.

The companion website for this book will be www.EWSolutions.com/book.asp. On this Web site we will have an updated list of MME vendors with links to their websites, the most comprehensive meta data information center with, links to hundreds of articles, meta data research study statistics, additional information about the authors, and much, much more.

PART

One

Presenting the Managed Meta Data Environment

Part One of this book is designed to assist government agencies and corporations of all sizes to implement a successful Managed Meta Data Environment (MME). In Chapter 1, we examine the genesis of the MME, the reasons why it is so vital to all enterprises, and the return on investment (ROI) that it can provide. Chapter 2 focuses on the six major architectural components of the MME and the fundamentals around them. Chapter 3 walks you through an MME, providing examples in several industries, and presents two corporations that have successfully built world-class MME implementations

Overview of the Managed Meta Data Environment

The key to your company's prosperity is how well you gather, retain, and disseminate knowledge. Managed meta data environments are the key to gathering, retaining, and disseminating knowledge. The Managed Meta Data Environment (MME) provides tremendous value to companies and government organizations that are struggling to effectively manage their data and their information technology (IT) applications. This chapter identifies the most common ways an MME can help corporations and government agencies achieve a strategic advantage over their competition. We begin with the evolution of the MME, then move on to discuss the common objectives and challenges that corporations must address today and how the MME can assist in meeting them.

Evolution of the Managed Meta Data Environment

Even the earliest computer systems contained knowledge that was necessary for building, using, and maintaining IT systems. Meta data existed throughout every organization, including:

- Enterprise systems (customer relationship management [CRM], enterprise resource planning [ERP], data warehousing, supply chain)

- Technical processes (operational systems, desktop applications, documents, spreadsheets)
- Business processes (corporate Web site, e-business)
- Messaging/transactions (Enterprise Application Integration [EAI], Web services, Extensible Markup Language [XML])
- Software tools
- Organizational policies
- People (business partners, vendors, customers, IT staff)

Chapter 2 discusses these meta data sources in more detail.

By the 1970s, we needed a place to store this information (or meta data). This required data about the data—or meta data—used in computer systems. For a more detailed discussion of this topic, refer to Chapter 1 of *Building and Managing the Meta Data Repository* (Wiley, 2000).

Many companies are rushing to begin building meta data repositories, in spite of a slow world economy where the technology industry, in particular, has shrunk dramatically. This is happening because companies are realizing that they need to make significant investments in their MME applications in order for their IT systems to provide sustainable value, to disseminate corporate knowledge, and to manage skyrocketing IT expenditures.

The MME has six major architectural components: a meta data sourcing layer, a meta data integration layer, a meta data repository, a meta data management layer, meta data marts, and a meta data delivery layer. Chapter 2 covers these in detail, but following is a brief overview. The meta data sourcing layer extracts meta data from its source and brings it into the meta data integration layer or directly into the meta data repository itself. The meta data integration layer takes the various sources of meta data, integrates them, and loads the meta data into the meta data repository. The meta data repository is responsible for the cataloging and persistent physical storage of the meta data and pointers to the meta data in a distributed meta data environment. The meta data management layer provides systematic management of the meta data repository and the other MME components, while the meta data marts provide a database structure, usually sourced from a meta data repository, designed for a homogenous meta data user group. Finally, the meta data delivery layer delivers the meta data from the repository to the end users and any applications or tools that require meta data.

Typical Managed Meta Data Environment Objectives

The managed meta data environment represents the architectural components, people and processes that are required to properly and systematically gather, retain and disseminate meta data throughout the enterprise. A sound MME architecture can meet the varied and complex meta data management requirements of even the largest organizations (see Figure 1.1). The key components of the MME are:

- Meta data sourcing layer
- Meta data integration layer
- Meta data repository
- Meta data management layer
- Meta data marts
- Meta data delivery layer

Chapter 2 discusses each component of the MME in greater detail.

Chapter 3 looks at several industry-specific examples of how the MME provides significant value, including two world-class MME initiatives from Allstate and RBC Financial Group. Although these MME initiatives vary in scope and application, they all have one common thread: each clearly identifies and resolves specific business challenges. This begs the question: What is a good business objective for an MME? Good MME objectives include:

- Increase revenue and/or decrease costs
- Promote public health
- Adhere to regulations
- Improve national security
- Provide education
- Ensure public safety

The following sections discuss each of these objectives in greater detail.

Increase Revenue and/or Decrease Costs

Increasing revenue and decreasing costs are the most fundamental drivers for any MME initiative. These two distinct business drivers should govern any IT initiative, whether it is data warehousing, CRM, ERP, or a supply chain management (SCM) system.

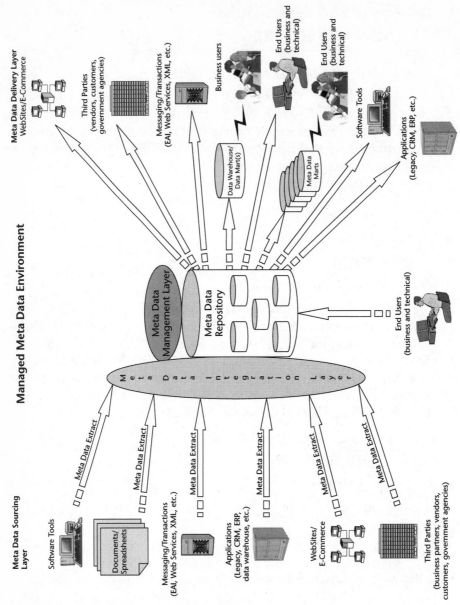

Figure 1.1   Managed Meta Data Environment.

The goal of most every senior executive is to increase shareholder value (stock price). Most have large financial incentives based on company stock performance. For example, in late 1978 Lee Iacocca took over automotive manufacturer Chrysler (now part of DaimlerChrysler). Chrysler had suffered tremendous corporate losses that required a government loan to keep the company financially viable. Lee Iacocca was hired to turn the company around and make it profitable again, a huge task indeed. One would imagine that such a job would pay the chief executive officer (CEO) very well. In Lee Iacocca's case, the starting salary that he negotiated was one dollar. He stated that he should only be paid if he increased shareholder value. Therefore, the bulk of his compensation depended on the stock price of the company. How much did Mr. Iacocca make during his tenure of running Chrysler? Over $20.5 million! ("The Dollar-a-Year Man," Ari Weinberg, http://forbes.com/2002/05/08/0508iacocca.html, May 8, 2002). This is slightly more than some of us had made during that same time period.

The majority of senior executive compensation is based on company performance, which leads to the question: How does an executive increase the stock price of his or her corporation? The obvious answer is by increasing revenues and decreasing costs.

When defining the business goals of your MME, it is critical that you illustrate how your MME effort increases revenues and/or decreases expenses. Defining how the company's MME will increase revenues and/or decrease costs increases the likelihood that your project will be approved and guarantees that you will have executive management's support.

Promote Public Health

For pharmaceutical companies, healthcare insurance providers, hospitals, and certain government agencies, a key objective is increasing customer health. Suppose that a pharmaceutical company is developing a new drug (the pharmaceutical industry refers to these as "compounds") that is designed to help people lose weight. However, the drug has a horrific side effect—it increases pancreatic cancer rates. If this drug were to make it successfully through the clinical trials and become widely marketed and sold, eventually this terrible side effect would be discovered. In addition to the public health issues, the impact of this situation would be devastating to the pharmaceutical company. Revenues would be greatly diminished for the new drug and the negative publicity could adversely affect sales of all of the company's drugs. In addition, costs would skyrocket because of the barrage of legal actions that would most likely follow.

Let's look at a more positive example of the value of saving lives. Suppose that a healthcare insurance provider could lower the mortality rates of its policyholders. This would have tremendous value to the corporation, because cost outlays for mortalities are significant. In addition, deceased policyholders, obviously, no longer pay for healthcare insurance. If you can build an MME that can address these types of issues, senior executives are very likely to fund and support your initiative.

Adhere to Regulations

Almost all corporations have to adhere to a variety of regulatory requirements. With the front-page scandals of Enron, Arthur Anderson, Adelphia, and Tyco (just to name a few), there is a movement to make government regulations more pervasive and punitive. Many newer forms of legislation are designed to do much more than just assign financial penalties to a corporation; they put executives in jail for more egregious infractions. Certainly industries like pharmaceuticals, insurance, automotive manufacturing, and banking and various government agencies are acutely aware of these regulations.

In the previous section, we walked through a hypothetical situation where a pharmaceutical company creates a new weight loss drug that inadvertently increases pancreatic cancer rates. If the pharmaceutical company violated one or more of the regulatory requirements during the clinical trial for that drug, senior executives could be imprisoned for violating the regulations of the FDA (Food and Drug Administration).

MMEs that facilitate the adherence to regulatory requirements will find a great deal of acceptance within companies, especially if they will keep the company's senior executives out of jail. Chapter 3 offers specific examples how companies are using MMEs to address government and industry regulations.

Improve National Security

Anyone working in a defense-oriented corporation or in any branch of the armed forces is keenly aware of the need for national security. During our work with several arms of the Department of Defense (DoD), one of the themes that became clear is that the return on investment (ROI) of national security is infinite. As the old saying goes, "You may have every treasure the world has to offer, but if you are not safe, than you have nothing."

Military organizations have two distinct modes of operation: wartime and peacetime. Often when people think of a military organization, they think of military conflict. However, the vast majority of military activities have very little to do with combat engagements. The U.S. military manages the world's largest distribution chain and performs a wide array of activities, including:

- Distributing food rations
- Humanitarian services
- Information gathering
- Security
- Rescues

- Transportation
- Combat operations

Despite the jokes we all know and the rhetoric of many politicians, military organizations are very concerned with decreasing costs (really). Along with this desire, these organizations are chiefly concerned with the wartime and peacetime activities in the previous list. Certainly an MME can target these activities, and there is a significant trend in many military organizations toward building MMEs.

Provide Education

Schools and universities are always concerned with decreasing costs; however, they are equally concerned with being perceived as exceptional centers of study and learning. The reputation of a university or school is critical for increasing enrollment, improving the quality of the accepted students, and increasing alumni donations. Most of these types of organizations have very small IT departments and pretty limited systems, but they still build MMEs to support their efforts. The scope of these MMEs is also small compared to that of the MMEs of Global 2000 companies and larger government agencies.

Ensure Public Safety

Ensuring public safety is a different objective from improving national security, which we discussed earlier. The major difference between these two drivers is the scope of the business objectives. Improving national security has a worldwide scope, while ensuring public safety has a more local flavor. For example, local police organizations and security organizations are highly focused on ensuring public safety. The U.S. National Guard and Coast Guard are focused at a national level, and the U.S. Army, Navy, Air Force, and Marines are focused on a worldwide scale.

Facing Corporate Challenges with an MME

The balance sheet of most any *Forbes* Global 2000 company would show entries for assets such as property, cash, equipment, and accounts receivable. Unfortunately, one item that is not seen in the asset section of the balance sheet is data. Data is every bit as valuable as property, equipment, and accounts receivable. Low-quality data, poorly understood data, mismanaged data, redundant applications, and poorly built applications prevent companies from effectively managing their other assets. How can a company convert accounts receivables into cash when the accounts receivable system has transaction records with data quality issues that prevent them from ever becoming billable? Moreover, all of the needlessly redundant applications create a substantial cost drain on the enterprise's cash assets (see the "Reduce IT Redundancy" section later in this chapter).

This is an especially important concept because all companies are desperately trying to increase shareholder value. Corporate executives spend numerous hours looking for ways to increase their company's value, because 95 percent of these executives' compensation is directly linked to shareholder value. They realize that shareholder value is tied not just to the assets on the balance sheet, but also to nonphysical factors (for example, intellectual capital, customer loyalty, brand recognition). Moreover, CEOs and CIOs are using successful technology implementations as trophies to improve shareholder value by enhancing the company's reputation as an innovator and by attracting better employee talent.

Understanding and leveraging technology is critical for any enterprise. The average company spends 5.3 percent of its gross revenues on its IT applications. This means that a company with $1 billion in revenues spends, on average, $53 million annually on their IT systems. Several *Fortune* 50 companies and large government organizations have IT budgets that approach or exceed $1 billion annually. These same organizations have implemented systems to manage almost every aspect of their business, including payroll systems, accounts receivable applications, order entry systems, marketing campaign management, human resources systems, logistics, invoicing applications, and even systems to track the placement of office furniture and employee holidays. In fact, a great number of the same organizations have systems (though unauthorized) that manage the weekly football pool. Despite this massive investment, most companies do not have an application to systematically manage their IT systems. This reveals a fundamental truth about data management:

> *We build systems to manage every aspect of our business, except one to manage the systems themselves.*

Despite spending these exorbitant amounts on IT, most companies still do not value data as an asset, whether on the balance sheet or in the board room. Most companies' IT development process can best be described as piecemeal. Typically, systems are built through "heroic effort" by a group of developers and business users who get together to implement a new application (for example, data warehousing, customer relationship management, enterprise resource planning). These heroes embark on a perilous journey to understand the existing (and often convoluted) system's architecture, work many long hours, make business assumptions with little or no common business understanding, and then hope that their efforts will be successful. This situation explains why 60 percent to 75 percent of large IT initiatives fail. Even successful initiatives may not be repeatable, because an application development process is not in place and the standards for building the application have not been formulated or documented. Moreover, even those companies whose IT processes are repeatable find that they can be repeated only by a single group of developers. Their work and effort cannot be transferred to other groups. Even with a failure rate so high and an investment in IT so great, most companies still do not manage their applications systematically.

An MME can manage a company's systems by cataloging all of the applications, data, processes, hardware, software (technical meta data), and business knowledge (business meta data) possessed by an organization. This information (meta data) can then be utilized to identify redundancies before they occur and to eliminate duplication that already exists. A world-class meta data management solution dramatically improves data quality by providing a full understanding of the data and is absolutely essential for having repeatable and transferable IT processes because it centrally and completely documents all data and applications. Business executives are beginning to realize the importance of managing their data as an asset and thus are starting to look to the MME as the key technical solution for data asset management.

The key to your company's prosperity is how well you gather, retain, and disseminate knowledge. Managed meta data environments are the key to gathering, retaining, and disseminating knowledge.

One of the chief challenges in building a successful MME is to decide on the specific business objectives for your MME. The rest of this section describes the most pressing challenges that organizations are currently facing:

- Provide IT portfolio management
- Reduce IT redundancy
- Prevent IT applications failure
- Reduce IT expenditures
- Enable knowledge management
- Adhere to regulatory requirements
- Enable enterprise applications

Chapter 3 shows specific MME applications to meet each of these challenges.

Provide IT Portfolio Management

Over the years, we have performed dozens of data warehousing assessments. During these assessments, clients are routinely asked how much they spend annually on data warehousing. Most cannot accurately estimate on what they actually spend. In order to manage these and any other costly IT initiatives, it is critical to measure each one, but it is impossible to measure them when most companies do not understand them (see Figure 1.2). This is where IT portfolio management enters the picture.

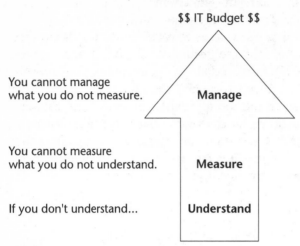

How to Manage IT

$$ IT Budget $$

You cannot manage
what you do not measure.   **Manage**

You cannot measure
what you do not understand.   **Measure**

If you don't understand...   **Understand**

Figure 1.2   How to manage IT.

IT portfolio management is the formal process for managing IT assets. An IT asset may be software, hardware, middleware, an IT project, internal staff, an application, or external consulting. As with other new disciplines, many companies are not setting up IT portfolio management efforts correctly (see sidebar "Red Light, Green Light, No Light"). Following are some of the keys to building successful IT portfolio management applications.

RED LIGHT, GREEN LIGHT, NO LIGHT

The October 1, 2001 *CIO Magazine* article titled "Red Light, Green Light" by Tracy Mayor presents an IT-project-tracking dashboard (type of IT portfolio management system) that is used by General Motors North America to track IT projects.

From the tone of the article and subsequent *expert* reviews of this IT project dashboard, it was clear that the application was being lauded as a best practice case study. As I continued reading the article, I discovered that the technology that they were using was a long way from best practices. "By design, the technology itself is as simple to use as possible: an Excel spreadsheet and PowerPoint presentation template." Excel spreadsheets and PowerPoint presentations are not best practices. These applications are highly simplistic and can only provide the most basic IT-portfolio-related information (meta data). In addition, the meta data in this technology cannot be linked to any other meta data. This is why IT portfolio management is a vital subject area of an MME and is the central topic of Chapter 6.

The information that portfolio management targets is meta data (both business and technical), and, as such, needs to be stored in the MME. The MME will allow the corporation to aggregate the portfolio-related meta data into an executive view so that it is clear which projects are proceeding well and which are lagging behind. It can also publish information to a Web site so that frontline IT staff can see the status of other projects. This will greatly aid their project timelines and planning.

It should be directly linked to the more granular business and technical meta data to allow developers to understand what IT projects are underway, what technology these projects are implementing, and what data sources they are accessing. Most large companies have a great deal of duplicate IT efforts (see the next section for more on this topic). This happens because the meta data is not accessible. EWSolutions, where author David Marco works, has a couple large clients whose only goal is to remove these tremendous redundancies, which translates into tremendous initial and ongoing IT costs.

Finally, the MME should contain both a business and a technical component. In most cases, the business component is more complicated than the technical. For example, a project manager communicates a project's funding, status, and technology to the group responsible for the portfolio management application. The meta data in the portfolio application is only as good as the information that these managers provide, so it is vital to integrate the IT portfolio application into the company's IT production turnover procedures. This ensures that the portfolio application stays current. See Chapter 6 for an IT portfolio management meta model walkthrough.

Reduce IT Redundancy

CIO is commonly defined as chief information officer; however, there is another possible meaning for this acronym—career is over. One of the chief reasons for this is that most IT departments are handcuffed by needless IT redundancy that too few CIOs are willing and able to fix.

There are several CIO surveys that are conducted annually. These surveys generally ask, "What are your top concerns for the upcoming year?" Data integration is usually high on the list. Data integration focuses on two key areas:

- Integration of data across disparate systems for enterprise applications
- Removal of IT redundancies

Some IT redundancy is a good thing. For example, during a power outage when one of your data centers is not operational, you need a backup. The discussion here focuses on *needless* IT redundancy, or IT redundancy that only exists because of insufficient management of the IT systems. I was working with a midwestern insurance company that, over a four-year span, had initiated various decision support efforts. After this four-year period, they took the time to map out the flow of data from their operational systems to their data staging areas and finally to their data mart structures. What they discovered is shown in Figure 1.3.

The typical response to Figure 1.3 is, "Where did you get a copy of our IT architecture?" If you work at a Global 2000 company or any large government entity, Figure 1.3 represents a simplified version of your IT architecture, which is actually no architecture at all. Poor architecture creates a litany of problems, including:

- Redundant applications, processes, and data
- Needless IT rework
- Redundant hardware and software

The following sections will discuss each of these problems in greater depth.

Typical IT Architecture

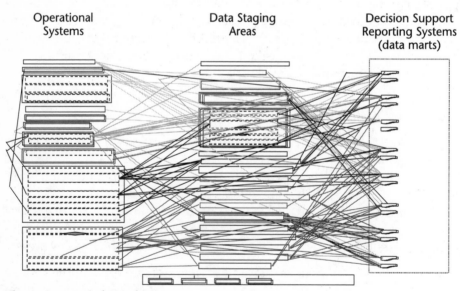

Figure 1.3 Typical IT architecture.

Redundant Applications, Processes, and Data

It has been our experience in working with large government agencies and *Forbes* Global 2000 companies that needlessly duplicated data is running rampant throughout organizations. One large banking client asked us to analyze its IT environment. During this analysis, we discovered a tremendous amount of application and data redundancy. The company had over 700 unique applications. During this analysis, we compared this client to a bank that is more than twice its size; however, this larger bank has a world-class MME and uses it to properly manage its systems. As a result, it has less than 250 unique applications. Clearly, the bank with more than 700 applications has a great deal of needless redundancy. The bank with the world-class MME was also 14 times more profitable than the one maintaining over 700 applications. Obviously, the less-profitable bank would become much more profitable if it removed its needless redundancy.

In our experience, a typical large organization's data has 60 percent to 75 percent needless data redundancy (see sidebar "Toyota: A Case Study in a Lack of Meta Data Management"). Some organizations have hundreds of *independent* data mart applications spread all over the company. Each one of these data marts is duplicating the extraction, transformation, and load (ETL) processes typically done centrally in a data warehouse. This greatly increases the amount of support staff required to maintain the data warehousing system, and these tasks are the largest and most costly data warehousing activities. Each data mart also copies the data, requiring even more IT resources. It is easy to see why IT budgets are straining under the weight of all of this needless redundancy.

Fortunately, these large organizations are beginning to realize that they can't continue to operate in this manner. Therefore, they are targeting MME technology to assist them in identifying and removing existing application and data redundancy. This can be accomplished because the MME can identify redundant applications through analysis of the data and the application's processes. These same companies are starting IT application integration projects to merge these overlapping systems, in conjunction with their MME initiatives to ensure that future IT applications do not proliferate needless redundancy.

TOYOTA: A CASE STUDY IN A LACK OF META DATA MANAGEMENT

In 1998, Toyota Motor Sales (TMS) used data from their Corporate Customer Information System (CCIS) to mail checks to Lexus owners to replace troublesome tires. Each check was over $400. Unfortunately, in some cases these checks were sent to people who didn't even own Lexuses. One errant check even found its way to a Toyota auditor for a vehicle he hadn't owned for a while. "You can imagine the repercussions of that," said John Gonzales, TMS data quality manager. "We can't afford to be giving money away to people who shouldn't be getting it."

Why did this happen? The CCIS stored customer data from "roughly 15 databases in different parts of company," according to Gonzales. There were many needlessly redundant systems, as well as a lack of knowledge about the data, the systems, and the data quality.

TMS worked feverishly to consolidate their redundant systems and to clean their data. "The amount of work to do was frightening," Gonzales said. "Some databases had wrong vehicles, wrong motors, wrong addresses." (Story and corresponding quotes are from an article in *Baseline Magazine* by Sean Gallagher at http://www.baselinemag.com/article2/0,3959,686,00.asp.)

Needless IT Rework

During the requirements-gathering portion of one MME initiative, an IT project manager brought up the challenges that he faced in analyzing one of the mission-critical legacy applications that fed the data warehousing application his team had been asked to build. During our interview he stated, "This has to be the 20th time that our organization is analyzing this system to understand the business rules around the data." This story is all too common, because almost all organizations reinvent the IT wheel with every new project. This situation occurs when separate teams build each of the IT systems without an MME, so the teams can't leverage each other's standards, processes, knowledge, and lessons learned. This results in a great deal of rework and reanalysis.

A good MME captures this invaluable IT information, including business rules, business processes, attribute definitions, entity definitions, and data lineage. This information is invaluable to an organization that is looking to maximize its IT investment. For more information on meta data sources and the types of meta data that they include, see Chapter 2 of *Building and Managing the Meta Data Repository* (Wiley, 2000).

Redundant Hardware and Software

All of this redundant application and IT work generates a great deal of needless hardware and software redundancy, forcing the enterprise to retain skilled employees (usually at great cost) to support each technology. In addition, more money is spent because standardization doesn't occur. Often software, hardware, and tools can be licensed at a considerable discount to an enterprise. These economies of scale can provide tremendous cost savings to the organization.

In addition, the hardware and software is not used in an optimal fashion. For example, one client purchases hardware for each individual IT project. As a result, they have a bunch of servers running at 25 percent capacity.

Software presents even more problems. One IT project leader responded to the question of what software vendors his company was standardized on with, "All of them!" This leads to the old joke "What is the most popular form of software on the market?" Answer: "Shelfware!" Shelfware is software that a company purchases and winds up never using, so it just sits on a shelf collecting dust.

Prevent IT Applications Failure

When a corporation looks to undertake a major IT initiative, such as a CRM, ERP, a data warehouse, or an e-commerce solution, the likelihood of project failure is between 65 percent and 80 percent, depending on the study referenced. This is especially alarming considering that these same initiatives traditionally have executive management support and cost many millions of dollars. For example, one large client was looking to roll out a CRM system (for example, Siebel, Oracle) and an ERP system (for example, SAP, People-Soft) globally within four years, with an initial project budget of over $125 million. In my opinion, they have a 0 percent probability of delivering all of these systems on time and on budget. When was the last time you saw an ERP or CRM initiative delivered on time or on budget?

When we examine the causes of project failure, the following themes become apparent. First, the company did not address a definable and measurable business need. This is the number one reason for project failure—data warehouse, CRM, MME, or otherwise. Second, it did not incorporate the existing IT environment and business rules. This includes custom applications, vendor applications, data elements, entities, data flows, data heritage, and data lineage.

An MME dramatically reduces the likelihood of IT project failure, because it allows a corporation or government agency to decipher its IT environment and to greatly speed up its IT development life cycles. The MME captures the key meta data around a company's IT applications and uses this meta data to generate an *impact analysis*. An impact analysis is a technical meta-data-driven report that shows the impact of a potential change to an organization's IT systems. Chapter 3 presents several MME use-case examples utilizing impact analysis. The MME case studies featured in that chapter also discuss impact analysis.

Reduce IT Expenditures

If your MME reduces the applications, processes, data, software, and hardware, and it lowers the likelihood for IT project failure and speeds up the IT development life cycle, then clearly it will greatly reduce your company's IT expenditures. The majority of MMEs are focused on reducing and managing IT expenditures.

Enable Knowledge Management

One of the most vital functions of any MME is to provide the technical architecture and processes to manage corporate knowledge. All corporations strive to become more intelligent. To attain a competitive advantage, a business needs its IT systems to manage more than just their data; they must manage knowledge (that is, meta data). As a corporation's IT systems mature, they progress from collecting and managing data to collecting and managing knowledge. Knowledge is a company's most valuable asset, and an MME is the key *technological backbone* for managing a company's corporate knowledge. For more information on knowledge management, refer to Chapter 11 of *Building and Managing the Meta Data Repository* (Wiley, 2000).

George Bernard Shaw once said, "The greatest problem in communication is the illusion that it has been accomplished." Executives often do not realize how not properly managing a company's knowledge (meta data) can negatively affect their bottom-line profits, or they are under the illusion that proper communication and understanding are occurring. This couldn't be further from the truth (see sidebar "NASA Mars Orbiter: A Case Study in a Lack of Meta Data Management").

Adhere to Regulatory Requirements

Every industry has its own dizzying array of regulatory requirements (see the next section of this chapter for more details on these requirements). Many companies look to MME architecture to assist them in meeting these requirements. Since most information stored in a company is stored electronically, an MME can greatly assist an organization in tracking, monitoring, and recording changes to its data and documents. Often this type of information is needed to meet regulatory requirements. Corporations must be able to meet these requirements, because the penalties can be severe. They range from large monetary fees to felony charges levied against the senior executives within the organization.

NASA MARS ORBITER: A CASE STUDY IN A LACK OF META DATA MANAGEMENT

On December 11, 1998, the National Aeronautics & Space Administration (NASA) launched the Mars Climate Orbiter to study the climatic conditions on the planet Mars. The engineers who worked on this mission calculated rocket firing using feet per second. However, the orbiter was programmed in Newtons per second (metric) of thrust. The difference between these calculations was 4.4 feet per second. "Each time there was a burn (rocket firing) the error built up," said Art Stephenson, Director of the Marshall Spaceflight Center and head of the NASA Investigation Team. "We entered the Mars atmosphere at a much lower altitude (than planned)," said Ed Weiler, NASA's chief scientist. "It (the spacecraft) either burned up in the Martian atmosphere or sped out (into space). We're not sure which happened."

This situation clearly illustrates a lack of meta data management. If NASA had an MME, they would have had meta data on the business rules programmed into the orbiter. The engineers would have known that it was programmed for metric measurements, rather than making incorrect assumptions. What was the cost of this lack of proper meta data management? The cost of this mission was over $250 million. Who paid for this mistake? The U.S. taxpayer. (Story and corresponding quotes are from Associated Press Science Writer Paul Recer http://www.anomalous-images.com/news/news537.html.)

Enable Enterprise Applications

Without an enterprise-wide MME, your organization does not have a common understanding of the data across its systems. How do you build an enterprise-wide application (that is, a CRM, a data warehousing, or an ERP system) without an enterprise-view understanding of the data? The answer for most companies is that they can't. This is why many research firms state that CRM initiatives fail over 90 percent of the time. In fact, Tom Siebel proclaimed that "There's no market for CRM. . . . It's not there. There are a lot of companies trying to get into the space. . . . But they are going after a market that doesn't exist." ("The Siebel Observer," http://www.siebelobserver.com/siebel/trends/vision.htm.)

Realistically, this is not the case, because there is a clear business need to understand and manage all of a customer's *touch points* (see sidebar "Mismanaging a Customer's Touch Points"). So why does the man who marketed CRM the most and made the most money from it claim that it is dead? Maybe it's because these CRM initiatives are highly complex and as a result have created a large number of expensive failures. These failures, along with a compressed IT economy, may have caused companies to abandon CRM. Personally, I don't expect Siebel Systems to stop making CRM software. On the other hand, I interpret Tom Siebel's comments to mean that we have to get ready for a new term for the same old thing. Chapter 2 will discuss CRM and its role in the MME in greater detail.

In the January 2000 article for *DM Review* ("Data Warehousing Trends for 2000"), I gave predictions for the future of the data warehousing industry. In writing this article, I realized that the most important thing that I could do was to make sure that my predictions were accurate. Therefore, the first prediction was that most large government agencies and Global 2000 companies would spend a great deal of time and money rebuilding their data warehousing investments. This was a simple and easy prediction to make. During the 1990s, corporations raced to build their data warehouses as quickly as they could. In their zeal to do this, many organizations neglected to build the architecture necessary to grow their systems over time. In many cases, these companies built "independent" data marts, which are directly sourced from operational systems without a data warehouse. These companies also neglected to implement an MME. Without an MME, it is exceedingly difficult, if not impossible, to maintain and enhance a data warehouse.

MISMANAGING A CUSTOMER'S TOUCH POINTS

One client (and fellow Chicagoan) wanted to purchase a winter coat from his favorite coat maker. It was during the Christmas holiday and this person did not want to battle the holiday shoppers, so he went to the company's Web site (touch point #1) to find the coat he wanted. He was successful in locating the exact coat that he wanted; unfortunately, when he tried to place this order online he was told that the coat was out of stock. Undaunted, he called the toll-free phone number (touch point #2) and was again told that the coat was out of stock.

A few days later, the client was in his local mall and walked past one of their stores (touch point #3). On a whim, he entered the store and discovered a rack full of the exact same coats he had seen on the Web. However, these coats were priced at $40 less than on the Web site. What happened is that the corporation in their rush to build a corporate Web site did not take the time to integrate their e-commerce system into their existing legacy order entry systems. As a result, their customer touch points were mismanaged. There is an old marketing rule that "A customer will tell two to four people when they are happy with the product/service you've given them. These same customers will tell 12 to 20 other potential customers when they are dissatisfied with your product or service."

THE CEO'S THREE ENVELOPES

The CEO of a company has just been fired from his job. As the old CEO is cleaning out his desk the new CEO arrives. The old CEO turns to the new CEO and hands this person three envelopes. The old CEO tells the new CEO that if he is ever in trouble all he has to do is open one of the envelopes, and it will solve whatever problem that he is facing. The new CEO takes the envelopes and, thinking that the old CEO is crazy, places the three envelops in his desk drawer.

The first six months of the new CEO's tenure went very well. However, after this six-month period, the new CEO's popularity is slipping and he realizes that there is a good chance that he is going to be fired. Late one night, the new CEO is trying to think of a way to save his job. While doing this he happens across the previous CEO's three envelopes. The new CEO thinks that he has nothing to lose and decides to open one of them. So, he opens the first envelope, and it says "Blame the last guy." He thinks, of course that is the answer! So, first thing the next morning he blames the previous CEO for all of the problems that the company is having. As a result, the new CEO becomes popular again. Unfortunately, this newfound popularity only lasts about another six months before his job is in jeopardy again, and he is back on the firing line. Late one night he thinks, "Well, that first envelope really helped me out, let me open the second envelope." He then opens the second envelope, and it says "Reorganize." He thinks that's it! I need to reorganize the company! So, the next morning he reorganizes the company, and once again his popularity becomes sky high. Of course, another six months go by, and once again his job is in trouble. He thinks, "I'd better open that last envelope." He opens the third envelope, and inside it says "Write out three envelopes."

I share this joke because it is important to understand that the average CIO and CEO only last about 18 to 24 months on the job. Those of you who have been in the business world long enough will notice that the scenario described in this joke is pretty accurate. Most new executives first blame the previous management group for their problems, then they reorganize, and then they are fired.

This is especially true if a company has implemented multiple, disparate data warehousing systems. Having multiple data warehouses can lead to the following problems:

- Duplicate data
- Duplicate reports and queries
- Increased strain on operational batch windows
- Multiple versions of the truth

An MME addresses the excessive IT redundancies in this type of environment and acts as the *glue* that binds the data warehouses together. This makes MMEs even more vital in a cluttered environment.

Global 2000 companies spend *billions* of dollars analyzing existing data warehousing systems for requirements and business rules, which have long since been forgotten. All of these requirements and business rules should have been initially managed in the MME. These same companies will continue to invest equally large expenditures into CRM and other enterprise-spanning applications. If you do not properly manage your meta data, you will have a very difficult time implementing enterprise-wide systems.

MMEs may not be as glamorous as CRM applications; however, these projects deliver real value as opposed to the 90 percent plus failure rate. Running a successful business is about concentrating single-mindedly on the fundamentals and then executing those fundamentals.

Summary

Now that we have a sound, high-level understanding of the MME and the value that it provides, we can start learning about the details around each of its components. Chapter 2 will discuss the components of the MME and give best practices for each. These best practices are critical; they usually make the difference between successful and unsuccessful MME implementations.

The Managed Meta Data Environment Architecture

Almost every corporation and government agency has already built, is in the process of building, or is looking to build an MME. Many organizations, however, are making fundamental mistakes. An enterprise may build many meta data repositories, or *islands of meta data* that are not linked together, and as a result do not provide as much value as they might (see sidebar "Where's My Meta Data Architecture?").

Let's take a quick meta data management quiz. What is the most common form of meta data architecture? It is likely that most of you will answer "centralized," but the *real* answer is "bad architecture." Most meta data repository architectures are built the same way that data warehouse architectures were built—badly. The data warehouse architecture issue resulted in many Global 2000 companies rebuilding their data warehousing applications, sometimes from the ground up. Many of the meta data repositories being built or already in use need to be completely rebuilt. The goal of this chapter is to make sure that your MME's architecture is constructed on a rock solid foundation that provides your organization's MME with a significant advantage over poorly architected MMEs.

WHERE'S MY META DATA ARCHITECTURE?

One of our clients is a large pharmaceutical company. Since knowledge is the lifeblood of any pharmaceutical company, these types of firms tend to have very large meta data requirements and staffs. This company had decided to have a *Meta Data Day*, so they had asked us to come on-site and give a keynote address to kick the day off. Between 60 and 80 people attended Meta Data Day.

After the keynote address, there was a series of workshops. We counted four separate meta data repositories in production and three other *separate* new meta data repository initiatives starting up—a classic *islands of meta data* problem. This is not an approach that leads to long-term positive results. None of these islands was linked to the others, which is a problem because much of the most valuable meta data functionality comes from the relationships that the meta data has with itself. For example, it is highly valuable to view a physical column name (technical meta data) and then drill-across to the business definition (business meta data) of that physical column name.

This chapter presents the complete managed meta data environment (MME), and walks you through each of the six components of the MME in detail and the sustaining of the MME. In addition, such critical topics as the Data Stewardship Framework and the data stewardship's role in the MME. Also during this chapter, I will look at the Systems Engineering Capability Maturity Model (SE-CMM). In this section, I will explain the SE-CMM and illustrate its importance from an MME perspective. Finally, we will walk through the Common Warehouse Metamodel (CWM) standard and show how it relates to this book.

MME Overview

The managed meta data environment represents the architectural components, people, and processes that are required to properly and systematically gather, retain, and disseminate meta data throughout the enterprise. The MME encapsulates the concepts of meta data repositories, catalogs, data dictionaries, and any other terms that people have thrown out to refer to the systematic management of meta data. Some people mistakenly describe an MME as a data warehouse for meta data. In actuality, an MME is an operational system and, as such, is architected in a vastly different manner than a data warehouse.

Companies that are looking to truly and efficiently manage meta data from an enterprise perspective need to have a fully functional MME. It is important to note that a company should not try to store all of its meta data in an MME, just as the company would not try to store all of its data in a data warehouse. Without the MME components, it is very difficult to be effective managing meta data in a large organization. The six components of the MME, shown in Figure 2.1, are:

- Meta data sourcing layer
- Meta data integration layer
- Meta data repository
- Meta data management layer
- Meta data marts
- Meta data delivery layer

MME can be used with either the centralized, decentralized, or distributed architecture approaches. A *centralized architecture* offers a single, uniform, and consistent meta model that mandates the schema for defining and organizing the various meta data stored in a global meta data repository. This allows for a consolidated approach to administering and sharing meta data across the enterprise. A *decentralized architecture* creates a uniform and consistent meta model that mandates the schema for defining and organizing a global subset of meta data to be stored in a global meta data repository *and* in the designated shared meta data elements that appear in local meta data repositories. All meta data that is shared and reused among the various local repositories must first go through the global repository, but sharing and access to the local meta data are independent of the global repository. A *distributed architecture* includes several separate and autonomous meta data repositories, which have their own meta models to dictate their internal meta data content and organization, with each repository being solely responsible for the sharing and administration of its meta data. The global meta data repository will not hold meta data that appears in the local repositories; instead, it will have pointers to the meta data in the local repositories and meta data on how to access it.

See Chapter 7 of *Building and Managing the Meta Data Repository* (Wiley, 2000) for a walkthrough of these approaches.

Meta Data Sourcing Layer

The meta data sourcing layer is the first component of the MME architecture. The purpose of the meta data sourcing layer is to extract meta data from its source and to send it into the meta data integration layer or directly into the meta data repository (see Figure 2.2).

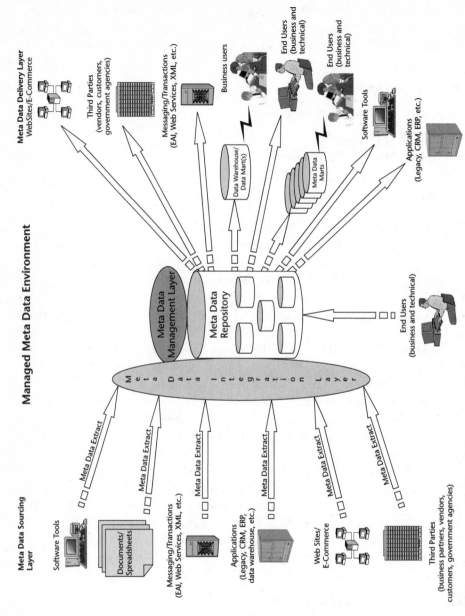

Figure 2.1   Managed meta data environment.

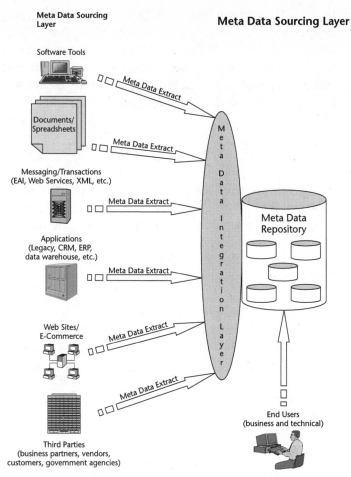

Figure 2.2 Meta data sourcing layer.

It is best to send the extracted meta data to the same hardware location as the meta data repository. Often meta data architects incorrectly build meta data integration processes on the platform that the meta data is sourced from (other than record selection, which is acceptable). This merging of the meta data sourcing layer with the meta data integration layer is a common mistake that raises a whole host of issues.

As sources of meta data are changed and added (and they will be), the meta data integration process is negatively affected. When the meta data sourcing layer is separated from the meta data integration layer, only the meta data sourcing layer is affected by this type of change. By keeping all of the meta data together on the target platform, the meta data architect can adapt the integration processes much more easily.

Keeping the extraction layer separate from the sourcing layer provides a tidy backup and restart point. Meta data loading errors typically happen in the meta data transformation layer. Without the extraction layer, if an error occurred the architect would have to go back to the source of the meta data and reread it. This can cause a number of problems. If the source of meta data has been updated, it may be out of sync with some of the other sources of meta data that it integrates with. The meta data source may also currently be in use, and this processing could have an impact on the performance of the meta data source. The golden rule of meta data extraction is:

> *Never have multiple processes extracting the same meta data from the same meta data source.*

In these situations, the timeliness and, consequently, the accuracy of the meta data can be compromised. For example, suppose that you have built one meta data extraction process (Process #1) that reads physical attribute names from a modeling tool's tables to load a target entity in the meta model table that contains physical attribute names. You also built a second process (Process #2) to read and load attribute domain values. It is possible that the attribute table in the modeling tool has been changed between the running of Process #1 and Process #2. This situation would cause the meta data to be out of sync.

This situation can also cause unnecessary delays in the loading of the meta data when the meta data sources have limited availability/batch windows. For example, if you were reading database logs from your ERP system, you would not want to run multiple extraction processes on these logs, since they most likely have a limited amount of available batch window. Although this situation doesn't happen often, there is no reason to build unnecessary flaws into your meta data architecture.

The number and variety of meta data sources will vary greatly depending on the business requirements of your MME. Though there are sources of meta data that many companies commonly use, we've never seen two meta data repositories that had exactly the same meta data sources. (Have you every seen two data warehouses with exactly the same source information?) The following are the most common meta data sources:

- Software tools
- End users
- Documents and spreadsheets
- Messaging and transactions
- Applications
- Web sites and e-commerce
- Third parties

Software Tools

A great deal of valuable meta data is stored in various software tools (see Table 2.1 for a limited list). Keep in mind that many of these tools have internal meta data repositories designed to enable the tool's specific functionality and are not designed to be accessed by meta data users or integrated into other sources of meta data. You will need to set up processes to go into these tools' repositories and pull the meta data out.

Of these tools, relational databases and modeling tools are the most common sources of meta data for the meta data sourcing layer. The MME usually reads the database's system tables to extract meta data about physical column names, logical attribute names, physical table names, logical entity names, relationships, indexing, change data capture, and data access.

Table 2.1   Software Tools Meta Data Sources

SOFTWARE CATEGORY	PRODUCT NAME	PRODUCT COMPANY
Databases	DB2/UDB	IBM
	SQL Server	Microsoft
	Oracle	Oracle
	Teradata	NCR
	Sybase	Sybase
	Teradata	NCR
Data Quality	INTEGRITY	Ascential Software
	Information Quality Suite	First Logic
	MetaPure	MetaGenix
	Trillium Software System	Trillium
EAI	MQ Series	IBM
	Integration Platform	WebMethods
ETL	DataStage Suite	Ascential Software
	Hummingbird ETL	Hummingbird
	PowerCenter Suite	Informatica
	Data Transformation Services	Microsoft
Modeling	Erwin	Computer Associates
	ER/Studio	Embarcadero
	Designer	Oracle
	Rational Rose	Rational Software
	System Architect	Popkin

(continued)

Table 2.1   *(continued)*

SOFTWARE CATEGORY	PRODUCT NAME	PRODUCT COMPANY
Portals	Info View	Business Objects
	Upfront	Cognos
	CleverPath Portal	Computer Associates
	WebSphere Portal	IBM
	SharePoint Server	Microsoft
	AS Portal	Oracle9i
	Enterprise Portal	PeopleSoft
	Plumtree Corporate Portal	Plumtree Software
	mySAP Enterprise Portal	SAP
	ONE Portal Server	Sun
Reporting/OLAP	BusinessObjects Suite	Business Objects
	Impromptu & PowerPlay	Cognos
	BI/Suite	Hummingbird
	Microstrategy	Microstrategy

End Users

End users are one of the most important sources of meta data that is brought into the MME. These users come in two flavors: business and technical. Figure 2.3 lists the types of meta data entry done by each group.

Often the business meta data for a corporation is stored in the collective consciousness of its employees as *tribal knowledge*. As a result, it is vital for the business users to input business meta data into the repository. The need for active and engaged business users ties into the topic of data stewardship, discussed later in this chapter.

The technical users also need direct access into the meta data repository to input their technical meta data. Because much of the technical meta data is stored in various software tools, it is not as difficult for technical users to input the technical meta data as it is for business users to input the business meta data.

The interface for both of these user groups should be Web-enabled. The Web provides an easy-to-use and intuitive interface that both of these groups are familiar with. It is critical that this interface be directly linked to the meta data in the repository. We strongly suggest the use of drop boxes and pick lists, because these are tools that users are highly familiar with. You should always use the referential integrity features that the database software provides.

Documents and Spreadsheets

A great deal of meta data is stored in corporate documents (Microsoft Word) and spreadsheets (Microsoft Excel). The requirements of your MME will have a great impact on the degree to which you need to bring in meta data from documents. Sometimes these documents and spreadsheets are located in a central area of a network or on an employee's computer. In most organizations though, documents and spreadsheets tend to be highly volatile, and lack standardized formats and business rules. As a result, they are traditionally one of the most unreliable and problematic sources of meta data in the MME. Sometimes business meta data for these sources can be found in the note or comment fields associated with the document or with a cell (if a spreadsheet). Technical meta data, such as calculations, dependences, or lookup values are stored in the application's (Microsoft Excel or Lotus 1-2-3) proprietary data store.

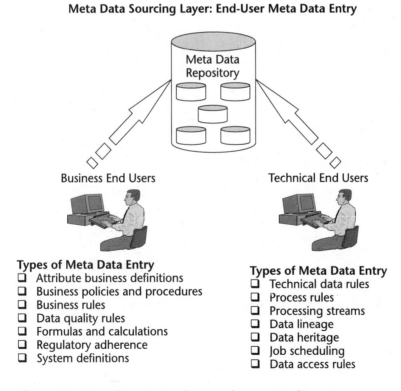

Meta Data Sourcing Layer: End-User Meta Data Entry

Meta Data Repository

Business End Users

Technical End Users

Types of Meta Data Entry
- ❑ Attribute business definitions
- ❑ Business policies and procedures
- ❑ Business rules
- ❑ Data quality rules
- ❑ Formulas and calculations
- ❑ Regulatory adherence
- ❑ System definitions

Types of Meta Data Entry
- ❑ Technical data rules
- ❑ Process rules
- ❑ Processing streams
- ❑ Data lineage
- ❑ Data heritage
- ❑ Job scheduling
- ❑ Data access rules

Figure 2.3 Meta data sourcing layer: end-user meta data entry.

For companies that have implemented a document management system, it's important to extract the meta data out of these sources and bring it into the MME's repository. Typically, when a company builds a document or content management system, it also purchases a software product to aid management of meta data on documents, images, audio, geospatial (geographical topography), and spreadsheets. It is important to have a meta data sourcing layer that can read the meta data in the document management tool and extract it out and bring it into the MME's repository. This task is extremely difficult because most document management companies do not understand that they are really meta data repositories and, as such, need to be accessible. Document management tools often employ proprietary database software to persist their meta data and/or their internal database structure is highly *abstract*, meaning that the structure of the meta data is not represented in the meta model, but is instead represented in program code. As a result, it can be difficult to build processes to pull meta data out of these sources (see Figure 2.4).

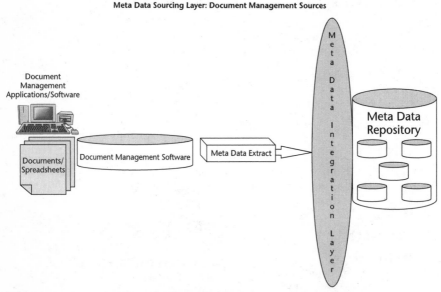

Figure 2.4   Meta data sourcing layer: document management sources.

Messaging and Transactions

Many companies are using some form of messaging and transactions, either Enterprise Application Integration (EAI) or Extensible Markup Language (XML) (sometimes EAI applications use XML), to transfer data from one system to another. The use of EAI and XML is a popular trend as enterprises struggle with the high cost of maintaining current point-to-point approaches to data integration. The problem with point-to-point integration is that the IT environment becomes so complex that it is impossible to manage it effectively or efficiently, especially if you do not have an enterprise-level MME. An EAI messaging paradigm should help companies unravel their current point-to-point integration approaches. Figure 2.5 shows an EAI messaging bus, which provides the technical engine for the EAI messages.

Although the vast majority of companies are not very advanced in their use and application of EAI and XML, these types of processes can be used to capture highly valuable meta data: business rules, data quality statistics, data lineage, data rationalization processes, and so on. Since the EAI tools are designed to manage the messaging bus, not the meta data around it, it is important to bring this meta data from the EAI tools into the MME to allow for global access, historical management, publishing, and distribution. Without a good MME, it becomes very difficult to maintain these types of applications. Large government organizations and major corporations, such as Allstate (see Chapter 3), are using their MMEs to address this challenge.

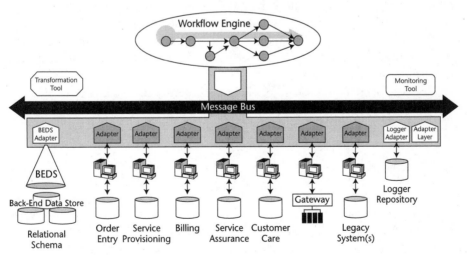

Figure 2.5 EAI messaging bus.

Applications

Within the wide array of applications a corporation uses, some will be custom-built by the enterprise's IT department (for example, data warehouses, general ledger systems, payroll, supply chain management), others will be based on packages (for example, PeopleSoft, SAP, Siebel), and some may be outsourced or based on an application service provider (ASP) model. This proliferation of applications can be quite voluminous. For example, we know of several corporations and government agencies whose applications number in the thousands.

Each of these applications contains valuable meta data that may need to be extracted and brought into the MME application. Assuming that the applications are built on one of the popular relational database platforms (for example, IBM, Oracle, Microsoft, Sybase, Teradata), the meta data sourcing layer can read the system tables or logs of these databases. There is also considerable meta data stored within these varied applications. Business rules and lookup values are buried within the application code or control tables. In these situations, a process needs to be built to bring in the meta data.

Web Sites and E-Commerce

One of the least used sources of meta data is corporate Web sites. Many companies forget the amount of valuable meta data that is contained (or should we say *locked* away) in Hypertext Markup Language (HTML) on Web sites. For example, healthcare insurance industry analysts need to know the latest information about the testing of a new drug for patient treatments. Research is typically conducted by a doctor working with a hospital. The doctor usually posts his findings on the hospital's Web site or portal, so it's important to capture meta data around these Web sites—for example, when the site was updated, what was updated, and so on.

This also applies to e-commerce. When a customer orders a product via the Web, valuable meta data is generated and needs to be captured and placed in the MME.

Third Parties

For many companies, it is a standard business process to interact heavily with third parties. Companies in the banking, healthcare, finance, and certain types of manufacturing and national-defense-related agencies need to interact with business partners, suppliers, vendors, customers, and government or regulatory agencies (such as the FDA and Census Bureau) on a daily basis. For every systematic interaction, these external data sources generate meta data (see Chapter 2 of *Building and Managing the Meta Data Repository* (Wiley, 2000) for a more detailed discussion of external meta data sources) that should be extracted and brought into the MME.

Meta Data Integration Layer

The meta data integration layer (see Figure 2.6) takes the various sources of meta data, integrates them, and loads the meta data into the meta data repository. This approach differs slightly from the techniques commonly used to load data into a data warehouse, because the data warehouse clearly separates the transformation (what we call integration) process from the load process. In an MME, these steps are combined because the volume of meta data is not nearly as large as in a typical data warehousing application. As a general rule, the MMEs hold between 5GB and 20GB of meta data; however, because MMEs are looking to target audit-related meta data, storage can grow into the 20GB to 75GB range, and over the next few years you will see some MMEs reach the terabyte range.

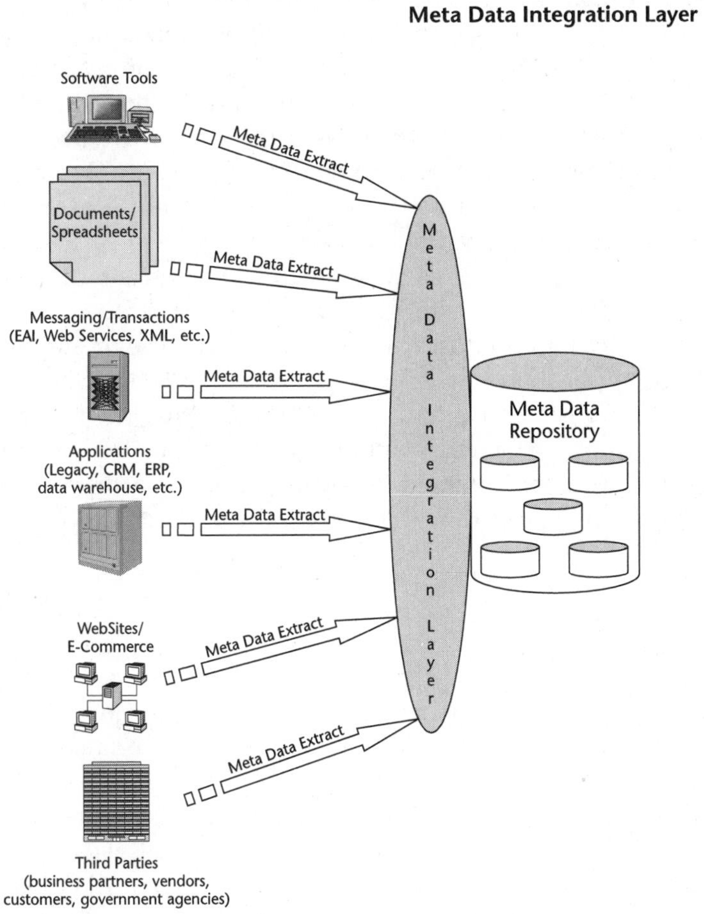

Meta Data Integration Layer

Figure 2.6   Meta data integration layer.

The specific steps in this process depend on whether you are building a custom process or if you are using a meta data integration tool to assist your effort. If you decide to use a meta data integration tool, the specific tool selection can also have a great impact on this process.

Meta Data Repository

A meta data repository is a fancy name for a database designed to gather, retain, and disseminate meta data. The meta data repository (see Figure 2.7) is responsible for the cataloging and persistent physical storage of the meta data.

The meta data repository should be *generic, integrated, current,* and *historical.* Generic means that the physical meta model stores meta data by meta data subject area as opposed to storing it in an application-specific way. For example, a generic meta model will have an attribute named "DATABASE_PHYS_NAME" that will hold the physical database names within the company. A meta model that is application-specific would name this same attribute "ORACLE_PHYS_NAME." The problem with application-specific meta models is that meta data subject areas change. To return to the example, today Oracle may be your company's database standard. Tomorrow you may switch the standard to SQL Server for cost or compatibility reasons. This situation would necessitate needless additional changes to the physical meta model. Chapters 4 to 8 offer sound physical meta models.

A meta data repository also provides an integrated view of the enterprise's major meta data subject areas. The repository should allow the user to view all entities within the company, and not just entities loaded in Oracle or entities that are just in the CRM applications.

Third, the meta data repository contains current and future meta data, meaning that the meta data is periodically updated to reflect the current and future technical and business environment. Keep in mind that a meta data repository is constantly being updated, and it needs to be in order to be truly valuable.

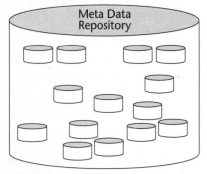

Figure 2.7 Meta data repository.

Finally, meta data repositories are historical. A good repository will hold historical views of the meta data, even as it changes over time. This allows a corporation to understand how its business has changed over time. This is especially critical if the MME is supporting an application that contains historical data, such as a data warehouse or a CRM application. For example, suppose that the business meta data definition for *customer* is "anyone who has purchased a product from our company within one of our stores or through our catalog." A year later, a new distribution channel is added as part of the business strategy. The company constructs a Web site to allow customers to order products. At that point in time, the business meta data definition for customer would be modified to "anyone who has purchased a product from our company within one of our stores, through our mail order catalog, or through the Web." A good meta data repository stores both of these definitions because they both have validity, depending on what data users are analyzing (and the age of that data).

It is strongly recommended that you implement your meta data repository on an open, relational database platform. Part Two offers physical meta models that can be used as templates for building your own meta data repository.

Meta Data Management Layer

The meta data management layer provides systematic management of the meta data repository and the other MME components (see Figure 2.8). As with other layers, the approach to this component greatly differs depending on whether a meta data integration tool is used or whether the entire MME is custom-built. If an enterprise meta data integration tool is used for the construction of the MME, than a meta data management interface will most likely be included within the meta data integration tool. If the software did not have a meta data management interface (which is highly unlikely), than you would have to custom build this layer.

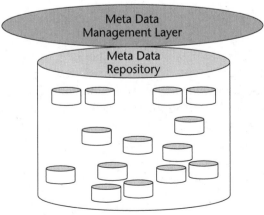

Figure 2.8 Meta data management layer.

The meta data management layer performs the following functions:

- Archiving
- Backup
- Database modifications
- Database tuning
- Environment management
- Job scheduling
- Maintenance of load statistics
- Purging
- Maintenance of query statistics
- Query and report generation
- Recovery
- Security processes
- Source mapping and movement
- User interface management
- Versioning

We will now discuss each of these functions in greater detail.

Archiving

The archive function allows the meta data architect to set the criteria or event that triggers the MME archiving process. It should be able to archive all of the meta data in the meta data repository and the related meta data marts, and it should allow for specific meta data tables to be archived when necessary.

Backup

Backup functionality is often confused with archiving. Archiving targets the storage of older and less-needed versions of the MME, while backing up refers to the process of making sure that the current MME is stored in a separate database so that if the production version of the MME is corrupted, or if any of its components fails, a backup version can be brought online. Often the backup strategy is implemented at a hardware level through the use of disk mirroring. Best practices in this area include storing the copy in a different physical location than the production version of the MME.

Database Modifications

Since the meta model is implemented in an open, relational database, often tables and columns within the meta model need to be added, modified, or deleted. The meta data management layer needs not only to assist in this process, but also to track the changes that have been made to the MME.

Database Tuning

Tuning of the meta data repository and its associated meta data marts is a very important part of the meta data management layer. First, identifying indexes ensures that reports run efficiently. When you are analyzing physical meta model structures, it is common to only see indexes on primary keys. This is typically a sign of poor or no indexing strategies.

Second, database tuning helps you identify and remove dormant meta data within the repository. A large MME that has been in production for a few years commonly has a good deal of dormant meta data. A sound MME will contain meta data that provides operational measurement statistics on the use of meta data in the MME to assist in the identification of dormant meta data.

Environment Management

Many meta data professionals make the mistake of believing that when they implement an MME, they are implementing and maintaining one system. In actuality, they are building and maintaining three (possibly more) systems:

- Production
- Testing
- Development

The production version of the MME is the system that is in the production environment of an organization and is the version of the MME that the end users are accessing. The testing environment is the version used to test changes made to the system in response to *bugs* found in the production version of the MME. The development version of the MME is used to test future, major MME enhancements.

The names and number of MME environments differ based on the organization's internal IT standards; however, the three environments just mentioned are the most common. In any event, a good meta data management layer can handle whatever number of environments and names are required. The environment management portion of the meta data management layer needs to organize and control the operation of and migration between these three versions of the system.

Job Scheduling

The program and process jobs that are executed to load the MME and to access the MME need to be scheduled and managed. The job-scheduling portion of the meta data management layer is responsible for both event-based and batch-triggered job scheduling.

Maintanence of Load Statistics

The meta data extraction and integration layers of the MME generate a great deal of valuable MME load statistics. These historical MME load statistics need to be stored within the meta data repository portion of the MME. Examples of the most common types of load statistics include:

- How long it takes a particular process tread to run (clock time and CPU time)
- How long the entire meta data extraction and integration layers takes to run (both clock and CPU time)
- What errors were encountered in the meta data extraction and integration layers
- What the categories (for example, informational, warning, severe, critical) of the errors were that were logged
- How many rows were inserted, changed, or deleted in each table of the meta model

Purging

This part of the meta data management layer defines the criteria for MME purging requirements. The MME's specific purging requirements and criteria will be governed by its business requirements. As a general rule, meta data that is inaccurate or improperly loaded should be purged; all other meta data should be archived.

Maintenance of Query Statistics

Once the various meta data delivery layer reports and queries are generated, it is important to capture the user statistics associated with the access to these reports and queries. At a minimum, the meta data management layer needs to historically capture:

- Who is accessing the report or query
- What report or query the user is accessing

- When the user is accessing the report or query
- How often the user is accessing the report or query
- How long the user accesses the report or query

Query and Report Generation

The reports and queries used in the meta data delivery layer are defined and generated in the report generation section of the meta data management layer. How this is accomplished depends on whether a custom meta data delivery application is developed or a meta data access tool is implemented. This component also needs to manage any publishing and subscribing capabilities that are required.

Recovery

There are many situations that can result in a company's having to recover or reload a previous version of its MME: hardware failure, database corruption, a power outage, errors in the meta data integration layer. The recovery process needs to be tightly tied to the backup and archiving facilities of the meta data management layer. Recovery processes may be manually built or utilize existing recovery processes within the meta data integration tool. Whichever approach is used, it needs to be integrated into the organization's existing application recovery processes.

Security Processes

The Security processes manage:

- Creating new MME users
- Grouping MME users
- Setting MME user privileges and profiles
- Implementing firewalls/infrastructures
- Managing passwords
- Verifying user locations
- Providing meta data masking (at the data level or access level)

How extensive the security processes are is dependent on the business requirements of the MME. For instance, the security requirements around a Department of Defense (DoD) or Federal Bureau of Investigation (FBI) MME are far greater than that of a bank.

Source Mapping and Movement

Meta data sources need to be mapped to the correct attributes and entities of the meta data repository. This mapping and movement process needs to be captured and managed in the meta data management layer of the MME.

User Interface Management

This is the process for building, managing, and maintaining the Web site (the recommended user interface) that the end users will visit to navigate through the MME. Typically, the view (version of the Web site) that end users see depends on their security privileges and profiles. A business user would not be interested in looking at program code changes, so it makes sense to not have meta data reports or queries related to highly technical meta data available to the traditional business user.

Versioning

As meta data is changed, added, and purged, it will be important for the meta data management layer to historically track (or version) it. There are two common techniques for meta data versioning. The first is the use of date stamps. Date stamping—assigning a date to each row of the meta model entities—allows a firm to make whatever changes are necessary to the meta data, while maintaining its historical relevance.

The second technique is to assign version numbers to each row of the meta model. Version numbers are merely generated unique values (for example, 1.1, 1.2, 1.a). Version numbers are more limiting than date stamping, which has more meaning to MME users. Version numbers can be associated with specific dates and times; however, this adds additional complexity to the loading of the meta data and an additional join in the access of queries and reports.

Another challenge of using versioning is capturing meta data that will become current at some point in time in the future. For example, a new physical table may be moved into the production environment at a future date. To handle these versioning situations, *effective dated rows* can be useful. Using effective dated rows is a process that allows data to be entered into a group (table) for subsequent processing when the effective date becomes current. Effective dated data can be historical, current, or future. Following are the key effective dated rows concepts:

Effective date.   The date on which the row of data becomes effective; the date it can be acted on.

Effective status.   Allows an application to select the appropriate effective dated rows when combined with the effective date (domain value list: *Active* or *Inactive*).

Current row. The first row of data with an effective date equal to or less than the system date and an effective status of *Active*. Only one row can be in this state.

Future row. Meta data rows that have a date greater than the system date.

Historical row. Rows of meta data that have an effective date less than the current row.

Table 2.2 illustrates the effective dated rows technique. In this example, the current system date is January 20, 2004. The meta data row dated "2004-01-27" has an effective status of "Inactive." However, once the current date reaches January 27, 2004, the meta data row dated "2004-01-18" will become an historical row, and the row dated "2004-01-27" will have its "Effective Status" changed from "Inactive" to "Active."

Meta Data Marts

A meta data mart is a database structure, usually sourced from a meta data repository, designed for a homogenous meta data user group (see Figure 2.9). *Homogenous meta data user group* is a fancy term for a group of users with like needs.

There are two reasons why an MME may need to have meta data marts. First, a particular meta data user community may require meta data organized in a manner other than the way it is in the meta data repository. Second, an MME with a large user base often experiences performance problems because of the number of table joins that are required for the meta data reports. In these situations, it is best to create meta data marts targeted specifically to meet those users' needs. The meta data marts will not experience performance degradation because they will be modeled multidimensionally. In addition, a separate meta mart provides a buffer layer between the end users and the meta data repository. This allows routine maintenance, upgrades, and backup and recovery of the meta data repository without affecting the availability of the meta mart.

Table 2.2 Effective Dated Rows

EFFECTIVE DATE	EFFECTIVE STATUS	EFFECTIVE STATUS COMMENTS
2003-12-01 12:00:00	Active	Historical row
2004-01-18 12:00:00	Active	Current row
2004-01-27 12:00:00	Inactive	Future row

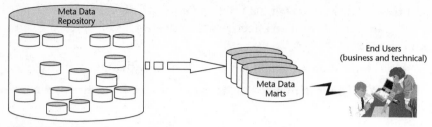

Figure 2.9 Meta data marts.

Meta Data Delivery Layer

The meta data delivery layer is the sixth and final component of the MME architecture. It delivers the meta data from the repository to the end users and any applications or tools that require meta data (see Figure 2.10). See Chapter 10 of *Building and Managing the Meta Data Repository* (Wiley, 2000) for a detailed discussion on meta data consumers and meta data delivery.

The most common targets that require meta data from the MME are:

- Applications
- Data warehouses and data marts
- End users (business and technical)
- Messaging and transaction applications
- Meta data marts
- Software tools
- Third parties
- Web sites and e-commerce

Applications

Quite often applications (CRM, ERP, and so on) need to receive meta data from the MME for their own use. In these situations, it is most common to have the meta data repository create an extract file that can be brought into the application. Typically, the repository will generate a flat file and place it in a holding area that, when it is ready, an application can read in.

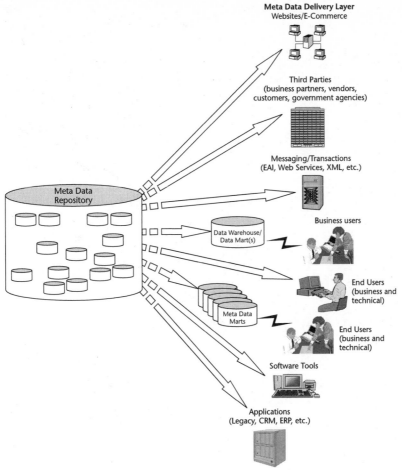

Figure 2.10   Meta data delivery layer.

Data Warehouses and Data Marts

The meta data delivery layer data warehouses and their associated data marts (usually query and reporting are executed at the data mart level) are separate from applications because of some subtle differences in the way they use meta data. Figure 2.11 shows the data mart query and report function bringing in meta data from the repository. Typically, data marts are accessed via front-end tools (Business Objects, Cognos, Hyperion, Microstrategy, and so on). These tools generate SQL code. Since the meta data repository is stored on an open, relational database, it is easy enough to *point* these tools at the repository and bring the meta data directly into the query/report (see Figure 3.5 for an example).

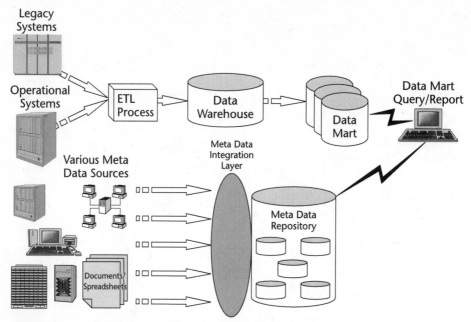

Figure 2.11   Meta data delivery layer: data warehouse and data marts.

For some date warehousing applications where the data in the data marts is voluminous or the number of end users is high, the overhead involved with going to a separate database may create too great a time delay for end users. These technical implementation issues can be remedied by loading the meta data directly into the data marts (see Figure 2.12).

End Users

The meta data delivery layer typically brings meta data directly to both business and technical end users. Usually, this meta data is delivered directly to the user's computer in the form of a document or spreadsheet or through a *thick or thin* client front-end meta data access tool.

Messaging and Transactions

As previously discussed, many companies use some form of messaging and transactions—whether EAI or XML—to transfer data from one system to another. Although most companies are not very advanced in their use and application of EAI or XML, these types of applications do utilize meta data. If companies continue to grow these applications, their need for meta data will continue to increase.

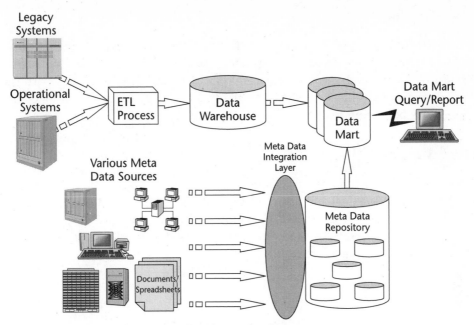

Figure 2.12   Loading meta data directly into the data marts.

Meta Data Marts

As discussed earlier in this chapter, there are situations where meta data will be extracted from the repository and brought into meta data marts. These meta data marts are a database structure designed for a huge group of meta data users.

Software Tools

The sharing and interchange of meta data among various software tools' internal meta data repositories is particularly desirable for global enterprises with dispersed teams trying to solve similar or related data analysis problems using an integrated computing approach (see Chapter 2 of *Building and Managing the Meta Data Repository* (Wiley, 2000) for a more detailed discussion on this topic). Hopefully, industry meta model standards, such as CWM, should make this effort easier. Today, most companies have to analyze the software tools' meta models and then build technical processes that will share meta data between these tools. Anyone who has had the opportunity to build and maintain these types of processes will attest to how difficult it is.

Third Parties

Some MMEs need to send meta data to third parties: vendors or suppliers, customers, government agencies or regulatory bodies, and business partners (see Figure 2.13). Typically, when meta data is exchanged with these third parties, it is done through the generation of a flat file; however, more and more companies are beginning to use XML as transportation syntax.

Web Sites and E-Commerce

Web sites and e-commerce applications also need meta data. Meta data-related Web sites are a very effective way to present meta data to the end users (see Chapter 3 for several examples). E-commerce—with its trend toward using XML and the necessity of interacting with customers and partners—will continue to need meta data for its processes.

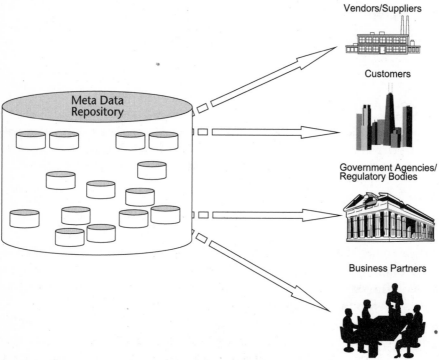

Figure 2.13 Meta data delivery layer: third parties.

MME Data Stewardship

Data is one of the most important assets in a corporation. In order for data to have value, it must be delivered quickly; be formatted properly; and be concise, accurate, and, most importantly, *understood*. The MME has become the key enabling technology for helping corporations manage meta data, but the technology is just one part of the knowledge management equation. The other parts are business ownership and active participation. These factors depend on the people responsible for the data to define and manage that meta data. As a result, the role of the data steward has grown considerably over the years.

Understanding Data Stewardship

The data steward acts as the conduit between IT and the business. The data steward (who is often not just one person, but a collection of people) align the business needs with the IT systems supporting them (both decision support and operational). The data steward has the challenge of guaranteeing that one of the corporation's most critical assets—its data—is used to its fullest capacity.

Some people may say that their company does not have any data stewards, but this is not true. Every company has a data steward. There is always someone within the company whom people turn to with questions about what the data means. This person is the data steward, even if he or she doesn't have the title.

Your company's size, organization, and industry dictates how much effort you will need to place in data stewardship. Organizations we have found to require greater data stewardship include pharmaceutical companies, certain government organizations (for example, military, energy), insurance, banking, and security brokerages and investment advisors.

Having had the opportunity to form several data stewardship organizations, we can attest that no two data stewardship groups are exactly the same. The Data Stewardship Framework provides guidelines for how these groups should be formed. This framework is designed to provide corporations and government entities with the strategies and guidelines necessary to implement a highly successful data stewardship organization. Chapter 7 provides the specific meta data elements that pertain to data stewardship.

Types of Data Stewards

Throughout this section, we use the term *data steward* to refer to the four types of data stewardship committee roles:

- Executive sponsor
- Chief steward

- Business steward
- Data steward

As each role is reviewed in the following sections, keep in mind that (with few exceptions) they are not full-time jobs.

Executive Sponsor

Any initiative that cuts across a company's lines of business must have executive management support. This is imperative in breaking down the barriers and the *ivory towers* that exist in all of our companies. Do not underestimate the obstacles that political challenges present; they are the greatest challenge that any data stewardship committee faces.

Good executive sponsors do not need to attend every data stewardship meeting, nor do they need to participate in tasks like defining data definitions. Instead, the executive sponsor needs to provide the appropriate level of support for his or her business or technical stewards.

It can be more difficult to find a business executive sponsor than it is to find a technical executive steward. Look for five key qualities in your executive sponsor:

- Someone willing to be an executive sponsor
- A person with an executive rank
- Someone with high credibility
- Someone knowledgeable about problems within the company
- A person willing to challenge the company status quo

A large financial institution was looking to implement an enterprise-level data stewardship committee. We had a technical executive sponsor; however, she had not identified a business executive sponsor. As part of our engagement with this client, we conducted a readiness assessment of their MME initiative. During this assessment, we interviewed a member of the company's executive management team. This person has worked at this company for over 20 years and was a very bright individual. He had a strong belief in his company's need for data stewardship, and he clearly understood how the lack of data stewardship had cost his company significant dollars. After this meeting, we went back to the client and stated that we found a business executive sponsor.

Chief Steward

The chief steward is responsible for the day-to-day organization and management of the data stewardship committee. Like any other organization, the data stewardship committee needs a leader or project manager. Typically, the chief steward will be someone at a senior management level, as opposed to the executive level.

The chief steward must be a highly credible person within the organization. He or she should have a sound knowledge of both the technical and the business sides of the corporation. This knowledge is vital because some stewards are from the business side and some are from the technical side. The chief steward needs to understand the politics within the organization and have insight on how to navigate around those challenges. Most importantly, the chief steward must have strong leadership and communication skills to help guide the data stewardship committee. This is most evident when this person needs to attain consensus across disparate groups.

Business Steward

The business steward is responsible for defining the procedures, policies, data concepts, and requirements of the enterprise. Keep in mind that the business stewards can be organized from a departmental level (for example, consumer lending, military branch, pharmacology) or by subject matter (for example, logistics, shipping).

Business stewards need to have a strong knowledge of the business requirements and policies of the corporation. They must make sound decisions and work with key members of their business in order to gain consensus on their organizations' business policies and requirements.

Technical Steward

The technical steward is a member of the IT department. Technical stewards focus on the technical meta data and data that needs to be captured by the data stewardship committee.

Preparing for Data Stewardship

The data stewardship committee must complete the following tasks before it can capture and define business and technical meta data:

1. Form a charter
2. Define and prioritize the committee's activities
3. Create committee rules of order
4. Establish roles for committee members
5. Design standard documents and forms

Form a Charter

The first task of the data stewardship committee is to create a documented charter for their activities. This charter states the business purposes that necessitated the data stewardship committee's formation. The data stewardship charter should not be a voluminous document, because this document's goal is to provide a clear indication of the committee's strategic business goals. This charter needs to target the specific concerns of and opportunities for the company.

TIP We like the data stewardship charter to fit on one single-spaced page. Anything longer is likely *too* long.

For example, pharmaceutical companies tend to have extensive and elaborate data stewardship committees. Their data stewardship charters traditionally focus on clinical trials, the process a pharmaceutical company goes through to research, develop, and attain government approval for new compounds (drugs). The average cost for developing a new drug is between $150 million and $250 million, and it takes over 10 years before a new drug can be brought to market. Every *day* that a new compound is delayed from reaching the market costs the company $1 million in lost revenue. This includes the extra time it will take to recoup sunk expenses (Did you ever see the interest expense on $150 million?) and the possibility of a competitor creating a competing compound.

During these trials, a new drug must meet rigorous standards from government agencies, such as the FDA, before it can gain approval. Passing these FDA (and other agency) tests is not easy. These organizations and their corresponding legislation require that a pharmaceutical company has very definitive definitions for their data elements. Clearly, a pharmaceutical company's data stewardship committee's charter will focus very heavily on how they can expedite the passing of the FDA audits.

Define and Prioritize Committee Activities

Once the charter has been created, the data stewardship committee needs to define the specific activities that it will be performing. It is vital that these activities support the strategic objectives of the data stewardship charter.

Once these activities have been defined, they must be prioritized so the data stewardship team knows what to tackle first. At this point in the process, we suggest using a matrix to show the possible activities. On the vertical axis, list which of these activities will be most beneficial to the organization (see Figure 2.14).

Possible Data Stewardship Activities	Projected Benefit to the Organization
Define physical domain values for each attribute on the primary applications.	Critical value to the organization
Define key business rules for all data warehousing and CRM applications throughout the organization.	Must be accomplished as per CIO edict
Identify potential data stewards in company that we are acquiring.	Important to accomplish but will be much more important next quarter

Figure 2.14 Prioritization matrix.

Create Committee Rules of Order

Once the activities of the data stewardship committee have been identified, the committee will have to create rules of order for the organization. Following is a sample of the types of rules of order that will need to be defined:

- Regular meeting schedule
- Meeting structure or agenda
- Issue documentation
- Issue resolution
- Meeting notes' capture and dissemination

Establish Roles for Committee Members

After the data stewardship committee has defined the rules of order, it will be important for this team to formally define the different data stewardship roles and responsibilities. Earlier, we defined four data stewardship roles: executive sponsor, chief steward, business steward, and technical steward. These roles are a good beginning set for any new data stewardship committee; however, you will want to tailor these roles, titles, and descriptions to suit your company's specific needs.

Design Standard Documents and Forms

Now it is time for the data stewardship committee to create any standard documents or forms that will support the data stewardship activities. This activity is important, because you do not want to have each steward creating his or her own documents for each activity.

One of the most commonly required documents is a change control document. Members of your company will use it to formally document their data stewardship tasks. For example, suppose that a key task of your data stewardship committee is to define business meta data definitions. You will have business stewards working on these definitions; however, some people who are not formally part of the data stewardship committee may want to recommend changes to the business definitions that your business stewards have defined. Clearly, you need a form (optimally Web-based, tied to a meta data repository of the MME) that will allow them to provide feedback.

Another common form is a data stewardship feedback mechanism. It is important that the data stewardship committee not be viewed a group that is isolated in their own ivory tower. Allowing feedback on the things that your data stewardship committee is doing well, as well as recommendations on what they can do better, helps to ensure that you are meeting the needs of your constituency.

Data Stewardship Activities

The specific activities of the data stewardship committee will vary from one organization to another and from industry to industry. However, there are some common activities:

- Define data domain values
- Establish data quality rules, validate them, and resolve them
- Set up business rules and security requirements
- Create business meta data definitions
- Create technical meta data definitions

The data stewards who work on these different activities will be primarily working with meta data; however, there will be occasions when they may need to work with actual data. The following sections walk you through these activities and provide a set of guidelines and best practices for performing them. We discuss the typical data stewards who perform each task. It is important to note that sometimes there are people who are highly knowledgeable about the data and the business policies related to the data, even though they do not belong to the particular stewardship group that I mention for the activity. For example, there may be some technical stewards who are as knowledgeable about the business policies and data values as any of the *official* business stewards. So, even though I state in my guidelines that the business stewards should be creating the business meta data definitions, obviously you would want these technical stewards working with the business stewards to generate the business meta data definitions.

For all of these activities, the chief steward will play a critical role in ensuring that they are properly completed. A good chief steward ensures that the technical and business stewards do their work thoroughly and expeditiously, understanding how easy it is for a group to fall into *analysis paralysis*. The chief steward will act as a project manager or guide in each of these activities. Most importantly, the chief steward aids committee members in resolving any conflicts—and there will be conflicts.

Define Data Domain Values

Once the business stewards define the key data attributes, they need to define the domain values for those attributes. For example, if one of the attributes is state code, then the valid domain values would be the two character abbreviations of the states (for example, CA, FL, IL, NY).

As with all data stewardship tasks, this meta data will be stored in the MME. It is highly recommended that a Web-based front end be developed so that the business stewards can easily key in this vital meta data.

In many cases, data modelers input attribute domain values into their modeling tool (for example, Erwin, Silverrun, System Architect). If this process has occurred in your company, you can create a process to export that meta data from the modeling tool and import it into the MME. This will allow the business stewards a good starting point in their process to enter domain values.

Establish Data Quality Rules, Validate Them, and Resolve Them

Data quality is the responsibility of both the business and technical stewards. It is the responsibility of the business steward to define data quality thresholds and data error criteria. For example, the data quality threshold for customer records that have errors during a data warehouse load process may be 2 percent. Therefore, if the percentage of customer records in error is greater than 2 percent, then the data warehouse load run is automatically stopped. An additional rule can be included that states that if the records-in-error rate is 1 percent or greater but less than 2 percent, then a warning message is triggered to alert the data warehouse staff; however, the data warehouse run is allowed to proceed. An example of data error criteria would be a rule defined for the HOME_LOAN_AMT field. This rule would state that the allowable values for the HOME_LOAN_AMT field is any numeric value between $0 and $3,000,000.

It is the responsibility of the technical stewards to make sure that during implementation the data quality rules are adhered to. In addition, the technical stewards will work with the business stewards on the specific data quality threshold and data error criteria.

Set Up Business Rules and Security Requirements

Business rules are some of the most critical meta data within an organization (see Chapter 7). Business rules describe how the business operates with its data. A business rule describes how the data values were derived and calculated, if the field relates (cardinality) to other fields, what the data usage rules and regulations are, and if there are any security requirements around a particular entity or attribute.

For example, a healthcare insurance company may have a field called POLICY_TREATMENTS. This field may list the specific medical treatments that a policyholder has undergone. The business rule for this field is an alphanumeric 20-byte field, whose *system of record* is System A. In addition, there may be security requirements on this field. Most health insurance companies provide coverage to their employees, so the security requirement for this field is that the IT department cannot view this field or associate it with any fields that would identify the policyholder. When security rules like these are broken, the corporation is vulnerable to legal action.

Create Business Meta Data Definitions

One of the key tasks for the business stewards is to define the business meta data definitions for the attributes of a company. It is wise to begin by having the business stewards define the main *subject areas* of their company. Subject areas are the *nouns* of the corporation: customer, product, sale, policy, logistics, manufacturing, finance, marketing, and sales. Typically, companies have 25 to 30 subject areas, depending on the industry. Once the business stewards define the subject areas, each of these areas can be further drilled down. For example, a company may distinguish between the different lines of business or subsidiaries.

Some data elements require calculation formulas of some sort. Your company may have a data attribute called NET_REVENUE. NET_REVENUE may be calculated by subtracting *gross costs* from *gross revenues*. Any calculation formulas should be included in the business meta data definitions.

Once the key data elements have been identified, the business stewards can begin working on writing meta data definitions on the attributes. The process for capturing these definitions needs to be supported by an MME. The MME includes meta data tables with attributes to hold the business meta data definitions. In addition, a Web-based front end would be given to the business stewards to key in the business meta data definitions. The MME captures and tracks these meta data definitions historically, using *from* and *to* dates on each of the meta data records. A *meta data status code* is also needed on each row of meta data. This status code shows if the business meta data definition is approved, deleted, or pending approval.

TIP Status codes are important because it is poor policy to delete meta data rows. The second you delete a row of meta data, the user wants it back.

When the first business meta data definitions are entered, it is common practice to mark them as *pending*. This allows the business data stewards to gain consensus on these elements before changing their status to *approved*.

Create Technical Meta Data Definitions

The technical stewards are responsible for creating the technical meta data definitions for the attributes of a company. It is important to understand that technical meta data definitions will differ fundamentally in form from business meta data definitions. Business meta data definitions are targeted at the business users; technical meta data definitions are targeted at an organization's IT staff. Therefore, it is perfectly acceptable to have SQL code and physical file and database locations included in the technical meta data definitions.

Usually, it is too much work to have the technical stewards list *all* of the physical attributes within the company. Instead, begin by having the technical stewards list their key data attributes. By identifying the core data attributes, the IT department can focus technical meta data definitions on only the most important data attributes. Once your technical stewards have defined these initial physical attributes, they can start working on the remaining attributes.

The process for capturing these technical data definitions is a mirror image of the process for capturing business meta data; in fact, the Web-based user screens should look very similar. The same functionality described in the business meta data definitions above (from and to dates, status codes, and so on) should be included.

Once both the business and technical stewards have defined their meta data definitions, any discrepancies will almost immediately come to light—and there will be discrepancies. For example, the business stewards may define *product* as any product that a customer has purchased. The technical stewards may define *product* as a product that is marked as active. These two definitions are clearly different. In the business stewards' definition, any product (active or inactive) that is currently on an open order for a customer would be valid. The IT staff will want to work with the business users to repair such hidden system defects.

Capability Maturity Model and the MME

Every corporation wants IT systems that are robust enough to meet their current requirements and flexible enough to adapt to their changing business needs. However, most corporations have very poorly designed IT applications; thus, when they need to implement a major enhancement to their existing systems or build new applications, the probability of project failure is exceedingly high (65 percent to 80 percent according to most surveys). This failure rate is surprising, because the average company spends approximately 5.3 percent of its annual revenue on IT-related activities.

Executives need to understand why their major IT initiatives fail at such a high rate, and why seemingly simple changes to their applications are so costly and time-consuming. They need a technique for comparing their IT development methods with those of other firms. These needs fuel the popularity of the Software Engineering Institute's (SEI) Systems Engineering Capability Maturity Model (SE-CMM). In this section, we:

- Define what the SE-CMM is

- Describe each of the six SE-CMM levels

- Apply the SE-CMM to data warehousing and provide metrics for each level

- Illustrate why an MME is the most vital application for any company looking to move up the SE-CMM levels

What Is the Capability Maturity Model?

There are many different applications of the Capability Maturity Models. Models target software development, staffing, and so on. In this section, we focus on the Systems Engineering Capability Maturity Model (SE-CMM). The SE-CMM was developed by the SEI, the Department of Defense, and a host of other entities. The SEI Web site (http://www.sei.cmu.edu/) contains more information about the various applications.

The SE-CMM is designed to be an easy-to-understand methodology for ranking a company's IT related activities. The SE-CMM has six levels (0 to 5):

- Level 0 – Not Performed

- Level 1 – Performed Informally

- Level 2 – Planned and Tracked

- Level 3 – Well-Defined

- Level 4 – Quantitatively Controlled

- Level 5 – Continuously Improving

The purpose of these levels is to provide a *measuring stick* for companies and organizations looking to improve their system development processes.

Why Is the SE-CMM Valuable?

The SE-CMM is fairly simple and easy to understand, making it a useful tool for presenting projects to the executives of a corporation. Many corporate executives are already familiar with this model. Over the years, we have used this model successfully to illustrate major IT issues and concepts to senior executives. It can be a very valuable tool for attaining project funding for key initiatives such as enterprise data asset management and meta data repository development.

Since a company cannot jump from Level 2 directly to Level 4, it is forced to develop a strategy to move up the levels sequentially.

Many large companies and government institutions are actively using this model to compare themselves with other entities. In fact, many corporations have IT goals centered on the SE-CMM levels. The SE-CMM also gives a company a mechanism to compare itself to its competitors.

Some government or agency contracts for application development now require the bidding contractor to be certified up to a given SE-CMM level in order to participate.

Purpose of SE-CMM

Before we walk through the SE-CMM's six levels, it is important to understand five key concepts:

Consistency.   This means that a task is performed much more frequently than it is not performed. If the majority of your company's IT projects use written project plans, then this activity would be performed consistently. It is important to note that consistency does not address quality or value that the task provides. Therefore, some IT staff will prepare written project plans using Microsoft Project, some will use Microsoft Excel, and some will write them out by hand. Also, the level of detail in the project plans will vary.

Repeatable.   Repeatable refers to an IT activity that provides value and is regularly performed by a particular project team or group within the company. For example, a data warehousing team may have a standard method for constructing project plans (tool, level of detail, resource naming, and so on).

Tranferable.   Transferable means that the IT activity is standardized and followed throughout the company. As a result, the success of a task is transferable across groups within the company. For example, all project plans throughout an organization should be standardized, formatted consistently, and have the same level of granularity.

Quantitative.   This refers to the objective measuring of an IT activity. For example, the time it takes to construct each project plan could be measured and captured.

Qualitative.   This refers to the subjective evaluation how well a task was accomplished. Was the project plan accurate? Was it followed by the team?

SE-CMM Levels

The SE-CMM is designed to be an easy-to-understand methodology for ranking a company's IT related activities. The SE-CMM has six levels, as described in the earlier *What Is the Capability Maturity Model?* section. The levels are explained in detail in this section.

Level 0: Not Performed

Level 0 is common for companies that are just entering the IT field. At this level, there are few or no best practices. Some IT activities are not even performed, and all deliverables are done in *one-off efforts*. Typically, new applications are built by a small number of people (possibly even one person) in a very isolated fashion.

Level 1: Performed Informally

At Level 1, consistent planning and tracking of IT activities is missing, and deliverables are generated via heroic effort. *Heroic effort* means that a team might work long hours in order to build a particular application; however, there are very few IT standards and reuse/sharing is minimal. As a result, IT deliverables are adequate; however, the deliverables are not repeatable or transferable.

As a general rule, the amount of money that a company spends on its IT applications does not affect what SE-CMM level it is at. The only exception to this rule is the move from Level 0 to Level 1. A company can move from Level 0 to Level 1 as a by-product of elevated IT spending. Moving beyond Level 1 is not affected by money spent. A corporation could be spending well over $500 million on application development and be at Level 1. Indeed, the vast majority of Fortune 500 companies and large government organizations are at a SE-CMM of Level 1.

Level 2: Planned and Tracked

At Level 2, IT deliverables are planned and tracked. In addition, there are some defined best practices within the enterprise (defined IT standards and documents or program version control, for example). Some repeatable processes exist within an IT project team, but the success of this team is not transferable across the enterprise.

Level 3: Well-Defined

IT best practices are documented and performed throughout the enterprise. At Level 3, IT deliverables are repeatable *and* transferable across the company. This level is a very difficult jump for most companies. Not surprisingly, this is also the level that provides the greatest cost savings.

Level 4: Qualitatively Controlled

Companies at Level 4 have established measurable process goals for each defined process. These measurements are collected and analyzed quantitatively. At this level, companies can begin to predict future IT implementation performance.

Level 5: Continuously Improving

At Level 5, enterprises have quantitative (measurement) and qualitative (quality) understanding of each IT process. It is at this level that a company understands how each IT process is related to the overall business strategies and goals of the corporation. Every programmer should understand how each line of SQL will assist the company in reaching its strategic goals.

Applying SE-CMM to Data Warehousing

We will now apply the SE-CMM model to data warehousing and provide you with metrics to rank your company's data warehousing efforts on SE-CMM's six levels.

Level 0: Not Performed

If your company has not built a data warehouse or has tried but failed to build a data warehouse, then your company is at SE-CMM Level 0. Even if your company has built a data warehouse, it is still possible to be at a SE-CMM Level 0. Companies at this level have few or, most likely, no best practices around their data warehouses. Their data warehouses are built by a fairly small number of people (possibly even one person) in a very isolated fashion. Also there will be a very limited understanding or testing of the quality of the data in the data warehouse. Finally, there will be low levels of business value being provided.

Following is a questionnaire that tests your company's readiness level. If you answer *yes* to more than one of the questions, it is likely that your company is at a SE-CMM Level 0 for data warehousing. If you answer *no* to all of these questions, then please proceed to SE-CMM Level 1.

Level 0 Questionnaire

1. Does your company's IT group have no dedicated data warehousing department?

2. Does your company use nonstandard terms to refer to its data warehouse (for example, data repository, data dumpster, data store)?

3. Is there a lack of understanding of the architectural differences between data warehouses, data marts, and operational data stores?

4. Are independent data marts the *standard* data warehousing architecture?

5. Does the data warehouse have no or limited error-handling processes?

Level 1: Performed Informally

At SE-CMM Level 1, consistent planning and tracking of data warehousing activities are missing. In addition, data warehousing projects are run in a heterogeneous manner, with few standards and instances of reuse or sharing. As a result, one team will build their data warehouse in one manner, and the next will build a data warehouse in a completely different manner.

This level creates extreme data, process, and technology redundancy. Many times, redundant or needless data marts and data warehouses are constructed. For example, one client built eight independent data marts. After we analyzed each, we were able to consolidate them into only two data marts. What we found was that each data mart's data and processes were fundamentally redundant with those of the other data marts. The only differences were how the data was filtered and organized on the end-user's reports.

Technology redundancy is also rampant at this level. The most popular software category is *shelfware* (software that is purchased but only sits on the shelf and is not actively used). These same companies purchase lots of redundant software. There isn't a business or technical reason for a company to have licenses for SQL Server, Oracle, DB2, Teradata, Sybase, and Informix, but the majority of Fortune 500 companies have all six. This needless redundancy requires IT resources to be knowledgeable about (not to mention available for) each of these technologies. Obviously the software vendors enjoy these spending patterns a great deal.

At SE-CMM Level 1, some data warehousing projects are successful, some projects fail miserably, many projects are unnecessary, and all of them are overly expensive. Often, data warehousing projects that are initially successful cannot be sustained. Thus, they may be successful in the first few years of operation but then will not be able to scale to meet the end users' demands or an increase in data volumes.

Companies that are at a SE-CMM Level 1 in data warehousing typically spend a great deal of money. It is important to understand that regardless of how much money a company spends on its data warehousing applications, it will not move the company past SE-CMM Level 1, unless it is spent wisely. In fact, the most costly data warehousing implementations reside at Level 1, including those of the vast majority of Fortune 500 companies and large government organizations that have data warehouses.

Level 1 Questionnaire

1. Is your company just beginning to understand that there are considerable data quality issues in the data warehouse?

2. Is your company spending extreme amounts on data warehousing (40 percent to 60 percent of the entire IT budget)?

3. Does your company not know how much it is spending on data warehousing?

4. Does your company have multiple, large (8 to 15 staff members) data warehousing departments?

5. Does your company lack a global understanding of all of their data warehousing initiates?

6. Are independent data marts the *standard* data warehousing architecture?

7. Does the data warehouse have no or only limited error-handling processes?

Level 2: Planned and Tracked

At Level 2, independent data marts are less prevalent than at Level 1; however, they are still the most common form of data warehousing architecture used in the company. Successful data warehousing projects tend to stay successful and run in a fairly efficient manner. For example, a company may have many disparate data warehousing activities; however, a particular department or line of business has implemented a sound data warehouse with the appropriate supporting teams and processes. This group plans and tracks their IT deliverables and has defined some best practices (for example, a meta data repository, defined IT standards and documents, program version control, a dedicated data warehousing team, data quality tracking). These repeatable processes exist within the department or line of business; however, these processes and standards are only followed by the group and not used throughout the organization. As a result, the success of this group is not transferable across the enterprise.

Although they have some success, organizations at this level have many failed projects and many unnecessary projects, which creates an overly expensive IT organization.

Level 2 Questionnaire

1. Is there a successful data warehouse implementation within your company?

2. Is the successful data warehouse sustainable?

3. Do you have a meta data repository that, at a minimum, contains and manages data-warehousing-related meta data?

4. Has the successful data warehouse implemented development standards (see the preceding paragraph for examples)?

5. Is it true that the entire enterprise does not support or have centralized procedures/standards?

6. Is your company spending extreme amounts on data warehousing (30 percent to 60 percent of the entire IT budget)?

7. Does your company have multiple, large (8 to 15 staff members) data warehousing departments?

Level 3: Well-Defined

The jump from Level 2 to Level 3 is the most difficult for a large company or government entity. At Level 3, IT's best practices are documented and performed throughout the enterprise. In addition, IT deliverables are repeatable *and* transferable across the company. This is also the level that provides the greatest cost savings.

At Level 3, the organization has already invested in centralized IT organizations (centers of excellence, standards bodies, and so on), and standards are religiously adhered to. At Level 3, independent data marts are few and far between, and data warehousing project success is more common than project failure. In addition, an enterprise-wide meta data repository has been constructed and is a central part of any IT effort. At this level, the data warehousing investments are truly becoming efficient.

Level 3 Questionnaire

1. Are there very few independent data marts?
2. Do your data warehousing initiatives succeed more often than they fail?
3. Is there a successful data warehousing implementation within your company?
4. Is the successful data warehouse sustainable?
5. Does your company know how much they are spending on data warehousing?
6. Does your company have centralized IT groups?
7. Does your company have an enterprise-wide meta data repository that supports the data warehouse and the operational systems?

Level 4: Qualitatively Controlled

Companies at Level 4 have established measurable process goals for each defined data warehousing process. These measurements are collected and analyzed quantitatively. At this level, companies can begin to predict future IT implementation performance.

At this level, data warehousing efforts are consistently successful, and an organization can begin to accurately forecast the future performance of these efforts. Existing data warehousing efforts are improving in terms of data quality and value to the business.

Level 4 Questionnaire

1. Can you measure each of your data warehousing processes?
2. Are your data warehousing efforts consistently successful?
3. Has the quality of the data within your data warehouse been improving over time?
4. Can you accurately predict (within 10 percent) what future data warehousing efforts will take?
5. Is technology, data, and process redundancy minimal throughout the organization?

Level 5: Continuously Improving

At Level 5, enterprises have *quantitative* (measurement) and *qualitative* (quality) understanding of each data warehousing IT process. It is at this level that a company understands how each IT process is related to the overall business strategies and goals of the corporation. For example, every programmer should understand how each line of SQL will assist the company in reaching its strategic goals.

Level 5 companies experience very low levels of data, process, and technology redundancy. The redundancy that does exist is documented, and why it exists is understood. Data warehousing investments are becoming optimized.

Level 5 Questionnaire

1. Can you measure each of your data warehousing processes?
2. Can you measure the quality of each of your data warehousing processes and compare changes in that quality over time?
3. Has the quality of the data within your data warehouse been improving over time?
4. Is your data warehousing investment very efficient?
5. Does your company have a very strong understanding of the quality of each and every data warehousing process?
6. Do your programmers understand their role in helping the company reach its goals?

As you can see from Figure 2.15, we have never seen a SE-CMM Level 5 data warehousing initiative. However, some firms have attained SE-CMM Level 5 in application development.

Data Warehouseing –CMM Levels

Figure 2.15 Data warehousing: SE-CMM levels.

MME and the Common Warehouse Metamodel

The Common Warehouse Metamodel (CWM) is the current open standard for the interchange of data-warehouse-related meta data. It supports tool interoperability across systems via a shared meta model. CWM is owned and supported by the Object Management Group (OMG, www.omg.org), which is a consortium of over 800 companies. The OMG's most well-known standard is the Common Object Request Broker Architecture (CORBA), which allows object-oriented programs to interoperate on distributed systems. They concentrate on object technology and distributed applications, and now they also have custody of the Unified Modeling Language (UML) specification. The OMG board approved the CWM specification in June 2000. It is based on other OMG technology and focused on being vendor-neutral.

CWM borrows some of its designs from the Open Information Model (OIM), which was from the Meta Data Coalition (MDC). The OIM was originally engineered by Microsoft and Texas Instruments in 1996. In 2001, the MDC OIM was officially merged into the OMG effort. The CWM was meant to be specific to the data warehouse and business intelligence meta data areas, whereas the OIM covered this plus more general IT areas such as business rules and business processes.

Integrating meta data provided by different software tools (for example, ETL tools, OLAP tools, databases) is complex, since each tool has its own design for relevant meta data. The CWM is a model for data warehouse and business intelligence meta data. It is intended to be used by vendors of data warehousing and business intelligence software so that the tools can communicate with each other in a standard way. Most meta data integration requires difficult work to transform and integrate one tool's meta data into another tool's meta data. The CWM aims to simplify this task, to reduce the cost of creating and maintaining a data warehouse, and to increase the effectiveness of using it by managing the meta data integration problems. As CWM is adopted by a wider range of software vendors, the standard is expected to enable the interoperability of the various data warehousing tools and to significantly assist in the development of the data warehousing field as a whole. In addition, CWM aspires to aid MMEs to more easily integrate meta data from data warehousing tools.

As we previously stated, CWM only covers data warehousing and business intelligence meta data, but it has a limited scope in other ways too. CWM is not a repository standard; it only specifies the shared models along with some supporting underlying technologies. Thus, it does not specify repository functions that are needed to support the real operations of MMEs. Also, it is independent of the architecture of the MME, whether centralized, decentralized or distributed. See Chapter 7 of *Building and Managing the Meta Data Repository* (Wiley, 2000) for more information.

IMPACT OF CWM ON THIS BOOK

In writing this book, it was a central goal to not tie any of the meta models to a particular vendor or standard. However, the philosophy of designing for common meta data concepts that allow uniform treatment is a powerful modeling concept, and it has been applied here. The incorporation of this philosophy becomes very important when the models of the various areas in an IT environment need to relate to each other. For example, a deployed software module may provide access to any kind of physical data resource such as a relational database or an XML file. Using a common concept means that the software module meta data does not need to have different structures for the different data types.

Where the design areas of this book and CWM overlap, great effort was taken to make them structurally compatible without negatively affecting the structure or design of the meta models in this book. The models are based on using a relational database as the final implementation technology, whereas the CWM is based on the MOF.

CWM Solution for Interchange Requirements

The CWM has technology for addressing each of the three requirements for interchanging meta data between data warehousing tools that do not have their own adapters. The requirements are:

Common meta models.   CWM wants the basic data warehouse subject areas to have the same meta model. As a result, CWM's core functionality is the mappings, files, expressions, and so on that are needed to exchange data warehousing artifacts. This is the most critical functionality of CWM.

A common definition language for these models.   Just like SQL, data definition language (DDL) can be used to define relational databases; a standard language is needed to represent the models. The language also needs a manipulation component (such as SQL) in order to access and update the meta data. This language is called the Meta Language Facility (MOF). MOF also allows the CWM models to be extended for new functionality.

A wire protocol to send the models between the applications.   The meta data needs a defined representation in terms of bits to be exchanged. This is XML Metadata Interchange (XMI) language. Essentially XMI is a serialization into XML of the MOF language.

CWM Technology and Approach

The CWM technology and approach encompasses a layered architecture and other supporting technology.

Layered Architecture

The CWM design covers most aspects of the data warehousing and business intelligence. The structure of CWM includes several layers, where each layer provides a grouping of information. The layers have components called *packages*, which are narrowed to a particular area. The component packages in each layer are:

Foundation.   The foundation layer comprises three components: business information, data types, and software deployment. Business information covers documents, descriptions, and contacts that can be attached to any other element. Data types describe the types of data used in the various systems, such as a specific relational database, and how one type can be coverted to another type. Software deployment tracks what software packages are installed on what hardware.

Resource.   The resource layer has five key components: relational, file, XML, object-oriented database (OODB), and COBOL. These five components describe the finer structure of these data resources.

Analysis.   The analysis layer comprises four important components: transformation, OLAP, data mining, and information visualization. The transformation component describes the structure of expressions and the mappings of data resources to other data resources that may use the data types for conversions. OLAP defines the logical structure of OLAP cubes and dimensions. These logical structures can then be mapped to physical data resources. The data-mining component defines a structure to hold driving parameters for data-mining algorithms and to hold the results of that mining. Information visualization covers the structure used in controlling a display of information and the structure of reports.

Data warehouse management.   The data warehouse management layer has two key components: warehouse process and warehouse operations. The purpose of the data warehouse process component is to define how the processes that run the loading of a data warehouse are structured. The data warehouse operations component defines how the executions of the data warehouse processes are recorded.

Supporting Technology

An important implementation point for CWM is its definition language, MOF. Whereas relational database structures are defined with ANSII SQL, the OMG saw different requirements that needed a different technology. MOF is a data-centric object-oriented language. MOF allows for the direct use of abstractions that do not exist in relational databases, but that correspond to some abstractions used in logical- or conceptual-level models. MOF provides a direct implementation of these and other modeling concepts that are not provided by a relational database, including:

- An individual identity for each entity is provided. This is like a single surrogate key for each entity
- Entity subtypes
- Multiple inheritances, where an entity can be a direct subtype of more than one entity
- Implementation of many-to-many relationships
- Ordering of relationships—the *many* side of a relationship can have an ordering to it
- Examination of the structure of the models through reflection. This is the meta level for the models. MOF supports this examination directly, similarly to the way you can get the structure of a database and then dynamically create SQL
- The semantics of MOF support the distribution of data across multiple machines
- A standard direct serialization of the language into XML

The MOF language provides a powerful platform for modeling the complex structures required of a comprehensive meta data design. It can be viewed as a specification of an object-oriented database that can only do data definition, accessing, and updates.

There are some drawbacks, however:

- OODB structures can have a performance penalty, depending on the design; however, the size of meta data is usually small and manageable, and thus performance should not be an issue in most cases
- It is a new and relatively unknown language and currently has only a few implementations
- There are currently few people proficient in using MOF and who understand the CWM structure, especially compared to the pool of talent for SQL-based technology

The use of a language such as MOF is natural for the OMG. MOF supports working with distributed objects, which was the prime motivation for the original creation of the OMG.

The Future of the CWM

The CWM is a target meta data solution for data warehousing and business intelligence, because it handles the complexity of the subject area well and supports the distributed nature of some meta data architectures. The Web Services protocol standard is aimed at making distributed computing easier to implement. Making a distributed system had been a difficult task that required specialized knowledge and skill. Web Services is a protocol standard designed to accomplish ease of use. A significant technological direction for CWM is to utilize Web Services to support distributed meta data architectures.

Another major direction is the specification of interchange patterns so that the various data warehousing tools can interoperate via the standard. For example, if two repositories or tools exchange meta data about a relational database, at what granularity should the meta data be transferred?

Summary

Now that you have a solid understanding of the six major components of the MME, we will present the types of applications that a MME can provide. Chapter 3 presents MME applications across varied industries, along with case studies of two world-class MME implementations.

Managed Meta Data Environment Applications

Having delivered over 100 keynote speeches and courses on meta data management and the MME concepts, we have learned that it is vital to show specific applications in which the MME can be used. This chapter presents several practical applications of the meta models found in Part Two. In the first section, we will use fictitious data from several industries and government agencies.

In the last part of this chapter, we will look at two world-class MME initiatives that illustrate the fundamentals presented in Chapters 1 and 2.

> **NOTE** All data used in this section of the book is fictitious and not based on any client site.

MME Application Examples

This section walks you through several specific applications for an MME. The following applications are covered throughout the examples in this section:

- Business meta data and knowledge management
- Data quality analysis
- IT impact analysis

- IT systems consolidation and migration
- Mergers and acquisitions
- Regulatory adherence
- Security analysis

Some of the applications will show meta data in standalone reports. In other examples, meta data will be directly integrated into a data warehousing environment. These applications are a good cross-industry selection, including:

- Banking and finance
- Healthcare insurance
- Manufacturing
- National defense organizations
- Pharmaceuticals
- Retail
- Telecommunications

You may find these application examples so familiar that it will seem as if they were taken right from your own company's history. Rest assured that all of our examples are based on actual MME implementations; however, the industries, data, and specific applications have been changed.

Banking and Finance Industry Example

Banking and financial organizations were early adopters of MME technology. One of the reasons for this trend is that banking and financial institutions have additional complexities that have been brought into their IT departments because of the extensive mergers and acquisitions that take place in this industry segment. All of these mergers and acquisitions leave your typical large bank with several versions of each of their core processing and strategic decision-making systems.

This problem is compounded by the fact that most of these companies are not managed from an enterprise view. Instead, each line of business has a great deal of autonomy, including a separate budget and, in some cases, a separate IT department. This situation creates even more application, process, software, hardware, and data redundancy.

BUSINESS META DATA FOR THE CUSTOMER

A client is in the business of supplying information to large corporations. The information is provided in data-mart-like structures. This company competes against other large firms in very long and complex sales cycles. When the data in these data-mart-like structures was delivered to the clients, a great deal of training was required to understand the data in the structures. The company's typical approach (and their competitors' approach) was to train a group of four to six *superusers* to, in turn, educate the thousands of people who would end up using this data. This situation was problematic for all of the customers because it is very difficult to have four to six superusers manually disseminate information to thousands of end users. We decided to define global business meta data for the industry that they compete in. Then, we would use this global business meta data as a template and create a copy of the template and tailor it to the specific requirements of each client.

What value did this MME, which focused on business meta data, provide to the company?

◆ The company could offer this business meta data to the clients as part of its information offerings. This provided the company with a competitive advantage in the marketplace.

◆ The competition did not have this capability. As a result, our client had an extra *bullet* in its sales arsenal that the competition was missing.

◆ This feature was so valuable that the company could charge a premium for it. As a result, the MME was generating new revenues for the company. As you can imagine, this project had the complete support of the senior managers of the company and is viewed as a huge success.

◆ There were considerable savings in reduced training time for the company's customers.

This is an outstanding example of an MME that targets, not the employees of a company, but the customers of the organization.

Application Scenario

In order to penetrate the Wisconsin market, BigCity Bank recently acquired Small Town Bank, which had a significant local presence. In fact, the majority of the services that BigCity Bank offers is only a part of Small Town Bank's core product offerings. This acquisition comes with some challenges, the first and foremost being a whole new set of redundant applications that Small Town

Bank has. Clearly, BigCity needs to migrate Small Town to the BigCity systems as soon as possible, since the maintenance costs are significant. In addition, this migration will be critical for helping the Small Town employees adapt to the BigCity environment.

Fortunately for BigCity, several years ago it invested in building an enterprise-wide MME application. This application is targeted at capturing and managing technical meta data throughout all of their systems. Therefore, the first step in this migration was to bring in the technical meta data from Small Town Bank into BigCity's MME environment. This was no small task; but once it was completed it allowed BigCity to significantly assist their Small Town IT migration team. The IT team doing the Small Town migration wanted an impact analysis that would take the core BigCity columns and tables and map them to the corresponding Small Town columns and tables (see Figure 3.1).

This report is invaluable to the migration team, because they need to know which Small Town systems they need to analyze in order to migrate them over. For example, BigCity uses *Cust_Nbr* as its key attribute of record for unique customer numbers. Small Town has three attributes (*CUSTNUM*, *Purchase_No*, and *Borwr_No*) that need to be migrated over to BigCity's *Cust_Nbr*. This type of information is absolutely critical to the migration team, because it is fundamental to the process for retiring Small Town Bank's systems.

Once this analysis is completed, the migration team will want to get more detailed in their study. They will want to know the specific transformation rules that will be necessary to move the Small Town columns into the BigCity systems. Figure 3.2 shows a technical meta-data-driven impact analysis that shows each of the key BigCity columns with the corresponding Small Town columns, along with any transformation rules.

Figure 3.2 illustrates a classic MME application. Notice how each domain value for *Cust_Tbl* is mapped to the corresponding transformation rule, keeping in mind that each of the values for *Cust_Tbl* has a slightly different transformation rule. The *Cust_Tbl* attribute is set to "1" when Small Town's customer record has attribute *CUSTCDE* equal to "3" and the *CUSTBAL* is greater than $500,000. This analysis has been made much easier because BigCity has a bankwide (global) definition for affluent customers. For them, an affluent customer is one with a balance greater than $500,000. Now that the migration team has this meta data, the task for integrating all of the Small Town Bank's systems into theirs is much easier.

Banking MME Report: Systems Consolidation

BigCity Bank				Small Town Bank		BigCity Bank	BigCity Bank
Attribute Name	Attribute Definition	Entity Name	System Name	Attribute Name	Attribute Definition	Entity Name	System Name
Cust_Nbr	Cust_Nbr is the attribute of record for BigCity Bank customer numbers.	Cust_Tbl	Central Customer System	CUSTNUM	Customer numbers from the deposit system	CUSTTABLE	CUSTAPPL
				Purchase_No	Customer numbers from the purchase in the legacy deposit system	Purch_Tbl	CUSTSYS
				Borwr_No	Customer numbers from the loan system	Borrower_File	LoanSys
Cust_Type	Cust_Type is the attribute of record for BigCity Bank customer types (affluent, upward, standard, high risk).	Cust_Tbl	Central Customer System	CUSTCDE	Customer Types from the general ledger system	GL_CUST	GLAPPL
Cust_Card_Ind	Cust_Card_Ind is the attribute of record for Big City Bank customers who have a BCB credit card.	Cust_Tbl	Central Customer System		None applicable		
Cust_Crdt_Ratg	Cust_Crdt_Ratg is the attribute of record for BigCity Bank customer credit ratings (Superior Risk, Low Risk, Standard Risk, High Risk, Extreme Risk).	Cust_Tbl	Central Customer System	Credit_Rate	Customer rate is from the general ledger system and refers to the credit rating/worthiness of a customer	GL_CUST	GLAPPL

Figure 3.1 Banking MME report: systems consolidation.

Banking MME Report: Column Analysis

| Systems Consolidation Report | | | | | August 15, 2003 | | |
| BigCity Bank | | | | | Small Town Bank | | |
Entity Name	Attribute Definition	Attribute Name	Domain Value	Transformation Rules	Attribute Name	Domain Value	Entity Name
Cust_Tbl	Cust_Type is the attribute of record for BigCity Bank customer types: 1 = affluent 2 = upward 3 = standard 4 = high risk	Cust_Type					
			1	Cust_Tbl = 1 WHEN CUSTCDE = 3 AND CUSTBAL > 500,000	CUSTCDE	3	GL_CUST
					CUSTBAL	High cardinality field	GL_CUST
			2	Cust_Tbl = 2 WHEN CUSTCDE = 4 AND CUSTBAL <= 500,000 AND CUSTBAL > 200,000	CUSTCDE	3	GL_CUST
					CUSTBAL	High cardinality field	GL_CUST
			3	Cust_Tbl = 3 WHEN CUSTCDE = 1 or 2 AND CUSTBAL <= 200,000 AND CUSTBAL > 75,000	CUSTCDE	3	GL_CUST
					CUSTBAL	High cardinality field	GL_CUST
			4	Cust_Tbl = 4 WHEN CUSTCDE = 0 AND CUSTBAL < 75,000 AND Credit_Rate < 22	CUSTCDE	3	GL_CUST
					CUSTBAL	High cardinality field	GL_CUST
					Credit_Rate	High cardinality field	GL_CUST
Cust_Card_Ind	Cust_Card_Ind is the attribute of record for BigCity Bank customers who have a BCB credit card.	Cust_Tbl					

Figure 3.2   Banking MME report: column analysis consolidation.

Healthcare Insurance Industry Example

Healthcare insurance companies were also early adopters of MME applications. Healthcare insurance companies must adhere to a number of regulations. For example, many healthcare companies insure their employees. While this makes sense, it does create a problem: an insurance company cannot view the individual claims made by its employees.

For example, imagine that an employee is receiving treatments and submitting valid insurance claims for a drug-related problem. If an unauthorized employee looks at the employee's claims, this would violate several privacy statutes and could create potentially serious legal exposure for the insurance company.

Application Scenario

Discount Health Company (DHC) wants to make sure that there isn't any unauthorized access to sensitive company reports. DHC has implemented a fairly limited scope MME that captures user IDs and user names for each report that users access. DHC then uses this MME to generate a report that shows the restricted queries, user IDs, user names, and security privileges (see Figure 3.3).

Notice that this report shows that several users are accessing the highly sensitive *DHC Employee Claims* query. In viewing these users, it is clear that *Larry Williams* does not have the correct security privileges to be accessing this query. In addition, Larry did not access this report one time; he has accessed it 22 times over the past month.

This is a situation that needs to be handled on multiple fronts. First, there is a gap in the IT department's security process. The IT department needs to revisit its client/role security access. Second, a conversation needs to take place with Mr. Williams to determine why he has accessed the employee claims report over 20 times. Using an MME gives DHC an opportunity to catch this problem early, before other people obtain access via the gap in the security process, and it will help reduce the likelihood of Mr. Williams talking about what he has been viewing.

Manufacturing Industry Example

As the size of a manufacturing firm grows, the need for an MME also grows. For example, there is not a major automobile manufacturer that doesn't have some sort of MME initiatives in production or development (although some of these initiatives could be architected and designed better). Our application scenario will focus on an automotive manufacturer.

Healthcare MME Report: Security Analysis

Query Security Report (October)   Discount Health Company (DHC)   November 20, 2003

Query name	Query Definition	User ID & Name	Query Requests	
DHC Employee Claims	This query shows all DHC employees who are covered by DHC health plans. Fields on this query include employee number, Social Security number, employee name, episode of care (EOC), EOC date, and EOC treatment on a monthly basis.	00010 Clay Johnson	34	EMP –Std employee AEMP –Employee admin. EHLTHAD –Employee health plan admin.
		00015 Gwen Gaines	7	EMP –Std employee HLTHAD –Global health plan admin.
		00023 Larry Williams	22	EMP –Std employee
DHC Employee Payroll	This query shows all DHC employees and the salary, commission, and bonuses that they have received on a yearly basis. Fields on this query include employee number, Social Security number, employee name, base salary, sales commissions, and employee bonuses.	00007 Kim Melvin	27	EMP –Std employee AEMP –Employee admin.
		00015 Gwen Gaines	10	EMP –Std employee HLTHAD –Global health plan admin.
		00034 Lenny Moore	19	EMP –Std employee EPAYAD –Employee payroll admin.

Figure 3.3   Healthcare MME report: security analysis.

Application Scenario

FirstRateMotors (FRM) is a major automobile manufacturer that has a full range of automobiles but tends to specialize in sports/performance and sport utility vehicles (SUVs). Like any manufacturer, FRM schedules and runs national marketing campaigns to help promote vehicle sales. FRM has an MME that targets business meta data, specifically to support a marketing campaign management data warehouse. This data warehouse contains many marketing reports, including auto sales by auto type and by marketing campaign (see Figure 3.4).

A report like the one presented in Figure 3.4 is a critical tool for any vice president of marketing or marketing director to understand the effectiveness—or ineffectiveness—of his or her marketing campaigns. Such marketing decision-makers use this report to make strategic decisions about the campaigns that they want to run. The ability to *hotkey* (that is, **right-click and press F1**) on a row of data and receive data quality statistics would have a tremendous value. Figure 3.5 shows how an end user can bring up these statistics.

Suppose that you are trying to make a strategic decision about your *0 Down and 0% Interest* marketing campaign. As you look at the sales numbers, you can see that the technical meta data shows that 2.3 percent of the records were not loaded into the data warehouse. As a result, there is a skew percentage of 2.3 percent associated with this field. A senior decision-maker in the Marketing department would want to know that the numbers are skewed and by how much.

National Defense Organization Industry Example

National defense organizations (such as, the FBI; the U.S. Army, Navy, Air Force, Marines, and Coast Guard; and Britain's Royal Navy) have some of the most extensive MME requirements of any type of organization. These groups are absolutely dependent on the information from their systems and the proper functionality of their immense IT applications. This is doubly important to understand because the activities that these organizations engage in place people in harm's way. Our application scenario maps the IT system's data elements to the functional information elements for interfaces between the major IT systems.

Application Scenario

A key task of the National Security Organization is to deliver medical supplies to various theaters of operation. They want to see which branches of the military utilize what interfaces and elements to accomplish this task (see Figure 3.6). This type of report is highly valuable when problems or enhancements need to be resolved/made across the IT systems.

Manufacturing MME Report: Automotive Report

Campaign Analysis Query

FirstRateMotors

January 20, 2004

Campaign Dates	Campaign Name	Campaign Description	Auto Sales	Auto Type
01/01/2003 – 03/31/2003	Buy Now, Pay Later	The "Buy Now, Pay Later" campaign was a nationwide campaign. This campaign offered customers the option not to begin payments for a new car purchase until January 1, 2004. This offer was only applicable for those customers with better than standard credit ratings.	7,045	ECON – Smaller, cheaper, economy car line
			9,500	MID – Midsize sedan automobiles
			22,010	SPTS – Sports/performance cars
			14,700	SUV – Sport utility vehicles
		Grand Total	**53,255**	
04/01/2003 – 06/30/2003	Buy One, Get a Free Scooter	The "Buy One, Get a Free Scooter" campaign was a nationwide campaign. This campaign offered customers a free scooter with the purchase of a new car. Dealer could only discount cars, up to $1,000 above the customer-shown invoice.	5,205	ECON – Smaller, cheaper, economy car line
			7,250	MID – Midsize sedan automobiles
			17,888	SPTS – Sports/performance cars
			10,900	SUV – Sport utility vehicles
		Grand Total	**41,243**	
07/01/2003 – 09/30/2003	$1,000 Minimum Trade-In	The "1,000 Minimum Trade-In" campaign was a nation-wide campaign. This campaign offered customers a $1,000 minimum trade-in, regardless of the condition of their trade-in vehicle, only for those customers purchasing a new car.	6,102	ECON – Smaller, cheaper, economy car line
			8,330	MID – Midsize sedan automobiles
			19,750	SPTS – Sports/performance cars
			12,400	SUV – Sport utility vehicles
		Grand Total	**46,582**	
10/01/2003 – 12/31/2003	0 Down and 0% Interest	the "0 Down and 0% Interest" campaign was a nationwide campaign. This campaign offered customers standard car discounts, with 0 Down and 0% Interest for only those customers with standard or better credit ratings.	6,700	ECON – Smaller, cheaper, economy car line
			8,925	MID – Midsize sedan automobiles
			20,820	SPTS – Sports/performance cars
			13,220	SUV – Sport utility vehicles
		Grand Total	**49,665**	

Figure 3.4 Manufacturing MME report: automotive report.

Automotive Report: Data Quality Statistics

Campaign Analysis Query **FirstRateMotors** **January 20, 2004**

Campaign Dates	Campaign Name	Campaign Description	Auto Sales	Auto Type
01/01/2003 – 03/31/2003	Buy Now, Pay Later	The "Buy Now, Pay Later" campaign was a nationwide campaign. This campaign offered customers the option not to begin payments for a new car purchase until January 1, 2004. This offer was only applicable for those customers with better than standard credit ratings.	7,045	ECON –Smaller, cheaper, economy car line
			9,500	MID –Midsize sedan automobiles
			22,010	SPTS –Sports/performance cars
			14,700	SUV –Sport utility vehicles
		Grand Total	**53,255**	
04/01/2003 – 06/30/2003	Buy One, Get a Free Scooter	The "Buy One, Get a Free Scooter" campaign was a nationwide campaign. This campaign offered customers a free scooter with the purchase of a new car. Dealer could only discount cars, up to $1,000 above customer shown invoice.	5,205	ECON –Smaller, cheaper, economy car line
			7,250	MID –Midsize sedan automobiles
			17,888	SPTS –Sports/performance cars
			10,900	SUV –Sport utility vehicles
		Grand Total	**41,243**	
07/01/2003 – 09/30/2003	$1,0... Trade...	...paign was a ...ign offered ...-in, regardless ...hicle, only for ...ew car. ...hose customers...	6,102	ECON –Smaller, cheaper, economy car line
			8,330	MID –Midsize sedan automobiles
			19,750	SPTS –Sports/performance cars
			12,400	SUV –Sport utility vehicles
		Grand Total	**46,582**	
10/01/2003 – 12/31/2003	0 Down and 0% Interest	the "0 Down and 0% Interest" ca... ...was a nationwide campaign. This campaign ...e and customers standard car discounts, with 0 ...rd 0% Interest for only those customers with stan... or better credit ratings.	6,700	ECON –Smaller, cheaper, economy car line
			8,925	MID –Midsize sedan automobiles
			20,820	SPTS –Sports/performance cars
			13,220	SUV –Sport utility vehicles
		Grand Total	**49,665**	

> **Data Quality Statistics**
>
> 2.3% of the records were not loaded in the data warehouse batch runs.
>
> **Skew percentage equals 2.3%**

Figure 3.5 Automotive report: data quality statistics.

National Security MME Report: Systems Interfaces Report

Systems Interfaces Reports		National Security Organization		February 10, 2004
Functional Task Name	IT Systems Involved	Interface between IT Systems	Functional Information Elements Needed for Interface	IT System Information Elements Needed for Interface
Deliver Medical Supplies	Air Force –Air Force Transport Systems (AFTS)	AFTS to ATS	Airplane Attributes	Airplane Cargo Capacity
				Airplane Status
			Truck Attributes	Truck Cargo Capacity
				Truck Miles per Gallon
		AFTS to NTS	Airplane Attributes	Airplane Cargo Capacity
				Airplane Status
			Boat Attributes	Boat Capacity
	Army –Army Transport Systems (ATS)	ATS to AFTS	Truck Attributes	Truck Capacity
				Truck Volume
			Airplane Attributes	Airplane Cargo Capacity
				Airplane Fuel Capacity
		ATS to NTS	Truck Attributes	Truck Cargo Capacity
				Truck Volume
			Boat Attributes	Boat Capacity
				Boat Status
	Navy –Navy Transport System (NTS)	NTS to AFTS	Boat Attributes	Boat Capacity
				Boat Status
			Airplane Attributes	Airplane Cargo Capacity
				Airplane Fuel Capacity
		NTS to ATS	Boat Attributes	Boat Capacity
				Boat Status
			Train Attributes	Train Capacity
				Train Fuel Used

Figure 3.6 National security MME report: systems interfaces report.

Pharmaceutical Industry Example

Chapter 2 examined the clinical trial process for developing new compounds (drugs). There is a regulation, Title 21 CFR Part 11, that has a significant impact on a clinical trial for a pharmaceutical company. Let's look at the following passage from the FDA, Department of Health and Human Services, entitled "Title 21 CFR Part 11, Electronic Records; Electronic Signatures; Final Rule" dated Thursday, March 20, 1997:

> *The Food and Drug Administration (FDA) is issuing regulations that provide criteria for acceptance by FDA, under certain circumstances, of electronic records, . . . the pharmaceutical industry met with the agency to determine how they could accommodate paperless record systems . . . to develop a uniform approach by which the agency could accept electronic signatures and records in all program areas . . . . The final rule provides criteria under which the FDA will consider electronic records to be equivalent to paper records, and electronic signatures equivalent to traditional handwritten signatures.*

Compliance with FDA regulations such as this is no small task, and almost every pharmaceutical company is struggling to adhere to this regulatory rule. This rule will be the focus point of our application scenario.

Application Scenario

TheGreatPharma Company is a large pharmaceutical company that is running a clinical trial on a new compound. In order to pass various Title 21 CFR Part 11 audit compliance regulations, they must track every instance where a person changed any data within the clinical trial. The meta data captured in this process includes what data was changed, who changed it, when it was changed, what its prior value was, what its new value is, and why it was changed. The audit compliance report shown in Figure 3.7 could be generated directly from the MME and provided to the FDA to assist in expediting the process of FDA approval.

Retail Industry Example

Retail companies were early adopters of data warehousing technology. Interestingly, they have been lagging somewhat on the adoption of MME compared to industries like healthcare and banking, which were also early data warehouse adopters. The need for MME applications in the retail industry is absolutely critical, because retail companies have inflated IT budgets and there is a great deal of decision-making and client interfacing that occurs among various stores.

Title 21 CFR Part 11 MME Report: Audit Compliance

Audit Compliance Report					The Great Pharma Company						Clinical Research Organization	August 15, 2004
In-House Clinic							**Clinical Research Organization**					
Attribute Name	Who Changed Data?	When Changed	Current Value	Prior Value	Reason for change	Attribute Name	Who Changed Data?	When Changed	Current Value	Prior Value	Reason for Change	
Subject's Date of Birth	Data Screener A	May 1, 2003	July 2, 1985	July 2, 1958	Input error, transposed last 2 digits of year	Subject's Date of Birth	Data Screener 1	June 4, 2003	April 4, 1955	July 4, 1945	Input error, entered wrong value	
DateTime Treatment Given	Data Screener B	May 10, 2003	March 9, 2003 10:05AM	March 9, 2003 10:05PM	Input error, should have been PM instead of AM	DateTime Treatment Given	Data Screener 2	May 10, 2003	March 9, 2002 10:05AM	March 9, 2002 10:05PM	Input error, should have been PM instead of AM	
Subject's Weight at Screening	Data Screener C	May 12, 2003	210 pounds	195 pounds	Equipment error, scale wasn't calibrated correctly	Subject's Weight at Screening	Data Screener 3	May 14, 2003	210 pounds	195 pounds	Equipment error, scale wasn't calibrated correctly	
						Subject's Weight at Screening	Data Screener 3	May 14, 2003	164 pounds	146 pounds	Input error, transposed last 2 digits	
						Subject's Weight at Screening	Data Screener 3	May 14, 2003	164 pounds	146 pounds	Input error, transposed last 2 digits	
Subject's Height at Screening	Data Screener D	June 18, 2003	64.2 inches	42.6 inches	Input error, reversed the numbers	Subject's Height at Screening	Data Screener 4	June 21, 2003	55.5 inches	555 inches	Input error, skipped decimal point	

Figure 3.7 Title 21 CFR Part 11: audit compliance.

Application Scenario

MegaMart is a large, nationwide retailer with over a thousand stores. A few years ago, MegaMart was wise enough to build an MME that would manage both technical and business meta data around its systems. MegaMart has a corporate goal of consolidating three of its current systems into a new ERP system. In order to accomplish this task, MegaMart needs to know where its customer data resides within these systems. Figure 3.8 shows where customer data exists, by attribute, with the attribute definition and the estimated number of records.

If the ERP implementation team didn't have the MME, they would have to do the impact analysis shown in Figure 3.8 manually. Typically, this degree of manual impact analysis takes months to accomplish. An impact analysis generated from the MME takes only hours or days.

Telecommunications Industry Example

Telecommunications is a particularly challenging industry. A great number of regulations have an impact on the telecommunications industry. Moreover, it is quite common for firms in this space to pay literally tens and even hundreds of millions of dollars in penalty fees for not adhering to these regulations.

Retail MME Report: Systems Analysis

Systems Analysis Report			MegaMart	October 12, 2003
System Name	Entity Name	Estimated Records	Attribute Name	Attribute Definition
CUSTAPPL	Cust_Tbl	1,025,000	Cust_Nbr	Cust_Nbr is the attribute of record for MegaMart customer numbers. Customer number is a unique number that is assigned by the CUSTAPPL system during the customer creation process.
			Cust_Addr	Cust_Addr is the attribute of record for MegaMart customer mailing addresses. Customer addresses are assigned by the CUSTAPPL system during the customer creation process.
			Cust_Type	Cust_Type is the attribute of record for MegaMart customer types. Customer is assigned by the CUSTAPPL system during the customer creation process.
	Cust_Tbl	254,000	Cust_Card_Ind	Cust_Card_Ind is the attribute of record that indicates that the MegaMart customer has a MegaCard credit card.
GLSYS	Customer_Tbl	3,561,128	Cust_Purch_Bal	Cust_Purch_Bal is the attribute of record that stores each individual MegaMart customer's purchase amounts in U.S. currency.

Figure 3.8   Retail MME report: systems analysis.

Application Scenario

NoTeleCo is a large telecommunications company that provides long-distance and local phone service (usage). NoTeleCo has an extensive MME that targets business and technical meta data. In addition, NoTeleCo has a data warehouse that focuses on phone usage. When a customer places a call through a telephone service provider, the phone lines that are used typically are not owned by one service provider. Usually, the phone call will go across several telecommunications companies' equipment. As a result, NoTeleCo needs a report (see Figure 3.9) that shows the amount of phone usage by their customers that is occurring on other carriers' (telecommunications service providers) lines.

A knowledge worker at NoTeleCo would be working with this report and might want to better understand the Discounted Usage column. Figure 3.10 shows the worker hotkeying on the Discounted Usage column to get a business meta data definition for the field.

Carrier/Usage Summary Report			NoTeleCo		November 20, 2003
Month	Carrier Name	Usage Type	Regular Usage (M seconds)	Discounted Usage (M seconds)	Total Usage (M seconds)
December	BigTeleCo	Long Distance	7,201	4,288	11,489
		Local	72,033	42,000	114,033
	TeleBell	Long Distance	630	777	1,407
		Local	23,000	17,255	40,255
	NewBell	Long Distance	220	310	530
		Local	1,100	757	1,857
December	BigTeleCo	Long Distance	6,400	4,000	10,400
		Local	73,450	42,702	116,152
	TeleBell	Long Distance	645	750	1,395
		Local	23,500	17,923	41,423
	NewBell	Long Distance	124	175	299
		Local	1,175	703	1,878
December	BigTeleCo	Long Distance	6,220	4,010	10,230
		Local	71,207	41,918	113,125
	TeleBell	Long Distance	652	754	1,406
		Local	20,010	15,500	35,510
	NewBell	Long Distance	92	110	202
		Local	1,177	708	1,885

Figure 3.9   Telecommunications report.

Telecommunications MME Report: Business Meta Data

Carrier/Usage Summary Report			NoTeleCo		November 20, 2003
Month	Carrier Name	Usage Type	Regular Usage (M seconds)	Discounted Usage (M seconds)	Total Usage (M seconds)
December	BigTeleCo	Long Distance		4,288	11,489
				42,000	114,033
	TeleBell			777	1,407
				17,255	40,255
	NewBell			310	530
		Local	1,100	757	1,857
December	BigTeleCo	Long Distance	6,400	4,000	10,400
		Local	73,450	42,702	116,152
	TeleBell	Long Distance	645	750	1,395
		Local	23,500	17,923	41,423
	NewBell	Long Distance	124	175	299
		Local	1,175	703	1,878
December	BigTeleCo	Long Distance	6,220	4,010	10,230
		Local	71,207	41,918	113,125
	TeleBell	Long Distance	652	754	1,406
		Local	20,010	15,500	35,510
	NewBell	Long Distance	92	110	202
		Local	1,177	708	1,885

> **Discounted Usage:** Any local or long-distance phone usage that has a discount applied to it. Discounts include **non-prime, holiday** and **rate specials**.
>
> Last Updated: 3/31/2003, Bob Jones

Figure 3.10 Telecommunications MME report: business meta data.

As the knowledge worker is looking through the business meta data definition for "Discounted Usage," he sees that discounted usage is defined as "non-prime, holiday and rate specials." Notice in this meta data definition that "non-prime," "holiday," and "rate specials" are bolded. This formatting lets the user know that business meta data definitions exist for these fields and that the end user can click on these fields to receive a business meta data definition. This type of functionality is common in well-designed MMEs.

In our example, this worker may want to learn when non-prime phone usage rates apply by clicking the "non-prime" field to get a business meta data definition for this field. Figure 3.11 shows the definition for "non-prime." What the user discovers is that non-prime time is defined as phone usage between 8:00 P.M. and 7:00 A.M.

Telecommunications MME Report: Business Meta Data

Carrier/Usage Summary Report		NoTeleCo			November 20, 2003
Month	Carrier Name	Usage Type	Regular Usage (M seconds)	Discounted Usage (M seconds)	Total Usage (M seconds)
December	BigTeleCo	Long Distance		4,288	11,489
				42,000	114,033
	TeleBell			777	1,407
				17,255	40,255
	NewBell			310	530
			1,100	757	1,857
December	BigTeleCo	Long Distance	6,400	4,000	10,400
			73,450	42,702	116,152
			645	750	1,395
			23,500	17,923	41,423
			124	175	299
		Local	1,175	703	1,878
December	BigTeleCo	Long Distance	6,220	4,010	10,230
		Local	71,207	41,918	113,125
	TeleBell	Long Distance	652	754	1,406
		Local	20,010	15,500	35,510
	NewBell	Long Distance	92	110	202
		Local	1,177	708	1,885

Discounted Usage: Any local or long-distance phone usage that has a discount applied to it. Discounts include **non-prime, holiday** and **rate specials.**

Last Updated: 3/31/2003, Bob Jones

Non-Prime Usage: Any local or long-distance phone usage that occurs between the time of 8:00 pm and 7:00 am.

Last Updated: 1/08/2003, Tony Ragone

Figure 3.11   Telecommunications report.

Case Studies: Two World-Class MME Initiatives

Allstate and RBC Financial Group are two world-class corporations. Not surprisingly, they both feature world-class MME initiatives. These are large, international, and complex corporations. Both of their MME implementations contain enterprise meta data for all of their IT applications. One of the key contributors to their success is that both MMEs had strong, ongoing support from their executive management.

Allstate

Over the last several years, Allstate's MME has been recognized as a world-class meta data management initiative that has garnered multiple meta data management awards. Like any great success, it took a precise focus and a great deal of hard work to make this system a reality.

Company Background

The Allstate Corporation is the nation's largest publicly held personal lines insurer. Widely known through the "You're in Good Hands with Allstate" slogan, Allstate provides insurance products to more than 16 million house-holds and has approximately 12,300 exclusive agents and financial specialists in the United States and Canada. Customers can access Allstate products and services through Allstate agents, or in select states at allstate.com and 1-800-Allstate. Encompass and Deerbrook Insurance brand property and casualty products are sold exclusively through independent agents. Allstate Financial Group includes the businesses that provide life and supplemental insurance, retirement, banking, and investment products through distribution channels that include Allstate agents, independent agents, and banks, and securities firms.

Challenges and Opportunities

Corporations that lack effective data management practices experience many difficulties as they attempt to integrate systems into their IT environments. In the early 1990s Allstate, like most large corporations, found itself challenged with managing disparate systems to satisfy its IT needs. Allstate wanted its applications to be able to talk across platforms. Unfortunately, systems that have different coding schemes for common codes and mismatches in field types and sizes cannot interchange data easily. Also, the rise in popularity of data warehousing demanded a precise understanding and knowledge of the data that the analysts of the data warehouse would utilize. For these reasons and more, Allstate embarked on an Enterprise Data Architecture project in 1995 and all meta data management processes that Allstate follows today grew from that initiative. Allstate's Area Leader of Data Management, Doug Stacey, commented, "Managing the data assets of a corporation of Allstate's size and complexity is no small task. Unlike our competitors, we realized that a sound meta data management practice and process would provide our company with a significant advantage in our marketspace."

Need to Manage Code Data

The insurance industry is a very *code-driven* environment because every state has its own regulatory statutes to which Allstate must adhere. Without a sound data management strategy across different applications and many departments, it is highly time-consuming and difficult to integrate systems because projects would take longer to deliver and costs would be higher. The use of sound meta data management techniques was expected to reduce or eliminate IT rework, speed up projects, and lower their overall costs.

Enable Data Warehousing Application

Also, with the advent of the data warehousing initiative, data quality was suddenly more important than ever. It was no longer left to subject matter experts in an application area to know what the data represented, what it actually meant, and how to use it. This data was now going to be presented to actual end users, and one cannot afford to have user *interpretations* of what the data *may* mean be used to make real live business decisions! Again, the expectation was that a strong, centralized data management environment would be the basis for consistent data driving high-quality decisions by end users.

MME Solution Overview

Allstate realized that it needed a meta data repository to persistently store the meta data that it was collecting. In addition, it made sure to develop the appropriate processes in the meta data sourcing layer to properly populate and maintain the repository (see Figure 3.12).

Allstate's initial focus was the management of the codes that permeated its systems. While a commercially available meta data integration tool was chosen to handle much of the meta data, there was no product on the market that allowed Allstate to both identify enumerated domains (those for which a set list of values can be listed) and define the various coding schemes that were found in the different applications and the associated business values. This led to the development of a custom portion of Allstate's MME solution called the Codes Management System (CMS). CMS, which started out as a simple prototype in a Microsoft Access database, allowed Allstate's Codes Analysts group to do their job more effectively. This group would be engaged by application teams to research all the codes and values of the application and to document them in the CMS repository. The codes analysts, along with a group of data administrators, then became the nucleus of the Enterprise Data Management group. While they were out assisting an application area research and documenting their codes, they were also keeping an enterprise perspective by documenting each unique domain they encountered and storing it in the repository. As they worked with subsequent projects, they were able to see where the same data had been encoded differently between applications. When this happened, rather than create a duplicate domain, they would simply add another "collection" or physical coding scheme to the already existing domain.

This custom development of CMS allowed Allstate's MME a great deal of flexibility and extensibility, so much so that Allstate deployed its custom-developed repository to replace the commercial meta data integration product with which it began. Of course, the downside to this type of approach is the cost of development and maintenance.

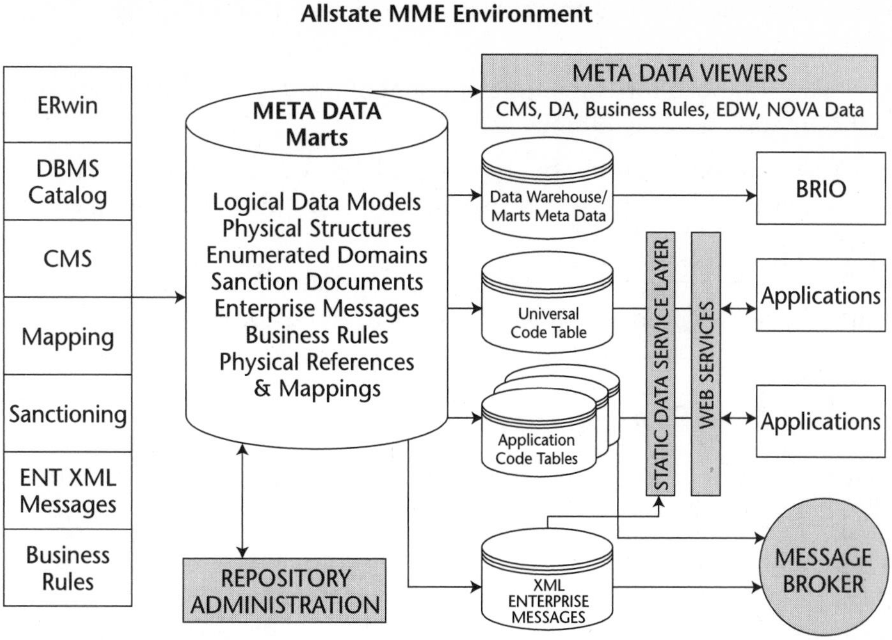

Allstate MME Environment

Figure 3.12 Allstate MME environment.

Data Stewardship

Allstate's Data Stewardship Council (DSC) is a cross-business-unit team established in January, 1997 and focused on the business aspects of managing data as a valued enterprise asset. It is a part-time, virtual team of Allstate employees who have strong business knowledge, vision, and the ability to look horizontally across the enterprise. These data stewards are focused on addressing the business issues behind key data resource management objectives: managing data redundancy, implementing data shareability and standardization, and managing and improving data integrity.

As its first priority, DSC is addressing the issue of consistency of shared information through the development of enterprise definitions. This group has developed a process by which enterprise agreement is achieved. As part of this process, a business data steward is assigned ongoing responsibility to be the *enterprise point person* for a particular data subject. The data steward follows several basic principles for managing data resources of any type; these include the following:

- Requirements for the resource must be anticipated and fulfilled proactively.

- Allstate cannot afford an infinite amount of the data resource; therefore, the amount must be optimized.

- The data resource should be shared and leveraged in as many ways as possible in order to maximize its value while diminishing its overall costs.

- The data resource must be carefully managed to ensure that its use in the business is prudent, efficient, effective, and secure.

MME Meta Data Sourcing Layer

Allstate has many different meta data sources that are being brought into its MME. These sources include:

- Logical data models
- Physical data models
- Codes
- Logical-to-physical data mapping
- Messaging for EAI

Logical Data Models

One primary means of populating meta data in Allstate's MME is through the process of logical data modeling. Application development teams engage (and fund) the data administrator to help identify and model the entities, attributes, relationships, and constraints on their data. They also create English-readable names and definitions for entities, attributes, and nonenumerated domains. A data model is then created in one of the popular modeling tools and extracted and *checked into* the MME.

To accomplish the import, Allstate defined an XML schema that represents the data in the repository. An import utility was created to take that XML schema and load it into the repository. Whenever they need to get data into the repository, they just create a file or extract one from another tool in their standard format, and then the load can be easily accomplished.

Physical Data Models

Technical meta data describing the physical structure of data is extracted directly from the source database system files. This process is relatively straightforward because an extraction of meta data (database, table, column, and keys) is made from the database system files, and then through the meta data integration layer it is loaded into the MME.

Codes

Another major source of meta data is from the codes analysts and their use of the CMS application. The codes analysts research and document any data found to be in codes, creating new enumerated domains to represent the codes when needed, but with a focus on the reuse of existing domains whenever possible.

What codes analysts often find is that the same data in two different applications is represented in two entirely different ways. This extends not only to the naming of the fields or columns, but also to both the codes and the values as well. The codes analysts will document the codes and business values used for each of the applications as well as the physical representation of the code for each. These distinct physical representations are called collections.

An enumerated domain can have one or more collections associated with it. The different collections are different ways in which the information that a particular domain represents is implemented across the enterprise. The codes analysts will often designate one of the collections as *preferred* and encourage any new use of that domain to use that particular physical representation. The important thing though is to ensure, through rigorous definition of the domains, that what is actually the same data is not mistakenly represented by two different domains.

Logical-to-Physical Data Mapping

One of the most manual exercises involved in the population of the MME is the data-mapping function for Allstate's data warehousing environment. Mapping is what allows data warehouse users to view what normally would be difficult-to-read physical column names (technical meta data) as easy-to-read logical names (business meta data). It also allows the business definitions for entities and attributes captured in the logical model to be viewed by the data warehouse users.

Mapping is performed by a data warehouse analyst primarily in two cases. The first is to map the physical and logical structures together. Through the MME, analysts simply access the meta data repository to pull up a list of tables on one side of the screen and a list of entities on the other, and proceed to match table/columns with entity/attributes. This *tie* is then captured in the MME. The second type of mapping is where table join keys are identified in different tables and *mapped* together.

Messaging for EAI

In any Global 2000 company or large government agency, system integration is always a major concern. Over the years, Allstate has successfully implemented many point-to-point systems. As with any large organization, this point-to-point approach is expensive to maintain.

At Allstate instead of this point-to-point approach, messages that are deemed to be of interest or significance to the enterprise are now defined and the meta data about those messages is stored in the MME. This capability allows an existing application to only perform one translation, from its own internal format (for the message content) to the *common* Allstate format for a given event, and it will be able to communicate with all other applications that use the same event. Likewise, a receiving application simply needs to translate from the common format to its own format to process the event. XML is used as the transportation syntax, and XML tag names are assigned to each item of data that the messages contain. (For a detailed discussion of XML messaging see Chapter 5.)

The common messages are created through analysis of the two applications seeking to exchange the messages with a focus towards the reuse of the messages throughout Allstate's other applications. This process ensures consistency and reusability of these common messages. In addition, it leverages the codes information stored in the MME. When two applications exchange a message that contains codes, typically two different coding schemes are being utilized. While the message is being created, a new common code translation is used in these cases. All applications write code that either translates from their collection to the common collection or from the common collection to theirs, depending on their need. This eliminates point-to-point solutions and allows greater reusability of the messages across the enterprise.

MME Meta Data Delivery Layer

Allstate's MME has a sophisticated meta data delivery layer, which has several different meta data delivery mechanisms. These mechanisms include:

- Meta data for the data warehouse
- Static data management
- DTDs and schemas
- Viewers

Meta Data for the Data Warehouse

Allstate's data warehouse is the most popular application of its meta data and certainly its MME's driving force. The data warehouse's end-user query tool is directly linked to the meta data in the MME. This allows Allstate's data warehouse users to view English names (from the logical data model in the MME) rather than the cryptic physical names that would normally appear. The end users can view the descriptions created during the logical data modeling. In addition, all of the business values discovered through the analysis of the codes analysts are passed in the meta data to the end-user query tool, so that instead of a data warehouse user having to view "03" as a code, he or she can see the value of "automobile."

Static Data Management

As Allstate collected domain information and documented the valid codes and values, the application areas within the company started to ask if they could leverage this meta data directly in their applications. This led Allstate to create the ability to request the generation of *static data tables*. A static data table is simply the valid codes and values for one or more domains deployed to a table so that an application may use the data.

Over the years, when speaking and writing about meta data management, we discussed the idea that a future MME architectural trend is the desire of corporations to implement a *closed loop* functionality. Closed-loop MME architecture feeds meta data from the MME directly into a corporation's IT applications[1]. At the time of these lectures, I stated that this approach is a natural progression of MME architecture; however, I was not aware of any corporation that had implemented this advanced technique. That is, up until now. Allstate's MME has implemented closed-loop functionality in its MME architecture. Allstate extended its MME's capabilities by implementing a universal code translation (UCT) table. This table is populated with multiple enumerated domains and all their associated collections. This allows an application to utilize this table to translate from its *language,* or representation of the code, to any other *language.* Typically, they'd translate into another application's specific representation of that code if they were doing a point-to-point, or the common Web front-end. This table is maintained by the Enterprise Data Management group and replicated to all nine regional operating centers throughout Allstate. Once an application implements the UCT, it no longer has to make any program changes when new codes are deployed. Allstate's team leader of Codes Analysts and Meta Data Services, Pam Gardell, commented, "Centralizing our ability to manage code data through linking our MME directly into Allstate applications has reduced the tremendous costs of managing these codes and greatly increased our flexibility to changing those codes over time."

DTD and Schemas

As the meta data for common messages is captured in the MME, the meta data is also generated from the repository and imported by the message broker product used by Allstate. This common event description is the basis for Allstate's "common namespace." This is the format that a sending application needs to translate *to,* and *from* which a receiving application must translate.

---

[1]For more information on closed-loop architecture, please see Chapter 7 of Building and Managing the Meta Data Repository (Wiley, 2000).

Viewers

The MME has a great deal of value as a reference tool for both application developers and business users alike. As a result, Allstate custom developed a generic Web-browser-based tool, the *Metadata Viewer*, which allows anyone in the enterprise to view the meta data in the MME. For example, if someone needs to know the Accident Type codes used in the Claims system or Vehicle Classifications in Property and Casualty, the information is now readily available.

The scope of the meta data can be a bit overwhelming for a user browsing the information, so application-specific *views* have been constructed and made available through the creation of custom viewers. Currently, Allstate has deployed a *CMS Viewer* that presents the same information as in the Metadata Viewer but is oriented in its display toward a user who is only interested in the code information from the MME.

Allstate's Future MME Directions

While many corporations would be happy to rest on their laurels, this is not the case with Allstate as it is constantly looking to build on its success.

Business Rules

Allstate believes that business rules are another area where it can add value to its enterprise. Rules engines from various vendors are likely to show up in an organization of Allstate's size. Rather than struggle to impose a particular engine on a specific application, Allstate's approach is to define and capture the common meta data around a business rule in which it has interest. Allstate plans to extend its MME to accommodate this additional meta data and provide a central place on which users can rely to get information on what rules may already exist concerning a specific topic.

ETL Tool Integration

Allstate has recently chosen an enterprise solution for its ETL needs. It is now working on a bidirectional meta data bridge that will push logical model information and codes and values to the ETL tool and pull back transformation meta data. This will be stored centrally in Allstate's MME and passed through the same meta data generation process into its data warehousing environment. In addition, Allstate will also gather load statistics and data quality statistics from actual runs of the ETL tool, and plans to present that information to business users of key reports.

Process Definitions

Process definitions and data about processes are other areas where Allstate is considering expansion. Allstate currently has a group that will help its business area document and subsequently improve its current process.

Taxonomies

Another group within Allstate is exploring the creation of an enterprise taxonomy, or classification scheme, to be used for searching and general knowledge management of Allstate's Internet and intranet offerings. Allstate's Vincent DiGiannantonio, team leader of Data Administration and Common Name Space, observes, "In general, we listen closely to what our application services people, and ultimately our business community, is saying. We position ourselves to provide tangible benefits to the community through our work, thus enabling us to continue to add value to the corporation."

MME Challenges

Allstate's MME implementation is one of the most advanced meta data management applications in existence. An application of this magnitude requires sufficient upfront investment and sustained organizational support. It has been Allstate management's unwavering support that has allowed this effort to prosper. Linda Hall, Director of Enterprise Data Management and Data Warehousing, stated, "You must have an excellent vision, coupled with a strong development team . . . . We have real strong visionaries, and those visionaries have continued to support us. They continue to set our sights onto the future."

MME ROI

Allstate calculated the cost for the development and maintenance of the infrastructure needed to build and support the MME. Added to that is the cost of all groups responsible for working with the application areas and gathering the meta data to populate the repository. Allstate's company policy prohibits the publication of actual costing numbers; however, like any major IT initiative, it is not a minor investment. Linda Hall mentioned, "Now we get lots of IT reuse, and this shows up in faster and cheaper application development."

While the investment in meta data management is not trivial, Allstate's tremendous success has provided it an equally impressive return through the IT reuse. Doug Stacey commented, "Consider the effort that goes into researching codes for an application. If we did not have the repository as a base for this information, we would be forced to repeat that effort every time a new requirement for the application arises or a set of codes changes. This savings is significant and results in real dollars to our organization." Allstate is currently achieving a reuse factor of 7.5, meaning that for every domain in production mapped to a physical column it is actually mapped to an average of 7.5 columns. In addition, over 50 percent of the domains captured in the MME are mapped to more than one physical column.

Allstate has estimated both the costs of the MME and the savings realized through reuse and feels comfortable stating that it has achieved a significant return on investment. Doug Stacey stated, "Our repository has been invaluable to our company. The ability to manage our systems in a more flexible manner has made the repository pay for itself several times over."

RBC Financial Group

RBC Financial Group's MME is an enterprise meta data repository that provides an inventory of the company's information assets, a documentation facility for RBC Financial Group's IT applications, the capability for enterprise-wide impact analysis, and a map for data movement. This meta data management solution was directly supported by RBC Financial Group's executive management.

Deployed in 1993, RBC Financial Group's MME provides value to both business and technical users via a customized Web front end. It implemented a vendor's meta data integration tool to assist it in the meta data sourcing and integration layers; however, it has significantly extended this product to meet its specific and unique meta data requirements. The MME's use has grown significantly in recent years and has become ingrained into the work processes at the bank.

Company Background

RBC Financial Group uses the initials RBC as a prefix for its businesses and operating subsidiaries, which operate under the master brand name of RBC Financial Group. RBC Financial Group is Canada's largest financial institution as measured by market capitalization and assets, and is one of North America's leading diversified financial services companies. It provides personal and commercial banking, wealth management services, insurance, corporate and investment banking, and transaction processing services on a global basis. The company employs 60,000 people, who serve more than 12 million personal, business, and public sector clients through offices in North America and some 30 countries around the world.

A recognized leader in technology innovation and eBusiness, RBC Financial Group currently has more than 2.1 million active Canadian online customers. RBC Financial Group has formed strategic alliances with industry leaders, including AOL Canada, Interactive Technologies Inc., and CashEdge, using new technologies to improve service and enhance value for its customers. RBC Financial Group's e-business products, services, and technology infrastructure have been recognized for excellence in the external marketplace by a number of top industry technology and research firms, including Gartner Group Inc., Forrester Research Inc., and Speers & Associates, among others.

Challenges and Opportunities

RBC Financial Group's Data Warehouse Environment (DWE) consists of five databases and contains more than 5 terabytes of data. Data warehouse end users required a tool to gain knowledge of the data content as well as an understanding of the data sources to effectively utilize the Data Warehouse Environment. As Mohammad Rifaie, RBC Financial Group's Group Manager for Enterprise Information Solutions, explained, "To further a body of knowledge for a culture, you must have a common language and it must be well documented. Data is the language of the business. We can't further the body of knowledge of business unless the data is well documented."

Any company the size of RBC Financial Group has hundreds of applications, all interfacing and sharing data. As a result, it is critical for this company to be able to reduce the risk and effort necessary to modify its IT systems during application changes. In addition, in order to improve its product's time to market, business solutions analysts require an easy mechanism to understand the data they are working with.

Finally, many applications within the organization are well known by only a handful of key individuals. Therefore, RBC Financial Group understands that it is necessary to capture this information (meta data) from these individuals before the corporate knowledge is lost.

MME Solution Overview

RBC Financial Group's meta data management solution is focused on enabling its Data Warehouse Environment; however, its MME was implemented before its data warehouse was built. This may come as a surprise to some, but as I have discussed in several of my columns, it *is* the optimal and correct approach[2]. Mohammad Rifaie commented, "The repository was in the bank before the warehouse. Meta data repositories are considered a key process for data and information management. In order to do IRM (information resource management) properly, you must have an inventory of your data assets and we must share these assets. *Obviously you cannot share the unknown. The place for this inventory is the repository, and it needs to be in one place.*"

RBC Financial Group's MME persistently stores over 6 GB of meta data, has over 200 applications, 1.35 million data elements, and over 20 million data relationships. The repository provides more than 1,000 unique end users 24×7 access to the meta data. Moreover, its meta data delivery layer had over 450,000 unique visits in 2002. It is easy to see why this company's MME has garnered so many industry awards and is one of the world's most extensive meta data management applications.

---

[2]"Which Should Come First the Chicken or the Egg (Meta Data Repository or the Data Warehouse)?" David Marco, DM Review, September 2001.

RBC Financial Group's MME resides on a DB2 OS/390 database platform and is dynamically accessed and updated via a meta data integration tool, ASP (Active Server Pages) Web pages, and Focus processes. It has focused its repository on documenting its data warehouse's source applications, allowing RBC Financial Group to create impact analyses around the data warehousing environment.

The application is accessible to any individual via the bank's intranet; however, a security meta model was developed to secure sensitive marketing meta data and to protect against unauthorized updating of the meta data. All other meta data is generally available. It is important to note that only business meta data may be updated via the MME's Web site because all of the technical meta data is maintained via the meta data sourcing and integration layers.

Finally, RBC Financial Group has created global naming standards for all physical tables and columns. Clearly, it is not feasible to enforce these naming standards for existing legacy applications; however, all new applications must use the naming standards as a part of its data model certification process.

MME Meta Data Sourcing Layer

RBC Financial Group's meta data sourcing layer is a highly sophisticated process that is directly integrated into its data warehousing environment. In fact, data is not loaded into the data warehouse until the meta data is in the repository. RBC Financial Group has many different meta data sources that are being brought into its MME. These sources include:

- Logical and physical data models
- Mainframe meta data
- Interface meta data
- Application change notification
- Business meta data
- Rationalized data elements
- Data transformations
- Standard XML tags

Logical and Physical Data Models

RBC Financial Group's MME holds technical meta data on the company's logical and physical data models. Its meta data management solution uses ERwin as the modeling tool. The MME has a certified process to extract the meta data on logical and physical models out of ERwin and into the repository.

There is a section of the MME's meta model to store the logical data models and a separate section to store the physical data models. Each data model is loaded into the repository as a separate and distinct entity. Logical and physical data models are explicitly related at the entity and attribute levels. Data models used in a specific application are loaded with a status code to separate them from data models used in other applications.

RBC Financial Group's meta data access layer looks to make implicit relationships for attributes and entities that have the same name since these data models are loaded on the same tables in the repository. The certification process ensures that these implicit relationships will be available. Impact analysis across data models can now be performed with a simple name search. The status will identify the applications affected. It is important to note that this process will work even if the data models are created using different modeling tools. Some form of data rationalization can be performed to build more explicit relationships, for example, if the physical name has to change due to restrictions within the modeling tool.

Mainframe Meta Data

Mainframe meta data is captured nightly from RBC Financial Group's mainframe change management tool for the job control language (JCL), copybooks, and source and executable code (COBOL) for its mainframe environment. Its MME automatically scans this change management tool to capture the critical technical meta data across over 200 operational applications.

Interface Meta Data

This company's interface meta data is derived from the MME via a weekly batch process. Approximately 4,900 batch interfaces are extracted from the mainframe meta data loaded into the repository. The process queries the meta data in the meta data management solution, identifying data sets shared between the batch jobs. These interfaces are collected and stored in an extension to the repository. The interfaces used and provided by an application are displayed on the MME's Web site. This provides the IT staff with a high-level impact analysis for changes to their applications.

Application Change Notification

The MME is used to identify changes to operational applications that affect the data warehousing environment. When the MME identifies a change to a source application that feeds the Data Warehouse Environment, an email is sent to data warehouse personnel notifying them of impending changes. RBC Financial Group's Meta Data Management team is also notified of changes to the data warehouse, where meta data maintenance processes are then initiated.

Business Meta Data

RBC Financial Group's knowledge workers manually enter business meta data directly into the MME via its Web site. The author of inserted and updated meta data is stored during the update process. These workers provide the business meta data definitions, audit notes, user comments, application documentation, and valid domain values. Art D'Silva, Manager of Information Architecture and Strategies, commented, "We wanted to empower our business users to make decisions, and meta data is a key contributor to making that happen. Users must understand the data. *This is not an IT issue anymore—it is a business issue."*

There is a certification process in place that ensures that the business meta data is usable by the business users. Due to the abundance of application meta data, RBC Financial Group's application groups are given the responsibility of monitoring the quality of its meta data (another example of an MME best practice).

All users accessing the MME have the ability to enter user comments. This gives each end user the ability to provide input into the definition of a data element. This is necessary functionality because it is the end users who use the data who should be documenting it.

An inventory of IT applications is captured and published in the MME. This meta data describes the application, technology used, interfaces, responsible manager, and other pertinent information. RBC Financial Group's project manager manually inputs this information into the MME. All users have access to obtain information related to a particular application. This allows the enterprise to maintain a persistent corporate knowledge base of all applications.

Rationalized Data Elements

In a company the size of RBC Financial Group, presenting rationalized elements was challenging due to the large number of data elements in the MME (over 1.35 million elements). Rationalization takes these elements and standardizes the cryptic element names using a data quality tool, then a relationship is made from the standardized name to the actual name. Only 70,000 standardized elements are required to relate to approximately 850,000 actual elements.

Web pages were developed to present this meta data, but can be cumbersome at times due to the large volume of data elements. Most of the time, impact analysis using the rationalized elements is performed using reports generated outside of the MME's Web site. As new data elements are added to the repository, the rationalization process can be rerun to standardize and relate these new elements.

Data Transformations

RBC Financial Group's data warehousing environment has an extensive ETL process for bringing data into the Enterprise Data Warehouse application. This process captures meta data on the source to target data mappings. A meta data exchange file is generated from the ETL procedure and loaded into the MME as part of the development process. This information is critical for data warehouse users to understand the source of the data within the data warehousing environment. Without this knowledge, the data in the warehouse would not be trusted. These mappings are displayed on request via the MME's Web site.

Standard XML Tags

RBC Financial Group is building an IT infrastructure that allows the use of current technology to standardize the collection and delivery of information to its clients. The infrastructure will use XML to identify the data being exchanged between applications. It decided to develop a list of standard XML data tags that IT developers could use to avoid extensive translation. Using the meta data from the data warehouse and data mart, and the rationalized elements, 1,600 of the most common elements were identified. The XML data tags were derived from the standard names of the elements and published via the MME.

Throughout RBC Financial Group, all new IT development using XML uses this set of standard data tags. Any data elements required for new development but not on the list will be researched by the meta data team and added to the list.

MME Meta Data Delivery Layer

The Web interface has been the key component in the meta data delivery layer as well as the capture of meta data in the meta data integration layer. The MME's Web site has been developed in-house to deliver the right meta data to the right user at the right time, while hiding the complexity of meta data management application from those who do not care to see it. RBC Financial Group's Information Management Web site is divided into four different categories:

- Data dictionary
- MME base applications
- Hosted applications
- Utilities

Its MME's Web site has a feedback process directly integrated into it. Todd Moore, RBC Financial Group's Meta Data Management Team's Project manager, stated, "The feedback process is critical. The users must have the ability to comment on the information that they are viewing . . . . This feedback must be immediate and controlled by the application."

Data Dictionary

The data dictionary category includes the functionality for access to more than 20 separate data dictionaries for operational applications, the Enterprise Data Warehouse, and various data marts. This includes the source-to-target mapping information extracted from the ETL process. This category accounts for 69 percent of all Web access to the MME.

MME Base Applications

The MME base applications category includes information for the operational applications (mainframe COBOL and JCL), data models, enterprise information model, enterprise standard elements, standard rationalized elements, and XML data tags. This category accounts for 28 percent of all Web site access.

Hosted Applications

Hosted applications are comprised of application inventory documentation, group contact lists, and vendor documentation manuals. This application is a recent addition to the MME's delivery layer and accounts for 1.5 percent of all Web access.

Utilities

The final category of its MME Web site is utilities. This category includes a number of utilities to extract, import, and administer the repository. Many of these utilities allow for the extraction and importation of large quantities of meta data with a single Web page access. This application comprises 1.5 percent of all Web access for the MME.

MME Challenges

RBC Financial Group's MME is one of the most highly respected meta data management solutions in the industry. It is admired by many corporations for its value to their organization and the shear size and complexity of its environment. Any application of this magnitude requires a fully staffed and highly knowledgeable development team and sustained support from the senior leaders of the organization.

Another challenge that RBC Financial Group faced was reaching *critical mass* in the MME. For the first three years of the repository, it only had three applications stored in it. This all changed in 1996 when during its Y2K conversion it gathered meta data on 135 applications throughout the enterprise. Interestingly, RBC Financial Group's Y2K vendor wanted them to discard this valuable meta data. Instead, its management and internal staff wisely loaded this meta data into its MME.

MME ROI

RBC Financial Group believes that the largest part of application support and maintenance is spent on manual impact analysis. Todd Moore stated, "Industry analysts have stated that 67 percent of the application support and maintenance budget is spent on impact analysis; therefore, even if the repository can cut this marginally this will help us dramatically on the bottom line." As a result, RBC Financial Group focused its MME on reducing the cost of its IT environment. Its award-winning repository accomplishes this by providing numerous benefits to the company including:

- Documentation, source-to-target mapping, and change notification for the DWE
- Identification, publication, and maintenance of over 4,900 batch interfaces among more than 200 applications
- Assisting applications in map and gap analysis. One particular project generated more than 10,000 hits to the Web site, preventing thousands of phone calls
- Rationalization of the repository data elements, which allows impact analysis across 200 applications and can be completed in hours or days as opposed to weeks or months
- Identification and publication of data element standards

By intelligently and effectively managing its meta data, RBC Financial Group has provided itself with a much greater ability to properly manage its IT environment. This becomes even more apparent when one sees that, typically, large banks spend 15 percent to 22 percent of noninterest expenses (NIE) on their IT systems, while RBC Financial Group spends approximately 13 percent of NIE on its IT systems (see Figure 3.13). This is a significant advantage in the marketplace (see the sidebar "RBC Financial Group's MME in Action").

It is obvious why RBC Financial Group's MME has been lauded for being a world-class MME. Todd Moore concluded, *"The growth in the number of people accessing our repository is a testament to its success."*

RBC FINANCIAL GROUP'S MME IN ACTION

In the late 1990's, a major credit card company asked RBC Financial Group to change its credit card number from 13 bytes to 16 bytes. This company assigned three people for four to six months to identify the 122 changes they needed to make in their systems for this key field expansion. RBC Financial Group, in contrast, used its world-class MME to identify 144 changes that would be needed to its systems and accomplished this analysis in 15 minutes. Rifaie commented, "Within our repository we had implemented meta data to identify these changes. We accomplished this in 15 minutes and we identified 144 changes. This report was better and more complete. This accounts for a very significant cost avoidance."

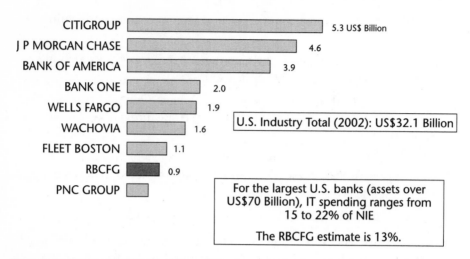

U.S. Banks' IT Spending

Projected 2002 IT Spending by U.S. Banks[1]

CITIGROUP — 5.3 US$ Billion

J P MORGAN CHASE — 4.6

BANK OF AMERICA — 3.9

BANK ONE — 2.0

WELLS FARGO — 1.9

WACHOVIA — 1.6

U.S. Industry Total (2002): US$32.1 Billion

FLEET BOSTON — 1.1

RBCFG — 0.9

PNC GROUP

For the largest U.S. banks (assets over US$70 Billion), IT spending ranges from 15 to 22% of NIE

The RBCFG estimate is 13%.

(1) IT spending defined as excluding Voice Telecom. RBC estimate is $1,484MM CAD less $130MM Voice Telecom = $1,354MM / 1.55 - $0.9 Billion USD

Figure 3.13   U.S. banks' IT spending.

Source: TowerGroup January 2002.

Summary

You should now have a good understanding of the MME, its architectural components, and the types of applications that an MME provides. Part Two of this book walks you through four physical meta models focused on a particular meta data subject area and one universal meta model.

PART

Two

Universal Meta Models for the Meta Data Repository Environment

Part One of this book introduced the Managed Meta Data Environment (MME). Chapter 2 listed the architectural components and showed how to systematically integrate meta data throughout the enterprise. Practical application areas were also examined, including return on investment measurement, the resource skills assessment required to implement and maintain the MME, real-world case studies on utilizing the MME, and a comparison to other models (CWM and CMM).

In Part Two, we dive into the details of the models that compose the MME environment and their major areas of interaction. Chapters 4 to 7 describe in detail the models composing the managed meta data environment.

These meta models include:

- Enterprise systems (Chapter 4)
- XML, messaging, and business transactions (Chapter 5)
- IT portfolio management (Chapter 6)
- Business rules, business meta data, and data stewardship (Chapter 7)

Chapter 8 consolidates the meta models from the other chapters into one summarized meta data model view.

Structure of Each Chapter in This Part

Each chapter in this part of the book uses the same structure to describe, apply, navigate, and compare the model. The chapter structure is:

1. **Purpose of the model.** This provides an introduction to the model's definition, including the business and technical questions that can be answered by the meta data model.

2. **Model assumptions.** This provides any guidance applicable to interpreting and implementing the meta data model

3. **Subject areas.** These provide detailed descriptions of each of the subject areas covered by the model and its interactions with other chapter models, as well as descriptions of each of its entities and attributes.

4. **Report from the meta model.** This provides examples of reports that can be generated from the models, including a discussion of the business and technical purposes and values.

5. **Summary of the model.**

Chapter 5 also contains an XML introduction after the model overview. This provides readers who may not be familiar with the technology the context for reviewing the rest of the chapter and its meta data model.

Assumptions Made in Part Two

We assume that you already have some knowledge of data-modeling principles (entities, attributes, relationships, subtypes, supertypes, foreign keys) and information engineering notation. Our intention is to educate you about data-modeling viewpoints through the examples provided. Data-modeling references through Part Two use specific conventions to highlight these areas for you. Entities are shown in capital letters (for example, DATA PACKAGE). Attributes are displayed in boldface lowercase (for example, **data packaged id**). Subject area names of the models are presented in title case (for example, Data Package). Finally, relationships are shown in boldface italic lowercase (for example, *is a subgroup in*).

Each model is intended to be a starting point for developing a logical MME meta model; they are not meant to be shrinkwrapped and ready for implementation. Each model is a litmus test for existing, planned, or purchased MME projects. Here are some additional considerations:

- The models use an information engineering (IE) data-modeling notation (see Appendix B for other assumptions applied to the models found on the CD in ERwin 3.5.2 format). See figure ii.1 for details on how to interpret the modeling notation.

- The models represent a logical view, not a physical implementation perspective. Physical-modeling transformation steps must be applied in order to implement the models (for example, subtyping resolution). The physical implementation of these models is beyond the scope of this book, because of space limitations. For example, a physical implementation using MS Access would require a different physical design than Oracle.

- No operational controls around versioning, history, or access controls exist in the models.

- The application of international, industry, or corporate standards for data naming and coding are left to the reader's discretion.

- Parent/child verb phrases used for relationships are shown as needed to help clarify the purpose of a modeling relationship.

IE Notation Components

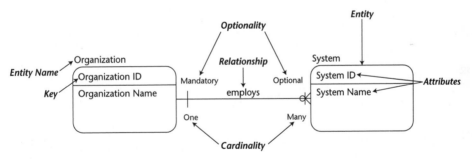

Figure ii.1   IE Notation.

Universal Meta Model for Enterprise Systems

We begin our exploration of the universal meta data models by looking at the database management components of the enterprise. However, what does the term *enterprise* mean here in relation to the MME? An enterprise is an organizational entity, usually large, that utilizes information technology. The term's use here goes beyond just the data found in operational or decision support applications; it includes all data stored and analyzed in an organization. This includes the data structures, data movements, data transformations, and expressions composing these components. These types of constructs are covered in the Enterprise Systems model.

Purpose of the Enterprise Systems Meta Model

The purpose of the Enterprise Systems meta model is to define all of the data structures in the enterprise and describe how these structures interrelate in the meta data domain. This model serves as the core for all subsequent submodels of the environment to control and manage both data and meta data enterprise-wide. The Enterprise Systems model offers insight into data, relationships, and the data movement and integration processes. The model serves as a single reference source for system semantics and data structures. By capturing and sharing the information about our systems, the model allows for a greater possibility of achieving integration throughout the enterprise.

Questions that need to be answered by the meta data of Enterprise Systems include:

- Where in the enterprise is a particular data attribute used? What is the attribute's definition? How is the attribute derived?
- What data attributes depend on the content of another attribute?
- Which data structures compose a particular application system?
- How many data sources indirectly and directly influence a particular target system?
- What is the impact on the enterprise of migrating from one DBMS to another?
- What is the data lineage of a database table or specific column?
- Which downstream applications feed the CRM system?
- Which applications receive data feeds from the ERP application?
- What is the complexity level of a specific set of source to target transformations?
- What is the percentage of transformation reuse for a data warehouse?
- Are data warehouse updates completed in the overnight batch window?
- What is the overall quality rate of data structures associated with a specific business area?
- What is the origin and subsequent processing history of a source data file?
- What is the average volume of transactions loaded into the target system?
- Which source systems have the highest reject/error percentages?
- Which systems have interoperability/consolidation opportunities?

Enterprise Systems Model Assumptions

The Enterprise Systems model assumes the following:

- Commonly found physical data structures can be represented in the model. Less common or proprietary data structures can be represented in the OTHER structure subtype or the DATA PACKAGE or DATA GROUP entities expanded to accommodate the particular format.

- General data transformation methods and characteristics are represented in the model. Other methods can be represented in associated subtype or the TRANSFORMATION GROUP entity expanded to accommodate the specific method. These characteristics are not intended to fully represent all details around a specific product or group of products.

Now, let us take a closer look at the Enterprise Systems model's subject areas, starting with the Data Package.

Enterprise Systems Subject Areas

The Enterprise Systems model encompasses six subject areas. Figure 4.1 illustrates the major subject areas of the Enterprise Systems model and the interaction points to other model entities. Each of these subject areas is explored in detail within the related subject area meta models.

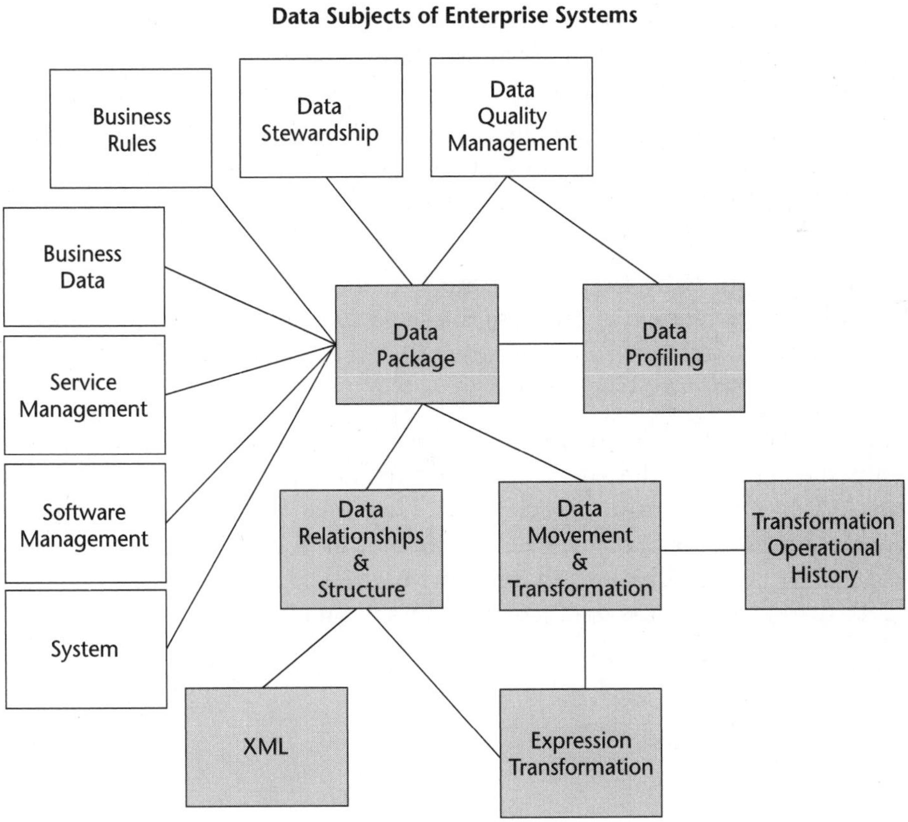

Figure 4.1   Enterprise Systems models subject areas.

The six subject areas of Enterprise Systems are:

Data Package.   This subject area covers the interrelationship of data and data structures to application systems, data stewards, and business rules, and data movement activities. Major entity areas include *Data Package, Data Group, Data Element,* and *Domain.*

Data Relationships to Structure.   This subject area details how the overall interrelationship of data relates to the physical structure or concrete subtypes. Major entity areas include *XML, Relational, Messaging, Flat File,* and *Other.*

Data Movement and Transformation.   This subject area documents the general mapping that a set of data sources has to a set of data targets. Major entity areas include *Source to Target Map, Transformation Package, Transformation Group, Transformation Process, Transformation Step,* and *Transformation Process Sequence.*

Expression Transformation.   This subject area supports data detail transformations through use of an expressions model using an abstract syntax tree method. This area also shows how the expression transformations integrate to Data Package entities. Major entity areas include *Expression Node, Operation, Operation Argument List, Element Node, Operation Node,* and *Constant Node.*

Transformation Operational History.   This subject area captures auditing information and data transformation related meta data. Major entity areas include *Transformation Package Audit, Transformation Process Audit,* and *Transformation Step Audit.*

Data Profiling.   This subject area supports the identification of domain violations in relation to business rules and data quality during detailed expression transformations. Major entity areas include *Invalid Domain* and *Invalid Domain Values Found.*

Each of these subject areas relates to the others. The Data Package subject area is the central focal area for the other universal meta models (Business Rules, XML, and IT Portfolio models). This key relationship of the Enterprise Systems model to the Business Rules, Data Stewards, and Subject Areas entities allows for the validation and reporting of the core data entities.

Let's now take a look at the first subject area: Data Package.

Data Package

The Data Package subject area includes the logical relationships of data abstracted for use in capturing and integrating data within the enterprise, detached from the source or target systems. This subject area provides the basis to control, manage, and integrate information and meta data throughout the enterprise.

The structuring of data in the enterprise model has three major components. Seeing how these objects relate to concrete structures such as a relational database provides insight into this generalization's workings. A packaging-level DATA PACKAGE holds high-level structures and corresponds to items such as relational database catalog, database schema, flat files, business transactions, and messaging. The DATA GROUP is the lowest level grouping of data and corresponds to a relational database table. The DATA GROUP holds a DATA ELEMENT, which is a unit of addressable data. The DATA ELEMENT corresponds to an attribute from a logical perspective and a column in a relational database table from a physical viewpoint. The DATA ELEMENT may a have a domain that describes the data values it may inherit. The relationship of the structures is shown in Figure 4.2.

The entry point of the model is the DATA PACKAGE, which has relationships with the DATA GROUP. The nonidentifying one-to-many relationship of DATA PACKAGE to DATA GROUP to DATA ELEMENT provides the key architecture for all data structures in the enterprise and the MME. The hierarchy of data, for the enterprise, is documented here, allowing data objects to be grouped, packaged, and reused in multiple occurrences. For example, customer name may be grouped into one of many data groups, such as customer contact or customer mailing address. These groups may become many data packages, such as customer or sales databases. The data model for DATA PACKAGE is shown in Figure 4.3.

The DATA PACKAGE representation in the physical world is shown through the relationship with SYSTEM, ENVIRONMENT, and DATA PACKAGE DEPLOYMENT. The relationship to these three entities allows the user to analyze business and technical meta data from an operational usage perspective plus see data reusability throughout the enterprise.

A many-to-many relationship exists from DATA PACKAGE, DATA GROUP, and DATA ELEMENT to DATA STEWARD. This relationship provides a means to identify the individual or group that is responsible for defining the use of these data objects.

Generic Structure of Data in the Enterprise

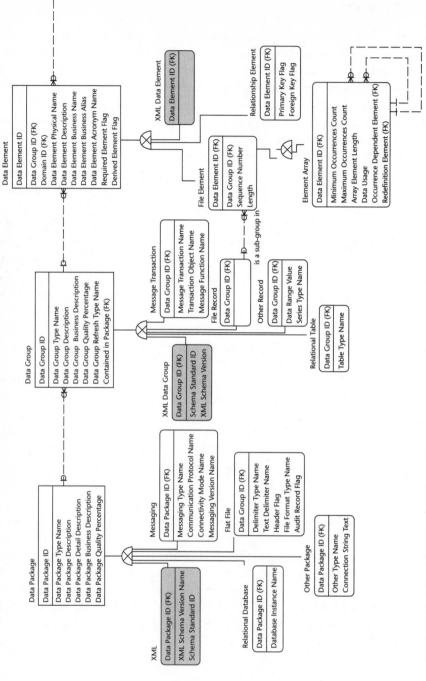

Figure 4.2 Generic structure of data in the enterprise.

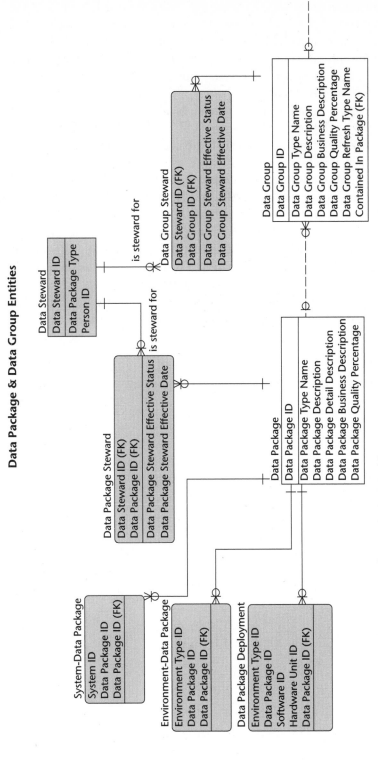

Data Package & Data Group Entities

Figure 4.3   DATA PACKAGE and DATA GROUP entities.

The many-to-many relationship between SUBJECT AREA and DATA GROUP (see Figure 4.4) provides a means to apply business user understanding to a particular set of DATA ELEMENT groupings for analysis and reporting purposes. From an information delivery perspective, this allows the user to drill down into the enterprise data from a business view, providing a more complete and accurate perspective.

Business rules apply broadly in daily business activities and the enterprise. The many-to-many relationship between DATA GROUP and DATA ELEMENT allows tracking to various levels in a subject area for impact and reporting analysis, as shown in Figures 4.4 and 4.5.

DOMAIN has a nonidentifying one-to-many relationship with DATA ELEMENT, as shown in Figure 4.6. DOMAIN and child entity DOMAIN VALUE contain the enterprise perspective of business and technical meta data about a data object. Changes made to these entities are reflected across the enterprise to ensure data standardization and provide ease of maintenance. For example, if all "Amount" data elements are defined in a common domain, then changing a domain value can be done once instead of finding each occurrence. The recursive nature of DOMAIN provides a means for understanding the dependency that different data objects have on each other that affect content.

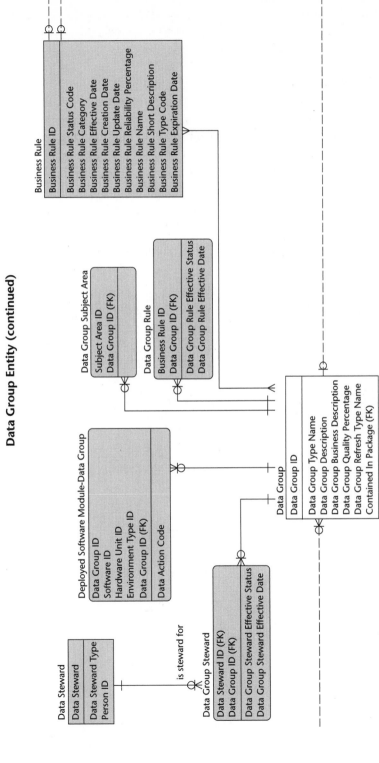

Data Group Entity (continued)

Figure 4.4   DATA GROUP entity (continued).

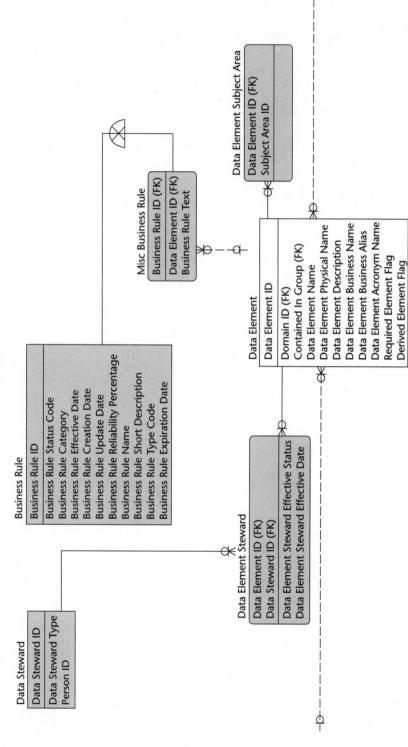

Figure 4.5 DATA ELEMENT entity.

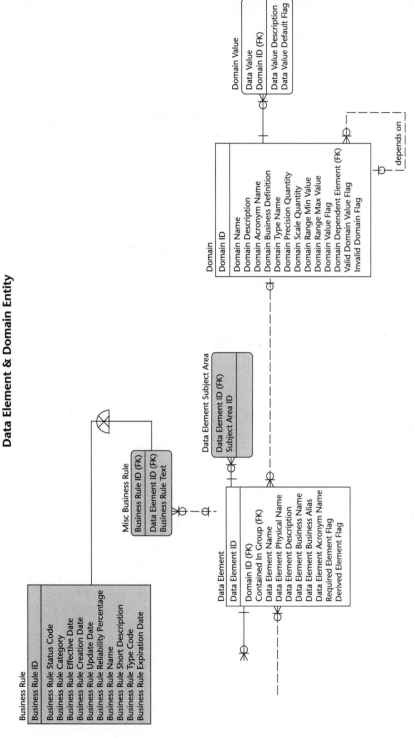

Data Element & Domain Entity

Figure 4.6   DATA ELEMENT and DOMAIN entities.

Table 4.1 shows more details about the entities of the Data Package subject area.

Table 4.2 shows more detail about the attributes of the Data Package subject area.

Table 4.1 Data Package Entities

ENTITY NAME	ENTITY DEFINITION
DATA PACKAGE	A collection of information organized to accomplish a business function in the enterprise: the DATA PACKAGE provides context and scope to the DATA GROUPS, DATA ELEMENTS, and the relationships between these items.
DATA GROUP	A combination of data elements that represents a complete set of information or business transaction.
DATA ELEMENT	A specific item of information; the smallest unit of information.
DOMAIN	A method of identifying and grouping types of data elements for the standardization and maintenance of business and technical meta data.
DOMAIN VALUE	The total possible set of values for a domain.
SYSTEM	Refer to Table 6.1 for entity definition.
DATA STEWARD	Refer to Table 7.5 for entity definition.
BUSINESS RULE	Refer to Table 7.1 for entity definition.
SUBJECT AREA	Refer to Table 7.3 for entity definition.

Table 4.2 Data Package Attributes

ENTITY NAME	ATTRIBUTE NAME	ATTRIBUTE DEFINITION
DATA PACKAGE	data package	System-generated, nonintelligent designator that uniquely specifies the DATA PACKAGE; a collection of information organized to accomplish a business function in the enterprise.
	data package type name	Describes what data format the data package is represented in (for example, XML, Relational, Message, or Flat File).
	data package description	Textual description describing the data package.

Table 4.2 *(continued)*

ENTITY NAME	ATTRIBUTE NAME	ATTRIBUTE DEFINITION
	data package detail description	Detailed textual description describing the data package.
	data package business description	Textual description describing the data package from a business perspective.
	data package quality percentage	Denotes the data quality confidence level of the data package expressed as a percentage.
DATA GROUP	data group	System-generated, nonintelligent designator that uniquely specifies the data group; a combination of data elements that represents a complete set of information or business transaction.
	data group type name	Describes what data format the data package is represented in (for example, XML Type Definition, XML Element Declaration, Relational Table, File Record, Message Transaction, or Other).
	data group description	Textual description describing a data group.
	data group business description	Detailed textual description describing a data group.
	data group quality percentage	Denotes the data quality confidence level of the data group expressed as a percentage.
	data group refresh type name	Indicates the frequency with which the data group content is refreshed (for example, Real Time, Near-Real Time, Hourly, Intraday, Daily, Weekly, Monthly, Annually, or Other).
	contained in package	Collection of information organized to accomplish a business function in the enterprise.

(continued)

Table 4.2   *(continued)*

ENTITY NAME	ATTRIBUTE NAME	ATTRIBUTE DEFINITION
DATA ELEMENT	**data element id**	System-generated, nonintelligent designator that uniquely specifies the DATA ELEMENT; a DATA ELEMENT is a specific item of information, and is the smallest unit of information.
	domain id	System-generated, nonintelligent designator that uniquely specifies the DOMAIN; a DOMAIN identifies and groups types of data elements for standardization and maintenance of business and technical meta data.
	contained in group	A collection of information organized to accomplish a business function in the enterprise.
	data element physical name	Represents the physical data group name of the data element.
	data element description	Contains the detailed explanation of the business meaning of the element in the context of the enterprise.
	data element business name	Contains the common name of the element that is recognized by business users.
	data element business alias	Contains a common alternative name of the element recognized by the enterprise.
	data element acronym name	Contains a common acronym coding of the element.
	required element flag	Indicator that denotes if the element instance or value is required to have content (not null).
	derived element flag	Denotes a data element instance whose value is obtained from some expression or business rule dependency on other data elements.

Table 4.2   *(continued)*

ENTITY NAME	ATTRIBUTE NAME	ATTRIBUTE DEFINITION
DOMAIN	domain id	System-generated, nonintelligent designator that uniquely specifies the DOMAIN; a DOMAIN identifies and groups types of data elements for standardization and maintenance of business and technical meta data.
	domain name	Descriptive terms specific for the domain.
	domain description	Detailed definition information about the domain.
	domain acronym name	Common acronym used for the identifying the domain in the enterprise.
	domain business definition	Detailed text definition of the domain from a business perspective.
	domain data type name	Common generic data type associated with the domain (for example, String, Number, Datetime, Blob, or Other).
	domain precision quantity	Denotes the required degree of precision after the decimal point that the domain requires.
	domain scale quantity	Lists the required level of scale before the decimal point that the domain requires.
	domain range min value	Indicates the lower boundary of numeric values for the domain.
	domain range max value	Indicates the higher boundary of numeric values for the domain.
	domain value flag	Indicates whether the domain has domain values (lookup).
	domain dependent element name	Indicates a domain that may influence the contents or domain values (lookup) of another domain.

(continued)

Table 4.2   *(continued)*

ENTITY NAME	ATTRIBUTE NAME	ATTRIBUTE DEFINITION
	valid domain value flag	Indicates that a data element value is a valid domain value.
	invalid domain flag	Indicates that a data element value is not a valid domain value.
DOMAIN VALUE	**data value**	Contains a specific value, code, identifier, or unit that the domain can contain.
	domain id	System-generated, nonintelligent designator that uniquely specifies the DOMAIN; a DOMAIN identifies and groups types of data elements for the standardization and maintenance of business and technical meta data.
	data value description	Contains a detailed definition of a specific data value of the domain.
	data value default flag	Denotes the default value of the domain.

Data Relationships to Structure

The Data Relationships to Structure subject area encompasses the concrete or physical representation of the generalized data objects shown in the Enterprise Systems subject area. For example, a DATA PACKAGE becomes a relational database; a DATA GROUP, a relational table; and a DATA ELEMENT, a relational column. Figures 4.7 and 4.8 show the data model for the Data Relationships to Structure subject area.

A DATA PACKAGE can be represented physically as a RELATIONAL DATABASE, XML SCHEMA (described in Chapter 5), MESSAGE, FLAT FILE, or some OTHER unconventional or proprietary format. Physical characteristics of each of these formats are captured in these subtype entities. For example, characteristics of a flat file, such as its delimiter character and the existence of a header row, provide more details about the specific data package. These details can be used for informational and analysis purposes when selecting and using data integration tools.

Data Package & Data Groups Subtypes

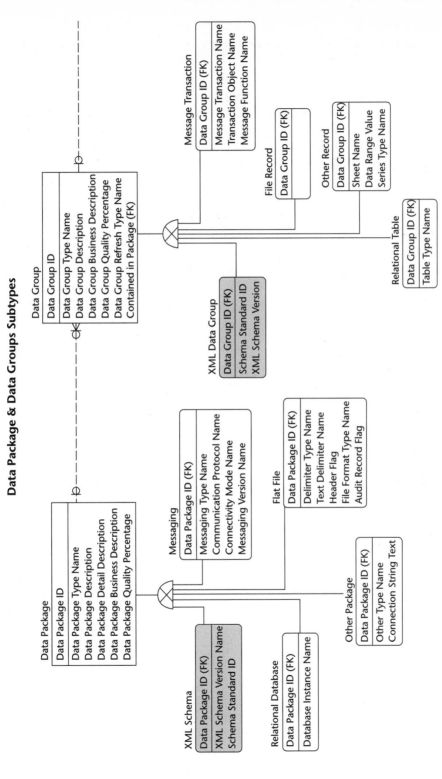

Figure 4.7 DATA PACKAGE and DATA GROUP subtypes.

A DATA GROUP can be represented physically as a RELATIONAL TABLE, XML DATA GROUP (described in Chapter 5), MESSAGE TRANSACTION, FLAT FILE RECORD, or some OTHER RECORD format. In some cases, a FILE RECORD can be decomposed into a nested group of elements, for example in a COBOL REDEFINE statement in a copy library (see Figure 4.9). The *is a sub-group in* relationship between a FILE RECORD and a FILE ELEMENT provide for this special case. The element **data group id** acts as both a record and element in the two entities to accommodate any decomposition level in a nested group of elements. The FLAT ELEMENT could be further subtyped to allow explicit arrays, as in COBOL. A COBOL structure can reidentify the composition of an existing element that in the model is handled by the relationship from the redefining element. The relationship between FILE RECORD and FILE ELEMENT allows you to perform lineage tracing and impact analysis.

A data element can be represented physically as a RELATIONAL ELEMENT (or column), XML DATA ELEMENT, FLAT FILE ELEMENT (or field). In some cases, a group of file elements can be part of a repeating group of elements, as in an array—for example, a repeating group of fields in a COBOL OCCURS statement in a copy library, as shown in Figure 4.8. The second-level subtype relationship shown between the entities FILE ELEMENT and ELEMENT ARRAY handles this special case. The attributes in ELEMENT ARRAY allow the capturing of how many times the group repeats, and identify the dependent element that indicates how many positions are in the array

Data Group & Data Element Subtypes

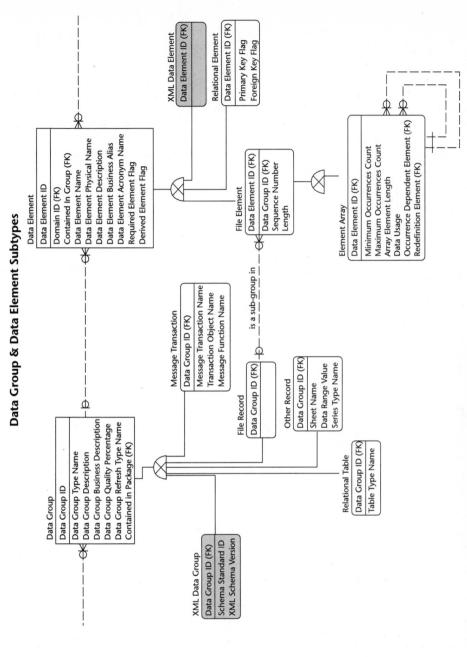

Figure 4.8 DATA GROUP and DATA ELEMENT subtypes.

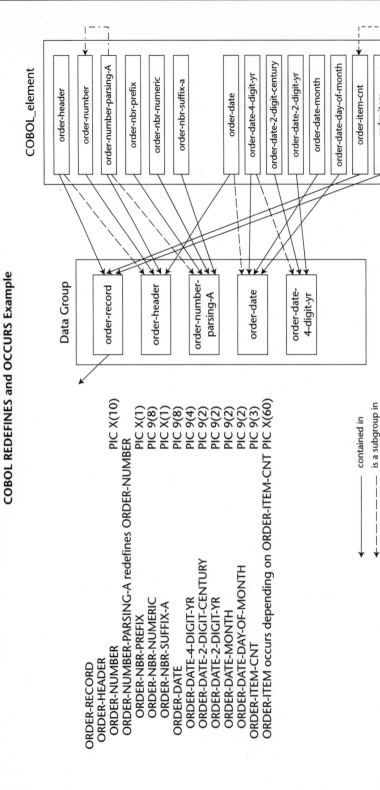

COBOL REDEFINES and OCCURS Example

ORDER-RECORD
ORDER-HEADER
ORDER-NUMBER   PIC X(10)
ORDER-NUMBER-PARSING-A redefines ORDER-NUMBER
  ORDER-NBR-PREFIX   PIC X(1)
  ORDER-NBR-NUMERIC   PIC 9(8)
  ORDER-NBR-SUFFIX-A   PIC X(1)
ORDER-DATE   PIC 9(8)
  ORDER-DATE-4-DIGIT-YR   PIC 9(4)
  ORDER-DATE-2-DIGIT-CENTURY   PIC 9(2)
  ORDER-DATE-2-DIGIT-YR   PIC 9(2)
  ORDER-DATE-MONTH   PIC 9(2)
  ORDER-DATE-DAY-OF-MONTH   PIC 9(2)
ORDER-ITEM-CNT   PIC 9(3)
ORDER-ITEM occurs depending on ORDER-ITEM-CNT PIC X(60)

—————— contained in
—·—·—·— is a subgroup in
········· occurs depends on
—··—··— redefines

Figure 4.9   COBOL REDEFINES and OCCURS example.

Table 4.3 shows more details about the entities of the Data Relationships to Structure subject area.

Table 4.3 Data Relationships to Structure

ENTITY NAME	ENTITY DEFINITION
XML SCHEMA (DATA PACKAGE subtype)	Refer to Table 5.2 for this entity's definition.
MESSAGING (DATA PACKAGE subtype)	An assemblage of data groups and data elements sent or received together between applications; messaging uses messages to communicate with different applications to perform an operation or set of operations.
RELATIONAL DATABASE (DATA PACKAGE subtype)	A collection of data groups and data elements organized to facilitate efficient data retrieval by an application.
FLAT FILE (DATA PACKAGE subtype)	A text document without a structured interrelationship between its data groups and data elements.
OTHER (DATA PACKAGE subtype)	An alternate method of assembling data groups and/or data elements.
XML DATA GROUP (DATA GROUP subtype)	Refer to Table 5.2 for this entity's definition.
MESSAGE TRANSACTION (DATA GROUP subtype)	A data grouping that includes a single operation performed on a single message.
FILE RECORD (DATA GROUP subtype)	A set of file elements that grouped together represent a complete set of information; a file comprises a set of records.
RELATIONAL TABLE (DATA GROUP subtype)	A set of data elements arranged into rows and columns like in a spreadsheet.
OTHER RECORD (DATA GROUP subtype)	An alternate method of assembling and/or selecting data elements.
XML DATA ELEMENT (DATA ELEMENT subtype)	Refer to Table 5.2 for this entity's definition.
FILE ELEMENT (DATA ELEMENT subtype)	Describes specific attributes of a flat file data element.
RELATIONAL ELEMENT (DATA ELEMENT subtype)	Describes specific attributes of a relational database data element.
ELEMENT ARRAY (DATA ELEMENT subtype)	Used to denote data organization methods where a data group contains repeating groups or arrays of data elements (for example, COBOL).

Table 4.4 shows more detail about the attributes of the Data Relationships to Structure entities.

Table 4.4   Data Relationships to Structure Attributes

ENTITY NAME	ATTRIBUTE NAME	ATTRIBUTE DEFINITION
MESSAGING	data package	System-generated, nonintelligent designator that uniquely specifies the DATA PACKAGE; a DATA PACKAGE is a collection of information organized to accomplish a business function in the enterprise.
	messaging type name	Describes the messaging service type being used (for example, MQ Series, JMS, Tibco, FTP, CORBA, COM/DCOM, SOAP, ebXML, JAXM, or others).
	communication protocol name	Denotes the communication protocol used for messaging (for example, TCP/IP, HTTP, HTTPS, SMTP, Wireless, WDSL, Java, ActiveX, C/C++, or others).
	connectivity mode name	Describes the communication mode used for messaging (for example, LAN, WAN, VPN, Internet, or others).
	messaging version name	Documents the version number of the messaging package being used.
RELATIONAL DATABASE	data package	System-generated, nonintelligent designator that uniquely specifies the DATA PACKAGE.
	database instance name	Denotes the physical name of the database instance, if available.
FLAT FILE	data package	System-generated, nonintelligent designator that uniquely specifies the DATA PACKAGE.
	delimiter type name	Denotes the element separator, delimiter, value used to separate elements in the file (for example, quote double quote, pipe, colon, space, tab, carat, and others).

Table 4.4 *(continued)*

ENTITY NAME	ATTRIBUTE NAME	ATTRIBUTE DEFINITION
	text delimiter name	Describes a secondary delimiter used specifically to separate string elements; typically, quotes or double quotes are used for this task.
	header flag	Indicates whether the file contains a header row that contains labels describing the elements.
	file format type name	Denotes the character-encoding format used to create the file (for example, ASCII, EBCDIC, Binary, VSAM, and others).
	audit record flag	Denotes whether an audit row exists in the flat file that can be used to verify a completed file transport.
OTHER	data package	System-generated, nonintelligent designator that uniquely specifies the DATA PACKAGE.
	other type name	Describes an alternate data package method (for example, MS Excel, proprietary, or others).
MESSAGE TRANSACTION	data group id	System-generated, nonintelligent designator that uniquely specifies the DATA GROUP; a DATA GROUP is a combination of data elements that represents a complete set of information or a business transaction.
	message transaction name	Denotes the actual physical name attached to the transaction.
	transaction object name	Describes the label established with the messaging service.
	message function name	Denotes the function call, or verb, of the messaging service application program interface (API).

(continued)

Table 4.4 *(continued)*

ENTITY NAME	ATTRIBUTE NAME	ATTRIBUTE DEFINITION
FILE RECORD	**data group id**	System-generated, nonintelligent designator that uniquely specifies the DATA GROUP.
RELATIONAL TABLE	**data group id**	System-generated, nonintelligent designator that uniquely specifies the DATA GROUP.
	table type name	References the usage type the table has in the database management system or data store structure (for example, Control, Dimension, Fact, Snowflake, System, Transaction, Operational, View, Temp, Scratch, or others).
OTHER RECORD	**data group id**	System-generated, nonintelligent designator that uniquely specifies the DATA GROUP.
	data range value	Denotes a grouping of data elements and labels within the data package.
	series type name	Describes the organization method used in the data package for data elements and labels (for example, rows, columns, hierarchical, or others).
FILE ELEMENT	**data element id**	System-generated, nonintelligent designator that uniquely specifies the DATA ELEMENT; a DATA ELEMENT is a specific item of information; it is the smallest unit of information in a data package.
	data group id	System-generated, nonintelligent designator that uniquely specifies the DATA GROUP.
	sequence number	A unique identifier for a specific data element in a hierarchal group (for example, the decomposition of data element into subelements found in COBOL copylibs).

Table 4.4 *(continued)*

ENTITY NAME	ATTRIBUTE NAME	ATTRIBUTE DEFINITION
	length	Length of a specific subelement in a hierarchal data group.
RELATIONAL ELEMENT	data element id	System-generated, nonintelligent designator that uniquely specifies the DATA ELEMENT.
	primary key flag	Indicates whether the data element is a primary key in the associated data group. A data element that has a unique value for each data group instance.
	foreign key flag	Indicator between two data groups in a data package that signifies that a relationship exists between two data groups; a foreign key is a primary key of one data group that is propagated to another data group to identify instances of the relationship.
ELEMENT ARRAY	data element id	System-generated, nonintelligent designator that uniquely specifies the DATA ELEMENT.
	minimum occurrences count	Describes the minimum number of occurrences of a data element in an array.
	maximum occurrences count	Describes the maximum number of occurrences of a data element in an array.
	array element length	Denotes length of a single occurrence of the array in the data element.
	data usage	The number of times the array repeats in the data group.
	occurrence dependent element	Uniquely identifies the element in the array.
	redefinition element	Uniquely identifies the element in the array.

Data Movement and Transformation

The Data Movement and Transformation subject area describes the general types of data integration and mapping activities that occur in the enterprise, as well as the tools and processes used to perform the tasks required. The transformations fall into two categories:

- Black-box, where the exact structure of the expression may not be known
- White-box, where the expression used for the transformation is parsed and mapped out explicitly

The black-box corresponds to the SOURCE TO TARGET MAP entity, and the white-box to the Expression Transformation subject area.

The SOURCE TO TARGET MAP entity (see Figure 4.10) provides the ability to map a set of sources to a set of targets. Mappings are accommodated through the many-to-many relationships of the SOURCE TO TARGET MAP entity to the DATA GROUP and DATA ELEMENT entities. The *group source*, *group target*, *source element*, and *target element* relationships allow mappings to be represented at a data group and/or an individual data element level, depending on your data integration needs. Specific details or comments about a particular mapping are captured in the **mapping comment text** and provide additional analysis and reporting information. For example, you can create an analysis report that documents which source tables were used to produce columns in a specific table.

For example, a SOURCE TO TARGET MAP entry could indicate that customer table column firstname and column lastname were source elements for an XML schema target of element customername. There could be many SOURCE TO TARGET MAP entries to complete the mapping of the customer information to XML, and each could specify a single element target, or more than one. That group is represented by the TRANSFORMATION GROUP entity.

Maps are grouped for an individual transformation in the TRANSFORMATION GROUP entity, as shown in Figure 4.11. The subtype entities ETL, EAI, SQLENGINE, XSLT (detailed in Chapter 5), and OTHER provide specific characteristics about the data integration method employed. For example, the **etl transformation name**, **etl repository name**, and **etl folder name** provide specific method details about the extraction, transformation, and load (ETL) process. The characteristics detailed in these subtypes are supposed to be representative of most methods.

MESSAGE-ORIENTED MIDDLEWARE

Message-oriented middleware (MOM) allows applications on heterogeneous hardware, operating systems, and networks exchange information dependably and securely. Data is transferred from an application to a message queue, where the MOM server may then modify the message and allow other applications to retrieve it from the queue. No direct connection between the sending and receiving applications needs to occur. The system provides fault-tolerant guaranteed messaging for applications across a variety of operating systems, even when the receiving applications are unavailable, by using queues to maintain the message securely. This is an asynchronous form of communication, and occurs in real time from one application to others, in contrast to synchronous, or request-based communication.

There are different types and protocols available with MOM servers. There is point-to-point (P-P), which involves one receiver per message, and publish/subscribe, which can be used to retrieve multiple messages based on a subscription data type. A message queue is written to by applications, and other applications can be notified about messages and read from the queue.

The MOM systems usually have transformation capabilities on the messages. A message send to a queue can be transformed and processed by the MOM server before distribution. MOM messages have a header and a body. The header specifies how the message is to be processed and may indicate the format of the body. The header form is typically vendor-proprietary, but some standards exist for Java and XML messaging. The form of the message body can be anything that is agreed to by the sender and receiver. XML messages are increasingly used for messaging. Many MOM servers allow use of XSLT for XML transformations of messages.

MOM systems are represented in the model by separating the adapter functions that applications use to communicate with a queue from the queue management and transformation functions. This is indicated on the TRANS-FORMATION GROUP - EAI by either the **manager flag** or the **adapter flag** being true. A message queue can be treated like any other data source, and the source to target maps are used as the adapters write or read from the message queues. The maps are grouped by TRANSFORMATION GROUP - EAI. The management and transform part of MOM systems also uses the source to target maps, but these are grouped by an EAI subtype, where the manager flag is true. The set of transformations and processing for the manager is then represented under the TRANSFORMATION PACKAGE.

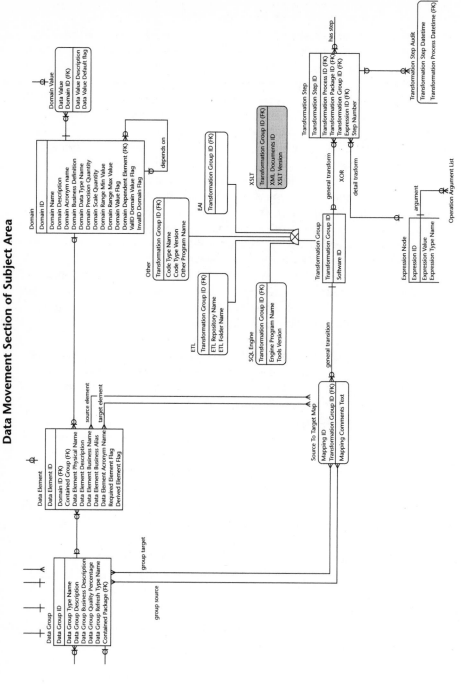

Figure 4.10   Data movement section of subject area.

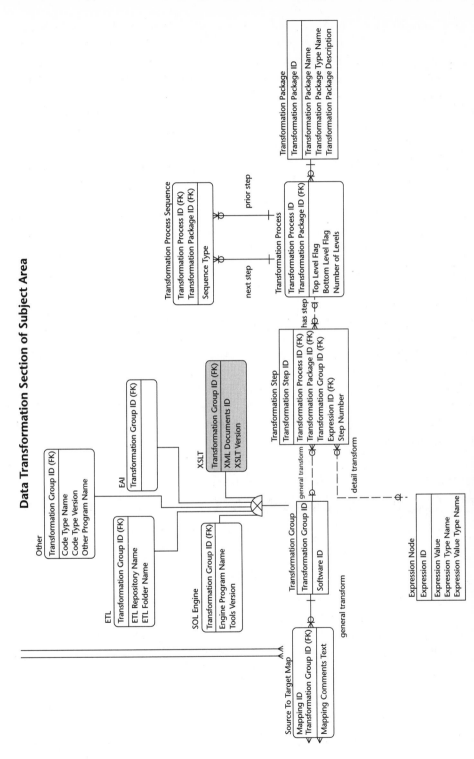

Figure 4.11   Data transformation section of subject area.

A TRANSFORMATION GROUP performs work by transporting and transforming data. In ETL processes and other data integration applications, this process can be reused by multiple processes, and the components need to be grouped and sequenced. For example, in dimensional schema processing for a data warehouse, the dimension tables need to be updated before the fact tables. This is sequence control. A single process may be responsible for one dimension table, and that process must be done before the fact table processing starts. The model covers this process of grouping and sequence control.

The relationship between TRANSFORMATION GROUP and TRANSFORMATION STEP provides for the transformation mapping to be done in one operation. The relationship between TRANSFORMATION PROCESS and TRANSFORMATION STEP entities provides reuse of the mapping operation. The TRANSFORMATION GROUP and TRANSFORMATION STEP entities provide the linkage between general source to target mappings and a specific transformation expression if used one is in the operation. More on expression transformation follows in the next section of this chapter. The double relationship (*next step*, *prior step*) between the TRANSFORMATION PROCESS and TRANSFORMATION PROCESS SEQUENCE entities allow processes to be reused with multiple parents. The sequence type attribute in the TRANSFORMATION PROCESS SEQUENCE entity is used to denote failure path processing. A set of transformation steps is accomplished through the TRANSFORMATION PACKAGE entity. This entity is the object that would be scheduled to run periodic updates to data structures.

Table 4.5 shows more details about the entities of the Data Movement and Transformation subject area.

Table 4.5   Data Movement and Transformation Entities

ENTITY NAME	ENTITY DEFINITION
SOURCE TO TARGET MAP	Contains the cross-reference mapping and semantic resolution between the source system and the target system in the enterprise.
TRANSFORMATION GROUP	The grouping of source to target map(s) for a single transformation.
ETL (TRANSFORMATION GROUP subtype)	Describes specifics about the extraction, transformation, and load (ETL)–based utility used to perform data transformations, usually associated with data warehouse implementations.

Table 4.5   *(continued)*

ENTITY NAME	ENTITY DEFINITION
EAI (TRANSFORMATION GROUP subtype)	Describes specifics about the enterprise application integration (EAI)–based utility used to perform data transformations, perform message routing, and provide adapters, usually associated with e-business, application integration, or Web Services.
SQL ENGINE (TRANSFORMATION GROUP subtype)	Describes specifics about the SQL-engine-based utility used to perform data transformations.
XSLT (TRANSFORMATION GROUP subtype)	Refer to Table 5.5 for this entity's definition.
OTHER (TRANSFORMATION GROUP subtype)	Describes specifics about the programming language or other methods used to perform data transformations. Typically, these are internally developed programs coded in a familiar programming language.
TRANSFORMATION STEP	A grouping of transformation maps used to perform a single operation that may be reusable in other transformation processes and that may use an expression.
TRANSFORMATION PROCESS	A set of transformation steps.
TRANSFORMATION PROCESS SEQUENCE	Allows transformation processes to be reused with multiple parents.
TRANSFORMATION PACKAGE	A set of transformation steps that can be scheduled for processing.

Table 4.6 shows more detail about the attributes of the Data Movement and Transformation subject area.

Table 4.6   Data Movement and Transformation Attributes

ENTITY NAME	ATTRIBUTE NAME	ATTRIBUTE DEFINITION
SOURCE TO TARGET MAP	**data group id**	System-generated, nonintelligent designator that uniquely specifies the DATA GROUP; a DATA GROUP is a combination of data elements that represent a complete set of information or business transaction.

(continued)

Table 4.6   *(continued)*

ENTITY NAME	ATTRIBUTE NAME	ATTRIBUTE DEFINITION
	mapping id	Unique identifier for a mapping a set of sources to targets.
	transformation group id	Unique identifier for a grouping of source to target map(s).
	mapping comments text	Describes any additional instructions required for mapping a source to target groups and/or elements.
TRANSFORMATION GROUP	**transformation group id**	Unique identifier for a grouping of source to target map(s).
	software id	Identifier used by the particular transformation method to designate a transformation step or map.
ETL (TRANSFORMATION GROUP subtype)	**transformation group id**	Unique identifier for a grouping of source to target map(s).
	etl repository name	Database name of the ETL product's transformation repository where the detailed transformation steps, processes, and packages are stored.
	etl folder name	The directory folder name in the ETL product's transformation repository where the detailed transformation steps, processes, and packages are stored.
EAI (TRANSFORMATION GROUP subtype)	**transformation group id**	Unique identifier for a grouping of source to target map(s).
	manager flag	Indicates whether the manager functions for queue management and transformations functions are in use.

Table 4.6 *(continued)*

ENTITY NAME	ATTRIBUTE NAME	ATTRIBUTE DEFINITION
	adapter flag	Indicates whether functions that applications use to communicate with a queue are in use.
SQL ENGINE (TRANSFORMATION GROUP subtype)	transformation group id	Unique identifier for a grouping of source to target map(s).
	engine program name	Program name recognized by the SQL engine transformation.
	tools version	The SQL engine tool's product version.
OTHER (TRANSFORMATION GROUP subtype)	transformation group id	Unique identifier for a grouping of source to target map(s).
	code type name	Product or source code name of the utility used to perform source to target mappings (for example, COBOL, SQL, Script, Awk, Perl, and others).
	code type version	Version number of the product or source code utility used to perform source to target mappings.
	other program name	Program name of the product or source code utility used to perform source to target mappings.
TRANSFORMATION STEP	transformation step id	System-generated, non-intelligent designator that uniquely specifies a specific TRANSFORMATION STEP.
	transformation group id	System-generated, nonintelligent designator that uniquely specifies the TRANSFORMATION GROUP; a TRANSFORMATION GROUP is a grouping of source to target map(s) for a single transformation.

(continued)

Table 4.6 *(continued)*

ENTITY NAME	ATTRIBUTE NAME	ATTRIBUTE DEFINITION
	transformation process id	System-generated, nonintelligent designator that uniquely specifies the TRANSFORMATION PROCESS; a TRANSFORMATION PROCESS is a set of transformation steps.
	transformation package id	System-generated, nonintelligent designator that uniquely specifies the TRANSFORMATION PACKAGE; a TRANSFORMATION PACKAGE is a set of transformation steps that can be scheduled for processing.
	expression id	System-generated, nonintelligent designator that uniquely specifies the EXPRESSION; an EXPRESSION is a data structure representing a transformation step that requires parsing that is independent of the source syntax.
	step number	Sequence number of an individual element mapping.
TRANSFORMATION PROCESS	**transformation process id**	System-generated, nonintelligent designator that uniquely specifies the TRANSFORMATION PROCESS.
	transformation package id	System-generated, nonintelligent designator that uniquely specifies the TRANSFORMATION PACKAGE.

Table 4.6 *(continued)*

ENTITY NAME	ATTRIBUTE NAME	ATTRIBUTE DEFINITION
	top level flag	Navigates directly to the highest step in a process.
	bottom level flag	Navigates directly to the lowest step in a process.
	number of levels	Identifies the number of the steps, or depth, of a process.
TRANSFORMATION PROCESS SEQUENCE	transformation process id	System-generated, nonintelligent designator that uniquely specifies the TRANSFORMATION PROCESS.
	transformation package id	System-generated, nonintelligent designator that uniquely specifies the TRANSFORMATION PACKAGE.
	sequence type	Indicates if a transformation process is part of a failure path.
TRANSFORMATION PACKAGE	transformation package id	System-generated, nonintelligent designator that uniquely specifies the TRANSFORMATION PACKAGE.
	transformation package name	Short descriptive name of the transformation package.
	transformation package type name	Indicator for the type of transformation processing that is being performed (for example, Interface, Conversion, Data Warehouse ETL, Business Transaction, or others).
	transformation package description	Detailed description of the purpose of the transformation package in the enterprise.

Expression Transformation

The Expression Transformation subject area provides a detail breakdown of those transformation steps that are expression based. Expressions contain two types of components, operands, and operators. Operands are the items that are changed, and operators are the symbols that represent specific processing. For example, in the expression, x - 1, "-" is an operator and X and 1 are operands. All expressions have at least one operand. An EXPRESSION NODE is denoted as an identifier, string literal, constant, string constant, array specification, a function or procedure call, or any combination of these, in order with operators. Expression elements are parsed and stored as OPERATION ARGUMENT LIST, OPERATION NODE, ELEMENT NODE, or CONSTANT NODE in an abstract syntax tree structure (as shown in Figure 4.12).

Every EXPRESSION NODE is differentiated by an **expression value** and **expression value type name** (see Figure 4.13). An **expression value** denotes the calculation type of the expression (Direct, Nested, Conditional, Other). The **expression value type name** indicates the return type of expression being used (for example, Boolean, integer, or string). A unary expression contains one operand and a unary (single element) operator. A binary expression contains two operands separated by one operator. A conditional expression is a compound expression that contains a condition. An assignment expression stores a constant value in the variable designated by the left operand. It uses an abstract syntax tree to store the structure of the expression.

Simple Abstract Syntax Tree

((32 / 4) −13) + (6 * 5)

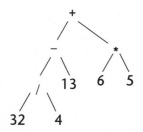

Figure 4.12   Simple abstract syntax tree.

ABSTRACT SYNTAX TREE

An abstract syntax tree is a data structure used to represent an expression that has been parsed into its primary elements without regard for the source syntax. It contains all the fundamental elements of the original expression but organized for easy access. This representation of information contains a node for each token identified during the parsing operation. Each abstract syntax tree consists of a root node and subnodes. Each subnode may also have its own subnodes. Elements such as parentheses and semicolons, while syntactically significant, are omitted because they have no semantic meaning.

The parenthesis-free mathematical notation, Polish notation, is used for evaluation of the expression. Using Polish notation, the operator is listed first, then the operands. For example, the following arithmetic statement ((32 / 4) −13) + (6 * 5) would be represented explicitly in Polish notation as + − / 32 4 13 * 6 5.

The OPERATION ARGUMENT LIST entity stores each type of argument composing the expression. Some languages, such as LISP and Perl, can provide named parameters so that the order of the argument list is not important. Most languages, however, use position in the argument list to determine the meaning of a parameter. The **argument sequence** handles the position in the argument lists and **argument parameter name** provides a unique name for each argument for languages requiring names. Objects are created for higher and higher levels of arguments, forming a tree structure needed to represent the expression. The entity allows for access to subarguments of an argument either as members of the expression or explicitly by name.

OPERATION entity supports the typical arithmetic operators, which take the operands of any numeric data type. There are also comparison operands, which take the operands of any data type with the data type of the result always being Boolean. In addition, there are Boolean operators that take Boolean operands and return in a Boolean result. The CONSTANT NODE entity stores the static values of components comprising the expression. The ELEMENT NODE entity stores the association of an element, in an expression, to the Data Package subject area through the relationships to DATA PACKAGE REFERENCE, DATA GROUP REFERENCE, and DATA ELEMENT REFERENCE, as shown in Figure 4.14.

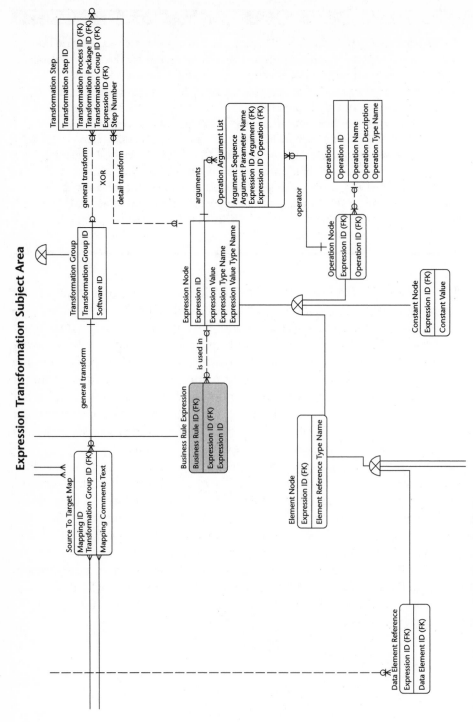

Figure 4.13   Expression Transformation subject area.

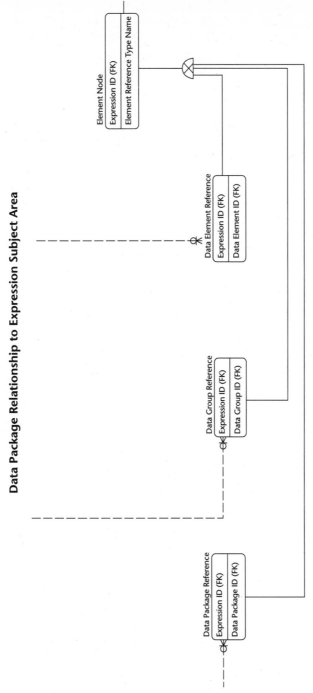

Data Package Relationship to Expression Subject Area

Figure 4.14 Data package relationship to Expression subject area.

Figure 4.15 illustrates how the components of an example expression would be parsed and distributed into an abstract syntax tree using the EXPRESSION subtypes OPERATION NODE, ELEMENT NODE, and CONSTANT NODE.

Table 4.7 shows more details about the entities of the Expression Transformation subject area.

Expression Abstract Syntax Tree

assign (col_A, IF (EQUAL (col_C, 1), col_B, 2))

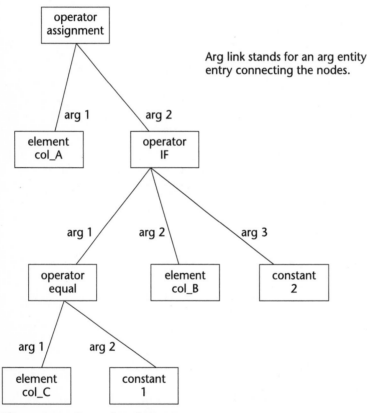

Figure 4.15 Expression abstract syntax tree.

Table 4.7   Expression Transformation Entities

ENTITY NAME	ENTITY DEFINITION
EXPRESSION NODE	A data structure representing a transformation step that requires parsing and is independent of the source syntax.
OPERATION ARGUMENT LIST	Contains the inheritance hierarchy of the expression.
OPERATION	Contains the operations or operands available to the expression.
OPERATION NODE (EXPRESSION NODE subtype)	The relationship of the operation to its node position on the syntax tree.
CONSTANT NODE (EXPRESSION NODE subtype)	The relationship of the constant value to its node position on the syntax tree.
ELEMENT NODE (EXPRESSION NODE subtype)	The relationship of the element to its node position on the syntax tree.
DATA PACKAGE REFERENCE (EXPRESSION ELEMENT subtype)	Denotes the relationship of a data package to a particular transformation expression.
DATA GROUP REFERENCE (EXPRESSION ELEMENT subtype)	Denotes the relationship of a data group to a particular transformation expression.
DATA ELEMENT REFERENCE (EXPRESSION ELEMENT subtype)	Denotes the relationship of a data element to a particular transformation expression.

Table 4.8 shows more detail about the attributes of the Expression Transformation subject area.

Table 4.8   Expression Transformation Attributes

ENTITY NAME	ATTRIBUTE NAME	ATTRIBUTE DEFINITION
EXPRESSION NODE	**expression id**	System-generated, nonintelligent designator that uniquely specifies the EXPRESSION; an EXPRESSION is a data structure representing a transformation step that requires parsing that is independent of the source syntax.

(continued)

Table 4.8 *(continued)*

ENTITY NAME	ATTRIBUTE NAME	ATTRIBUTE DEFINITION
	expression value	Grouping of operands, values, and operators; actions that represent a value.
	expression type name	Type of expression based on the operation being performed (for example, Direct, Nested, Conditional, or others).
	expression value type name	Type of expression determined by its content or value (for example, Unary, Binary, Conditional, or Assignment).
OPERATION ARGUMENT LIST	argument sequence	Denotes the order or precedence in which the arguments are evaluated.
	argument parameter name	Variable that takes on the value of the corresponding argument.
	expression id	System-generated, nonintelligent designator that uniquely specifies the EXPRESSION.
OPERATION	operation id	System-generated, nonintelligent designator that uniquely specifies the OPERATION; an OPERATION contains the operations or operands available to the expression.
	operation name	Name of the operation or operator that represents a specific action (for example, Addition, Subtraction, Multiplication, Division, Less Than, Less Than or Equal To, Greater Than, Greater Than or EqualTo, Equal To, Not Equal To, Not, Or, or And).
	operation description	Describes the action that the operation or operator represents.
	operation type name	Type of operation or operator determined by the action performed on the operands (for example, Boolean or Numeric).

Table 4.8   *(continued)*

ENTITY NAME	ATTRIBUTE NAME	ATTRIBUTE DEFINITION
OPERATION NODE (EXPRESSION NODE subtype)	**expression id**	System-generated, nonintelligent designator that uniquely specifies the EXPRESSION.
	operation id	System-generated, nonintelligent designator that uniquely specifies the OPERATION.
CONSTANT NODE (EXPRESSION NODE subtype)	**expression id**	System-generated, nonintelligent designator that uniquely specifies the EXPRESSION.
	constant value	Contains the content of a value in an expression.
ELEMENT NODE (EXPRESSION NODE subtype)	**expression id**	System-generated, nonintelligent designator that uniquely specifies the EXPRESSION.
	element reference type name	The element portion of an expression.
DATA PACKAGE REFERENCE (EXPRESSION ELEMENT subtype)	**expression id**	System-generated, nonintelligent designator that uniquely specifies the EXPRESSION.
	data package	System-generated, nonintelligent designator that uniquely specifies the DATA PACKAGE; a DATA PACKAGE is a collection of information organized to accomplish a business function in the enterprise.
DATA GROUP REFERENCE (EXPRESSION ELEMENT subtype)	**expression id**	System-generated, nonintelligent designator that uniquely specifies the EXPRESSION.
	data group id	System-generated, nonintelligent designator that uniquely specifies the DATA GROUP; a DATA GROUP is a combination of data elements that represent a complete set of information or a business transaction.

(continued)

Table 4.8   *(continued)*

ENTITY NAME	ATTRIBUTE NAME	ATTRIBUTE DEFINITION
DATA ELEMENT REFERENCE (EXPRESSION ELEMENT subtype)	**expression id**	System-generated, nonintelligent designator that uniquely specifies the EXPRESSION.
	data element id	System-generated, nonintelligent designator that uniquely specifies the DATA ELEMENT a DATA ELEMENT is a specific item of information; it is the smallest unit of information in a data package.

Transformation Operational History

The Transformation Operational History subject area captures operational meta data, or the actual executions of the transformations and the groupings that executed them. This is pertinent information collected during the transformation procedure used for measuring status, processing efficiency, capacity planning, source data quality analysis, historical comparison, error diagnosis, and other purposes. Operational meta data is collected for both the general transformations (the relationship to TRANSFORMATION GROUP) and for detailed transformations (the indirect relationship to EXPRESSION NODE). Meta data is collected at each hierarchal level of the transformation through the relationships *transformation step→transformation step audit, transformation process→transformation process audit*, and *transformation package→ transformation step package,* as shown in Figure 4.16. The relationship of a package audit to one or many process audits and process audits to one or many steps is captured through the hierarchy relationship between the entities.

Meta data related to status, data quality, historical, and capacity planning is captured in the **records processed** and **records rejected** attributes in each of the three entities for this subject area. By comparing the records processed over time to a particular target table, you can forecast expected growth for a particular table or target database. Transformation efficiency is measured through the **elapsed time** and **cpu time** attributes in each entity. Timing values captured at the DATA PACKAGE level can be used to plan and schedule transformation processing windows. The *return code name* and *return code message* relationships, if available through the specific TRANSFORMATION GROUP, provide insights into trouble shooting of transformations at the various levels.

Table 4.9 shows more details about the entities of the Transformation Operational History subject area.

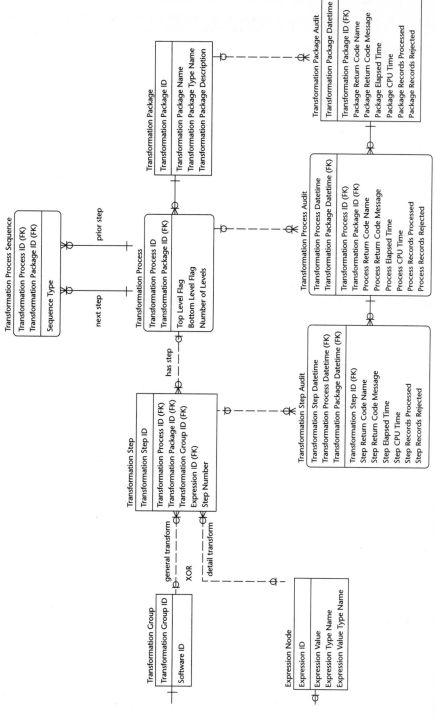

Figure 4.16   Transformation operational history.

Table 4.9   Transformation Operational History Entities

ENTITY NAME	ENTITY DEFINITION
TRANSFORMATION STEP AUDIT	Contains the operational meta data collected about the source to target mapping transformation step.
TRANSFORMATION PROCESS AUDIT	Contains the operational meta data collected about the transformation process.
TRANSFORMATION PACKAGE AUDIT	Contains the operational meta data collected about the transformation package.

Table 4.10 shows more detail about the attributes of the Transformation Operational History subject area.

Table 4.10   Transformation Operational History Attributes

ENTITY NAME	ATTRIBUTE NAME	ATTRIBUTE DEFINITION
TRANSFORMATION STEP AUDIT	**transformation step date time**	The date and time the transformation step was processed.
	transformation step id	A system-generated, nonintelligent designator that uniquely specifies the TRANSFORMATION STEP.
	transformation group id	A unique identifier for a grouping of source to target map(s).
	transformation process id	A system-generated, nonintelligent designator that uniquely specifies the TRANSFORMATION PROCESS; a TRANSFORMATION PROCESS is a set of transformation steps.
	transformation package id	A system-generated, nonintelligent designator that uniquely specifies the TRANSFORMATION PACKAGE; a TRANSFORMATION PACKAGE is a set of transformation steps that can be scheduled for processing.

Table 4.10   *(continued)*

ENTITY NAME	ATTRIBUTE NAME	ATTRIBUTE DEFINITION
	step return code name	The code returned by the transformation step indicating the final state of the step (for example, Failed, Succeeded, Warning, or Other).
	step return code message	The STEP RETURN CODE MESSAGE is the description of the return code value sent back from the transformation step, if available.
	step elapsed time	The amount of clock time the transformation step took to complete.
	step cpu time	The amount of computer resource time the transformation step took to complete.
	step records processed	The total number of records that were processed successfully by the transformation step.
	step records rejected	The total number of records that were processed and rejected by the transformation step.
TRANSFORMATION PROCESS AUDIT	**transformation process datetime**	The date and time the transformation process occurred.
	transformation process id	A system-generated, nonintelligent designator that uniquely specifies the TRANSFORMATION PROCESS; a TRANSFORMATION PROCESS is a set of transformation steps.
	transformation package id	A system-generated, nonintelligent designator that uniquely specifies the TRANSFORMATION PACKAGE; a TRANSFORMATION PACKAGE is a set of transformation steps that can be scheduled for processing.

(continued)

Table 4.10   *(continued)*

ENTITY NAME	ATTRIBUTE NAME	ATTRIBUTE DEFINITION
	process return code name	The code returned by the transformation process indicating the final state of the process (for example, Failed, Succeeded, Warning, or Other).
	process return code message	The description of the return code value sent back from the transformation process, if available.
	process elapsed time	The amount of clock time the transformation process took to complete.
	process cpu time	The computer resource time the transformation process took to complete.
	process records processed	The total number of records that were processed successfully by the transformation process.
	process records rejected	The total number of records that were processed and rejected by the transformation process.
TRANSFORMATION PACKAGE AUDIT	transformation package datetime	The date and time the transformation package was processed.
	transformation package id	A system-generated, nonintelligent designator that uniquely specifies the TRANSFORMATION PACKAGE; a TRANSFORMATION PACKAGE is a set of transformation steps that can be scheduled for processing.
	package return code name	The code returned by the transformation package indicating the final state of the package (for example, Failed, Succeeded, Warning, or Other).

Table 4.10 *(continued)*

ENTITY NAME	ATTRIBUTE NAME	ATTRIBUTE DEFINITION
	package return code message	The description of the return code value sent back from the transformation package, if available.
	package elapsed time	The amount of clock time the transformation package took to complete.
	package cpu time	The amount of computer resource time the transformation package took to complete.
	package records processed	The total number of records that were processed successfully by the transformation package.
	package records rejected	The total number of records that were processed and rejected by the transformation package.

Data Profiling

The Data Profiling subject area provides the MME with the capability to identify and historically track business rule and domain value violations in enterprise's data brought into the enterprise during transformations. This subject area also provides valuable relationships from domains and business rules to data quality metrics that may need to be further assessed. Measurement is performed against the quality of element values (single values, range specification, or pattern) in data stores. The subject area performs this function through relationships to the DATA QUALITY MEASURE and BUSINESS RULE EXPRESSION entities, as shown in Figure 4.17.

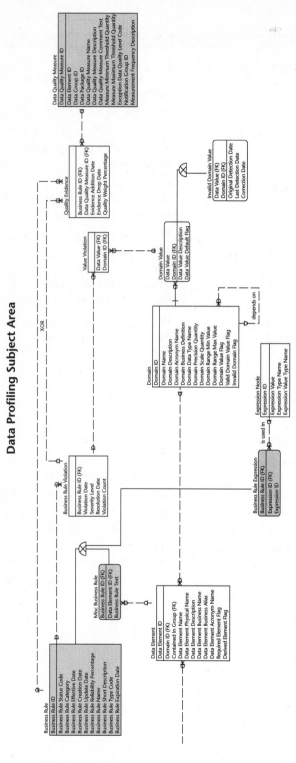

Figure 4.17 Data profiling.

This linkage provides MME users with a catalog of the enterprise data objects and also with a means to weigh the quality of the content so that corrective actions can be taken. This involves comparison between known values in the DOMAIN VALUE entity and those encountered during transformation processing. Corrective actions may involve changes to the source or target data structures (Data Package subject area) or modifications to detailed transformation expressions (Expression Transformation subject area). For example, in data warehousing, extract, transform, and load (ETL) transformation processing accesses source stores against expected domain values to uncover data quality defects or changes to business rules.

Business rules are associated with data elements through MISC. Business Rule entity's relationship. This relationship handles the simple case where a single element has a domain violation. Depending on the implementation method chosen, there could be a different business rule for each data element that has a violation, or there could be a single general rule for all single element violations. Complex business rules that span multiple data elements or data groups are identified through the relationships to the BUSINESS RULE EXPRESSION entity. The assumption in this relationship is that the associated expression must validate to true for the elements to be valid. An example of a complex rule could be:

If (AARP_discount = true) then age>50.

The QUALITY EVIDENCE entity relates the DATA QUALITY MEASURE entity for evaluation to the business rules and value violations. The DATA QUALITY MEASURE references to BUSINESS RULE VIOLATION and BUSINESS RULE relationship is mutually exclusive (XOR); data quality can be associated with either BUSINESS RULE VIOLATION or BUSINESS RULE, but not both. The relationship between DATA QUALITY MEASURE and BUSINESS RULE entities allows you to know which business rules apply to a particular data quality measure. This, in turn, allows you to know which business rule violations may be important to review. Business rule violations of any type are stored in the BUSINESS RULE VIOLATION entity. This entity uses the **violation date**, **resolution date**, **severity level**, and **violation count** attributes for tracking and measurement. The VALUE VIOLATION entity associates business rule violation records with valid or invalid domain values relevant to the violation.

Table 4.11 shows more details about the entities of the Data Profiling subject area.

Table 4.11 Data Profiling Entities

ENTITY NAME	ENTITY DEFINITION
BUSINESS RULE VIOLATION	Catalogs invalid domain value business rule violations.
QUALITY EVIDENCE	Associates data quality evaluations to business rules and business rule violations.
VALUE VIOLATION	Associates the business rule violation to the related valid or invalid domain value.
INVALID DOMAIN VALUE (DOMAIN VALUE subtype)	Captures invalid domain values.

Table 4.12 shows more detail about the attributes of the Data Profiling subject area.

Table 4.12 Data Profiling Attributes

ENTITY NAME	ATTRIBUTE NAME	ATTRIBUTE DEFINITION
BUSINESS RULE VIOLATION	business rule id	Refer to Table 7.2 for this attribute's definition.
	violation date	Date the business rule domain value variance occurred.
	severity level	Indicates the relevance of the business rule violation and the priority it should be given for resolution (for example, High, Medium, or Low).
	resolution date	Date the business rule domain value violation was rectified.
	violation count	Total occurrences of a particular business rule domain value violation.
QUALITY EVIDENCE	business rule id	Refer to this attribute's definition in Chapter 7.
	data quality measure id	Refer to Table 6.10 for this attribute's definition.

Table 4.12 *(continued)*

ENTITY NAME	ATTRIBUTE NAME	ATTRIBUTE DEFINITION
	evidence addition date	Date the data quality measure association to business rules or business rule violation was established.
	evidence drop date	Date the data quality measure association to business rules or business rule violation was abandoned.
	quality weight percentage	Indicates impact on data quality variance.
VALUE VIOLATION	**data value**	Contains a specific value, code, identifier, or unit that the domain can contain.
	domain id	System-generated, nonintelligent designator that uniquely specifies the DOMAIN; a DOMAIN identifies and groups types of data elements for standardization and maintenance of business and technical meta data.
INVALID DOMAIN VALUE	**data value**	Contains a specific value, code, identifier, or unit that the domain can contain.
	domain id	System-generated, nonintelligent designator that uniquely specifies the DOMAIN; a DOMAIN identifies and groups types of data elements for standardization and maintenance of business and technical meta data.
	original detection date	The date the first invalid domain value was discovered.
	last detection date	The date the last invalid domain value was discovered.
	correction date	The date the domain value was rectified.

Reports from the Enterprise Systems Meta Model

Mark Twain once said, "Few things are harder to put up with than the annoyance of a good example." To provide a better understanding of how to use the Enterprise Systems meta model, we will now examine examples of relevant reports that can be generated from this information. What real usable information and knowledge can be obtained from this portion of the MME?

Data Definition by System by Environment Report

One of the key functions of the MME (first presented in Chapter 1) is to enable the enterprise to share and reuse knowledge it assimilates. This provides the organization with a competitive advantage by allowing it to exploit this knowledge asset. The Data Definition by System by Environment report shown in Figure 4.18 provides a mechanism for sharing and reusing this resource. The report provides a central means for acquiring and using meta data from various corporate applications to promote the transfer of knowledge acquired from other implementations and to avoid the costs associated with the rediscovery and acquisition of this information. Information on previous used and pending business definitions can be reviewed across applications in the enterprise. All business and technical meta data, both previous and current, on an MME object can be reviewed through this report.

Data Structure Hierarchy Report

The hierarchical structure of data in the MME and its interdependent relationship to applications, transformations, and other data movement activities can be explored in the Data Structure Hierarchy report (see Figure 4.19). This report provides the means to review the data structures of a particular application at a concrete, or physical, level. As opposed to the previous report, only enough business and technical meta data is provided on the report to illustrate the data structures. The report could be easily extended into a hierarchical graph to improve the readability of the data relationships and illustrate common data types. The report provides business users with a means to better understand the structure of data in the enterprise, while providing technical users with insight into dependencies.

Data Definition by System by Environment

Data Definition by System by Environment																				October 3, 2003
Effective Date	Effective Status	System	Environment	Data Package Type	Data Package Technical Name	Data Group Name	Data Group Technical Name	Data Element Name	Data Element Technical Name	Business Description	Acronym	Required Element Flag	Derived Element Flag	Unit Type	Data Type	Precision/ Scale	Min/Max Value	Dependency Flag
9/1/2003	Active	Financial	Production	Database	HF00004P	Revenue	H_REVENUE	Total Revenue	TOT_REVN_AMT	The total revenue amount obtained from all consulting resourse (consultant, machine, fixed fee, miscelleaneous)		Y	Y	Dollars ($USD)	Decimal	10.2	–	N
1/1/2004	Active	Financial	Test	Database	HF00004P	Revenue	H_REVENUE	Total Revenue	TOT_REVN_AMT	The total revenue amount obtained from all consulting resourse (consultant, machine, fixed fee, miscelleaneous, writeups, writeoffs, billing)		Y	Y	Dollars ($USD)	Decimal	10.2	–	N
4/1/2003	Active	HRMS	Production	Database	HH00007P	Employee	H_EE	Employee Status	EE_STAT_CD	The current status of the employee with the employer	EESTAT	Y	N	N/A	Character	1	–	N
10/1/2003	Non-Active	HRMS	Test	Database	HH00019T	Employee	H_EE	Employee Status	EE_STAT_CD	The current status of the employee with the employer	EESTAT	Y	N	N/A	Character	2	–	N
2/1/2002	Active	Payroll Interface	Production	Flat File	PR_INF_ 00321.DAT	Compensation	COMP	Annual Rate	ANL_RT_AMT	The annual base rate of compensation for an employee		Y	Y	Euro (€ EUR)	Decimal	10.6	–	Y
1/1/2000	Active	Payroll Interface	Test	Flat File	PR_INF_ 00321.DAT	Compensation	COMP	Annual Rate	ANL_RT_AMT	The annual base rate of compensation for an employee		Y	Y	Dollars ($USD)	Decimal	10.2	–	Y

Figure 4.18   Data Definition by System by Environment report.

Data Structure Hierarchy

Data Structure Hierarchy	System	Environment	Data Package	Data Group	Data Element — October 3, 2003
Business Name		Production	Internal Production HR	Employee	First Name
Technical Name			HH00007P	H_EE	FIRST_NM
Type			Database	Table	Column
Effective Date			4/1/2003	4/1/2003	4/1/2003
Status			Active	Active	Active
Business Name					Full Name
Technical Name					FULL_NM
Type					Column
Effective Date					9/1/2003
Status					Active
Business Name				Compensation	Annual Rate
Technical Name				H_COMP	ANL_RAT_AMT
Type				Table	Column
Effective Date				5/1/2003	4/17/2003
Status				Active	Active
Business Name					Monthly Rate
Technical Name					MNTH_RAT_AMT
Type					Column
Effective Date					4/17/2003
Status					Active
Business Name	Payroll Interface	Production	Employee Personal Feed	Address	Street Address
Technical Name			PR_INF_00321.DAT	ADDRESS	ADDR_TXT
Type			Flat File	Record	Field
Effective Date			1/1/2000	1/17/2000	1/17/2000
Status			Active	Active	Active
Business Name					City
Technical Name					CITY_NM
Type					Field
Effective Date					1/17/2000
Status					Active

Figure 4.19   Data Structure Hierarchy report.

System Data Quality Assessment Report

One key insight that most companies cannot easily access is the quality of data in their enterprise. This lack of knowledge leaves open the possibility of making poor business decisions or interpretations based on faulty information. The System Data Quality Assessment report (see Figure 4.20) provides users with a means to evaluate the quality of this knowledge resource. Data quality factoring assessments are gathered from throughout the enterprise model to aggregate a quality factor based on SYSTEM, ENVIRONMENT, DATA PACKAGE, and DATA GROUP. The data quality meta tags assigned to each row of the information in the MME allow this type of evaluation to occur based on the source. Low-quality sources, such as spreadsheets, personal databases, or the Web, have poorer indicators than other applications. This provides a means to examine data quality throughout your enterprise, looking for opportunities for improvement, which results in better business decisions, helping the bottom line.

Data Profiling Exceptions Report

Due to changing business climates and strategies, organizations are often forced to change direction quickly to respond to pressures in the marketplace. Companies must quickly make changes in their applications and data movement rules. These changes are often communicated poorly, if at all, to the business and technical users using the enterprise systems. The Data Profiling Exceptions report (see Figure 4.21) utilizes the business and technical rules of the enterprise to detect exceptions or changes. Invalid lookup values for data elements are flagged and listed in this report, allowing users to take appropriate action. This may result in changes to a source application or interface, or another data movement activity. This can also result in changes to the business rules stored in the MME that govern information usage for the business.

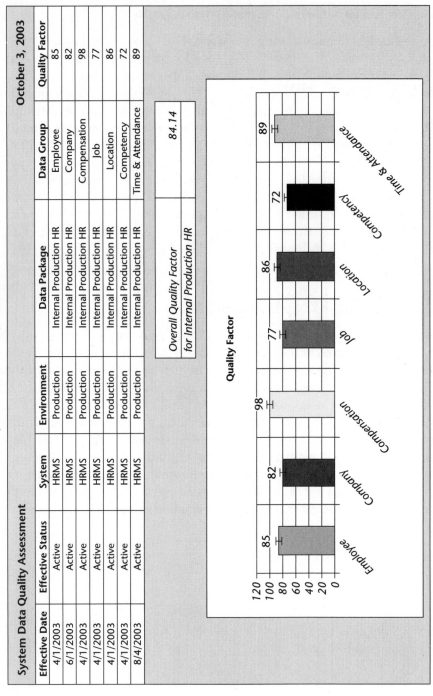

System Data Quality Assessment

System Data Quality Assessment   October 3, 2003

Effective Date	Effective Status	System	Environment	Data Package	Data Group	Quality Factor
4/1/2003	Active	HRMS	Production	Internal Production HR	Employee	85
6/1/2003	Active	HRMS	Production	Internal Production HR	Company	82
4/1/2003	Active	HRMS	Production	Internal Production HR	Compensation	98
4/1/2003	Active	HRMS	Production	Internal Production HR	Job	77
4/1/2003	Active	HRMS	Production	Internal Production HR	Location	86
4/1/2003	Active	HRMS	Production	Internal Production HR	Competency	72
8/4/2003	Active	HRMS	Production	Internal Production HR	Time & Attendance	89

Overall Quality Factor for Internal Production HR	84.14

Figure 4.20 System Data Quality Assessment report.

Data Profiling Exceptions

Data Profiling Exceptions										October 1, 2003
Effective Date	Effective Status	System	Environment	Data Package	Data Group	Data Element	Data Element Data Steward	Business Rule ID	Invalid Domain Value	Detection Date
4/1/2003	Active	HRMS	Production	Internal Production HR	Employee	Employee Status	Timothy Steward	314	ZA	9/25/2003
								314	Z	9/7/2003
								314	11	9/7/2003
								314	?	8/14/2003
11/1/2003	Active	Payroll Interface	Production	Internal Production HR	Employee Personal Feed	State	Mathew Rule	271	XT	9/4/2003
								271	XT	
								271	X	9/6/2003

Figure 4.21   Data Profiling Exceptions report.

Data Impact Analysis Report

Every action in the enterprise has a consequence; some are positive, some negative. Yet many organizations make changes to their enterprise applications that run their business without having any insight into the impact. The Data Impact Analysis report (see Figure 4.22) is one method for assessing the impact of a change to a data object. It provides a means for reviewing the total impact on the MME from a data structure, application, environment, business rule, and data movement perspective. This allows both business and technical users the ability to make informed decisions on what changes offer the best opportunity to improve efficiency in the enterprise. The report provides a very granular level of impact analysis down to the expression argument or token level.

Data Lineage Analysis Report

One of the most common business and technical questions asked of information in the enterprise is, "Where did this data come from?" The Data Lineage Analysis report (see Figure 4.23) allows the users to explore what data-associated movement activities resulted in the final data set. Users can review the entire history of a data object to determine its impact on the enterprise. Analysis can reveal areas of opportunity, where applications can be modified, resulting in increased efficiency.

Data Impact Analysis

Domain Name	Data Type	Precison/ Scale	Data Element	Data Group	Data Package	Environment	System	Business Rule ID	Data Steward	Expression Node	Transformation Step	Transformation Type
Name	Character	50	Full Name	Employee	Internal Production HR	Production	HRMS	192	Timothy Steward		2105	SQL Engine
								231	Timothy Steward		2105	SQL Engine
								192	Timothy Steward		2105	SQL Engine
			Full Name	Personnel	Personnel Feed	Production	HRMS	192	Mathew Rule		2105	EAI
			Employee Name	Employee History	HR Enterprise Warehouse	Production	HR DW	192	Karen Entity		4391	ETL
			Employee Name	Employee	HR Compensation Data Mart	Production	HR DW	192	Karen Entity		6721	ETL
Salary	Decimal	10.2	Annual Rate	Employee	Internal Production HR	Production	HRMS	367	Timothy Steward	11073	2105	SQL Engine
			Annual Salary	Employee	Payroll Feed	Production	HRMS	255	Cathy Attribute	21305	2105	EAI
			Base Compensation	Employee	HR Enterprise Warehouse	Production	HR DW	763	Cathy Attribute	35483	4391	ETL

Figure 4.22 Data Impact Analysis report.

Data Lineage Analysis

Data Lineage Analysis															October 1, 2003
DATA SOURCE					→ TRANSFORMATION →						TARGET				
System	Environment	Data Package	Data Group	Data Element	Transformation Group	Transformation Type	Transformation Step	Expression	System	Environment	Data Package	Data Group	Data Element		
Recruiting	Production	Recruitment	Candidate	Candidate Name	765	EAI	2189		HRMS	Production	Internal Production HR	Employee	Full Name		
HRMS	Production	Internal Production HR	Employee	Full Name	834	ETL	4389		HR DW	Production	HR Enterprise Warehouse	Employee History	Employee Name		
HRMS	Production	Internal Production HR	Employee	Full Name	532	EAI	6039		Corporate AAP	Production	Affirmative Action Plan	Employer	Employee Name		
HRMS	Production	Internal Production HR	Job	Job Salary	439	SQL Engine	4385	34567	Recruiting	Production	Recruitment	Position	Position Salary		
Recruiting	Production	Recruitment	Position	Position Salary	466	SQL Engine	6533	34888	HRMS	Production	Internal Production HR	Employee	Annual Rate		

Figure 4.23   Data Lineage Analysis report.

Summary

You have looked at the six subject areas within Enterprise systems. You have seen that the physical structures that an enterprise uses for data occur in many forms. Relational databases, XML files, flat files, Excel files, and COBOL files are common data forms. Enterprise applications move data bidirectionally to one or more of these forms. This data interchange is a central concept for the enterprise and for the MME models. This concept for modeling data movement among different data structures is made nonspecific and useful for treating different data forms (relational data bases, XML, COBOL, and so on), as common structures that the mapping models and other models can exercise.

By using this general structure for data, the related models for data movement do not need to address the actual physical type of the data. The general structures have subtypes that correspond to each of the physical categories such as a relational database or an XML file structure. This generalization allows data movement from many heterogeneous sources. Data insertion occurs broadly into a multiplicity of targets. A transformation that transports data from a relational database to an XML file is modeled exactly the same as one that moves data from a COBOL file. This concept provides the basis for reviewing the other models representing the MME. The next chapter explores the meta data definitions and details of the Universal Meta Model for XML, Messaging, and Business Transactions.

Universal Meta Model for XML, Messaging, and Business Transactions

Chapter 4 looked at the ways in which data and its transformation and movement can be represented in the meta model of the MME. However, different types of data sources have different levels of representation complexity, and Extensible Markup Language (XML) data can carry very complex structures. More and more Global 2000 companies and large government agencies are moving toward data interchange and system integration utilizing XML. The problems encountered in moving data around and having it understood by the systems are difficult and expensive to overcome. They are not unlike a problem Mark Twain had in France when he said, "In Paris they simply stared when I spoke to them in French; I never did succeed in making those idiots understand their language."

Although it is doubtful that XML would have helped Mr. Twain in Paris, it is a useful technology that can assist in the integration of information systems. This chapter provides the meta models for XML structure, transformation, classification, and business process specification. However, XML is a complex technology with aspects that are not familiar to many people; thus, this chapter will deviate slightly from the other chapters. Following the model assumptions section, there is an overview of XML technology that covers: the structural form and specification of XML documents, XML categories for documents and data, standards, and Web Services. This overview is then followed by the detailed information for each of the subject areas listed in the overview section. We've also included longer explanations of XML Schema and the Business Transactions subject area, because they are both complex topics.

Some of the critical business questions you can answer using this meta model are:

- What systems are affected by a change in the XML document schema?

- What existing XML elements can I reuse when dealing with a particular business area such as shop floor data collection for my new XML schemas?

- What XML document types do we exchange with our supply chain via particular protocols such as RosettaNet?

- What security levels control those XML documents?

- What systems support particular XML processes such as the Web Services purchase process?

- What XML schemas can process a given root element? You may have an XML document and want to know what XML schemas may apply to it.

- What XML schemas in a particular subject area have a specific word or phrase in their description? This is one way of locating relevant document schemas.

- What downstream XML schemas are affected by a change in a specific XML schema?

- Where did this XML schema import this XML element definition?

- What was the definition of a XML schema on a particular date?

- What other data structures are sourced from XML documents conforming to this XML schema? This query uses information contained in Chapter 4 to track the use of data.

- To what database tables and columns does this XML schema map XML documents?

- What software systems are affected by a change in this XML schema? The impact analysis of XML schema dependencies can be extended to the software systems that utilize them. The software systems are defined in Chapter 6.

Purpose of the XML Meta Models

Most major corporations and government institutions are using some form of XML-based technology. Nearly all software packages have some degree of XML compatibility. There are hundreds of software tools to manipulate XML. XML is truly a ubiquitous technology in IT applications. XML documents are used in a variety of places and for many processes throughout the enterprise, including data transport between applications and specifying the utilization of

Web Services. Managing the proliferation of these documents can be difficult because they are so broadly used. The structure, use, and role of these documents in the enterprise must be managed to prevent redundant efforts and the creation of incompatible systems. Management of the XML artifacts is a critical part of managing enterprise information systems, thus the MME must model the XML uses.

Model Assumptions

The use of XML is widespread, but like the proverbial elephant and the five blind men who come to different understandings of what an elephant is based on the different parts of the elephant they encounter, there is a great deal of confusion about XML and its true business uses. To clear up that confusion, we begin in the "Introduction to XML" section with an exploration of some important XML concepts and then show how XML is structured and integrated into our system for data transfers, transformations, and the control of business processes. If you are already familiar with XML, you may want to skip this section and go straight to the "XML, Messaging, and Business Transactions Subject Areas" section.

Introduction to XML

Everyone knows something about XML. The shelves of bookstores devote many linear feet to XML-related topics, and it is utilized across more and more companies and government agencies. So what is it, and why is it important?

Surprise! XML is not a clothing size, although there is an XML standard that covers clothing sizes. XML, is a system for defining, validating, and sharing document formats. It is a simplified subset of the Standard Generalized Markup Language (SGML), with a few additional syntax rules. XML is a project of the World Wide Web Consortium (W3C, www.w3c.org), originally started to make the Web a more useful resource. Its application is critical on the Web, but its domain now covers most aspects of IT. For our meta data purpose of modeling XML document structures, the actual nature of XML is a bit trickier to pin down because it is used for so many applications. In one sense, XML is a very simple concept but there is a complicated side to it, and we need to look at both briefly to understand XML fully.

As defined by the W3C, an XML document is simply a text string with some syntactic requirements that make it "well formed." It uses *tags* to mark document structures and uses attributes to encode other information. The tags indicate elements in the document. The element and attribute names identify what the values mean. For example:

```
<elementNameA  attribute1="a quoted string"> The element content
</elementNameA>
```

There is one element named "elementNameA" with one attribute named "attribute1." The attribute has simple content string of "a quoted string," and the element content is the string "The element content." This shows most of the basic parts that make up the XML document standard. In addition, the begin and end tags match, empty elements are marked, attribute values are nicely quoted, and elements are properly nested. (For more information on well-formed XML, see http://www.w3.org/TR/REC-xml.)

XML Schema Example

XML Schema (XSD) defines the elements and the structure of valid XML documents. Although XSD is a complicated standard, an example can illustrate much of how it works. Look at the following examples for a segment of a purchase order XML document and part of a schema that would be used for that document. These segments have a lot of information stripped from them that would normally specify versions, header information, and namespaces, which, if included, would hinder the understanding of the relevant structures.

Here is the Purchase Order XML document, greatly reduced:

```
<purchaseOrder orderdate="01JAN2003">
        <shipTo  xsi:type="US-Address">
                <name>George Washington</name>
                <title>President</title>
                <street>1600 Pennsylvania Ave. NW</street>
                <city>Washington</city>
                <state>DC</state>
                <zip>20006</zip>
        </shipTo>
                <!-- Other PO stuff would be here.-->
</purchaseOrder>
```

Here is the Purchase Order XML schema, reduced:

```
<schema>
  <element name="purchaseOrder" type="PurchaseOrderType"/>
  <complexType name="PurchaseOrderType">
    <sequence>
      <element name="shipTo" type="Address"/>
      <element name="invoiceTo" type="Address"/>
      <element name="Items" type="Items"/>
    </sequence>
    <attribute name="orderDate" type="date"/>
  </complexType>
```

```
<complexType name="Address">
  <sequence>
    <element name="name" type="string" minOccurs="0"/>
    <element name="title" type="string" minOccurs="0"/>
    <element name="street" type="string"/>
    <element name="city" type="string"/>
  </sequence>
</complexType>
<complexType name="US-Address">
  <complexContent>
    <extension base="Address">
      <sequence>
        <element name="state" type="US-State"/>
        <element name="zip" type="positiveInteger"/>
      </sequence>
    </extension>
  </complexContent>
</complexType>
<!-- Would have other address types and PO stuff defined -->
</schema>
```

In this sample schema, one top-level element (*purchaseOrder*) is declared with a type of *PurchaseOrderType*, that is composed of the subelements *shipTo*, *invoiceTo*, and *items*. *ShipTo* is of type *address*. *US-address* is an extension type of *Address*, and the XML example specifies the type of the address in the *shipTo* element using the attribute *xsi:type*. The *"xsi:"* prefix refers to a namespace that would have been declared earlier that specifies names used in schema definitions, such as *type*. There are many details of XML schema that cannot be covered here, but this shows enough to provide an understanding of the basics and their relationships in the model.

The essential structure of an XML document is simple. It is made of elements that have names, attributes, and content. It is all text, so numbers as content or for attributes are represented in a printable string. This can make for a lot of redundant text. This form makes both the strengths and the weaknesses of XML clear. The strengths are that the XML document carries a lot of information about its own structure and that being only text, it is independent of other representations. The weaknesses are the verbosity of the document and the need to convert numbers to and from strings for data exchange. In most cases, the strengths have been found to outweigh the weaknesses; however, applications that are very sensitive to data size or performance may need modifications in how they use XML or may need to use a different technology.

So, if XML is so simple, why are there so many books dedicated to this topic? In the next section, we examine the complexities of XML.

XML Categories

To better understand the use of XML, we need to classify some basic areas of XML. The first classification is the separation of document-centric and data-centric philosophies of XML use. The difference is first easily seen in examples; a sales order document is data-centric, and a Word document in XML is document-centric. We will now examine these aspects of XML in more detail.

Document-centric XML documents are critical in providing unstructured content to people, and thus have to be managed. They are likely to be persisted as XML. The ordering of the subelements of an element is important in document-centric XML. You can think of document-centric XML as mostly text with the XML elements marking up the text. Generally, document-centric XML documents will carry some data-centric information too. This could be in the header of the document, used to hold elements such as author and title, or the document could carry structured tables that may be data-centric, but it would still be a document-centric XML document.

NOTE When we refer to an XML document as a document, we are not saying that it is document-centric, merely that it is XML-compliant. No more will be done with document-centric XML in this book.

Data-centric XML documents carry structured data. Often, these data-centric XML documents are used only as a means of data transport between applications. They are generally of more interest in IT applications because most of these applications deal with the exchange of data rather than unstructured documents. In data-centric XML, unlike document-centric XML, the order of the subelements of an element is not important; they can be reordered, and the meaning of the document remains the same.

For example, in the purchase order example, the order of the *shipTo* and the *invoiceTo* elements does not matter to the meaning of the document. In addition, as opposed to the document-centric view of an XML document being text with markups, in data-centric XML the elements are the important part and text is just used to indicate values. However, a data-centric document may have parts that are document-centric-oriented. For example, a purchase order document may have large sections of marked-up text as descriptions of items, but the overall document is still data-centric; it just has some document-centric subparts. Although XML originated from document-centric roots, the data side is driving the majority of IT development.

Data-Centric XML: Data Structure vs. Process

Data-centric XML has two categories:

- The specification of data structure
- The specification of processes

Examples will help make this difference clear. A purchase order would structure customer information such as name and address as well as the items of the order and other information. This purchase order is a data structure form of XML. Data in relational databases can be easily formed into an XML document and would then clearly be a data structure form of XML. An example of process description XML would be an XML document that describes how that purchase order is processed by a supplier. It may govern workflow for how the purchase order is received and responded to. Another example of process description XML would be an XML document that describes how other XML documents should be transformed.

XML for data structure is well suited to convey data between applications, since XML elements carry the structure of the data that is in the applications, such as a purchase order in the sales system. The applications need to agree on the XML document structure and its meaning, since each application will map the XML document to its own internal data structures. This necessary agreement underscores the importance of standards, which dictate the names, structure, and meaning of the elements. The exchange of data between applications that use XML is this data structure type, which is fairly easy to understand and use. For data structure XML documents, XML schema is critical because it specifies the structure and is used for determining how those documents are mapped to other kinds of data structures in the information chain, such as relational databases.

In process description, XML elements have a semantic meaning that implies an action or behavior that is carried out by an application. In IT circles, this is considered a programming language, and programming languages can get rather complex. These XML documents are not used directly for data exchange; rather, they specify actions that may relate to other documents and data exchanges. The action's arguments, sequencing, and control just happen to be nicely described in an XML document. The document, in conjunction with the application it drives, is much more than a data document. However, it can be sent around as any other data-carrying document, which is critical for interoperative systems. For example, a Web Service may have a document describing its sequence of actions as Web Service Conversation Language (WSCL) XML. Client systems can use that document to interact with the Web Service and need to access the document and interpret it in order to use the

Web Service. While these process XML documents have an XML schema definition, it is not used as it is in data structure XML for transformation mapping. The business transaction model and the XSLT sections of this chapter are instances of process description XML. There may be other process areas that are important to you that would need to be modeled separately.

The separation of data structure XML and process XML is important because the largest use of XML in the IT world is for data structure conveyance, and this is well covered by the XML schema and integrated with the Enterprise Systems model for data transformation and movement. However, process XML documents are where the power of XML can be really seen; it allows the easy creation, dissemination, and interpretation of standards for many complex areas. However, each area covered by a process XML standard needs to have an accurate model if it is to be integrated with the Enterprise Systems model meta data.

XML Standards

XML is useful as is for integrating systems, but its value for integration really lies in the myriad standards that have developed over the last several years. Meaning is attached to the element names in a XML standard. For example, in the standard for HR-XML (human resources), the element "Relocation" denotes a relocation preference. The real complexity and power of XML is in the standards.

There are hundreds of XML standards, including XML schema definitions, XML transforms, human resources, Web Services, security, business processes, UML, and remote procedure calls (RPCs)—to name a few. Each area may have several XML standards that disagree on their overlapping parts, as standards often do. The real power of diverse standards becomes apparent as they are used together to solve business problems. For example, Web Services Description Language (WSDL), Web Services Conversation Language (WSCL), Universal Description, Discovery and Integration service (UDDI), Web Services Security (WS-Security), and Web Services Transactions (WS-Transactions) join forces to create a powerful combination of Web Services that may deliver additional services based on an application standard such as Human Resources XML (see Table 5.1 for more information on locating standards and the standard-setting bodies).

Some standards are meant for both document-centric and data-centric XML, such as the Dublin Core metadata initiative (http://dublincore.org/), which defines 15 standard item tags such as title, creator, and description that document processors can extract. However, most standards are for data-centric XML. Some standards are only for data structuring data-centric XML such as the XML Metadata Interchange (XMI) standard from OMG (see Table 5.1) or

UDDI. Many complex standards are used for both data structuring and process description, such as ebXML for electronic B2B commerce, XPath for selecting parts of an XML document, WSCL, and XSLT, to name just a few. With this complexity in the XML standards, you can see the need for the many books on XML.

Web Services revolve around XML. Web technologies are used more and more for application-to-application communication; in other words, the Internet enables distributed computation. This use of XML is the essence of Web Services—the programmatic interfaces used to do that form of distributed computing. This makes the definition of a Web Service pretty amorphous. You send a request to a URL and get back a reply with the payload. The original idea was that there are many interesting Web sites that provide useful information and it would be useful to get hold of the information in a programmatic way instead of just through a browser.

This is a simple concept, but there are many elements to distributed computing that need to be handled—and that is where the complexity arises. There are other standards for distributed computing, but Web Services are different because they rely on XML as a basic interchange standard and require the use of standard Internet protocols such as HTTP (Hypertext Transfer Protocol) or SMTP (Standard Mail Transfer Protocol). This makes Web Services applicable to any type of Web environment: internet, intranet, or extranet.

There are some minimum requirements to do distributed computation, and Web Services have existing or pending standards for them. The most basic requirement, after XML and the transfer protocol, is the form of service calls and replies. This is covered by the SOAP (Simple Object Access Protocol) standard, which allows a service to be called by name, arguments to be supplied, and a response to be returned. The other requirements for basic distributed computing are being able to locate a desired service and determining the exact forms of the services in terms of locations, names, arguments and responses. These are given by the UDDI and WSDL standards, respectively. These are all W3C-approved standards.

Say a developer wants to use a Web Service to retrieve book descriptions. He queries the UDDI Registry, searching for a business that offers the type of service that he wants. From the various entries for the service type and specific services, the developer can obtain the WSDL descriptions describing the service interface, the service bindings, and access points. Then, using the WSDL descriptions, the developer can construct a SOAP client interface that can communicate with the Web Services via the Internet and that will provide the book descriptions. That construction can be automated with tools that understand the standards.

However, enterprise distributed computing is not really that easy; in fact, it gets incredibly complex. Applications such as the one for retrieving and displaying book descriptions or one for performing and returning Google searches are simple and very useful, but the needs of enterprise computing for, say, running a manufacturing system are much deeper. Enterprise distributed computing also needs the following:

Reliable messaging. The Internet is not a reliable message delivery mechanism. You need to be sure that some messages are received and processed by their intended recipient.

Security. You do not want just anybody to get at your enterprise applications, so important services need many levels of security for authorization, authentication, and nonrepudiation for both service providers and requesters. In addition, the Internet has other security vulnerabilities, such as replay capability, that may need protection.

Transactions. Many enterprise systems need transactions to protect the integrity of the business processes.

Workflow of the services. Distributed computing is much more complicated than finding a stock price. Complicated interactions for, say, the scheduling and delivery of a product require a conversation between the participating entities. The processes become much more complicated as transactions are added.

Various organizations are developing the XML standards for all these areas, and the situation gets very complicated pretty quickly, especially since there are competing standards for each area. The standards will hopefully be reduced to one for each area in the near future.

Of the various subparts of distributed computing, the workflow area is the newest and has great potential for allowing the integration of various systems, both inside and outside the enterprise. This area is covered in this chapter.

The core ideas of WSDL, SOAP, and UDDI are simple, however. WSDL is needed so that users of a Web Service know how to prepare the arguments, how to call the service, and what the results will be for a given Web Service. SOAP defines the relationships of those parts and how they are sent. UDDI details how a Web Services directory protocol works so that a given Web Service can be located. The searching can be performed by function, name, or supplier, assuming that the supplier has registered with that UDDI registry. There is a global registry for UDDI just as there are name servers for Internet naming resolution. These core ideas for Web Services are simple, and thus many tools have been developed to automate Web Services' use.

Distributed computing is not new, and the neighborhood had competitors before Web Services came along. These included CORBA (Common Object Request Broker Architecture) from the OMG, DCOM from Microsoft, and the Java J2EE standards from SUN Microsystems. Each of these have ways of interfacing with Web Services protocols, which makes enterprise integration a little easier.

Web Services' main advantages over the competitive technologies are the use of XML for both data transfer and specification and the use of standard Internet protocols such as HTTP. Using XML lets you understand the content of the transferred data for debugging the applications, which is not the case when using a binary stream for other applications. The use of Internet protocols allows the use of the service from behind firewalls, which may block all connections other than HTTP. Strangely though, the main disadvantages are the same; the use of XML for data transfer and the use of standard Internet protocols. XML results in a bloated data stream compared to an application-specific binary stream and a network connection may be slow, thus imposing what could be a large performance penalty. The problem with most Internet protocols for Web Services is they are inherently stateless, that is, a connection between the participants only lasts for one round trip of a request and response. This necessitates additional work and standards for conversations that require multiple requests and responses. This complicates use. In addition, a stateless connection is harder to make secure against replay attacks. The competitive technologies usually use a connection protocol that lasts for the length of the conversation. Web Services has advantages and disadvantages, but the competitive technologies are more mature and cover all the needs for distributed computing. For enterprise distributed applications, the choice will be dependent on the requirements of the application.

Web Services technologies supply a distributed computing platform that is based on XML and Internet transfer protocols. The application of these Web Services is much easier than other distributed computing technologies for simple applications, and Web Services will be strong there. They are also strong contenders for enterprise distributed applications, depending on the needs of the applications and the continuing development of standards and tools for Web Services.

Web Services are modeled in the "XML for Business Transactions" section of this chapter.

Table 5.1 provides a listing of various XML resource sites on the Internet.

Table 5.1   Resource List for XML Standards

RESOURCE	DESCRIPTION
BPMI.org	BPMI.org (the Business Process Management Initiative) is a nonprofit corporation of member companies that promotes and develops business process management (BPM) by creating standards. They have created the Business Process Modeling Language (BPML) and the Business Process Query Language (BPQL). www.bpmi.org
HR-XML Consortium	This is a nonprofit organization for the development of XML specifications for human-resources-related data exchanges. http://www.hr-xml.org/channels/home.htm
OAG	The Open Applications Group is a nonprofit consortium working on XML for e-business and application integration. http://www.openapplications.org/
OASIS	Organization for the Advancement of Structured Information Standards is a not-for-profit, global consortium for e-business standards. OASIS is a joint sponsor of ebXML. Many XML vertical standards and other broader standards are produced by OASIS. http://www.oasis-open.org/ and http://xml.coverpages.org/ and http://www.xml.org:
OMG	The Object Management Group is a nonprofit consortium that has some open standards for metadata interchange. http://www.omg.org
RosettaNet	RosettaNet is a consortium creating standards for supply chain partners in the electronic industries. http://www.rosettanet.org/
W3C	World Wide Web Consortium develops interoperable technologies (specifications, guidelines, software, and tools) for the Web. They are the home for many of the basic XML standards. This is the first stop for searching for standards. http://www.w3.org/
XMLfiles.com	Nice resource for XML related material. http://www.xmlfiles.com/
XML industries	http://www.xml.org/xml/industry_industrysectors.jsp is fairly complete listing for locating XML standards for various vertical industries.

XML, Messaging, and Business Transactions Subject Areas

The areas covered by this chapter for the meta model are:

XML schemas (XSD) and DTDs. XML schema and DTDs describe the elements that may be used in XML documents that conform to that XML schema or DTD. The XML schema serves for both structuring documents and driving applications that interpret and parse XML documents. They are important for mapping the flow of XML data in the enterprise.

XML transformations (XSLT). XSLT is a transformation language in XML syntax that transforms other XML documents. This is a central piece of XML technology for data transfer and manipulation in the integration of systems.

Business Transactions. Electronic business processes function by exchanging data packages with other processes. The processes and their interactions can be specified by XML documents. XML can specify these processes from e-commerce standards to Web Services. The integration of external systems and internal systems can be done with this technology.

Classification Scheme. A document classification scheme is like the searchable catalog of a library. With lots of XML documents and XML schemas, locating relevant documents can be very difficult. A classification scheme is needed to help manage this task.

These four areas overlap in varying degrees. XML schema is of central importance and is referenced by the other areas. The classification scheme can be applied to many elements of XML Schema and to the business transaction area. Except for classification, the material on each has a connection to other chapters for information on transforms, data structuring, and software systems.

Let's now take a look at the first subject area, XML Schema and DTD.

XML Schemas and DTDs

XML schemas define the structure of valid XML documents and drive applications by describing the elements and XML types that may be used in a document (see http://www.w3.org/TR/xmlschema-0/ for an introduction to XML Schema). The relationship between schemas and their relationship to applications are modeled in the MME. The reasons for modeling XML schemas are simple: (1) to manage the dependency, use, and reuse of schemas, and (2) to understand the way that the structure of XML documents that conform to the schema are used as data sources and targets for applications and data warehousing.

The management of the use and reuse of XML schemas is critical because of their number and complexity. There are already many standards that cover both vertical industry and horizontal functions so that software can be standardized for both EAI and business-to-business transactions. In addition to using these external XML schema standards, businesses can create XML schema definitions to support their own internal and external data interchange needs. As a result, many companies have defined hundreds of XML schemas. The number of these internally defined XML schemas and imported standard XML schemas used by an enterprise could range from several hundred to several thousand. To help in the management of these schemas, the meta model tracks what has been defined, the life cycle of XML schemas, and how they are used. This information also assists users in defining new schemas via reuse.

The XML schemas often depend on the definition of other XML schemas because of reuse, thus the MME models the structure of schemas to track dependencies for the impact analysis of changes. For example, if a schema is scheduled to become obsolete, schemas that import parts of that schema will need to be updated.

The second purpose is important because XML documents are data-carrying structures and that data can be transferred to or from other data structures such as a relational database or perhaps even other XML documents. This is important information for ETL lineage and for the creation of system adapters, which differentiates XML from other systems. This lets XML be treated like any other data provider in the Enterprise Systems model discussed in Chapter 4.

XML Schema Structure

The model for XML Schema is shown in Figure 5.2. The entities and attributes are given in Tables 5.2 and Table 5.3. An XML document is composed of elements and their content. The elements may have attributes, and the value of the element is the content. The content can be one of four types: simple, empty, subelements, and mixed. Simple content is just a single unquoted string. Empty content means no content and has a special marking tag (/>) for the element. Subelements' content is composed only of subelements with no text. Mixed content is text with markup information contained in it and is used for document-centric XML sections.

The Simple Type content is a string that is to be interpreted as the type the element is defined with. For example, if the element content is defined in its Schema as an integer, then the string must be parsed as an integer.

XML PARSERS, APPLICATIONS, AND ADAPTERS

XML schemas can be used to drive XML parsers, applications, and adapters. Adapters move data into and from other applications as XML documents. A schema can also be utilized in the creation of applications by using it to generate the application framework. For example, the schema can be used to generate Java classes that are instantiated on parsing an XML document. The application can then use those class instances to do the required processing and, for example, produce another XML document. Many software packages are available to assist in these tasks.

The XML schema can define types and declare elements that are assigned to a particular type. The defined types can be simple, such as an integer, or complex with attributes and subelements (see the sample XML schema earlier in this chapter). XML types are important for two reasons. First, they can be imported from other schemas and used to declare the elements. Second, types can be derived from another type which is the equivalent of subtyping for objects or entities.

There are two methods to utilize the subtypes. One is shown in the XML document example in the "XML Schema Example" section, where the *ShipTo* element has an attribute indicating the type of the element content, which in this case is *US-Address*. The *ShipTo* element was defined as having an *Address* type and the *Address* type has a subtype, *US-Address*, that can be used in place of the base address type. *US-Address* has an added element, *zip*, that would need to be mapped. Having a document select the type of the element via an attribute requires the model to handle both XML elements and XML types as data groups, since the needed mapping is determined by the dynamic type of the element.

The mapping of data sources in Chapter 4 is based on treating different types of data sources as having a uniform top-level structure. The structures within that chapter are called: DATA PACKAGE, DATA GROUP, and DATA ELEMENT. In a relational database, they would be the database catalog, a table and a column, respectively. To handle this in the XML schema model, we have the following correspondences between the model in this chapter and the model in Chapter 4 (see Figure 5.1):

- The XML SCHEMA itself is a DATA PACKAGE.

- The XML ELEMENT DECLARATION and the XML TYPE DEF are DATA GROUPS.

- XML element attributes, **xml attribute def** and the element's simple content, **xml simple content**, are DATA ELEMENTS.

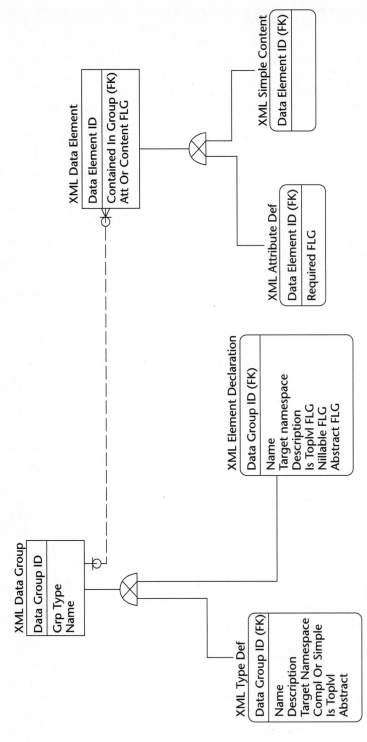

Figure 5.1   XML data subtypes.

Subtyping on the needed XML parts accomplishes the needed correspondences. XML ELEMENT DECLARATION and XML TYPE DEF are subtypes of XML DATA GROUP, which is a subtype of DATA GROUP (see Chapter 4). XML ATTRIBUTE DEF and XML SIMPLE CONTENT are subtypes of XML DATA ELEMENT. This allows the uniform treatment of XML ELEMENT DEC-LARATIONS and XML TYPE DEFINITIONS as DATA GROUPs and the uniform treatment of XML ELEMENT ATTRIBUTES and ELEMENT SIMPLE CONTENT as DATA ELEMENTs. The latter is required because the difference between attributes with values and the XML simple content value is nonexistent at a purely functional level for mapping information. For example, the following XML fragments could be considered equivalent for mapping purposes and information content.

```
1- <name  role="writer">Mark Twain</name>
2- <name  simpleContent="Mark Twain" role="writer"/>
```

In addition to XML SCHEMA being a subtype of DATA PACKAGE, it is also a subtype of XML DOCUMENT. XML schemas can be treated like any XML document, including being associated with another defining schema. That is, there may be XML schemas that determine the structure of XML Schema documents. For example, you can make an XML schema that restricts other XML Schema documents from defining elements that have a mixed content type.

DTD Structure

The model for XML DTD is shown in Figure 5.3. The entities and attributes are given in Table 5.3 and Table 5.4. XML schemas added much flexibility and solved many problems that were associated with document type definitions (DTDs), especially for data-centric applications. A fundamental difference between XML schemas and DTDs is that DTDs cannot define types and derived types, which are needed for more advanced applications. On the other hand, DTDs provide entity definitions, a concept that XML schemas do not have. An entity definition functions like a macro definition that is part of SGML (Standard Generalized Markup Language), the mother language of XML. Therefore, DTDs and XML schemas can both be used on a single XML document; however, the DTD would need to be applied first. Nearly all the standards in active use now provide an XML schema instead of a DTD. Other than entity definitions, the rest of the content of a DTD is easily converted to an XML schema definition.

While DTDs are not schemas, and in fact do not satisfy the requirements to be XML, they are used like schemas. Their power of definition is far less than schemas, but since they were a standard that preceded XML schema by many years, they are in common use. By fudging on the pedigree of DTDs and making them a subtype of schemas, the DTD gets the uniform treatment for mappings and dependencies, although they cannot be parsed like an XML document.

We start with XML documents, or XML DOC. Permanent XML documents may be held in the meta data repository in several ways. The text string of the XML document may be held directly in the repository, or the XML document may be held in an XML database and the database reference be held in the repository. An additional method is to use of a source version control system, which maintains all history and can reconstruct the source at will and a repository that holds that reference. XML SCHEMA is a subtype of XML DOC.

The XML SCHEMA itself can be supplied by some source, either an external body or an internally located one. This is indicated in the SCHEMA SOURCE entity. The XML SCHEMA is usually defined for a particular XML TARGET NAMESPACE. The namespace may be used to classify the various schemas (See the "Classification Scheme" section). The schema defines both the XML ELEMENT DECLARATION and XML TYPE DEFS. The definition of those XML ELEMENT DECLARATIONS and XML TYPE DEFS may be imported from another schema, which is handled by the IMPORT SCHEMA entity. The IMPORT SCHEMA is found via a URI LOCATOR. It is associated to an XML DOC, which must be a XML SCHEMA.

URI LOCATORS are handled as changeable references to XML DOCs. Changes can occur in the XML schemas and URIs. A URI can refer to something and then be changed. In addition, a document can be referred to by more than one URI. The URI LOCATOR entity handles these changes by having effective dating. Effective dating is supplied by a **Start Date** and an **End Date**. If the **End Date** is a special date, it corresponds to the current record. Using this, the XML documents and XML schemas can be chosen for their structure on a particular date. XML documents that were parsed in the past may have to be parsed by the new XML schema state. The link between an XML document and its possible defining schemas is made through the URI LOCATOR for the XML schema as the XML DOC TO SCHEMA LINK. The relationship is many-to-many, since an XML document can be parsed by more than one XML schema. To find the schemas that apply to a given XML document, use the XML DOC TO SCHEMA LINK to find all the URIs of the applying schemas. The URI locates XML documents, but the schema is a subtype of it.

The rest of the model deals with the real internal structure of an XML schema and the parts needed for mapping information. The XML schema defines the XML elements and XML type definitions. An XML element has an XML type that determines its attributes and allowed content type. If the content type is subelements only, they are defined by the XML SUBELEMENT DEF association entity as a sequence. If the element has only a simple content, it has an XML SIMPLE CONTENT entity that has a given simple type.

A XML TYPE DEF defines the XML ATTRIBUTES DEF, and each XML ATTRIBUTE DEF is a simple type. An XML element may have a simple content type denoted by an XML SIMPLE CONTENT entity. Since both the XML ATTRIBUTE DEF and XML SIMPLE CONTENT of XML elements can be mapped as DATA ELEMENTS, they have a common parent, XML DATA ELEMENT.

Table 5.2 shows more details of the entities of the XML Schemas and DTDs subject area.

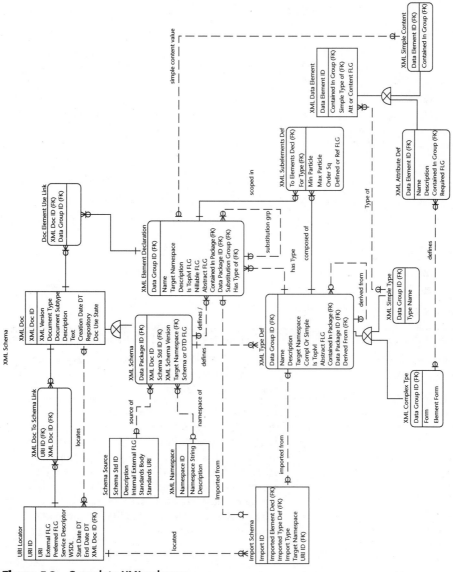

Figure 5.2   Complete XML schema.

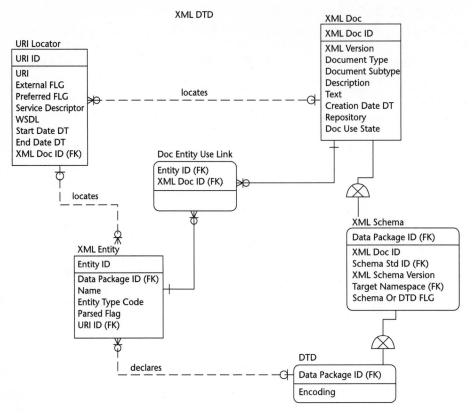

Figure 5.3 XML DTD.

Table 5.2 XML Schema Entities

ENTITY NAME	ENTITY DEFINITION
DOC ELEMENT USE LINK	DOC ELEMENT USE LINK is an associative entity used to show which XML documents use a particular XML element.
IMPORT SCHEMA	The IMPORT SCHEMA supplies XML element declarations and XML type definitions. A schema can import/include/redefine elements and types from another schema. The specified import schema usually has a definite link via a URI, but parsers are not required to use it. This is needed for tracking the impact of schema changes. If a schema changes, all schemas that import parts of it may be affected.

Table 5.2   *(continued)*

ENTITY NAME	ENTITY DEFINITION
SCHEMA SOURCE	The SCHEMA SOURCE is the source, or supplier, of the schema. It may be an outside standards body or internal.
URI LOCATOR	The URI LOCATOR is the indirection locator for URI. This handles the version changes of URIs. There can also be many URIs for a single given object. References to any version can also find the current version easily by using the URI plus the '31DEC9999' for the end date.
XML ATTRIBUTE DEF	XML ATTRIBUTE DEF holds a single XML attribute definition from this complex type. The XML COMPLEX TYPE can have 0 or more attributes defined. An XML attribute is defined in a complex type, and its value is required to be a simple XML type. Simple content also has a simple XML type, which is why the common supertype entity, XML DATA ELEMENT, carries the reference to XML SIMPLE TYPE.
XML COMPLEX TYPE	XML COMPLEX TYPE is used to define attributes for use by an element. The content type may be empty, mixed, simple, or element, but each may have possible attributes defined.
XML DATA ELEMENT	XML DATA ELEMENT is a common parent for attributes and simple content. It is a subtype of DATA ELEMENT (refer to Figure 4.8). It is needed for transform mapping simplicity. Attributes and simple content can only be simple types (such as string or integer), and the type is specified by this parent. This captures the idea that a data element is either an attribute value in the XML or is the simple content of the element, and it has values of a simple type.

(continued)

Table 5.2 *(continued)*

ENTITY NAME	ENTITY DEFINITION
XML DATA GROUP	XML DATA GROUP is the supertype of XML TYPE DEF and XML ELEMENT DEFINITION and is the subtype of DATA GROUP (refer to Figure 4.8). The subtype grouping allows both the XML TYPE DEFINTION and the XML ELEMENT DEFINITION to be mapped by the transforms. This captures the idea that a data group is either an element with content and attributes or it is a type definition. Both need to be mapped by transforms.
XML DOC	XML DOC is a text that follows the XML syntactic requirements. The actual text may be located here or in a source control system. This has many subtypes, but only a few are of interest in this system: XSD (schema), XSLT (transformation language), DTD (document type definition). Other types can be here and are identified by the type attribute.
XML DOC TO SCHEMA LINK	XML DOC TO SCHEMA LINK is an associative entity for M:M connection of an XML document and its schema. The link is made through a URI so that version control can be maintained. A document can be processed by more than one schema, and a schema can process many documents. The link to the schema is made through the URI entity so that version control can be maintained—that is, the schema can be found for a particular date. See the URI LOCATOR entity.
XML ELEMENT DECLARATION	XML elements are declared by the XML ELEMENT DECLARATION. They are defined in a schema or a DTD as a particular type. In the schema, they may have been imported from another schema definition but only top-level elements and type definitions may be imported or redefined directly. An element may be substituted for one of its ancestors in the substitution group in a document.
XML NAMESPACE	Schemas are given a target namespace that may be used for classification. This XML NAMESPACE defines that namespace and can also be classified by the classification system.

Table 5.2 *(continued)*

ENTITY NAME	ENTITY DEFINITION
XML SCHEMA	XML SCHEMA specifies the XML document structure. XML schemas are used by parsers of XML documents. They can be used to do document mapping and drive applications. This is a subtype of DATA PACKAGE from Chapter 4 and also a subtype of XML Doc. See Chapter 8 for an implementation discussion for multiple supertypes. XML SCHEMAS are XML documents and also used as packages for data in the Enterprise Systems model.
XML SIMPLE CONTENT	XML SIMPLE CONTENT gives the type of the simple content of an element. It is subtyped from XML DATA ELEMENT so that simple content of an XML element can be mapped uniformly with the XML attributes of an XML element. An element's simple content is restricted to being an XML simple type. That restriction is given by the supertype XML DATA ELEMENT.
XML SIMPLE TYPE	The XML SIMPLE TYPE is used by attributes and the value of a simple content element (for example, string, integer, double, date).
XML SUBELEMENTS DEF	This Identifies the subelements of an element definition. See the XML schema example. In XML schemas, XML elements always have a XML type, and it is the XML type that defines the subelements. The subelements may be defined in the scope of this element or by reference.
XML TYPE DEF	XML TYPE DEF is a supertype of XML SIMPLE TYPE and XML COMPLEX TYPE. An element is complex if it has attributes and/or elements as subelements. It may also be a mixed type, whereby the character value has markup information contained within it. The element, if it has attributes, may have a simple type for the element value. A type can be derived from another type definition. Simple types may only be derived from simple types. A complex type may be derived from either simple or complex types. W3 Schema supplies a set of base simple types.

Table 5.3 shows more details about the entities of the DTD's portion of the XML Schemas and DTDs subject area.

Table 5.4 shows more detail about the attributes of the XML Schemas and DTD subject area.

Table 5.3   DTDs Entities

ENTITY NAME	ENTITY DEFINITION
DOC ENTITY USE LINK	DOC ENTITY USE LINK is an associative entity link for the M:M link of XML DOCUMENT and XML ENTITY DEF for showing the use of the document.
DTD	DTD is the subtype of the schema for DTDs. DTDs are not really a true subtype of SCHEMA, but this allows the mapping in Chapter 4 to work on DTDs without any changes.
XML ENTITY	XML ENTITY is a physical substitution for the references in an XML document. They are only declared in a DTD document.

Table 5.4   Entity Attributes for XML Schemas and DTDs

ENTITY NAME	ATTRIBUTE NAME	ATTRIBUTE DEFINITION
DTD	data package id	data package id is the Subtype Key of DTD TO XML SCHEMA.
	encoding	encoding is the XML DTD Encoding that is defined by the W3C.
IMPORT SCHEMA	import id	import id is the Primary Key.
	imported element decl	imported element decl is a Foreign Key reference to XML Element Declaration.
	imported type def	imported type def is a Foreign Key reference to XML Type Def.
	import type	import type determines the actual Type of the import. It has values: import, include, redefine.
	target namespace	target namespace is the namespace of the import.
	uri id	uri id is a Foreign Key reference to URI Locator.
SCHEMA SOURCE	schema std id	schema std id is the Primary Key.

Table 5.4 *(continued)*

ENTITY NAME	ATTRIBUTE NAME	ATTRIBUTE DEFINITION
	description	This is a text description of the source.
	internal external flg	**internal external flg** indicates if the standards body is an internal committee or an external body.
	standards body	**standards body** is the standards body that made the XML schema. For example: W3C or HR-XML.
	standards uri	**standards uri** is the URI of the standards body—this is not an indirect locator.
URI LOCATOR	**wsdl**	**wsdl** is used for Web Services and contains the description language for the service.
	service descriptor	A URI may provide many services, such as: HTTP, FTP, GOPHER, Web Service, and so on. There are many services, and more will be added. **service descriptor** specifies the service.
	start date dt	**start date dt** is the date the URI is effective. In combination with the **end_date**, this will version the elements accessible via URIs. The actual Text of the documents can be either held here or preferably in a source control system and then given the start and end date, you can produce the Text of that time. Thus, if a document changes, it is given a new entry here. Therefore, documents parsed with a particular XML schema will have the schema definition available for when it was produced. An **end _date dt** of year 9999 indicates the current value of the URI.
	end date dt	**end date dt** is the date this URI changed to something else (see **start date**).

(continued)

Table 5.4 *(continued)*

ENTITY NAME	ATTRIBUTE NAME	ATTRIBUTE DEFINITION
	xml doc id	**xml doc id** is a Foreign Key reference to XML DOC that locates that document.
	uri id	**uri id** is the Primary Key.
	preferred flg	**preferred flg** indicates that this URI is the preferred URI for the resource.
	uri	**uri** is the text string of the URI.
	external flg	**external flg** indicates if the URI is located externally to the business.
XML ATTRIBUTE DEF	data element id	**data element id** is the Subtype Key to XML DATA ELEMENT.
	contained in group	**contained in group** is a Foreign Key reference to XML DATA GROUP, which is a subtype of DATA GROUP. For XML ATTRIBUTE DEF, this is the XML COMPLEX TYPE that defines this attribute definition.
	required flg	**required flg** indicates if the attribute is required in instance documents with the XML element.
XML COMPLEX TYPE	data group id	**data group id** is the Subtype Key to XML TYPE DEF.
	form	**form** gives the content type. It has the values empty, simple, mixed, or element.
	element form	**element form** is a subtype of Form. If form type is element, then this XML type has subelements, which are determined by **element form**. It can have the values sequence and choice.
XML DATA ELEMENT	data element id	**data element id** is the Primary Key.
	contained in group	**contained in group** is a Foreign Key reference to XML DATA GROUP, which is a subtype of DATA GROUP. XML DATA GROUP is either an XML TYPE DEF or an XML ELEMENT DECLARATION, which is the defining group for this XML DATA ELEMENT.

Table 5.4 *(continued)*

ENTITY NAME	ATTRIBUTE NAME	ATTRIBUTE DEFINITION
	simple type of	**simple type of** is a Foreign Key reference to XML SIMPLE TYPE. Both XML ATTRIBUTEs and XML SIMPLE CONTENT can only be simple types.
	att or content flg	**att or content flg** is the discriminator attribute for subtypes of XML ATTRIBUTE DEF and XML SIMPLE CONTENT.
XML DATA GROUP	**grp type**	**grp type** is the discriminator attribute for subtypes XML TYPE DEF and XML ELEMENT DEFINITION.
	name	**name** is the name of the XML DATA GROUP.
	contained in package	**contained in package** is a Foreign Key reference to XML SCHEMA, which defines this XML DATA GROUP.
	data group id	**data group id** is the Primary Key.
XML DOC	**xml doc id**	**xml doc id** is the Primary Key.
	xml version	**xml version** is the W3 version of the document.
	document type	**document type** gives the Type of this document (for example, XML schema, DTD, XSLT, SOAP envelop, or XMI). There are over 100 types.
	document subtype	**document subtype** gives the subtype of the Document Type if needed.
	description	This provides a text description of the document.
	text	**text**, if present, holds the actual Text of the document. This can get very large, or it can be a reference to the data repository location (see the **repository** attribute).
	creation date dt	**creation date dt** is the date the XML document was created.
	repository	If the Text is held elsewhere, **repository** gives the location and how to access it. This is dependent on the Repository system.

(continued)

Table 5.4   *(continued)*

ENTITY NAME	ATTRIBUTE NAME	ATTRIBUTE DEFINITION
	doc use state	**doc use state** gives the state of the document. It has the values active, retired, development, and test.
XML ELEMENT DECLARATION	**contained in package**	**contained in package** is a Foreign Key reference to XML SCHEMA, which defines the XML ELEMENT DECLARATION.
	abstract flg	**abstract flg** indicates that the element is an abstract element, which means that it cannot appear in an XML document. Only its dependents via a substitution group of the element may appear.
	nillable flg	**nillable flg** indicates that the element is nillable in a document, which means that it may have empty content. The XML term is nillable. It corresponds to nullable in SQL.
	substitution group	**substitution group** is a Foreign Key reference to XML ELEMENT DECLARATION, a recursive hierarchical reference. An XML element may be declared in a substitution group, then that element may be substituted for the parent element in an XML document.
	has type of	**has type of** is a Foreign Key reference to XML TYPE DEF. XML ELEMENTS are declared with an XML type (see the XML schema example).
	name	**name** is the name of the XML element defined by the XML ELEMENT DECLARATION.
	data group id	**data group id** is the subtype key to XML Data Group.
	is toplvl flg	**is toplvl flg** indicates that this element is defined at the global level of the schema. This means that it can be imported by other schemas.
	target namespace	**target namespace** is the namespace this element is defined in.

Table 5.4 *(continued)*

ENTITY NAME	ATTRIBUTE NAME	ATTRIBUTE DEFINITION
	description	This provides a text description of the element.
XML ENTITY	**entity id**	**entity id** is the Primary Key.
	data package id	**data package id** is a Foreign Key reference to DTD, which defines the XML ENTITY.
	name	**name** is the name of the XML entity.
	entity type code	**entity type code** indicates the XML entity Type, which is a W3C standard.
	parsed flag	**parsed flag** indicates if the entity is to be parsed, which is part of the W3C standard.
	uri id	**uri id** is a Foreign Key reference to URI LOCATOR, which locates this XML ENTITY.
XML NAMESPACE	**namespace id**	**namespace id** is the Primary Key.
	namespace string	**namespace string** is the text value of the namespace.
	description	This is a text description of the namespace.
XML SCHEMA	**data package id**	**data package id** is a Subtype Key from DATA PACKAGE in Chapter 4 Enterprise Systems model. It is the primary key for this entity.
	xml doc id	**xml doc id** is a Subtype Key to XML DOC. An XML schema is also an XML document.
	schema std id	**schema std id** is a Foreign Key reference to SCHEMA SOURCE, giving the source of this schema.
	xml schema version	**xml schema version** is the W3 schema Standard Version number of the XML schema doc.
	target namespace	**target namespace** is a Foreign Key reference to XML NAMESPACE. XML schemas are defined in a given namespace and this is useful for categorizing XML schemas.

(continued)

Table 5.4 *(continued)*

ENTITY NAME	ATTRIBUTE NAME	ATTRIBUTE DEFINITION
	schema or dtd flg	**schema or dtd flg** is the discriminator attribute for subtype DTD of XML SCHEMA.
XML SIMPLE CONTENT	data element id	**data element id** is the subtype Key to XML DATA ELEMENT.
	contained in group	**contained in group** is a Foreign Key reference to XML ELEMENT DECLARATION that contains this simple content.
XML SIMPLE TYPE	data group id	**data group id** is the subtype Key to XML TYPE DEF.
	type name	**type name** indicates the simple type. A simple type is string, integer, and so on.
	size	**size** gives the size of this type if applicable.
XML SUBELEMENTS DEF	to element decl	**to element decl** is a Foreign Key reference to XML ELEMENT DECLARATION, which is one of the subelements of the type. It is also part of the primary key.
	for type	**for type** is a Foreign Key reference to XML TYPE DEF, which is the type defining the subelements. **for type** is also part of the primary key.
	min particle	**min particle** gives the minimum occurrence of the subelement given by **to element decl**.
	max particle	**max particle** is the maximum occurrence of the subelement given by **to element decl**.
	order sq	**order sq** gives the order of definition of the subelements.
	defined or ref flg	**defined or ref flg** indicates if the subelement is defined by this Type or if it is referenced by the Type given by **for type**.

Table 5.4 *(continued)*

ENTITY NAME	ATTRIBUTE NAME	ATTRIBUTE DEFINITION
XML TYPE DEF	**abstract**	**abstract** indicates if the Type definition is abstract, which means that the type cannot be used directly; only elements in its substitution group may be.
	is toplvl	**is toplvl** indicates that the Type definition is at the top level of the XML schema. This allows it to be a root element and to be imported by other schemas.
	contained in package	**contained in package** is a Foreign Key reference to XML SCHEMA, which defines this XML TYPE DEF.
	derived from	**derived from** is a recursive Foreign Key reference to XML TYPE DEF. XML Types can be derived from another XML Type. That type may be in another XML schema, so it is important to track derivations.
	name	**name** is the name of this XML TYPE DEFINITION.
	data group id	**data group id** is the subtype Key to XML DATA GROUP, which is subtyped from DATA GROUP in Chapter 4.
	compl or simple	**compl or simple** is the discriminator attribute for the subtypes XML COMPLEX TYPE and XML SIMPLE TYPE.
	description	This is a text description of the type definition.
	target namespace	**target namespace** is the namespace this XML type definition is defined for.

XSLT: XML Transformation Language (XSLT)

The model for XSLT is shown in Figure 5.4. The entities and attributes are given in Tables 5.5 and 5.6. XSLT, a W3C standard, is a transformation programming language in XML syntax that drives an XSLT processor to transform XML documents. XSLT combines several processing paradigms and can appear to be quite complex. It is beyond the scope of this book to discuss this language; however, you can find details at http://www.w3.org/TR/xslt. This model allows you to ask:

- What parameters are taken by transforms that map to this schema?
- What transforms operate on documents of an XML schema type?
- What other transformations and mappings are associated with this XSLT in information chains?

The last two queries use the Enterprise Systems mode from Chapter 4 by having XSLT be a subtype of TRANSFORMATION GROUP. The SOURCE TO TARGET MAP entity of the TRANSFORMATION GROUP can indicate the documents of the transformation and the other transformations that affect those documents can then be located. XSLT can perform complete structural changes on an XML document, such as creating differing outputs from a single XML document. One output could be for browsers, another for PDA screens, and yet another for voice phones.

Generally, an XSLT for data-centric documents is created to operate on a particular document XML schema definition. It does not transform the XML schema; it transforms XML documents that conform to a particular XML schema and transforms them to XML documents conforming to another given XML schema. Thus, XSLT can be seen as a subtype of TRANSFORMATION GROUP in the Enterprise subject area of Chapter 4, and the data it operates on is the XML entities.

XSLT transformations are very powerful when used in conjunction with XML adapters and messaging. An XML adapter will map data to and from XML documents for other applications such as databases and ERP systems. XML messaging is middleware for the reliable communication of XML documents. Adapters and messaging are important elements in EAI. An XML adapter from a system creates a document that is then transformed by an XSLT specification into a different XML document. This document is then passed via middleware or transport mechanisms to its final destination, where another XML adapter interfaces to the destination application. Many adapters are now built into commercial software packages such as relational databases.

The MME model handles the structural information of XSLT and the way in which it is integrated with the other processes. An XSLT document is an XML document as well as a subtype of TRANSFORMATION GROUP from the Enterprise Systems model (see Chapter 4). This allows the modeling of its mapping nature and also the modeling of how and when it is executed. An XSLT document can define a set of parameters that drives the XSLT. XSLT documents can also import other XSLT documents for reuse. This dependency chain is modeled so that changes can be tracked.

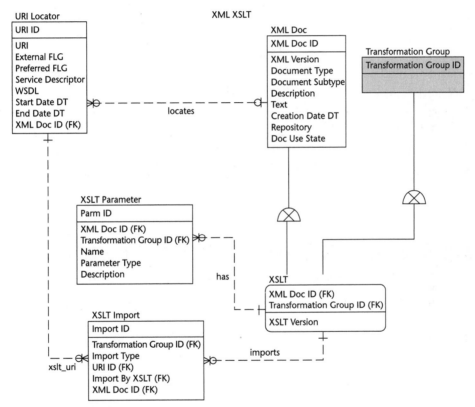

Figure 5.4 XSLT model.

Table 5.5   XSLT Entities

ENTITY NAME	ENTITY DEFINITION
XSLT	XSLT is an XML DOC interpreted as XSLT. XSLT defines a language that transforms XML documents to other XML documents. It can take a set of parameters in that transformation. It is a subtype of both XML Document and Transform Group from Chapter 4.
XSLT IMPORT	An XSLT document may import other XSLT documents. XSLT IMPORT shows the imported XSLT documents. The URI must reference another XSLT Type document. This is needed for impact analysis.
XSLT PARAMETER	An XSLT transform may take a set of parameters as global variables with a given Type. XSLT PARAMETER gives the parameter description.
TRANSFORMATION GROUP	Refer to Table 4.5 for this entity's definition.
URI LOCATOR	Refer to the "XML Schema and DTDs" section in this chapter for this entity's definition.

Table 5.6   Entity Attributes for XSLT

ENTITY NAME	ATTRIBUTE NAME	ATTRIBUTE DEFINITION
XSLT	**transformation group id**	**transformation group id** is a subtype Key to TRANSFORMATION GROUP in Chapter 4. This is a primary key.
	xslt version	**xslt version** is the version number of the XSLT standard from W3C.
	xml doc id	**xml doc id** is a Foreign Key/subtype reference to XML DOC. XSLT documents are also XML documents. This is an alternate key for XSLT.
XSLT IMPORT	**uri id**	**uri id** is a Foreign Key reference to URI LOCATOR, which locates the imported XSLT document.
	import by xslt	**import by xslt** is a Foreign Key reference to XSLT, which is the importing XSLT document.
	xml doc id	**xml doc id** is a Foreign Key reference to XSLT as the alternate key to XSLT.

Table 5.6   *(continued)*

ENTITY NAME	ATTRIBUTE NAME	ATTRIBUTE DEFINITION
	import id	**import id** is the Primary Key.
	import type	**import type** gives the how the other XSLT is imported. It is either include or import.
	transformation grp id	**transformation grp id** is a Foreign Key reference to XSLT as the importing XSLT.
XSLT PARAMETER	**name**	**name** is the name of this XSLT PARAMETER. XSLT takes named parameters.
	parameter type	**parameter type** is the simple XML Type of the parameter. This could be made a foreign key reference to XML SIMPLE TYPE.
	description	**description** is text for this attribute description.
	parm id	**parm id** is the Primary Key.
	transformation grp id	**transformation grp id** is a Foreign Key reference to XSLT, which is the XSLT this parameter is defined for.
	xml doc id	**xml doc id** is a Foreign Key reference to XSLT alternate key. It is the XSLT this parameter is defined for.

Business Transactions

A business transaction is the exchange of one or more electronic documents by two or more processes. For example, a purchase order document is exchanged between a customer process and a supplier process. Many of the exchanged documents are XML documents. Additionally, the specification of the processes can be contained in XML documents. However, not all data exchanges are in XML, and not all business transaction processes are specified by an XML document. Electronic data interchange (EDI) is an example of a non-XML-based standard. Examples of XML-based standards for governing business transactions are ebXML, RosettaNet, BPMI, Web Services Conversation Language (WSCL), and HR-XML. What these standards allow is the exchange of process information with business partners so that interactions can be automated. This is the essence of future business integration, the integration of processes.

Web Services can be seen as a type of business transaction process where XML documents are exchanged through interactions that are surfaced on a particular URL address. Web Services are also specified by XML documents. We model Web Services here by binding part of the process model, the INTER-ACTIONS, to a URL service address when needed.

Business transaction processes can be complex. A single process or a related set of processes may involve the exchange of tens or even hundreds of different documents. Some of these documents have requirements for security handling and control of messaging. They may also participate in certain commit transaction controls. Managing documents, business transactions, and other related processes is a difficult task. A company must manage and track how these processes interact with outside business partners as a fundamental requirement of doing business. In addition, this same approach can manage and track internal business process systems. Because process description XML documents control actions, they need to be modeled as a system, not as a data structure document. The MME model for this area manages this information by combining modeling concepts from the standards mentioned previously.

The models in Chapters 4 to 6 help you answer questions such as:

- What XML document types are sent out by ebXML?
- What systems have functionality surfaced as an external Web Service?
- What security is used on XML documents in the human resources system?
- What processes may involve sending a document that uses JMS messaging?
- In the exchange for the sales order type used in the example, where does the information in the order document come from
- What deployed software manipulates this document?

NOTE We use the term document in a very generic way to refer to any data package form. This use is consistent with the standards listed. XML documents will be referred to as XML documents and not as just documents.

Business processes describe what a business does and how it interacts with other entities, both internal and external. A business transaction results from two or more processes that interact in some determined sequence. These interacting processes may reside in one company or may belong to different companies that are transacting business. We can look to B2B commerce for an example. One company, say a retail store, has an automated system that has detected low supplies of corn flakes and wants to resupply them. It can send a message to its supplier ordering a quantity of corn flakes. The supplier's system may accept or reject the order, and if it is accepted, the supplier's system can send messages for invoices and shipping information. If the supplier's system rejected the order, it would send a rejection message to the ordering store (see Figure 5.5).

The exchanged messages can occur in many forms. XML is rapidly taking the dominant position, but EDI is a well-established process-message protocol that is not currently XML-based. However, the exchange of any document form still follows the same outline of interactions and processes.

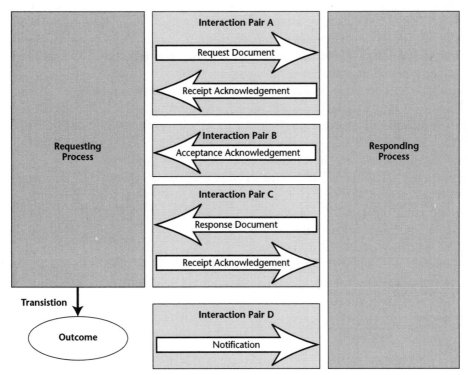

Figure 5.5   Interacting processes example.

Each participant in the transaction has a process that interacts with the other participant's process. In the given example, the store has a reordering process and the supplier has a matching accept order process. The interactions of those processes occur as an exchange of electronic documents in one or both directions, and the interactions follow the script of the processes. The processes can become very complex and detailed. Some of the added complexities can include sending acknowledgments as messages are received and handling errors and rejections.

To aid in understanding the model, there are two overview diagrams, Figures 5.6 and 5.7. Figure 5.8 gives a detailed view with all the elements visible. The entities and attributes are given in Tables 5.7 and 5.8.

A PROCESS is a set of specified INTERACTIONS that occur in a given TRANSITION pattern. INTERACTIONS are the centering concept of this area. The INTERACTIONS may be paired with an INTERACTION on another PROCESS. In the ordering example, the interaction of the store sending its order request and the supplier acknowledging the request is followed by another interaction pair that controls the accepting of the order. As shown in Figure 5.6, INTERACTIONS are performed by a SOFTWARE MODULE (from Chapter 6); they are part of a PROCESS, sequenced by TRANSITIONS, and they send and receive documents. In the detail view, PROCESSES are matched with other PROCESSES by the COORD PROCESS entity, and INTERACTIONS are matched by the COORD INTERACTIONS entity.

In the set of INTERACTIONS for a PROCESS, one INTERACTION is designated the initial INTERACTION, and it is used to start the PROCESS. One or more other INTERACTIONS can be designated the final INTERACTION, and when it is finished, the PROCESS is completed. PROCESS INTERACTION LINK is an associative entity between INTERACTIONS and PROCESSES that also designates the initial and final INTERACTIONS.

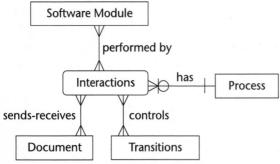

Figure 5.6 Overview of high-level interactions.

TRANSITIONS control the sequence of the INTERACTIONS. The TRANSI-TIONS entity indicates the successor INTERACTIONS of a source INTERAC-TION. For example, the ordering process interactions have an expected order, but a failure that occurs needs a different following INTERACTION.

The TRANSACTION CONTROL entity handles transaction integrity for the process's interaction transitions. The essence of transaction integrity is as follows: In a sequence of interactions and exchange of documents, certain events may occur that need to have other events finish to be considered correct. For example, if the supplier processes the order for completion and sends the acknowledgment to the orderer and then the orderer does not respond or rejects the order, the supplier may have already allocated stock for the order in his processing. The stock allocation should be restored. This is transaction integrity, and there are two types. One is considered atomic and occurs when the lifetime of the transaction is short. An example is the transaction integrity covering the sending and receiving of the relevant documents in the order process. The other type of transaction integrity is called *extended* and requires a compensating transaction to roll back the data to a consistent state. An example is a situation in which ordered goods were delivered and then rejected and returned. Other transactions are then needed to process the returns. Transaction integrity is maintained between different interactions of a single process.

Figure 5.7 shows a high-level view of the document structure that can be exchanged. The form of the documents in the exchange can be rather varied. The documents can have multiple parts and can require different levels of security for an exchange. For example, a document could consist of a SOAP envelope that is digitally signed, and it could contain an attachment that is digitally signed by another entity. Some of the document may be in XML, and other parts may be in encoded binary. A DOCUMENT ENVELOPE can have one or more BUSINESS DOCUMENTs as ATTACHMENTS and each attached BUSINES DOCUMENT may have its own security control in the DOCUMENT SECURITY entity. The documents can be of any form, not just XML. The method of sending the documents can be direct and unspecified or utilize a messaging service. The MESSAGING CONTROL entity specifies the service and protocol if messaging is used by the INTERACTION. It may refer to the MESSAGING entity from Chapter 4 for the message queue.

The security information indicates if the document is digitally signed if it is encrypted, the encryption method if it has additional security signatures, and if a protocol ensuring the identity of one side or the other has its claimed private key. The security control specification can be contained in an XML document that can be located via a URI. The BUSINESS DOCUMENTS and the DOCUMENT ENVELOPE may be XML documents that are defined by a XML schema that is located via a URI. Finally, the PROCESS, since it may be specified as an XML file, may also be located via a URI.

Web Services are a form of distributed computing that use XML for data exchange and for service specification, and use standard Internet protocols such as HTTP for communication. They specify interactions at particular URL addresses. Each address responds to XML document messages and returns an XML document. Standards are being created for Web Services that will add transaction control, security, reliable messaging, and workflow control. All of these parts are modeled here and will handle the differing standards. In this view, a Web Service is an INTERACTION that is surfaced to a URL address. The documents it will respond to are the document forms given by the INTER-ACTION DOC LINK entity, and the software that runs the service is in the SOFTWARE MODULE. As Web Services become more complex, they will utilize all of this model.

The WEB SERVICES BINDING entity indicates what INTERACTIONS are surfaced at a given URL with a given name. It also indicates which WSDL XML document, through a URI LOCATOR, is specifying this Web Service.

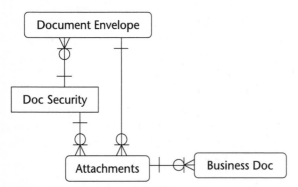

Figure 5.7   Overview of the document structure.

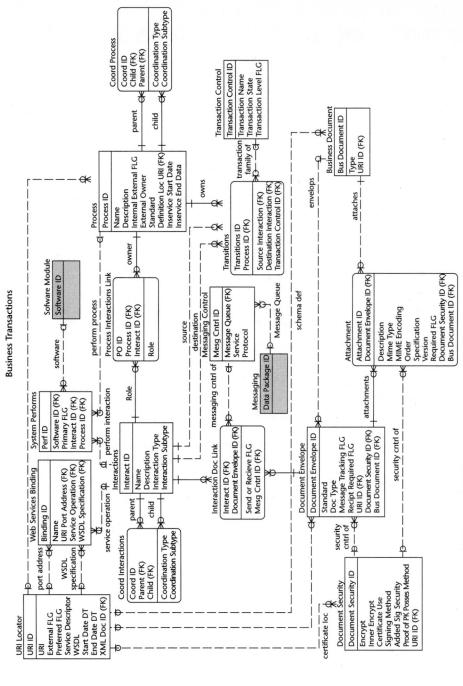

Figure 5.8   Business process and transactions.

Table 5.7 Business process and transactions entities

ENTITY NAME	ENTITY DEFINITION
ATTACHMENT	ATTACHMENT defines the payloads of the DOCUMENT ENVELOPE. Each payload may have its own security control.
BUSINESS DOCUMENT	BUSINESS DOCUMENT represents the abstract document. It may be of several types, including XML, EDI, or even an image.
COORD INTERACTIONS	COORD INTERACTIONS links Interactions that are coordinated. Not all interactions will have a coordinated part. The coordinated interactions may belong to different systems and processes. The coordination types can be complementary (such as the two sides of a process conversation) or transaction-reversing, or an intermediary connection.
COORD PROCESSES	COORD PROCESSES links PROCESSes that interact. For example, sales request and sales-taking processes. Processes may (often) reside on different systems.
DOCUMENT ENVELOPE	This is the envelope protocol for message exchanges. It may be an XML-based protocol such as SOAP or a binary protocol such as EDI.
DOCUMENT SECURITY	DOCUMENT SECURITY specifies security controls for documents. Messages can be encrypted in various ways, be signed, and have additional security to prevent replaying. It can provide integrity, confidentiality, and protection against replay attacks.
INTERACTION DOC LINK	INTERACTION DOC LINK is an associative entity connecting INTERACTIONS and DOCUMENT ENVELOPEs. COORDINATED INTERACTIONS exchange documents. An interaction may reference a set of sending documents and a set of receiving documents. The documents are transmitted via a given message protocol. This indicates if a system is sending or receiving the document.
INTERACTIONS	An INTERACTION is done by a SYSTEM for a PROCESS in a particular process transition. It specifies the documents to send and/or receive. TRANSITIONS are not needed, but will help determine allowed sequences of documents and the transactions involving them.

Table 5.7   *(continued)*

ENTITY NAME	ENTITY DEFINITION
MESSAGING	See Chapter 4, Table 4.5 for the definition of this entity. This represents a message channel that may be used by the messaging specification in messaging control.
MESSAGING CONTROL	Specifies the messaging Protocol and Service.
PROCESS	A PROCESS is a grouping of INTERACTIONS and TRANSITIONS. A PROCESS corresponds to one side of a conversation or a transaction; for example a sales request. A coordinating process for it would be the sales fulfillment process. A PROCESS may be external to the business or internal. Standards that can be modeled here include: XSCL, ebXML, UML, BPMI, XPDL, BPEL4WS.
PROCESS INTERACTIONS LINK	This links INTERACTIONS and the PROCESS. One INTERACTION is the initial one and another is the final one. The specifications of initial and final are not required for systems, but given them, the order in which documents flow can be determined.
SOFTWARE MODULE	SOFTWARE MODULE identifies the system that performs the INTERACTIONS and PROCESS. Refer to Table 6.3, for this entity's definition.
SYSTEM PERFORMS	SYSTEM PERFORMS is an associative entity for connecting the SOFTWARE MODULE with the INTERACTION or a PROCESS.
TRANSACTION CONTROL	TRANSITIONS can operate under TRANSACTION CONTROLS. The transactions span one or more TRANSITIONS and may be atomic or extended types.
TRANSITIONS	TRANSITIONS determine the order and flow of interactions. They belong to a PROCESS. TRANSITIONS are not needed, but will help determine the allowed sequences of documents and their parts in a transaction.
URI LOCATOR	Refer to Table 5.1 for this entity's definition.
WEB SERVICES BINDING	A Web Service is an operation that is surfaced on a URL address. It is specified by WSDL and is named. Multiple operations can be surfaced on one address. The operation is an INTERACTION and that INTERACTION specifies the document types it takes as input and output. A Web Services binding entity connects the service Interaction with the URL address and indicates the WSDL used.

Table 5.8 Entity Attributes for Business Transactions

ENTITY NAME	ATTRIBUTE NAME	ATTRIBUTE DEFINITION
ATTACHMENT	attachment id	**attachment id** is the Primary Key.
	document envelope id	**document envelope id** is a Foreign Key reference to DOCUMENT ENVELOPE, which contains this ATTACHMENT.
	description	**description** provides narrative explanation of the ATTACHMENT documents.
	mime type	**mime type** specifies the MIME Type of the ATTACHMENT documents if applicable.
	mime encoding	**mime encoding** specifies the Encoding.
	order	**order** gives the order of the attachments.
	specification	**specification** identifies the standards that the attachment must meet.
	version	This is the version of the Standard.
	required flg	**required flg** is true if this attachment is a required attachment.
	document security id	**document security id** is a Foreign Key reference to DOCUMENT SECURITY, which specifies the security needs of this ATTACHMENT.
	bus document id	**bus document id** is a Foreign Key reference to BUSINESS DOCUMENT, which is the document this Attachment will attach to the DOCUMENT ENVELOPE.
BUSINESS DOCUMENT	bus document id	**bus document id** is the Primary Key.
	type	**type** gives the business classification of document.
	uri id	**uri id** is a Foreign Key reference to URI LOCATOR, which is the URI information for this business document.
COORD INTERACTIONS	coord id	**coord id** is the Primary Key.

Table 5.8 *(continued)*

ENTITY NAME	ATTRIBUTE NAME	ATTRIBUTE DEFINITION
	parent	**parent** is a Foreign Key reference to INTERACTIONS, where INTERACTION is in the parent role specified in this coordination.
	child	**child** is a Foreign Key reference to INTERACTIONS, where INTERACTION is in the child role specified in this coordination.
	coordination type	**coordination type** has the values cooperation, reversing, mediation, communication, and security.
	coordination subtype	**coordination subtype** further specifies the Coordination Type and is standards-determined.
COORD PROCESSES	**coord id**	**coord id** is the Primary Key.
	parent	**parent** is a Foreign Key reference to PROCESS, where PROCESS is in the parent role specified in this coordination.
	child	**child** is a Foreign Key reference to PROCESS, where PROCESS is in the child role specified in this coordination.
	coordination type	**coordination type** has the values cooperation, reversing, mediation, communication, and security.
	coordination subtype	**coordination subtype** further specifies the coordination type and is standards-determined.
DOCUMENT ENVELOPE	**document envelope id**	**document envelope id** is the Primary Key.
	standard	This is the standards indication (for example, SOAP, EDI, SAP).
	doc type	**doc type** indicates the major type of the document, such as XML or EDI.
	message tracking flg	**message tracking flg** indicates that messages of this type are tracked by the sending protocol as an audit procedure.

(continued)

Table 5.8   *(continued)*

ENTITY NAME	ATTRIBUTE NAME	ATTRIBUTE DEFINITION
	receipt required flg	**receipt required flg** indicates if this document type requires a receipt from the receiver.
	uri id	**uri id** is a Foreign Key reference to URI Locator, which specifies this DOCUMENT ENVELOPE.
	document security id	**document security id** is a Foreign Key reference to DOCUMENT SECURITY, which specifies the security of the envelope. Attachments may need different levels of security or signatures.
	bus document id	**bus document id** is a Foreign Key reference to BUSINESS DOCUMENT, which can be the primary content of the envelope.
DOCUMENT SECURITY	document security id	**document security id** is the Primary Key.
	encrypt algor	**encrypt algor** specifies the algorithm to do encryption.
	inner encrypt	**inner encrypt** is used for an embedded encrypted symmetric key. The value is protocol specific.
	certificate use	**certificate use** indicates the type of certificate to exchange.
	signing method	**signing method** provides message integrity. Its value is protocol specific.
	added sig security	**added sig security** indicates additional security such as, time stamp, sequence number, expiration, message correlation. Its value is protocol specific.
	proof of pk posses method	**proof of pk posses method** is the protocol used to prove possession of a private key.
	uri id	**uri id** is a Foreign Key reference to URI LOCATOR, which is the URI of this document security document.

Table 5.8   *(continued)*

ENTITY NAME	ATTRIBUTE NAME	ATTRIBUTE DEFINITION
INTERACTION DOC LINK	**interact id**	**interact id** is a Foreign Key reference to INTERACTIONS and is part of the primary key.
	document envelope id	**document envelope id** is a Foreign Key reference to DOCUMENT ENVELOPE, which is a document used by this INTERACTION for sending or receiving.
	send or receive flg	**send or receive flg** indicates if the document is for sending or receiving. Although several documents can be specified, only one is sent at run time and only one is received at run time.
	mesg cntrl id	**mesg cntrl id** is a Foreign Key reference to MESSAGING CONTROL, which specifies the messaging service and protocol, if any, for this INTERACTION-DOCUMENT ENVELOPE pair.
INTERACTIONS	**interact id**	**interact id** is the Primary Key.
	name	**name** is the name of this interaction.
	description	**description** provides a narrative explanation of the INTERACTIONS.
	interaction type	**interaction type** is a major classification of interactions. It has values: bus_process, com_protocol, and security_protocol where: bus_process means that the interaction is part of a business process. com_protocol means that the interaction is part of a communication protocol, for example, receipt acknowledgment. security_protocol means that the interaction is part of a security exchange, such as proof of private key possession. Each of these Types has various subtypes controlling the exchange.

(continued)

Table 5.8   *(continued)*

ENTITY NAME	ATTRIBUTE NAME	ATTRIBUTE DEFINITION
	interaction subtype	**interaction subtype** gives subtype of the interaction type. The values are standards-dependent.
MESSAGING CONTROL	**mesg cntrl id**	**mesg cntrl id** is the Primary Key.
	message queue	**message queue** is a Foreign Key reference to MESSAGING (see Chapter 4, Enterprise Systems model), which is the Message channel or queue to use. It may be null.
	service	**service** is the provider of the messaging framework.
	protocol	**protocol** is the communication Protocol to be used (for example, HTTP and EDI).
PROCESS	**process id**	**process id** is the Primary Key.
	name	**name** is the name of this process.
	description	**descriotion** is the narrative detail about the process
	internal external flg	**internal external flg** indicates if the process is internal to the business or externally surfaced (for example, this process may be a Web Service provided to external customers).
	external owner	**external owner** indicates who provides the process if this process is only done by an external entity (for example a Web Service provided by another company).
	standard	The standard used in the definition of this process (for example, WSCL, BPMI, BPEL4WS, SAP, UML).
	definition loc uri	**definition loc uri** is a Foreign Key reference to URI LOCATOR, which is the XML document that specifies this process.
	inservice start date	**inservice start date** is the date that this process becomes active.
	inservice end date	**inservice end date** is the date this process is no longer active.

Table 5.8 *(continued)*

ENTITY NAME	ATTRIBUTE NAME	ATTRIBUTE DEFINITION
PROCESS INTERACTIONS LINK	**po id**	**po id** is the Primary Key.
	process id	**process id** is a Foreign Key reference to PROCESS.
	interact id	**interact id** is a Foreign Key reference to INTERACTIONS.
	role	**role** indicates the role of the interaction to process. It has the values initial, final, intermediate, and error.
SYSTEM PERFORMS	**perf id**	**perf id** is the Primary Key.
	software id	**software id** is a Foreign Key reference to SOFTWARE MODULE, which is found in Chapter 6, Table 6.3. The SOFTWARE MODULE is the software that can perform the PROCESS and/or INTERACTION. There can be multiple SOFTWARE MODULEs for this.
	primary flg	**primary flg** indicates that the system is the primary performer of the interaction or process.
	interact id	**interact id** is a Foreign Key reference to INTERACTION, which is an INTERACTION the SOFTWARE MODULE can perform.
	process id	**process id** is a Foreign Key reference to PROCESS, which is a PROCESS that the SOFTWARE MODULE can perform.
TRANSACTION CONTROL	**transaction control id**	**transaction control id** is the Primary Key.
	transaction name	**transaction name** names the transaction.
	transaction state	**transaction state** indicates the state change of the transaction. It has the values start, commit, and rollback.
	transaction level flg	**transaction level flg** indicates if the transaction is either atomic or extended.

(continued)

Table 5.8   *(continued)*

ENTITY NAME	ATTRIBUTE NAME	ATTRIBUTE DEFINITION
TRANSITIONS	transition id	**transition id** is the Primary Key.
	process id	**process id** is a Foreign Key reference to PROCESS, which owns this TRANSITION.
	source interaction	**source interaction** is a Foreign Key reference to INTERACTION, which plays the source role in the transition.
	destination interaction	**destination interaction** is a Foreign Key reference to INTERACTION, which plays the destination role in the TRANSITION.
	transaction control id	**transaction control** is a Foreign Key reference to TRANSACTION CONTROL, which specifies the transaction level of this TRANSITION.
WEB SERVICES BINDING	binding id	**binding id** is the Primary Key.
	name	**name** is the name of the service surfaced.
	uri port address	**uri port address** is a Foreign Key reference to URI LOCATOR, which is the URL that carries this service. Accessing that location may invoke this service.
	service operation	**service operation** is a Foreign Key reference to INTERACTIONS, which acts as the service to be surfaced.
	wsdl specification	**wsdl specification** is a Foreign Key reference to URI LOCATOR, which locates the XML document that specifies the WSDL used in specifying this service.

Classification Scheme

A document classification scheme is like the searchable catalog of a library. Although document classification is not related to an XML standard, it plays a critical role in information management. Much of the information contained in XML documents, XML schema parts, and business transaction parts needs to be classified if it is to be useful. Classification is necessary to reuse parts and locate relevant documents. The document classification model that I will use for this chapter's meta model is based on a proposal done at the National Institute for Standards and Technology (NIST, to be on OASIS-open.org when approved) and can be easily expressed and stored as an XML document.

A company may have hundreds or thousands of XML schemas, which can be provided by external bodies or created internally. Each of these XML schemas may have multiple definitions of XML elements and XML type definitions that can be used by other XML schemas. Reusing standard definitions via an XML schema importation is a good practice. However, given the large number of XML schemas, XML documents, and definitions of elements and types, locating relevant documents is nearly impossible without tool support. A common structure for locating material is a taxonomy or a classification scheme. Classifications are hierarchical structures. Library classifications, such as the Dewey Decimal system, are examples of such structures, as is the Linnaeus classification for biology.

A good classification system needs multiple classifications and to support multilevel classifications. Many documents can and will be classified under multiple classification schemes. For example, a reorder document may perhaps be classified under three classification schemes: a purchasing scheme, a legal document scheme, and a protocol scheme.

The model for classification is shown in Figure 5.9. The entities and attributes are given in Tables 5.9 and 5.10.

The classification system shown here supports this hierarchy requirement and also uses a subtyped link, so different entities can be classified. This system provides links to XML documents and thus to XML SCHEMAS, XML NAMESPACES, and XML DATA GROUPS, which are XML ELEMENT DECLARATIONS and XML TYPE DEFS. Implementations can easily add additional links as desired.

CLASSIFICATION SCHEME is the top level for classification and may have many CLASSIFICATION LEVELs. The CLASSIFICATION LEVEL is a hierarchy via the **parent level** attribute. CLASSIFICATION ITEM is the lowest level of a classification and is a child of the CLASSIFICATION LEVEL. The CLASSIFICATION ITEM is then associated with the items to be classified, such as XML document or XML Namespace, using the CLASSIFICATION LINK association entity and its subtypes. The CLASSIFICATION LEVEL defines the levels and CLASSIFICATION ITEM defines the members of the level. Thus CLASSIFICATION ITEM may have a parent CLASSIFICATION ITEM that belongs to the next level up. For example, an organization chart is a classification scheme. A company division level may be the parent level for department levels. This would be represented in the CLASSIFICATION LEVEL hierarchy. Now, a individual department such as the meta data support department may be in the IT division. These are represented by the CLASSIFICATION ITEM hierarchy, and each item also belongs to the appropriate level.

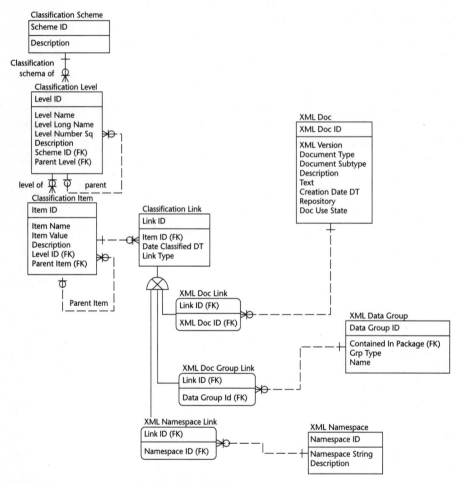

Figure 5.9   Document classification model.

Table 5.9   Document Classification Entities

ENTITY NAME	ENTITY DEFINITION
CLASSIFICATION ITEM	CLASSIFICATION ITEM gives the members of a classification level. For example, for the biology level kingdom, there are plants, animals, fungi, bacteria, and protists. This is also educational.
CLASSIFICATION LEVEL	CLASSIFICATION LEVEL is a hierarchical level of the classification item. For example, biology uses the levels: kingdom, phylum (plural phyla), class, order, family, genus, and species to classify organisms.
CLASSIFICATION LINK	This is an association entity that is a supertype for handling the linking of CLASSIFICATION ITEM and the particular entity to be classified, such as XML DOCUMENT, or XML NAMESPACE.
CLASSIFICATION SCHEME	The CLASSIFICATION SCHEME used (for example, department use, or business area, or business process).
XML DATA GROUP	Refer to Table 4.3 for entity definition.
XML DATA GROUP LINK	XML DATA GROUP LINK is a subtype of CLASSIFICATION LINK for XML DATA GROUPS that is a supertype for XML ELEMENT DECLARATIONS and XML TYPE DEFS.
XML DOCUMENT	Refer to Table 5.1 for entity definition.
XML DOC LINK	XML DOC LINK is a subtype of CLASSIFICATION LINK for XML DOCUMENTS.
XML NAMESPACE LINK	XML NAMESPACE LINK is a subtype of CLASSIFICATION LINK for XML NAMESPACES.
XML NAMESPACE	Refer to Table 5.1 for entity definition.

Table 5.10   Entity Attributes for Classification

ENTITY NAME	ATTRIBUTE NAME	ATTRIBUTE DEFINITION
CLASSIFICATION ITEM	**item id**	**item id** is the Primary Key.
	item name	**item name** is the name of the item at that level.

(continued)

Table 5.10 *(continued)*

ENTITY NAME	ATTRIBUTE NAME	ATTRIBUTE DEFINITION
	item value	**item value** is the designation for the CLASSIFICATION ITEM (for example in a biology scheme at the kingdom level, this could be 'Animal'.
	description	**description** provides the narrative explanation of the CLASSIFICATION ITEM.
	level id	**level id** is a Foreign Key reference to CLASSIFICATION LEVEL, which is the containing level of this CLASSIFICATION ITEM.
CLASSIFICATION LEVEL	level id	**level id** is the Primary Key.
	level name	**level name** is the level name (for example, in biology, kingdom).
	level long name	**level long name** is a long version of the level name.
	level number sq	**level number sq** is the level indicator. Numbering starts at the top level as 1.
	description	**description** is the narrative of the CLASSIFICATION LEVEL.
	scheme id	**scheme id** is a Foreign Key reference to CLASSIFICATION SCHEME, which is the containing classification container.
	parent level	**parent level** is a recursive Foreign Key reference to CLASSIFICATION LEVEL, which is the parent level to this CLASSIFICATION LEVEL.
CLASSIFICATION LINK	item id	**item id** is a Foreign Key reference to CLASSIFICATION ITEM, which is to be linked to some object for that classification.
	link id	**link id** is the Primary Key.

Table 5.10 *(continued)*

ENTITY NAME	ATTRIBUTE NAME	ATTRIBUTE DEFINITION
	date classified dt	**date classified dt** is the date time of the classification entry.
	link type	**link type** is the discriminator attribute for subtypes. The subtypes are XML Doc Link, XML Data Group Link, and XML Namespace Link.
CLASSIFICATION SCHEME	scheme id	**scheme id** is the Primary Key.
	description	**description** provides the narrative explanation of the CLASSIFICATION SCHEME.
XML DATA GROUP LINK	link id	**link id** is the subtype Key to CLASSIFICATION LINK.
	data group id	**data group id** is a Foreign Key reference to XML DATA GROUP, which is the Data Group to be classified.
XML DOC LINK	xml doc id	**xml doc id** is a Foreign Key reference to XML DOC, which is the document to be classified.
	link id	**link id** is the subtype Key to CLASSIFICATION LINK.
XML NAMESPACE LINK	link id	**link id** is the subtype Key to CLASSIFICATION LINK.
	namespace id	**namespace id** is a Foreign Key reference to XML NAMESPACE, which is the XML NAMESPACE to be classified.

Reports from the XML, Messaging, and Business Transactions Meta Model

At the beginning of this chapter, we posed a number of questions of importance to a business that can be answered by the meta data of XML/business transactions. The meta models from this area support many important queries on the use of XML schemas, the impact of changes in the business processes, and in the finding of important XML artifacts.

XML Use Report: XML Top-Level Elements

Figure 5.10 shows the XML element names that can be parsed with a particular XML schema.

A document has an outermost level element that can be processed by XML schemas that have that element identified as a top-level element. This is useful for determining possible XML schemas of an unknown document and for finding applicable XML schemas for reuse. The report would join the tables URI_LOCATOR, XML_DOC, XML_SCHEMA, XML_TYPE_DEF, SCHEMA_SOURCE, and CLASSIFICATION_ITEM.

XML Use Report: Schema Imports

XML schemas can import other XML schemas, as shown in the report in Figure 5.11. This makes changes in the imported XML schema affect the importing XML schema. This is a basic impact analysis report for XML schemas and is needed in other reports that also look at XML schema changes in other areas. The report would join the tables URI_LOCATOR, XML_DOC, XML_SCHEMA, IMPORT_SCHEMA, XML_TYPE_DEF, and XML_ELEMENT_DECLARATION.

XML Use Report: XML Top-Level Elements

Top-Level Elements of Schemas with Classification		August 15, 2003
schema_uri	element_name	classification_name
metadata/schema/purchaseOrder.XML	purchaseOrder	purchasing
		ebXML
		e-commerce
	address	
		e-commerce
	items	purchasing
		e-commerce

Figure 5.10   The top-level elements that current XML schemas can process.

XML Use Report: Schema Imports

Schema Imports of Schemas Report		August 15, 2003
uri_parent	Name	uri_imported	Imported Name
metadata/schema/purchaseOrder.xml	Purchase Order Form	metadata/schema/addressEuropean.xml	base address type
		metadata/schema/addressUS.xml	U.S. address type
		metadata/schema/addressEuropean.xml	European address type
		metadata/schema/items.xml	items list – order form
metadata/schema/invoice.xml	Invoice External	metadata/schema/addressBase.xml	base address type
		metadata/schema/addressUS.xml	U.S. address type
		metadata/schema/addressEuropean.xml	European address type

Figure 5.11   The dependencies of XML schema importing.

XML Use Report: XML Process Send

A business process is a set of interactions, where an interaction can send and/ or receive XML documents. You may be interested in knowing what documents are for what process so that security or messaging systems may be checked for them, as shown in Figure 5.12. The report would join the tables PROCESS, PROCESS_INTERACTION_LINK, INTERACTIONS, INTERACTION_DOC_ REL, MESSAGING_CONTROL, DOCUMENT_ENVELOP, BUSINESS_ DOCUMENT, ATTACHMENT, BUSINESS_DOCUMENT, and URI_LOCATOR.

XML Use Report: XML Process Impact

The business processes are executed by software that manipulates XML documents for message exchanges. When these XML documents are changed to reflect changing needs elsewhere in the business, you want to know the impact that this may have on other systems and software. The report shown in Figure 5.13 can utilize the previously made views for schema dependencies and the connection of processes to documents. The software systems can then be connected to the processes. The report would join the same tables as the previous query and add SOFTWARE_MODULE and SYSTEM_PERFORMS.

XML Use Report: XML Process Send

XML Documents Sent by Processes Report		August 15, 2003
process name	process description	Schema uri
receive order	internal for receiving and order	metadata/schema/acknowledgeLevel1.xml
		metadata/schema/rejectDoc.xml
		metadata/schema/deniedService.xml
acknowledge receipt of order	internal for when order is physically received	metadata/schema/OrderReceiptAck.xml
purchase	internal for placing orders	metadata/schema/purchaseOrder.xml

Figure 5.12   Documents that are sent by the business processes.

XML Use Report: XML Process Impact

Business Process and Systems Dependencies on Schema		August 15, 2003
process name	process description	Schema_uri
receive order	internal for recieving and order	metadata/schema/purchaseOrder.xml
		metadata/schema/invoice.xml
		metadata/schema/items.xml
		metadata/schema/acknowledgeLevel1.xml
acknowledge receipt of order	internal for when order is physically received	metadata/schema/ackGoodsReceipt.xml
purchase	internal for placing orders	metadata/schema/purchaseOrder.xml
		metadata/schema/invoice.xml
		metadata/schema/items.xml

Figure 5.13   Business systems affected by changes in the XML document schema.

Process XML: Order Flow Views

Another way of viewing the information in the models is graphically, which can present some information in a much clearer manner. This is similar to the viewing of a database design in an entity-relationship diagram versus a tabular listing of the tables and keys. This clearer presentation is especially true for the business transaction model instances. The level of interactions among the objects in that model is very high, and a graphical representation makes the relationships plain. The report views shown here are from a graphical browser for business transactions models. These views can help in debugging process flow problems or in understanding the sequence and details of document exchanges. The browser should allow the examination of the details and other information for each of the objects displayed (see Figure 5.14).

The scenario in these reports is as follows: A company may provide a Web Service for the internal purchasing of company supplies. The Web Service provided is the Receive Order process, and it has a coordinated process, the requesting service, or the Place Order process. The requesting process could be part of another, unrelated Web Service. The process boundaries are shown by a shaded box, and the internal interactions are boxes inside the process. The documents that are exchanged by the interactions are shown by boxes outside of the process boundaries. The people responsible for maintaining these systems are interested in the exchanged document structures because the system has not been performing adequately and they need to determine where the problem lies. They can use the browser to examine the flow of documents and look at their details. Figure 5.15 shows the browser with the information for the last XML document in a pop-up with the details of that document. The payload attachments and security protocols can be explored from the link in that pop-up. Figure 5.16 shows the browser with a pop-up on the Receive Order process with its details and access to the other coordinated processes, and the software modules that execute this process. This is useful for finding the coordinated processes, since the problem may be in them or in the software.

Using a universal browser for these process models overcomes the difficulty posed by the many standards that exist for the processes. Currently, the standards do not interoperate, and thus similar processes may be implemented in different standards. For example, the Web Service shown in the example could also be done with the ebXML standard. These related processes can be indicated as coordinated processes.

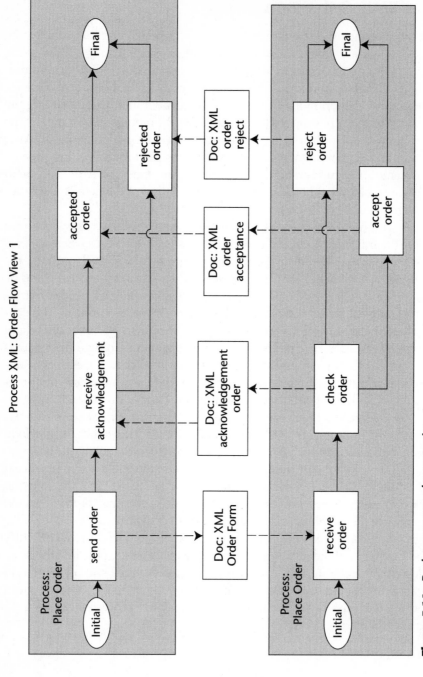

Figure 5.14 Business process browser view 1.

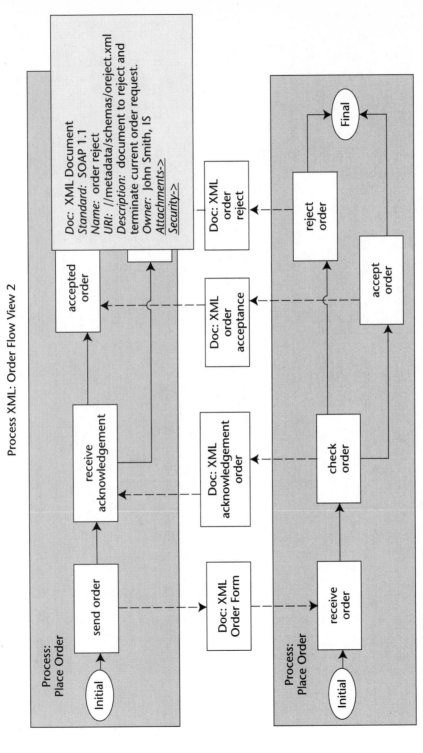

Process XML: Order Flow View 2

Doc: XML Document
Standard: SOAP 1.1
Name: order reject
URI: //metadata/schemas/oreject.xml
Description: document to reject and
terminate current order request.
Owner: John Smith, IS
Attachments->
Security->

Figure 5.15 Business process browser view 2.

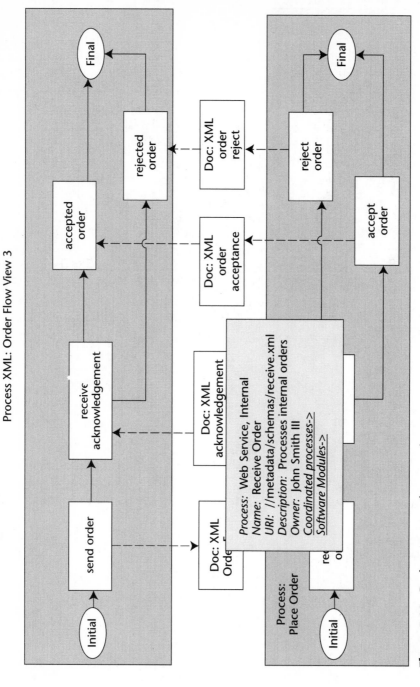

Figure 5.16 Business process browser view 3.

Summary

In this chapter, we covered the very broad applications of XML technologies and some of the major impacts they have on the functioning of an IT organization. The structure of XML documents is given by XML schemas, and they are modeled here for use in transformations and for the specification of interchange documents. XSLT XML documents can also specify transformations of other XML documents and are becoming widely used. These are modeled as a subtype of other IT applications as data transformation and movement. XML documents are also used to specify the operations of business processes according to various standards, and these were modeled here also. Web Services are modeled as a business process. Finally, documents and XML schema structures can be classified to help in finding and reusing the work involved in creating and maintaining XML documents and schemas.

XML schemas fit into this book's models as subtypes of a physical source for transformations, and XSLT fits in as a subtype for transformation. The classification systems shown in this chapter can be easily extended to also classify any other entity in the overall system, such as a person or hardware. This use would be dependent upon business needs. The XML business process specification models fit as a detailed extension for business processes that connect the documents used and the systems that use them. The modeling of those software systems is covered in the next chapter.

Universal Meta Model for IT Portfolio Management

In the preceding two chapters, we detailed meta data that directly pertains to the various structures of data when it is stored, processed, and transported. Now let's examine the meta data of the systems that store, process, and transport that data, and the meta data of those systems' components and management processes. Questions that need to be answered by the meta data for IT portfolio management include:

- Which applications access which tables and files, and which update the data as opposed to those that only read it?
- Which systems operate on obsolescent/unsupported hardware?
- What is the total processing and data storage capacity of each computing site?
- Which software patches have been installed on which systems and in which environments?
- What is our annual software license and maintenance liability by vendor?
- Which organizations submit the most trouble reports?
- Which system components have the most unscheduled maintenance?
- What types of staffing will be required—and how many staff members— by the portfolio of projects for the next 12 months?

- What is the business success rate of projects completed on time or within budget versus those that come in late or are over budget?
- Who are the most successful project managers?
- Which data is of questionable quality, and who needs to know about it?

Purpose of the IT Portfolio Management Meta Model

IT portfolio management is *the formal process for managing an organization's IT assets.* IT assets are things that are useful or valuable for an organization's IT department. These items include IT projects (maintenance and new development), software, hardware, middleware, internal staffing, and external consulting.

The IT Portfolio Management meta model supports IT management as a business function of the enterprise. IT is a complex endeavor that requires its own databases and applications just as much as any other functional area of the business. In the era of e-commerce and electronic integration of business processes, IT, increasingly, *is* the enterprise. IT is the mission-critical nervous system of the enterprise. If it does not run smoothly, the enterprise does not just feel the pain—it is paralyzed.

In this light, the objects of IT portfolio management may seem to fall into that gray area between meta data and "real" data. The objects of the IT portfolio—software, hardware, projects, vendors, and the like—are real business entities of the enterprise that are planned and managed as much as human resources, accounts, vehicles, and (dare we say) databases. So, what makes them *meta* data? The management of these objects is intimately intertwined with the management of the more stereotypical classes of meta data covered in Chapters 4 and 5—databases, tables, flat files, mappings, messaging—and IT portfolio objects are planned and managed together with them. Users and software access databases, software comes from vendors or is developed through internal projects, and the software runs on hardware that also comes from vendors and is connected via networks, all of which involve the people, places, and things of the enterprise. IT portfolio management is inextricably linked with understanding and managing the data, messages, and transactions of enterprise information systems, and therefore is an integral part of the MME.

Assumptions in the IT Portfolio Management Meta Model

The following assumptions govern the IT Portfolio Management meta model:

1. Operational fields such as data effective dates and audit fields (for example, create and update dates and user IDs) are not included in the meta model.

2. Tables for industry-standard global reference data, such as state codes, country codes, and the like are assumed to be available in the enterprise and to the MME, and are not included in the meta model.

3. Additional customary reference tables from operational systems are assumed to be available, and are not included in the meta model. For example, HARDWARE UNIT maintains a foreign key of Accounting Asset ID to a presumed General Ledger system table. Similarly LOCA-TION has a foreign key of Facility ID to a presumed Facilities Management system table. Such parent tables are assumed to be available in the enterprise and to the MME, and are not included in the meta model.

IT Portfolio Management Subject Areas

So what is the landscape of IT portfolio management? The IT portfolio management data model contains 68 distinct entities [(17 of them associative entities) (many-to-many attributed relationships)], plus more than 100 distinct foreign key relationships. These are too numerous to meaningfully display in a single entity-relationship diagram. Figure 6.1 shows the major data subjects of IT portfolio management and their most important conceptual relationships. Each of these interactions is explored in much fuller detail within each of the five highly related subject area meta models of IT portfolio management.

The five subject areas of IT portfolio management are:

Service Management.   This subject area covers the overall interrelationship of hardware, software, network, and database components that compose systems; the users who access those systems; their expectations for levels of service; and events that affect those systems or that service. Major data subjects are: *System, Hardware, Software, Network, Data Package, Service,* and *Person.*

Software Management.   This subject area details the computer programs of the enterprise and their relationships to each other, data, and other system components. Major data subjects are: *Software, Data Package, Person,* and *Vendor.*

Hardware and Network Management.   This subject area details the physical devices and communications links of IT. Major data subjects are: *Hardware, Network,* and *Vendor.*

Project Portfolio Management.   This subject area covers the major information objects of IT work initiatives and their resources. Major data subjects are: *Project, System,* and *Person.*

Data Quality Management.   This subject area supports the definition of data quality metrics, the recording of specific measurements, and the reporting of data quality exceptions to the business. Major data subjects are: *Data Quality Metric, Data Package,* and *Person.*

These five subject areas overlap to varying degrees. Many of the entities of Software Management and Hardware and Network Management overlap with Service Management. On the other hand, Project Portfolio Management and Data Quality Management overlap very little with the other subject areas, except where they use common reference entities such as PERSON, and to a lesser degree LOCATION, which are ubiquitous in the subject areas of IT portfolio management and are present as well as the subject areas of the Business Meta Data model (see Chapter 7 for a detailed discussion of this meta model).

Let's take a look at the first subject area, Service Management.

Data Subjects of IT Portfolio Management

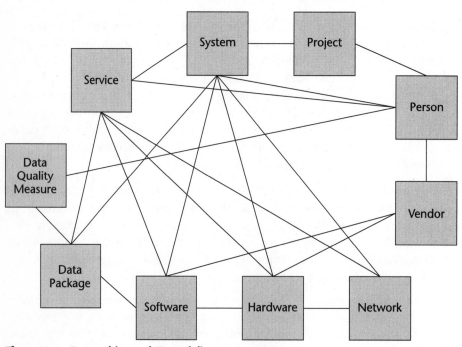

Figure 6.1   Data subjects of IT portfolio management.

Service Management

Service Management encompasses the interrelationship of hardware, software, network, and database components that compose systems; the users who access those systems; their expectations for levels of service; and events that affect those systems or that service. The data model for Service Management is shown in Figure 6.2. The heart of the model is SYSTEM. A SYSTEM is a logical aggregation of multiple components—software, hardware, databases, and so on—that together have a distinct identity for enterprise use and management. SYSTEM itself is a simple entity, with basic attributes such as **system name**, **description**, and **comment text**, plus a **system url** (Uniform Resource Locator) for Web-enabled applications. The simplicity of the SYSTEM entity belies its extensive reach, for it has definitive relationships with its subsidiary parts: HARDWARE UNIT, SOFTWARE MODULE, DATA PACKAGE, and NETWORK. Most of these relationships are M:M, for example, SYSTEM-HARDWARE—this notation means that a SYSTEM can operate on more than one HARDWARE UNIT, and conversely more than one HARDWARE UNIT can operate on a given SYSTEM. The same goes for SYSTEM and NETWORK (SYSTEM-NETWORK CONNECTION), and SYSTEM and DATA PACKAGE (SYSTEM-DATA PACKAGE).

In turn, these components of SYSTEMs themselves can be interrelated to one another. A SOFTWARE MODULE is deployed onto one or more HARDWARE UNITs in one or more ENVIRONMENTs—for example, Development, Test, or Production—and are thus designated as DEPLOYED SOFTWARE MODULEs. ENVIRONMENT is a small reference table containing the **environment ids** of standard **environment names**. Systems, software, databases, and networks can have identifiable physical locations as well, but only insofar as they themselves reside on HARDWARE UNITs. All these components of SYSTEM are explored in more detail in the *Software Management* subject area and the *Hardware and Network Management* subject area. The DATA PACKAGE is defined in detail in Chapter 4.

It is important to note that several objects in this subject area—HARDWARE UNIT, NETWORK, and LOCATION—have one-to-many recursive relationships, reflecting composition hierarchies (also commonly referred to as a *bill of materials* hierarchies) that enable multiple instances of an object to be grouped into a single, higher-order instance. For example, multiple specific mail delivery LOCATIONs may be grouped into a single building LOCATION, which in turn may be one of several building LOCATIONs grouped into a campus LOCATION, specified by **location group id**. Similarly, a single-server HARDWARE UNIT may be subdivided into multiple virtual server domains, denoted via **hardware group id**.

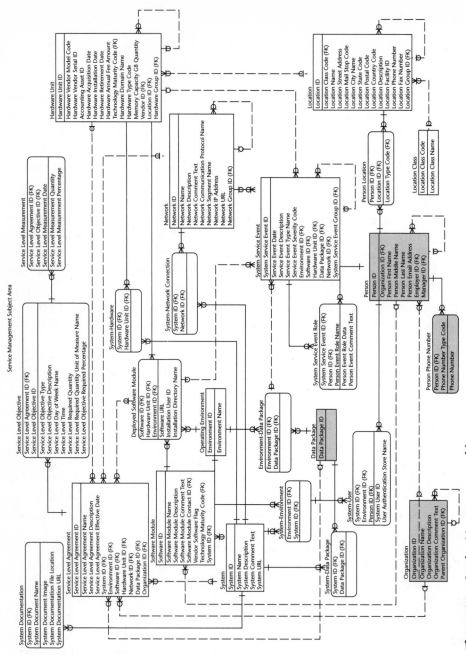

Figure 6.2 Service Management subject area.

SYSTEM also has a couple of additional subsidiary objects. Information about who is authorized to access a system is recorded in SYSTEM USER, a relationship between SYSTEM and PERSON (a general purpose meta entity described in more detail in Chapter 7) bearing the **system user ID** (that is, user name) used to access the system, and the **user authentication store** used to validate user access to the system. Additionally, documentation for a SYSTEM, such as run books or other operational procedures, is contained in SYSTEM DOCUMENTATION in the form of binary objects (such as PDF or word-processing documents) in **system document image,** or as a pointer to a **file location** on the local area network or a **system document url** on an intranet.

As the name implies, Service Management supports more than the inventory of system components. More vitally, it supports the management and delivery of services by IT, using SERVICE LEVEL AGREEMENTs and SYSTEM SERVICE EVENTs, such as help requests, trouble reports, maintenance events, and outages. It should be noted that the Service Management model is not intended to serve as the data model for a comprehensive help center system or system-monitoring tool. Rather, it supports service-related analysis and reporting in connection with other aspects of the IT portfolio. The MME complements the enterprise's operational tools and applications, and supports the management of service at a portfolio level. Much of the data in the Service Management subject area of the MME may in fact be imported from such operational tools.

Expected levels of system service (hours of availability, response times) are negotiated between system service providers and key representatives of system users. These commitments are formalized and recorded in the SERVICE LEVEL AGREEMENT and its detailed SERVICE LEVEL OBJECTIVEs. The SERVICE LEVEL AGREEMENT has a **name, description,** and specification of its **effective date**. More importantly, its optional relationships specify the **system, software, environment, hardware, data package, network,** or **organization** for which the SERVICE LEVEL AGREEMENT is in effect. Measurable targets are specified in SERVICE LEVEL OBJECTIVE, usually by **service level objective type** such as System Availability, Transaction Response Time, and Throughput. These objectives have **descriptions** and are explicitly detailed for certain days of the week (**service level day week name**) and times of day (**service level time**). For example, the committed availability of a given system for online transaction processing may be from 6 A.M. to 8 P.M. Monday to Friday. Any expected quantifiable metrics (for example, throughput in transactions per minute or system response time in minutes or seconds) are specified in **required quantity**, qualified by **required quantity unit of measure**, or in **required percentage**. For example, for Monday to Friday availability, the **required percentage** may be 99.5 precent of the time, the **required quantity** "2," and the **required quantity unit of measure** "maximum outages per week."

For comparison to SERVICE LEVEL OBJECTIVE, actual service levels should be measured and recorded in SERVICE LEVEL MEASUREMENT, which has an identifying **service level measurement date** and twin metrics of **service level measurement quantity** and **percentage**, tracked with the measures specified in SERVICE LEVEL OBJECTIVE.

Events occur that may affect the expected levels of system service specified in the SERVICE LEVEL AGREEMENT. Such a SYSTEM SERVICE EVENT may be a help request, trouble report, maintenance event, or system outage. It may involve a DEPLOYED SOFTWARE MODULE, a DATA PACKAGE, a HARDWARE UNIT, a NETWORK, or a combination of such components. SYSTEM SERVICE EVENT has optional relationships with all these entities, thereby identifying the parts of the IT portfolio involved in the event. DATA PACKAGE and SOFTWARE MODULE are recorded specifically to a particular OPERATING ENVIRONMENT. In addition to specifying what deployed software module (**software id, environment id, hardware id**), **data package**, **network**, and **hardware unit** are involved in the SYSTEM SERVICE EVENT, the event is captured by date-time (**service event date**), reported in detail (**description**), and categorized by **type** and **severity**. SYSTEM SERVICE EVENTs may also be aggregated into one or more larger events via the **system service event group**. For example, numerous individual trouble reports may relate to a single outage, which itself is a SYSTEM SERVICE EVENT instance.

Perhaps the most crucial relationship in Service Management is the interplay of human and machine: SYSTEM SERVICE EVENT ROLE. The relationship between SYSTEM SERVICE EVENT and PERSON identifies exactly who (**person id**) reported the event, who logged it, and who did what work on it via the **person event role**. Through this relationship not only are all involved PERSONs recorded, but also their **user IDs** (via SYSTEM USER) and the various items of information about PERSON available in the MME: their location (PERSON LOCATION by **LOCATION TYPE**, and LOCATION details), their contact numbers (PERSON **PHONE NUMBER** by **phone number type**), and their ORGANIZATION within the enterprise. PERSON, PERSON PHONE NUMBER, and ORGANIZATION are reviewed in more detail in Chapter 7. LOCATION supplies basic definition and descriptive information about the site of the PERSON or physical HARDWARE UNIT (**location name** and **description**), optional **facility id** and **location class** (for example, building or floor), the address (**street address**, **mail stop**, and **city, state, country**, and **postal codes**), and site-specific **phone** and **fax numbers**. By this rich reference information, various reports can be drawn regarding which organizations are affected by or involved in which kinds of service events.

Tables 6.1 and 6.2 describe the entities and attributes of the Service Management subject area.

Table 6.1 Service Management Entities

ENTITY NAME	ENTITY DEFINITION
DATA PACKAGE	Refer to Table 4.1 for this entity's definition.
DEPLOYED SOFTWARE MODULE	Deployed Software Module specifies the system Environment(s) of the Software Module and onto which Hardware Unit(s) it is operationally installed.
ENVIRONMENT-DATA PACKAGE	Environment-Data Package specifies a system Environment in which the Data Package is operationally installed.
HARDWARE UNIT	Hardware Unit is a piece of computer or network equipment.
LOCATION	Location is information about a place (physical or logical), associated Persons, computer Hardware, Vendors, and so on.
LOCATION CLASS	Location Class denotes the category or kind of Location, such as Campus, Building, Floor, or Mailstop.
NETWORK	Network is a computer or telephony system by which Hardware Units (and thereby Deployed Software Modules and ultimately System Users) are electronically interconnected and enabled to communicate and interoperate.
OPERATING ENVIRONMENT	Operating Environment is a reference table of standard system Environment names for use by all Systems as needed. Environment is the designated, discrete, and controlled system milieu for Deployed Software Modules (for example, Development, Quality Assurance, Stress Testing, System Acceptance Test, Production).
ORGANIZATION	Refer to Table 7.3 for this entity's definition.
PERSON	Refer to Table 7.3 for this entity's definition.
PERSON LOCATION	Person Location specifies one or more addresses (such as billing or shipping) associated with a Person.
PERSON PHONE NUMBER	Refer to Table 7.3 for this entity's definition.
SERVICE LEVEL AGREEMENT	Service Level Agreement is a formal document that specifies the negotiated and committed levels of performance (such as uptime, response time, throughput) of a System or a system component.
SERVICE LEVEL MEASUREMENT	Service Level Measurement records the quantified results of performing a measurement of actual service levels at a particular point in time to check compliance with Service Level Objectives.

(continued)

Table 6.1 *(continued)*

ENTITY NAME	ENTITY DEFINITION
SERVICE LEVEL OBJECTIVE	Service Level Objective is a quantified performance criterion that has been formalized in a Service Level Agreement.
SOFTWARE MODULE	Software Module is any unit of computer or network programming.
SYSTEM	System is a logical aggregate of Hardware, Software, Data Package, and Network components.
SYSTEM DOCUMENTATION	System Documentation is a file of some type (word-processing document, spreadsheet, PDF file, and so on) that provides pertinent information about a System.
SYSTEM SERVICE EVENT	System Service Event is detailed information about an occurrence or condition of a System, or of one or more system components such as Data Package or Hardware Unit. Examples include: a user request for help or service, a trouble report, or a maintenance event.
SYSTEM SERVICE EVENT ROLE	System Service Event Role specifies the responsibility or function of a Person in connection with a System Service Event (for example, one Person may be the Event Reporter, another the Event Logger, and yet others Telephone Assistance Providers, On-Site Service Provider, or Escalator).
SYSTEM-DATA PACKAGE	System-Data Package specifies the System(s) that access the Data Package (for example, both the Order Management System and the CRM system may access the Customer Database).
SYSTEM-ENVIRONMENT	System-Environment specifies an operating Environment (for example, Development, Test, Production) in which a given System is deployed.
SYSTEM-HARDWARE	System-Hardware specifies the operation of a System on one or more Hardware Units, and the operation of one or more Systems on a given Hardware Unit.
SYSTEM-NETWORK CONNECTION	System-Network Connection specifies the attachment of the System to one or more Networks, and the attachment of one or more Systems to a given Network.
SYSTEM-USER	System-User specifies the System-specific, Environment-specific login ID for a Person.

Table 6.2 Service Management Attributes

ENTITY NAME	ATTRIBUTE NAME	ATTRIBUTE DEFINITION
DEPLOYED SOFTWARE MODULE	**environment id**	**Environment id** specifies the Environment in which a Software Module has been deployed. An **environment id** is a system-generated, nonintelligent designator that uniquely specifies the Environment. An Environment is the designated, discrete, and controlled system milieu for Deployed Software Modules and Data Packages.
	hardware unit id	**Hardware unit id** specifies a Hardware Unit onto which a Software Module has been deployed in a particular Environment. A **hardware unit id** is a system-generated, nonintelligent designator that uniquely specifies the Hardware Unit. A Hardware Unit is a piece of computer or network equipment.
	installation directory name	**Installation directory name** is the root file directory in which the Deployed Software Module's program files were installed.
	installation user id	**Installation user id** is the system user id or username used to load and configure the software.
	software id	**Software id** specifies a Software Module that has been deployed in a particular Environment on a particular Hardware Unit. A **software id** is a system-generated, nonintelligent designator that uniquely specifies the Software Module. A Software Module is a unit of computer or network programming.
	software url	**Software url** is the Internet or intranet URL for the Deployed Software Module.
ENVIRONMENT- DATA PACKAGE	**data package id**	**Data package id** specifies a Data Package that is deployed in an Environment.

(continued)

Table 6.2   *(continued)*

ENTITY NAME	ATTRIBUTE NAME	ATTRIBUTE DEFINITION
	environment id	**Environment id** specifies an Environment associated with a Data Package. An **environment id** is a system-generated, nonintelligent designator that uniquely specifies the Environment. An Environment is the designated, discrete, and controlled system milieu for Deployed Software Modules and Data Packages.
HARDWARE UNIT	accounting asset id	**Accounting asset id** is the property tag number assigned by the enterprise's asset management function. The parent table for this identifier is in an operational system of the enterprise and is not shown in the MME meta model.
	hardware acquisition date	**Hardware acquisition date** denotes when the Hardware Unit was purchased or leased.
	hardware annual fee amount	**Hardware annual fee amount** is the yearly lease or maintenance amount due the Vendor of the Hardware Unit.
	hardware domain name	**Hardware domain name** is a designation of the Hardware Unit that uniquely identifies one or more IP addresses on the enterprise network. For example: a production Websphere server may be named WS001PROD.ACME.COM.
	hardware domain type name	**Hardware domain type name** denotes if the Hardware Unit is virtual or physical.
	hardware group id	**Hardware group id** denotes the **hardware id** of the larger Hardware Unit that encompasses the Hardware Unit in this record (for example, the Hardware Unit in this record may be "Disk Array 8," which may be a more specific Hardware Unit within the larger Hardware Unit of "Server Complex 20." Both Hardware Units would be in the Hardware Unit table. The **hardware unit id** of the latter would be found in the **hardware group id** (that is, parent Hardware Unit) of the former.

Table 6.2   *(continued)*

ENTITY NAME	ATTRIBUTE NAME	ATTRIBUTE DEFINITION
	hardware installation date	**Hardware installation date** denotes when the Hardware Unit was set up, configured, and made operational.
	hardware retirement date	**Hardware retirement date** denotes when the Hardware Unit was deactivated from use.
	hardware type code	**Hardware type code** denotes the kind of Hardware Unit (for example, Server, Storage, Network, Peripheral).
	hardware unit id	**Hardware unit id** is a system-generated, nonintelligent designator that uniquely specifies the Hardware Unit. A Hardware Unit is a piece of computer or network equipment.
	hardware vendor model code	**Hardware vendor model code** is the model number or model designation from the Vendor that sells the Hardware Unit.
	hardware vendor serial id	**Hardware vendor serial id** is the unique identifier or serial number of a Hardware Unit assigned by the Vendor.
	location id	**Location id** specifies the Location of the Hardware Unit. A **location id** is a system-generated, nonintelligent designator that uniquely specifies the Location. A Location is information about a place associated to Persons, computer Hardware, Vendors, and so on.
	memory capacity gb quantity	**Memory capacity gb** (gigabytes) quantity is the quantity of random access memory (RAM) contained in the Hardware Unit.

(continued)

Table 6.2 *(continued)*

ENTITY NAME	ATTRIBUTE NAME	ATTRIBUTE DEFINITION
	technology maturity code	**Technology maturity code** specifies the Technology Maturity of the Hardware Unit. **Technology maturity code** is a mnemonic designator that uniquely specifies the industry status of a given piece of Software or Hardware technology in terms of how developed it is for broad and robust commercial application, for use in determining its risk and appropriateness for use by the enterprise. Values include: E = Evolving, S = Stable, A = Aging, O = Obsolete/Unsupported. Technology Maturity designates the industry status of a given piece of Software or Hardware technology in terms of how developed it is for broad and robust commercial application, for use in determining its risk and appropriateness for use by the enterprise.
	vendor id	**Vendor id** identifies the Vendor of the HARDWARE UNIT. A **vendor id** is a system-generated, nonintelligent designator that uniquely specifies a supplier of the goods or services to the enterprise.
LOCATION	**location city name**	**Location city name** designates the city (or post office) of a domestic or international site or address.
	location class code	**Location class code** is a mnemonic designator that uniquely specifies the Location Class. A Location Class denotes the category or kind of Location, such as Campus, Building, Floor, or Mailstop.
	location country code	**Location country code** designates the standard two- or three-character ISO code for the nation of the Location. The code table for this code is assumed to be available in the enterprise and is not shown in the MME meta model.
	location description	**Location description** is definition information about the Location.

Table 6.2 *(continued)*

ENTITY NAME	ATTRIBUTE NAME	ATTRIBUTE DEFINITION
	location facility id	**Location facility id** is the building or site identifier assigned by the enterprise's facilities management function. The parent table for this identifier is in an operational system of the enterprise and is not shown in the MME meta model.
	location fax number	**Location fax number** specifies the main fax number (domestic or international) for the Location.
	location group id	**Location group id** denotes the **location id** of the Location that encompasses the Location in this record (for example, the Location in this record may be "Building 8"), which may be a more specific Location within the larger Location of "Omaha Campus." Both Locations would be in the Location table. The **location id** of the latter would be found in the **location group id** (that is, parent Location) of the former.
	location id	**Location id** is a system-generated, nonintelligent designator that uniquely specifies the Location. A Location is information about a place associated with Persons, computer Hardware, Vendors, and so on.
	location mail stop code	**Location mail stop code** is the number or code of a unit or mail stop within the street address.
	location name	**Location name** is the alphanumeric descriptive term specific for a specific Location. A Location is information about a place associated with Persons, computer Hardware, Vendors, and so on.
	location phone number	**Location phone number** specifies the main telephone number (domestic or international) for the Location.
	location postal code	**Location postal code** designates the standard U.S. postal code (that is, zip code) or international postal code of a site or address.

(continued)

Table 6.2 *(continued)*

ENTITY NAME	ATTRIBUTE NAME	ATTRIBUTE DEFINITION
	location state code	**Location state code** designates the uniform U.S. postal code of a U.S. state or the postal code of a Canadian province of a Location. The code table for this code is assumed to be available in the enterprise and is not shown in the MME meta model.
	location street address	**Location street address** is the Street Number and Street Name (or Post Office Box) of a domestic or international site or address.
LOCATION CLASS	**location class code**	**Location class code** is a mnemonic designator that uniquely specifies the Location Class. Location Class denotes the category or kind of Location, such as Campus, Building, Floor, Mailstop, and so on.
	location class name	**Location class name** is the alphanumeric descriptive term specific for the Location Class. Location Class denotes the category or kind of Location, such as Campus, Building, Floor, Mailstop, and so on.
NETWORK	**network comment text**	**Network comment text** is free-form, supplemental information or remarks about the Network.
	network communication protocol name	**Network communication protocol name** is the designation of the protocol the network carries (for example, TCP/IP).
	network description	**Network description** is definition information about the Network. A Network is a computer or telephony system by which Hardware Units (and thereby Deployed Software Modules and ultimately System Users) are electronically interconnected and enabled to communicate and interoperate.

Table 6.2   *(continued)*

ENTITY NAME	ATTRIBUTE NAME	ATTRIBUTE DEFINITION
	network group id	**Network group id** denotes the **network id** of the Network that encompasses the Network in this record. Both Networks would be in the Network table. The **network id** of the latter would be found in the **network id** (that is, parent) of the former. A **network id** is a system-generated, nonintelligent designator that uniquely specifies the Network.
	network id	**Network id** is a system-generated, nonintelligent designator that uniquely specifies the Network. A Network is a computer or telephony system by which Hardware Units (and thereby Deployed Software Modules and ultimately System Users) are electronically interconnected and enabled to communicate and interoperate.
	network ip address	**Network ip address** is the Internet Protocol locator of this Network (for example, 20.7.34.29).
	network name	**Network name** is the alphanumeric descriptive term specific for the Network. A Network is a computer or telephony system by which Hardware Units (and thereby Deployed Software Modules and ultimately System Users) are electronically interconnected and enabled to communicate and interoperate.
	network segment name	**Network segment name** is the intranet domain to which the Network belongs. An enterprise Network can be broken into many segments for functional and security purposes. For example, an internal network may have segments (certain IP address ranges) dedicated to Internet-facing applications versus internal-only facing applications. Access to mainframe hardware may also be controlled under its own IP segment.
	network url	**Network url** is the internet or intranet URL for the Network.

(continued)

Table 6.2 *(continued)*

ENTITY NAME	ATTRIBUTE NAME	ATTRIBUTE DEFINITION
OPERATING ENVIRONMENT	environment id	**Environment id** is a system-generated, nonintelligent designator that uniquely specifies the Environment. An Environment is the designated, discrete, and controlled system milieu for Deployed Software Modules and Data Packages.
	environment name	**Environment name** is the alphanumeric descriptive term specific to the system Environment for Deployed Software. Typically, it would be something like Development, Quality Assurance, System Acceptance Test, or Production.
PERSON LOCATION	location id	**Location id** specifies a Location associated with a particular Person. A **location id** is a system-generated, nonintelligent designator that uniquely specifies the Location. A Location is information about a place associated with Persons, computer Hardware, Vendors, and so on.
	location type code	**Location type code** is a mnemonic designator that uniquely specifies the Location Type. A Location Type specifies kinds of sites or addresses. For example: Primary Business, Billing, Shipping, Home, and so on.
	person id	**Person id** specifies an individual who has a Location of a particular type.
SERVICE LEVEL AGREEMENT	data package id	**Data package id** uniquely identifies the Data Package.
	environment id	**Environment id** specifies the Environment for which the Service Level Agreement applies. An **environment id** is a system-generated, nonintelligent designator that uniquely specifies the Environment. An Environment is the designated, discrete, and controlled system milieu for Deployed Software Modules and Data Packages.

Table 6.2 *(continued)*

ENTITY NAME	ATTRIBUTE NAME	ATTRIBUTE DEFINITION
	hardware unit id	**Hardware unit id** specifies the Hardware Unit for which the Service Level Agreement applies. A **hardware unit id** is a system-generated, nonintelligent designator that uniquely specifies the Hardware Unit. A Hardware Unit is a piece of computer or network equipment.
	network id	**Network id** specifies the Network for which the Service Level Agreement applies. A **network id** is a system-generated, nonintelligent designator that uniquely specifies the Network. A Network is a computer or telephony system by which Hardware Units (and thereby Deployed Software Modules and ultimately System Users) are electronically interconnected and enabled to communicate and interoperate.
	organization id	**Organization id** specifies the Organization for which the Service Level Agreement applies. **Organization id** is a system-generated, nonintelligent designator that uniquely specifies the Organization.
	service level agreement description	**Service level agreement description** is definition information about the Service Level Agreement. A Service Level Agreement is a formal document that specifies the negotiated and committed levels of performance (such as uptime, response time, throughput, and so on) of a System or a system component.
	service level agreement effective date	**Service level agreement effective date** denotes when the terms of the Service Level Agreement begin to apply.
	service level agreement id	**Service level agreement id** is a system-generated, nonintelligent designator that uniquely specifies the Service Level Agreement. A Service Level Agreement is a formal document that specifies the negotiated and committed levels of performance (such as uptime, response time, throughput, and so on) of a System or a system component.

(continued)

Table 6.2 *(continued)*

ENTITY NAME	ATTRIBUTE NAME	ATTRIBUTE DEFINITION
	service level agreement name	**Service level agreement name** is the alphanumeric descriptive term specific to the Service Level Agreement. A Service Level Agreement is a formal document that specifies the negotiated and committed levels of performance (such as uptime, response time, throughput, and so on) of a System or a system component.
	software id	**Software id** specifies the Software Module for which the Service Level Agreement applies. A software id is a system-generated, nonintelligent designator that uniquely specifies the Software Module. A Software Module is a unit of computer or network programming.
	system id	**System id** specifies the System for which Service Level Agreement applies. **System id** is a system-generated, nonintelligent designator that uniquely specifies the System. System is an aggregate of Hardware, Software, Data Package, and Network components.
	service level agreement id	**Service level agreement id** is a system-generated, nonintelligent designator that uniquely specifies the Service Level Agreement. A Service Level Agreement is a formal document that specifies the negotiated and committed levels of performance (such as uptime, response time, throughput, and so on) of a System or a system component.
	service level measurement date	**Service level measurement date** denotes when the Service Level Measurement was performed.
	service level measurement percentage	**Service level measurement percentage** records the proportion of time that the Service Level Objective was achieved, as specified.
	service level measurement quantity	**Service level measurement quantity** records quantitatively how much of the Service Level Objective was achieved.

Table 6.2   *(continued)*

ENTITY NAME	ATTRIBUTE NAME	ATTRIBUTE DEFINITION
	service level objective id	**Service level objective id** is a system-generated, nonintelligent designator that uniquely specifies the Service Level Objective. A Service Level Objective is a quantified performance criterion that has been formalized in a Service Level Agreement.
SERVICE LEVEL OBJECTIVE	service level agreement id	**Service level agreement id** is a system-generated, nonintelligent designator that uniquely specifies the Service Level Agreement. A Service Level Agreement is a formal document that specifies the negotiated and committed levels of performance (such as uptime, response time, throughput, and so on) of a System or a system component.
	service level day of week name	**Service level day of week name** is/are the day or days of the week for which the Service Level Objective is applicable (for example, Mon to Fri).
	service level objective description	**Service level objective description** is definition information about the Service Level Objective (for example, Class A transaction).
	service level objective id	**Service level objective id** is a system-generated, nonintelligent designator that uniquely specifies the Service Level Objective. A Service Level Objective is a quantified performance criterion that has been formalized in a Service Level Agreement.
	service level objective required percentage	**Service level objective required percentage** denotes the proportion of time that the Service Level Objective is committed to be achieved during the days and times specified.
	service level objective type	**Service level objective type** specifies the kind of Service Level Objective (for example, System Availability, Transaction Response Time, and Throughput).

(continued)

Table 6.2   *(continued)*

ENTITY NAME	ATTRIBUTE NAME	ATTRIBUTE DEFINITION
	service level required quantity	**Service level required quantity** is the expected quantified target of the Service Level Objective. (For example, 30 Seconds, for a response time objective; Seconds are specified in the Service Level Required Quantity Unit of Measure).
	service level required quantity unit of measure name	**Service level required quantity unit of measure name** specifies what the Service Level Required Quantity quantifies (for example: Seconds for a 30-second response time objective).
	service level time	**Service level time** specifies the times of day for which the Service Level Objective is applicable (for example, 0800 to 1700).
SOFTWARE MODULE	software id	**Software id** is a system-generated, nonintelligent designator that uniquely specifies the Software Module. A Software Module is a unit of computer or network programming.
	software module comment text	**Software module comment text** is free-form, supplemental information or remarks about the Software Module.
	software module contact id	**Software module contact id** is a unique identifier for an individual responsible for the software module
	software module description	**Software module description** is definition information about the Software Module. A Software Module is any unit of computer or network programming.
	software module name	**Software module name** is the alphanumeric descriptive term specific for the Software Module. A Software Module is any unit of computer or network programming.
	system id	**System id** specifies the System to which the Software Module belongs. A **system id** is a system-generated, nonintelligent designator that uniquely specifies the System. A System is an aggregate of Hardware, Software, Data Package, and Network components.

Table 6.2   *(continued)*

ENTITY NAME	ATTRIBUTE NAME	ATTRIBUTE DEFINITION
	technology maturity code	**Technology maturity code** specifies the Technology Maturity of the Software Module. **Technology maturity code** is a mnemonic designator that uniquely specifies the Technology Maturity state. Values include: E = Evolving, S = Stable, A = Aging, O = Obsolete/Unsupported. Technology Maturity designates the industry status of a given piece of Software or Hardware technology in terms of how developed it is for broad and robust commercial application, for use in determining its risk and appro-priateness for use by the enterprise.
	vendor software flag	**Vendor software flag** indicator for vendor provided software.
SYSTEM	system comment text	**System comment text** is free-form, supplemental information or remarks about the System.
	system description	**System description** is definitional information about the System. System is an aggregate of Hardware, Software, Data Package, and Network components.
	system id	**System id** is a system-generated, nonintelligent designator that uniquely specifies the System. System is an aggregate of Hardware, Software, Data Package, and Network components.
	system name	**System name** is the alphanumeric descriptive term specific for the System. System is an aggregate of Hardware, Software, Data Package, and Network components.
	system url	**System url** is the Internet or intranet URL for the System.
SYSTEM DOCUMEN-TATION	system document image	**System document image** is a document of some type (word-processing document, spreadsheet, PDF file, and so on) that provides pertinent information about the System. It is stored as a binary object.

(continued)

Table 6.2 *(continued)*

ENTITY NAME	ATTRIBUTE NAME	ATTRIBUTE DEFINITION
	system document name	**System document name** is the descriptive designation of a file supporting or describing an aspect of the System.
	system documentation file location	**System documentation file location** is the location of the System Document on a network file server.
	system documentation url	**System documentation url** is the Internet or intranet address of the System Document.
	system id	**System id** specifies a System for which System Documentation is maintained in the meta data repository. System is an aggregate of Hardware, Software, Data Package, and Network components.
SYSTEM SERVICE EVENT	data package id	**Data package id** specifies a Data Package, if applicable, involved in the Service Event.
	environment id	**Environment id** specifies the Environment involved in the Service Event. An **environment id** is a system-generated, nonintelligent designator that uniquely specifies the Environment. An Environment is the designated, discrete, and controlled system milieu for Deployed Software Modules and Data Packages.
	hardware unit id	**Hardware unit id** specifies a Hardware Unit, if applicable, involved in the Service Event. A **hardware unit id** is a system-generated, nonintelligent designator that uniquely specifies the Hardware Unit. A Hardware Unit is a piece of computer or network equipment.
	network id	**Network id** specifies the Network, if applicable, involved in the Service Event. A **network id** is a system-generated, nonintelligent designator that uniquely specifies the Network.
	service event date	**Service event date** denotes when the Service Event was logged.

Table 6.2 *(continued)*

ENTITY NAME	ATTRIBUTE NAME	ATTRIBUTE DEFINITION
	service event description	**Service event description** is definitional information about the Service Event. A System Service Event is detailed information about an occurrence or condition of a System, or of one or more system components such as a Data Package or Hardware Unit. Examples include: a user request for help or service, or a trouble report, or a maintenance event.
	service event severity code	**Service event severity code** denotes the type and level of business impact of the Service Event (for example, Mission-Critical Outage, Mission-Critical Degradation, Non-Mission-Critical Outage, Non-Mission-Critical Degradation, Unscheduled Maintenance, Scheduled Maintenance, Requested Upgrade, and so on).
	service event type name	**Service event type name** denotes the category of System Service Event (for example, outage report, user help, system maintenance, and so on).
	software id	**Software id** specifies a Software Module, if applicable, involved in the Service Event. A **software id** is a system-generated, nonintelligent designator that uniquely specifies the Software Module. A Software Module is a unit of computer or network programming.
	system service event group id	**System service event group id** denotes the **system service event id** of the System Service Event that encompasses the System Service Event in this record. A **system service event id** is a unique, system-generated, nonintelligent designator that uniquely specifies the Service Event. A System Service Event is detailed information about an occurrence or condition of a System, or of one or more system components such as Data Package or Hardware Unit. Examples include: a user request for help or service, or a trouble report, or a maintenance event.

(continued)

Table 6.2 *(continued)*

ENTITY NAME	ATTRIBUTE NAME	ATTRIBUTE DEFINITION
	system service event id	**System service event id** is a system-generated, nonintelligent designator that uniquely specifies the Service Event. A System Service Event is detailed information about an occurrence or condition of a System, or of one or more system components such as a Data Package or Hardware Unit. Examples include: a user request for help or service, or a trouble report, or a maintenance event.
SYSTEM SERVICE EVENT ROLE	person event comment text	**Person event comment text** is free-form, supplemental information or remarks about the Person Event Role.
	person event role date	**Person event role date** denotes when the Person began particular role in this Service Event.
	person event role name	**Person event role name** is the role the person plays with respect to the System Service Event (for example, Event Reporter, Event Logger, Telephone Assistance Provider, On-Site Service Provider, Escalator, and so on).
	person id	**Person id** specifies an individual who plays a particular role in a particular Service Event.
	system service event id	**System service event id** specifies a Service Event for which a Person has a particular role. A **service event id** is a system-generated, nonintelligent designator that uniquely specifies the Service Event. A System Service Event is **System service event id** specifies a detailed information about an occurrence or condition of a System, or of one or more system components such as a Data Package or Hardware Unit. Examples include: a user request for help or service, or a trouble report, or a maintenance event.
SYSTEM-DATA PACKAGE	data package id	**Data package id** identifies a Data Package associated with a System.

Table 6.2 *(continued)*

ENTITY NAME	ATTRIBUTE NAME	ATTRIBUTE DEFINITION
	system id	**System id** specifies a System associated with a Data Package. A **system id** is a system-generated, nonintelligent designator that uniquely specifies the System. A System is an aggregate of Hardware, Software, Data Package, and Network components.
SYSTEM-ENVIRONMENT	**environment id**	**Environment type id** specifies an Environment that is associated with a System. An **environment id** is a system-generated, nonintelligent designator that uniquely specifies the Environment. An Environment is the designated, discrete, and controlled system milieu for Deployed Software Modules and Data Packages.
	system id	**System id** specifies a System deployed in an Environment. A **system id** is a system-generated, nonintelligent designator that uniquely specifies the System. A System is an aggregate of Hardware, Software, Data Package, and Network components.
SYSTEM-HARDWARE	**hardware unit id**	**Hardware unit id** identifies a Hardware Unit that is associated with a System. A Hardware Unit is a piece of computer or network equipment.
	system id	**System id** identifies a System that is associated with a Hardware Unit. A **system id** is a system-generated, nonintelligent designator that uniquely specifies the System. System is an aggregate of Hardware, Software, Data Package, and Network components.
SYSTEM-NETWORK CONNECTION	**network id**	**Network id** identifies a Network that is associated with a System. A **network id** is a system-generated, nonintelligent designator that uniquely specifies the Network. Network is a computer or telephony system by which Hardware Units (and thereby Deployed Software Modules and ultimately System Users) are electronically interconnected and enabled to communicate and interoperate.)

(continued)

Table 6.2   *(continued)*

ENTITY NAME	ATTRIBUTE NAME	ATTRIBUTE DEFINITION
	system id	**System id** identifies a System that is associated with a Network. A **system id** is a system-generated, nonintelligent designator that uniquely specifies the System. System is an aggregate of Hardware, Software, Data Package, and Network components.
SYSTEM-USER	**environment id**	**Environment type id** specifies an Environment in which a Person is a user of a System. An **environment id** is a system-generated, nonintelligent designator that uniquely specifies the Environment. An Environment is the designated, discrete, and controlled system milieu for Deployed Software Modules.
	person id	**Person id** specifies an individual who is a user of a System in a particular Environment.
	system id	**System id** specifies a System that Person accesses as a user. A **system id** is a system-generated, nonintelligent designator that uniquely specifies the System. A System is an aggregate of Hardware, Software, Data Package, and Network components.
	system user id	**System user id** is the username or login ID of the person on this particular System.
	user authentication store name	**User authentication store name** denotes which entitlement store the user is authenticated against. Examples include: LDAP, NT, and ADSI.

Let us now take a closer look at the Software Management subject area.

Software Management

The Software Management portion of the IT Portfolio Management meta model describes the computer programs of the enterprise and their relationships to each other, data, and other system components. The data model for Software Management is shown in Figure 6.3. The heart of the model is, of course, SOFTWARE MODULE. A SOFTWARE MODULE has a **name, description,** and optional **comment text**. Documentation for a SOFTWARE MODULE, such as requirements or design documents or pseudo-code, is contained in SOFT-WARE DOCUMENTATION in the form of binary objects within **software document image,** or a pointer to a **file location** on the local area network or a **software document url** on an intranet. Another important item of information associated with a SOFTWARE MODULE is a **contact** person, generally a maintenance programmer or other technician who may be contacted in case of question or difficulty. Software is also classified according to the maturity of its technology (for example, Evolving, Stable, Aging, and Obsolete/Unsupported) through its **technology maturity code**, a reference to the TECHNOLOGY MATURITY entity. TECHNOLOGY MATURITY is simply a reference table, providing a **description** for the **technology maturity code**.

A SOFTWARE MODULE is deployed on a HARDWARE UNIT in an ENVIRONMENT and thereby designated as a DEPLOYED SOFTWARE MODULE (**software**, **hardware**, and **environment ids**). Because a SOFTWARE MODULE can be deployed in multiple ENVIRONMENTs and on multiple HARDWARE UNITs, one SOFTWARE MODULE can have multiple instances of DEPLOYED SOFTWARE MODULE. Additional characteristics of a DEPLOYED SOFT-WARE MODULE include information specific to loading and configuring the software—an **installation user id** and a file **directory name,** as well as the option of a specific **software url**, which may vary depending on where (environment and hardware) the software is deployed.

A SOFTWARE MODULE can have a programmatic relationship with other SOFTWARE MODULEs, depicted in SOFTWARE MODULE USAGE. Two SOFTWARE MODULEs are specified in SOFTWARE MODULE USAGE: a **using software id** and a **used software id**. SOFTWARE MODULE USAGE defines this M:M relationship in terms of one program *using* another in a direct call, a messaging interaction, or the like, denoted in **software use mode**. An identical construct exists at the DEPLOYED SOFTWARE MODULE level, this time including the identifying information of **environment id** and the **hardware ids** of the using and used SOFTWARE MODULEs.

A SOFTWARE MODULE may be either custom-developed internally in the enterprise or purchased as commercial off-the-shelf (COTS) software supplied by a VENDOR. COTS software is described in VENDOR SOFTWARE UNIT, a subtype of SOFTWARE MODULE. SOFTWARE MODULE contains a **vendor software flag** to indicate if it is further described in VENDOR SOFTWARE UNIT. The enterprise generally maintains the same information on acquired COTS software as it does on internally developed software, but additionally captures other details applicable only to acquired software products, recorded in VENDOR SOFTWARE UNIT. Of course, the supplier of the software must be identified by a **vendor id**, which points to the VENDOR table.

VENDOR maintains basic information about the supplier, such as **name** and **description**, plus **contract status** (for example, Pending, Complete, Terminated) and **dun bradstreet reference number**, useful for linking external information

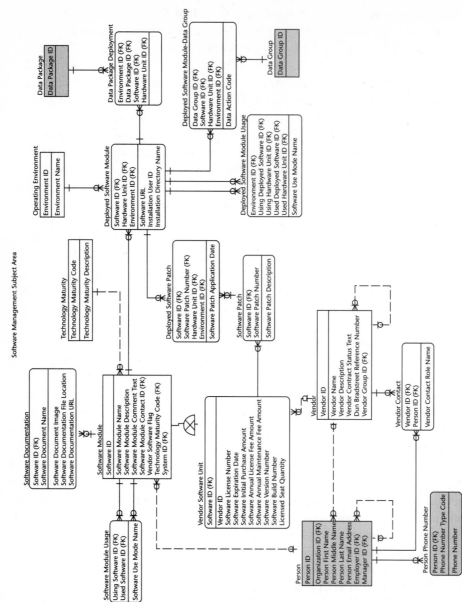

Figure 6.3 Software Management subject area.

about the vendor. Additionally, VENDOR—like HARDWARE UNIT, NETWORK, and LOCATION described in the previous section on Systems Portfolio Management—has a recursive relationship that supports grouping multiple vendor units into a single, higher-order VENDOR (identified with a **vendor group id**).

The VENDOR SOFTWARE UNIT also specifies the **software version** and **build numbers**, and various items of information about the license and maintenance terms, including the **license number** and **expiration date**, the number of **seats licensed**, and three key cost figures: **initial purchase**, **annual license**, and **annual maintenance amounts**. Vendor software may also require the application of a SOFTWARE PATCH, tracked as a dependent entity of VENDOR SOFTWARE UNIT. A SOFTWARE PATCH is identified by the **software patch number** or identifier provided by the vendor, and what the patch is expected to address is defined in a detailed **description**. The software patch is applied to deployed instances of software. This fact is recorded in DEPLOYED SOFTWARE PATCH, a relationship with DEPLOYED SOFTWARE MODULE, and specifies the **application date** that the patch was installed.

Contacts for software are maintained in two ways in this model, both via relationships to PERSON (described in more detail in Chapter 7). As you have seen already, the SOFTWARE MODULE itself may have a single designated contact (typically a maintenance programmer). Alternatively, the VENDOR of the VENDOR SOFTWARE UNIT may have assigned various VENDOR-CONTACTs, ranging from account managers to support engineers. Through these two relationships the contact PERSONs for the software module are identified. And through the PERSONs' relationships, additional information about these contacts is available as well: their locations (PERSON LOCATION by **LOCATION TYPE**, and LOCATION details), their contact numbers (PERSON **PHONE NUMBER** by **phone number type**), and their ORGANIZATION within the enterprise. PERSON, PERSON PHONE NUMBER, and ORGANIZATION are reviewed in more detail in Chapter 7. See the preceding *Service Management* section of this chapter for a more detailed description of LOCATION.

Finally, the Software Management model also specifies the relationship of DEPLOYED SOFTWARE MODULE to data objects, specifically DATA GROUPs (tables, flat file records, and the like) and DATA PACKAGEs as a whole (databases and files). A DEPLOYED SOFTWARE MODULE may access more than one database or file (DATA PACKAGE), as reflected in the simple M:M relationship of DATA PACKAGE DEPLOYMENT. Similarly, DEPLOYED SOFTWARE MODULE has an associative entity with DATA GROUP, specifically DEPLOYED SOFTWARE MODULE-DATA GROUP, which includes a **data action code**. The **data action code** specifies the create, retrieve, update, and delete (CRUD) functions that the program may perform on the table or record (DATA GROUP), enabling an inventory of CRUD matrix details at the physical level. DATA GROUP and DATA PACKAGE are explored in detail in Chapter 4.

Tables 6.3 and 6.4 describe the entities and attributes of the Software Management subject area.

Table 6.3 Software Management Entities

ENTITY NAME	ENTITY DEFINITION
DATA PACKAGE	Refer to Table 4.1 for this entity's definition.
DATA PACKAGE DEPLOYMENT	Data Package Deployment specifies the use of a Data Package by a Deployed Software Module. For example, a Customer Management Database is used by a CRM application module in the Production environment in Server Complex Beta.
DEPLOYED SOFTWARE MODULE	Refer to the Service Management section of this chapter for entity definition.
DEPLOYED SOFTWARE MODULE USAGE	Deployed Software Module Usage specifies the interrelationship of two Deployed Software Modules, one that uses the other in some fashion (specified in Software Use Mode).
DEPLOYED SOFTWARE MODULE-DATA GROUP	Deployed Software Module-Data Group specifies a Deployed Software Module that can use a given Data Group.
DEPLOYED SOFTWARE PATCH	Deployed Software Patch specifies a Software Patch applied to a given Deployed Software Module.
OPERATING ENVIRONMENT	Refer to the Service Management section of this chapter for entity definition.
PERSON	Refer to Table 7.3 for this entity's definition.
PERSON PHONE NUMBER	Refer to Table 7.3 for this entity's definition.
SOFTWARE DOCUMENTATION	Software Documentation is a file of some type (word-processing document, spreadsheet, PDF file, and so on) that provides pertinent information about the Software.
SOFTWARE MODULE	Refer to the "Service Management" section of this chapter for this entity's definition.
SOFTWARE MODULE USAGE	Software Module Usage specifies the interrelationship of two Software Modules, one that uses the other in some fashion (specified in Software Use Mode).
SOFTWARE PATCH	Software Patch is a modification applied to the Software Module, usually to correct a known bug.
TECHNOLOGY MATURITY	Technology Maturity designates the industry status of a given piece of Software or Hardware technology in terms of how developed it is for broad and robust commercial application, for use in determining its risk and appropriateness for use by the enterprise (for example, Evolving, Stable, Aging, and Obsolete/Unsupported).

Table 6.3 *(continued)*

ENTITY NAME	ENTITY DEFINITION
VENDOR	A Vendor is any company that provides goods or services to the enterprise.
VENDOR CONTACT	Vendor Contact specifies an individual (Person) who serves in a given capacity or position (Role) for a given Vendor.
VENDOR SOFTWARE UNIT	Vendor Software Unit is a specific type of Software Module with characteristics detailing its configuration and acquisition from a Vendor.

Table 6.4 Software Management Attributes

ENTITY NAME	ATTRIBUTE NAME	ATTRIBUTE DEFINITION
DATA PACKAGE DEPLOYMENT	**data package id**	**Data package id** specifies a Data Package accessed by a particular Deployed Software Module.
	environment id	**Environment type id** specifies the Environment in which a particular Data Package is deployed. An **environment id** is a system-generated, nonintelligent designator that uniquely specifies the Environment. An Environment is the designated, discrete, and controlled system milieu for Deployed Software Modules and Data Packages.
	hardware unit id	**Hardware unit id** specifies a Hardware Unit of a Deployed Software Module that accesses a particular Data Package. A **hardware unit id** is a system-generated, nonintelligent designator that uniquely specifies the Hardware Unit. A Hardware Unit is a piece of computer or network equipment.
	software id	**Software id** specifies a Software Module that has been deployed and accesses a particular Data Package. A **software id** is a system-generated, nonintelligent designator that uniquely specifies the Software Module. A Software Module is a unit of computer or network programming.

(continued)

Table 6.4 *(continued)*

ENTITY NAME	ATTRIBUTE NAME	ATTRIBUTE DEFINITION
DEPLOYED SOFTWARE MODULE USAGE	environment id	**Environment id** specifies the Environment in which the Using and Used Software Modules have been deployed. An **environment id** is a system-generated, nonintelligent designator that uniquely specifies the Environment. An Environment is the designated, discrete, and controlled system milieu for Deployed Software Modules and Data Packages.
	software use mode name	**Software use mode name** specifies the using relationship of one Deployed Software Module over another. For example: Dynamic Call.
	used deployed software id	**Used deployed software id** specifies the Deployed Software Module used by another. A **software id** is a system-generated, nonintelligent designator that uniquely specifies the Software Module. A Software Module is a unit of computer or network programming.
	used hardware unit id	**Used hardware unit id** specifies the Hardware Unit on which the Used Deployed Software Module resides. A **hardware unit id** is a system-generated, nonintelligent designator that uniquely specifies the Hardware Unit. A Hardware Unit is a piece of computer or network equipment.
	using deployed software id	**Using deployed software id** specifies the Deployed Software Module that uses the other. A **software id** is a system-generated, nonintelligent designator that uniquely specifies the Software Module. A Software Module is a unit of computer or network programming.
	using hardware unit id	**Using hardware unit id** specifies the Hardware Unit on which the Using Deployed Software Module resides. A **hardware unit id** is a system-generated, nonintelligent designator that uniquely specifies the Hardware Unit. A Hardware Unit is a piece of computer or network equipment.

Table 6.4   *(continued)*

ENTITY NAME	ATTRIBUTE NAME	ATTRIBUTE DEFINITION
DEPLOYED SOFTWARE MODULE-DATA GROUP	data action code	**Data action code** specifies the procedural or declarative action of the Software Module on the Data Group (or individual Data Elements within the Data Group) (for example, R for Read (retrieval) only, U for Update, CUD for Create/Update/Delete, and so on).
	data group id	**Data group id** specifies a Data Group that is accessed by a Deployed Software Module.
	environment id	**Environment id** specifies an Environment in which a Deployed Software Module accesses a particular Data Group. An **environment id** is a system-generated, nonintelligent designator that uniquely specifies the Environment. An Environment is the designated, discrete, and controlled system milieu for Deployed Software Modules and Data Packages.
	hardware unit id	**Hardware unit id** specifies a Hardware Unit onto which a Software Module has been deployed and accesses a particular Data Group. A **hardware unit id** is a system-generated, nonintelligent designator that uniquely specifies the Hardware Unit. A Hardware Unit is a piece of computer or network equipment.
	software id	**Software id** specifies a Software Module that has been deployed in a particular Environment and accesses a particular Data Group. **Software id** is a system-generated, nonintelligent designator that uniquely specifies the Software Module. Software Module is any unit of computer or network programming.
DEPLOYED SOFTWARE PATCH	environment id	**Environment id** specifies an Environment in which a Software Module has been deployed. An **environment id** is a system-generated, nonintelligent designator that uniquely specifies the Environment. An Environment is the designated, discrete, and controlled system milieu for Deployed Software Modules and Data Packages.

(continued)

Table 6.4 *(continued)*

ENTITY NAME	ATTRIBUTE NAME	ATTRIBUTE DEFINITION
	hardware unit id	**Hardware unit id** specifies a Hardware Unit on which a Software Module has been deployed. A **hardware unit id** is a system-generated, nonintelligent designator that uniquely specifies the Hardware Unit. A Hardware Unit is a piece of computer or network equipment.
	software id	**Software id** specifies a Software Module for which a particular Software Patch has been applied in a particular Environment. A **software id** is a system-generated, nonintelligent designator that uniquely specifies the Software Module. A Software Module is a unit of computer or network programming.
	software patch application date	**Software patch application date** denotes when the software patch was applied to the Deployed Software Module. A Software Patch is a modification applied to the Software Module, usually to correct a known bug.
	software patch number	**Software patch number** specifies a Software Patch that has been applied to a particular Deployed Software Module. A Software Patch is a modification applied to the Software Module, usually to correct a known bug.
SOFTWARE DOCUMEN-TATION	**software document image**	**Software document image** is a document of some type (word-processing document, spreadsheet, PDF file, and so on) that provides pertinent information about the Software Module. It is stored as a binary object.
	software document name	**Software Document Name** is the descriptive designation of a file supporting or describing an aspect of the Software.
	software documentation file location	**Software documentation file location** is the location of the Software Document on a network file server.
	software documentation url	**Software documentation url** is the Internet or intranet address of the Software Document.

Table 6.4   *(continued)*

ENTITY NAME	ATTRIBUTE NAME	ATTRIBUTE DEFINITION
	software id	**Software id** specifies a Software Module for which Software Documentation is maintained in the meta data repository. A **software id** is a system-generated, nonintelligent designator that uniquely specifies the Software Module. A Software Module is a unit of computer or network programming.
SOFTWARE MODULE USAGE	software use mode name	**Software use mode** specifies the using relationship of one Software Module over another (for example, Dynamic Call).
	used software id	**Used software id** specifies the Software Module used by another. A **software id** is a system-generated, nonintelligent designator that uniquely specifies the Software Module. A Software Module is any unit of computer or network programming.
	using software id	**Using software id** specifies the Software Module that uses another. A **software id** is a system-generated, nonintelligent designator that uniquely specifies the Software Module. A Software Module is a unit of computer or network programming.
SOFTWARE PATCH	software id	**Software id** specifies a Software Module for which a Software Patch exists. A **software id** is a system-generated, nonintelligent designator that uniquely specifies the Software Module. A Software Module is any unit of computer or network programming.
	software patch description	**Software patch description** is definitional information about the Software Patch.
	software patch number	**Software patch number** is the unique identifier or code or number denoting the Software Patch. A Software Patch is a modification applied to the Software Module, usually to correct a known bug.
TECHNOLOGY MATURITY	technology maturity code	**Technology maturity code** is a mnemonic designator that uniquely specifies the Technology Maturity state. Values include: E = Evolving, S = Stable, A = Aging, O = Obsolete/Unsupported.

(continued)

Table 6.4   *(continued)*

ENTITY NAME	ATTRIBUTE NAME	ATTRIBUTE DEFINITION
	technology maturity description	**Technology maturity description** is definition information about the Technology Maturity state.
VENDOR	**dun bradstreet reference number**	**Dun Bradstreet reference number** is the identifier of the Vendor within the Dun and Bradstreet commercial information base.
	vendor contract status text	**Vendor Contract Status Text** specifies the current standing of enterprise's binding legal agreement with the Vendor. Examples include: Pending, Complete, Terminated, and so on.
	vendor description	**Vendor description** is definition information about the Vendor. A Vendor is any company that provides goods or services to the enterprise.
	vendor group id	**Vendor group id** denotes the **vendor id** of the Vendor that is the parent of the Vendor in this record. Both Vendors would be in the Vendor table. A **vendor id** is a system-generated, nonintelligent designator that uniquely specifies a Vendor. A Vendor is any company that provides goods or services to the enterprise.
	vendor id	**Vendor id** is a system-generated, nonintelligent designator that uniquely specifies a Vendor. A Vendor is any company that provides goods or services to the enterprise.
	vendor name	**Vendor name** is the alphanumeric descriptive term specific to the Vendor. A Vendor is any company that provides goods or services to the enterprise. Typically, this will be the company's legal name used in contracts (for example, Acme Software, Inc.).
VENDOR CONTACT	**person id**	**Person id** specifies an individual who is a type of contact for a Vendor.
	vendor contact role name	**Vendor contact role name** provides contextual information about the Person's responsibilities in connection with the Vendor. For example, the Person may have a Vendor Contact Role Name of *Account Manager*.

Table 6.4   *(cointinued)*

ENTITY NAME	ATTRIBUTE NAME	ATTRIBUTE DEFINITION
	vendor id	**Vendor id** specifies a Vendor for which a Person is a type of contact. A **vendor id** is a system-generated, nonintelligent designator that uniquely specifies a Vendor. A Vendor is any company that provides goods or services to the enterprise.
VENDOR SOFTWARE UNIT	**licensed seat quantity**	**Licensed seat quantity** is the number of authorized users (usually concurrent users) of the software permitted under the license.
	software annual license fee amount	**Software annual license fee amount** is the yearly license amount due the Vendor of the Software.
	software annual maintenance fee amount	**Software annual maintenance fee amount** is the yearly maintenance amount due the Vendor of the Software.
	software build number	**Software build number** specifies the Vendor's designated physical build of the licensed software. **Software build number** is more specific than Version number.
	software expiration date	**Software expiration date** denotes when the Software license is due to end.
	software id	**Software id** is a system-generated, nonintelligent designator that uniquely specifies the Software Module. A Software Module is a unit of computer or network programming.
	software initial purchase amount	**Software initial purchase amount** is the original acquisition or license amount paid the Vendor for the Software.
	software license number	**Software license number** is the reference identifier of the licensing contract or order with the Vendor for this Software.
	software version number	**Software version number** specifies the Vendor's designated version or release of the licensed software.
	vendor id	**Vendor id** is a system-generated, nonintelligent designator that uniquely specifies a Vendor. A Vendor is any company that provides goods or services to the enterprise.

Let's now take a look at the Hardware and Network Management subject area.

Hardware and Network Management

Hardware and Network Management provides a detailed description of the physical devices and communications links of IT. The data model for Hardware and Network Management is shown in Figure 6.4. The model identifies several different types of HARDWARE UNIT: SERVER, STORAGE, NETWORK, and PERIPHERAL COMPONENTs. Let's examine HARDWARE UNIT itself, and then examine the rest of these hardware types more closely.

Unlike most entities in the MME, a HARDWARE UNIT is a tangible thing and must be clearly identifiable as such. Usually, such identification consists of a **vendor id**, a **model code**, and identifying **serial id** (that is, a serial number) from the manufacturer, plus an **asset management id** assigned by the enterprise and generally bar-coded onto the device. See the previous section on Software Management for a more detailed description of VENDOR. Because a HARDWARE UNIT is ultimately a physical thing, it resides in a particular LOCATION within the enterprise, specified by the **location id**. See the *Service Management* section of this chapter for a more detailed description of LOCATION and LOCATION TYPE. Certain calendar dates are vital items of information about the HARDWARE UNIT, specifically when it was purchased or leased (**acquisition date**), put into service (**installation date**), and decommissioned (**retirement date**). Only one amount field is carried here, the **annual fee amount**, representing yearly lease and maintenance fees that are typically expensed by the IT department. Additional amounts related to the hardware, such as actual hardware purchase costs and depreciation amounts, are typically tracked in capital accounting systems rather than in the Managed Meta Data Environment and are therefore not reflected in this model. In relation to the idea of tracking IT's investment in technology, the hardware is classified according to the overall status of its technology (for example, Evolving, Stable, Aging, or Obsolete/Unsupported) in the industry and the enterprise. Just as we saw with software in the preceding section, this is specified through the hardware's **technology maturity code**, a reference to the TECHNOLOGY MATURITY entity that you saw in the preceding *Software Management* section.

A handful of technical characteristics of the HARDWARE UNIT are also maintained: its **domain name** (representing its IP address on the enterprise network) and **domain type** (indicating if it is a physical or virtual domain), and its **memory capacity** in gigabytes. The latter is included at the level of generic HARDWARE UNIT rather than a specific subtype because, increasingly, all types of hardware, not just servers, can be equipped with RAM used

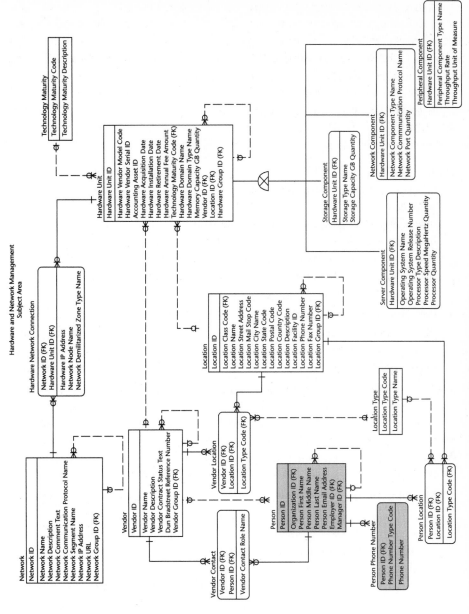

Figure 6.4   Hardware and Network Management Subject Area.

in the performance of their functions. Additionally, a HARDWARE UNIT also has a recursive relationship to itself, supporting a hierarchy of HARDWARE UNITs, denoted via a **hardware group id**. For example, several CPUs (SERVER COMPONENTs) and disk arrays (STORAGE COMPONENTs) can be identified as an aggregate complex. Additionally, an individual SERVER COMPONENT may be subdivided into multiple virtual server domains, each with its own identity as a HARDWARE UNIT.

All subtypes of HARDWARE UNIT inherit the common attributes we have just described. Each subtype also has specialized characteristics:

- The SERVER COMPONENT subtype of HARDWARE UNIT describes computer processing units, ranging from workstations to mainframe computers. A SERVER COMPONENT is further characterized by its **operating system** (**name** and **release number**), and its computing capacity. Computing capacity is specified by **processor type** (for example, x86) and quantified in terms of **processor speed** in megahertz and **processor quantity**, that is, the number of processors contained in the unit.

- The STORAGE COMPONENT subtype of HARDWARE UNIT describes data storage hardware. **Storage type** denotes what kind of device it is, such as a direct access storage device (DASD), optical disk drive, magnetic tape device, a related controller, or the like. **Storage capacity** quantifies, in gigabytes, how much data the device can hold.

- The NETWORK COMPONENT subtype of HARDWARE UNIT describes specialized communications processing units. **Network component type** specifies what kind of device it is: network switch, router, hub, bridge, firewall, encryption accelerator, and so on. It is further characterized by **network protocol** and the number of physical networking interfaces available on it (**port quantity**).

- The PERIPHERAL COMPONENT subtype of HARDWARE UNIT describes all other devices in the computing environment that are not covered by the other subtypes. **Peripheral component type** specifies whether it is a printer, fax machine, scanner, and so on. Most peripheral hardware processes data or documents at a certain rate, specified by **throughput rate**, qualified by **throughput unit of measure** (for example, pages per minute or characters per second). These devices are typically connected either to individual SERVER COMPONENTs directly or to a NETWORK (via the HARDWARE NETWORK CONNECTION), making them accessible to many other HARDWARE UNITs.

HARDWARE NETWORK CONNECTION depicts the M:M relationship between HARDWARE UNIT and NETWORK, reflecting that a HARDWARE UNIT can connect to more than one NETWORK, and conversely more than one NETWORK can connect to a given HARDWARE UNIT. This entity characterizes the network-specific aspects of a HARDWARE UNIT: its **hardware ip address**, its **node name** on the network, and what class of **network demilitarized zone** the hardware resides in (that is, Router, Web Server, Application, Database, Internal, and so on).

NETWORK itself bears a variety of information items independent of it hardware components. In addition to its **name**, **description**, and **comment text**, NETWORK contains information about the **network protocol** it runs on (for example, TCP/IP) and its various network addresses: **segment name** (intranet domain), **ip address** (internet location), and **url** (uniform resource locator on the intranet or the Internet).

Tables 6.5 and 6.6 describe the entities and attributes of the Hardware and Network Management subject area.

Table 6.5 Hardware and Network Management Entities

ENTITY NAME	ENTITY DEFINITION
HARDWARE NETWORK CONNECTION	Hardware Network Connection specifies the operational link between a Network and a given Hardware Unit.
HARDWARE UNIT	Refer to the *Service Management* section of this chapter for this entity's definition.
LOCATION	Refer to the *Service Management* section of this chapter for this entity's definition.
LOCATION TYPE	Location Type specifies kinds of sites or addresses. Examples include: Primary Business, Billing, Shipping, and Home.
NETWORK	Refer to the *Service Management* section of this chapter for this entity's definition.
NETWORK COMPONENT	Network Component is a type of Hardware Unit that is used to process digital or analog signal for the purpose of switching or routing electronic transmissions (for example: bridges, routers, firewalls, switches, or encryption accelerators).
PERIPHERAL COMPONENT	Peripheral Component is a type Hardware Unit, such as a printer, fax machine, scanner, and so on.
PERSON	Refer to Table 7.3 for this entity's definition.
PERSON LOCATION	Refer to the *Service Management* section of this chapter for this entity's definition.

(continued)

Table 6.5 *(continued)*

ENTITY NAME	ENTITY DEFINITION
PERSON PHONE NUMBER	Refer to Table 7.3 for this entity's definition.
SERVER COMPONENT	Server Component is a type of Hardware Unit that contains general-purpose computer processing chips and is used for executing software.
STORAGE COMPONENT	Storage Component is a type of Hardware Unit that is used primarily for storage and providing input/output (I/O) of the data.
TECHNOLOGY MATURITY	Refer to the *Software Management* section of this chapter for this entity's definition.
VENDOR	Refer to the *Software Management* section of this chapter for this entity's definition.
VENDOR CONTACT	Refer to the *Software Management* section of this chapter for this entity's definition.
VENDOR LOCATION	Vendor Location specifies one or more addresses (billing, shipping, and so on) of a Vendor.

Table 6.6 Hardware and Network Management Attributes

ENTITY NAME	ATTRIBUTE NAME	ATTRIBUTE DEFINITION
HARDWARE NETWORK CONNECTION	hardware ip address	**Hardware ip address** is the Internet Protocol (IP) locator of the Hardware Unit on a specific Network (for example, 20.7.34.29).
	hardware unit id	**Hardware unit id** specifies the Hardware Unit that is connected to a specific Network. A **hardware unit id** is a system-generated, nonintelligent designator that uniquely specifies the Hardware Unit. A Hardware Unit is a piece of computer or network equipment.
	network demilitarized zone type name	**Network demilitarized zone type name** denotes the network demilitarized zone (DMZ) in which the hardware unit resides. A DMZ is a computer host or small network inserted as a "neutral zone" between a company's private network and the outside public network. Values include: Router, Web Server, Application, Database, and Internal.

Table 6.6 *(continued)*

ENTITY NAME	ATTRIBUTE NAME	ATTRIBUTE DEFINITION
	network id	**Network id** specifies a Network to which a Hardware Unit is connected. A **network id** is a system-generated, nonintelligent designator that uniquely specifies the Network. A Network is a computer or telephony system by which Hardware Units (and thereby Deployed Software Modules and ultimately System Users) are electronically interconnected and enabled to communicate and interoperate.
	network node name	**Network node name** is the name a Hardware Unit is designated on a particular Network.
	location type code	**Location type code** is a mnemonic designator that uniquely specifies the Location Type. A Location Type specifies kinds of sites or addresses (for example, Primary Business, Billing, Shipping, Home, and so on).
LOCATION TYPE	location type name	**Location type name** is the alphanumeric descriptive term specific for the Location Type. A Location Type specifies kinds of sites or addresses (for example, Primary Business, Billing, Shipping, Home, and so on).
NETWORK COMPONENT	hardware unit id	**Hardware unit id** is a system-generated, nonintelligent designator that uniquely specifies the Hardware Unit. A Hardware Unit is a piece of computer or network equipment.
	network communication protocol name	**Network communication protocol name** is the designation of the protocol the network carries (for example, TCP/IP).
	network component type name	**Network component type name** denotes the kind of Network component. Examples include: hubs, bridges, routers, firewalls, switches, and encryption accelerators.
	network port quantity	**Network port quantity** is the number of physical networking interfaces supported by the Network Component for the purpose of connecting to one or more Networks or other Hardware Units.

(continued)

Table 6.6 *(continued)*

ENTITY NAME	ATTRIBUTE NAME	ATTRIBUTE DEFINITION
	hardware unit id	**Hardware unit id** is a system-generated, nonintelligent designator that uniquely specifies the Hardware Unit. A Hardware Unit is a piece of computer or network equipment.
PERIPHERAL COMPONENT	**peripheral component type name**	**Peripheral component type name** denotes the kind of Peripheral component. Examples include: printer, fax machine, and scanner.
	throughput rate	**Throughput rate** is the quantity of pages (or other units) that the peripheral is capable of processing in a specified period of time. The Throughput Rate's unit and the time period of measure are specified in the **throughput unit of measure**—for example, characters per second (cps) or pages per minute (ppm).
	throughput unit of measure	**Throughput unit of measure** is the unit and the time period of measure used in **throughput rate**. Examples include: characters per second (cps) or pages per minute (ppm).
SERVER COMPONENT	**hardware unit id**	**Hardware unit id** is a system-generated, nonintelligent designator that uniquely specifies the Hardware Unit. A Hardware Unit is a piece of computer or network equipment.
	operating system name	**Operating system name** is the designation of the computer software used to operate and manage the Hardware Unit. Examples include: Unix, Linux, NT.
	operating system release number	**Operating system release number** specifies the Vendor's designated version of the operating system software for the Hardware Unit.
	processor quantity	**Processor quantity** specifies the number of discrete computing units employed in the Hardware Unit.

Table 6.6   *(continued)*

ENTITY NAME	ATTRIBUTE NAME	ATTRIBUTE DEFINITION
	processor speed megahertz quantity	**Processor speed megahertz quantity** specifies the computing capacity of the processor(s) employed in the Hardware Unit.
	processor type description	**processor type description** specifies the type of discrete computing units employed in the Hardware Unit.
STORAGE COMPONENT	**hardware unit id**	**Hardware unit id** is a system-generated, nonintelligent designator that uniquely specifies the Hardware Unit. A Hardware Unit is a piece of computer or network equipment.
	storage capacity gb quantity	**Storage capacity gb quantity** is the persistent data capacity of the Storage Unit in gigabytes.
	storage type name	**Storage type name** denotes the kind of electronic storage device. Examples include: Direct Access Storage Device (DASD, that is, fixed disk), tape cartridge drive, and CD-ROM drive or juke box.
VENDOR LOCATION	**location id**	**Location id** specifies a Location that is associated with a Vendor. A **location id** is a system-generated, nonintelligent designator that uniquely specifies the Location. A Location is information about a place associated to Persons, computer Hardware, Vendors, and so on.
	location type code	**Location type code** is a mnemonic designator that uniquely specifies the Location Type. A Location Type specifies kinds of sites or addresses. For example: Primary Business, Billing, Shipping, Home, and so on.
	vendor id	**vendor id** specifies a Vendor that is associated with a Location. A **vendor id** is a system-generated, nonintelligent designator that uniquely specifies a Vendor. A Vendor is any company that provides goods or services to the enterprise.

Project Portfolio Management

Project Portfolio Management encompasses the major information objects of IT work initiatives and their resources. The data model for Project Portfolio Management is shown in Figure 6.5. The pivotal entity of the Project Portfolio Management model is, of course, PROJECT itself. It should be noted that this model is not intended to serve as the data model for a comprehensive project management tool. Rather, it supports project-related analysis and reporting in connection with other aspects of the IT portfolio. The MME complements the enterprise's project management tools. Such tools are used operationally at the individual project level, while the MME supports the management of projects at a portfolio level. Much of the data in the Project Portfolio Management subject area of the MME may in fact be imported directly from project management tools.

PROJECT houses basic project-specific information that a project manager would know: **name, description, current [project] phase**, and **status** (for example, Active, Planned, Cancelled). PROJECT also contains four key dates that may be derived or maintained in a project management tool: **estimated** and **actual project start** and **completion dates.** Additional facts to be maintained for a PROJECT are key cost figures: **estimated** and **actual** amounts for four major categories of project expense: **hardware cost, software cost, internal expense**, and **consulting expense amounts**. Four additional facts are derived: **actual** and **estimated duration** (calculated from the actual or estimated dates), an **on-time** (or late) **flag**, and a **within budget** (or over budget) **flag**. These are useful in reporting and statistical analysis. These project facts enable managers to perform robust analysis of the portfolio of IT projects according to various *dimensions* and dimensional attributes such as **current [project] phase, status, system**, and even project resource (such as project manager or DBA) via PROJECT RESOURCE ASSIGNMENT.

A PROJECT can support one or more SYSTEMs, and conversely a SYSTEM may be involved in more than one PROJECT, reflected in the M:M relationship of SYSTEM-PROJECT. As we have seen in other entities in the IT Portfolio data model, PROJECT has a 1:M recursive relationship, reflecting an open-ended hierarchy that allows a single PROJECT (**project group id**) to be explicitly subdivided into several subprojects, each with their own project-specific information. For example, an enterprise data warehousing project may be planned and managed as several releases, each implementing a major subject area of the business, each a project managed in its own right, with overlapping timelines and resources. Supplemental documents or files for a PROJECT, such as a scope document or project charter or a project plan, are contained in PROJECT DOCUMENTATION in the form of binary objects in **project document image,** or a pointer to a **file location** on the local area network or a **project document url** on the intranet.

Besides PROJECT itself, the other pivotal entity of the Project Portfolio Management model is the project resource (PERSON). Fully half the entities in this subject area support the identification of staffing resources—planned or

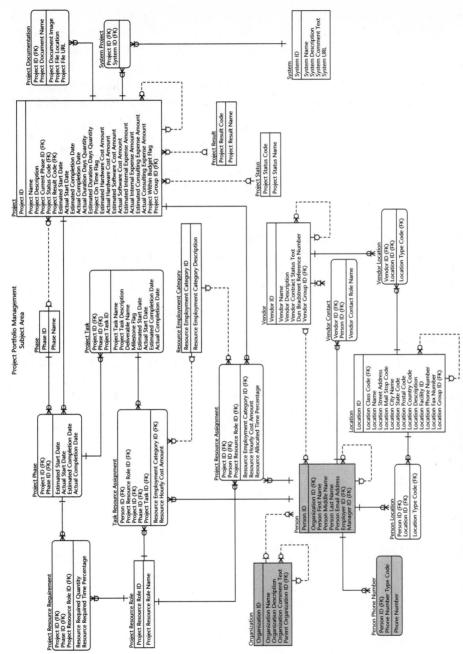

Figure 6.5   Project Portfolio Management subject area.

actual—needed in support of IT projects or their components. These components of PROJECT are sub-PROJECT (that is, a PROJECT that is a subdivision of another PROJECT via **project group id**), PROJECT PHASE, and PROJECT TASK. PROJECTs and sub-PROJECTs can be broken down into one or more standard project phases—for example, Orientation, Feasibility, Design, Development, User Acceptance Test, and Rollout—reflected in PROJECT PHASE, the M:M relationship between PROJECT and PHASE. Like the project itself, a PROJECT PHASE can have **estimated** and **actual start** and **completion dates**, but these are specific to a particular **project id** and **phase id**. PROJECT also has a direct single relationship with PHASE to denote the **current phase** of the project. Prior to assigning actual named PERSONs to a PROJECT, generic resources can be identified within PROJECT RESOURCE REQUIREMENT by project phase (**project id** and **phase id**) and specified as to **required quantity** and **required time percentage** of a particular **project resource role**.

A more granular component of a PROJECT PHASE is the PROJECT TASK (identified by **project** and **phase** plus a distinguishing **task id**). Like a PROJECT PHASE, a PROJECT TASK may have **estimated** and **actual start** and **completion dates**. Additional information of interest for the PROJECT TASK includes a **name** and **description** of the task, an optional **deliverable**, and a **milestone flag** to denote if it is a milestone (with no start dates, only completion dates) or a task with specified duration. It is at the task level that real people (**person id**) are typically assigned to projects in specific roles (**project resource role id**), reflected in the three-way relationship TASK RESOURCE ASSIGNMENT. This assignment is further characterized by the resource's **hourly cost amount** and the resource's **employment category** (for example, Internal FTE, Consultant, or External Contractor) from RESOURCE EMPLOYMENT CATEGORY. A less granular resource assignment may be made for a specific resource (**person id**) at the whole project level (**project id**) reflected in another three-way relationship, PROJECT RESOURCE ASSIGNMENT, with the added specification of **project resource role [id]**. As in the TASK RESOURCE ASSIGNMENT, the assigned resource in PROJECT RESOURCE ASSIGNMENT can be tagged with an **hourly cost amount** and **employment category** in addition to their **required time percentage**.

The entities we have just reviewed reflect the fact that IT projects are inherently people-intensive. For this reason, we include not just skeletal identifiers of the project's human resources, but also detailed information about each resource. Via PERSON's relationships, much additional information about the resources is available: their locations (PERSON LOCATION by **LOCATION TYPE**, and LOCATION details), their contact numbers (PERSON **PHONE NUMBER** by **phone number type**), and their internal ORGANIZATION or external VENDOR details. PERSON, PERSON PHONE NUMBER, and ORGANIZATION are reviewed in more detail in Chapter 7. See the preceding *Service Management* and *Software Management* sections of this chapter for more detailed descriptions of LOCATION and VENDOR, respectively.

Tables 6.7 and 6.8 describe the entities and attributes of the Project Portfolio Management subject area.

Table 6.7   Project Portfolio Management Entities

ENTITY NAME	ENTITY DEFINITION
LOCATION	Refer to the *Service Management* section of this chapter for this entity's definition.
ORGANIZATION	Refer to Table 7.3 for this entity's definition.
PERSON	Refer to Table 7.3 for this entity's definition.
PERSON LOCATION	Refer to the *Service Management* section of this chapter for this entity's definition.
PERSON PHONE NUMBER	Refer to Table 7.3 for this entity's definition.
PHASE	Phase is a standard project phase name for use by all Projects as needed. A Phase is a discrete segment of a Project. A Phase typically consists of one or more Tasks. Phases generally occur sequentially but can overlap if needed. For example: Planning, Requirements, Design, Build, System and Acceptance Test, or Deployment.
PROJECT	A Project is a distinct work undertaking or initiative with defined start and end dates. A Project may have resources (time or expenses) allocated to it and tracked for it. Other aspects of a Project that may be planned and managed include the commencement, completion, and dependencies of specific activities and deliverables.
PROJECT DOCUMENTATION	Project Documentation is a file of some type (word-processing document, spreadsheet, PDF file, and so on) that provides pertinent information about the Project (for example, scope, requirements, risk assessment, or project plan).
PROJECT PHASE	Project Phase specifies one or more Project Phases of a given Project.
PROJECT RESOURCE ASSIGNMENT	Project Resource Assignment specifies the allocation of individual Persons to a particular Project. A Person may be assigned to more than one Project. A Person may also have multiple assignments to the same Project, varying by Project Resource Role.
PROJECT RESOURCE REQUIREMENT	Project Resource Requirement specifies the Project Resource Roles needed for a given Project in a given Phase.

(continued)

Table 6.7 *(continued)*

ENTITY NAME	ENTITY DEFINITION
PROJECT RESOURCE ROLE	Project Resource Role describes a staffing position or function used or needed on a Project (for example, Project Manager, DBA, or Network Administrator).
PROJECT RESULT	Project Result is the outcome of a completed or canceled IT project in terms of its favorability and benefit to the business.
PROJECT STATUS	Project Status denotes a standard category of a Project by its standing in a project life cycle (for example, Active, Planned, Cancelled, or Completed).
PROJECT TASK	Project Task is a defined activity within a Project Phase to which specific resources (Persons) may be assigned for a specific purpose and duration.
RESOURCE EMPLOYMENT CATEGORY	Resource Employment Category is the type of employment or contractual arrangement of a given project resource (Person) (for example, Internal FTE, Consultant, or External Contractor).
SYSTEM	Refer to the *Service Management* section of this chapter for this entity's definition.
SYSTEM PROJECT	System Project specifies the relationship of a Project to a System. A given System may involve multiple Projects, and a given Project may involve multiple Systems.
TASK RESOURCE ASSIGNMENT	Task Resource Assignment represents the appointment of a resource (Person) to a specific Project Task in a particular Role (for example, Programmer).
VENDOR	Refer to the *Software Management* section of this chapter for this entity's definition.
VENDOR CONTACT	Refer to the *Software Management* section of this chapter for this entity's definition.
VENDOR LOCATION	Vendor Location specifies one or more addresses (billing, shipping, and so on) of a Vendor.

Table 6.8 Project Portfolio Management Attribute Walkthrough

ENTITY NAME	ATTRIBUTE NAME	ATTRIBUTE DEFINITION
PHASE	**phase id**	**Phase id** is a system-generated, nonintelligent designator that uniquely specifies the Phase. A Phase is a discrete segment of a Project.

Table 6.8   *(continued)*

ENTITY NAME	ATTRIBUTE NAME	ATTRIBUTE DEFINITION
	phase name	**Phase name** is the alphanumeric descriptive term specific for a discrete segment of a Project. A Phase is a discrete segment of a Project. Examples include: Planning, Requirements, Design, Build, and Testing.
PROJECT	actual completion date	**Actual completion date** denotes when the Project ended.
	actual consulting expense amount	**Actual consulting expense amount** is the expended cost of external consulting resources in support of the implementation of this Project.
	actual duration days quantity	**Actual duration days quantity** is the calculated difference in days between the Actual Start Date and the Actual Completion Date.
	actual hardware cost amount	**Actual hardware cost amount** is the expended cost of hardware acquisition in support of the implementation of this Project.
	actual internal expense amount	**Actual internal expense amount** is the expended cost of internal enterprise resources in support of the implementation of the Project.
	actual software cost amount	**Actual software cost amount** is the expended cost of software acquisition in support of the implementation of this Project.
	actual start date	**Actual start date** denotes when the Project commenced.
	estimated completion date	**Estimated completion date** denotes the planned end date of the Project.
	estimated consulting expense amount	**Estimated consulting expense amount** is the planned cost of external consulting resources in support of the implementation of the Project.
	estimated duration days quantity	**Estimated duration days quantity** is the calculated difference in days between the Estimated Start Date and the Estimated Completion Date.

(continued)

Table 6.8 *(continued)*

ENTITY NAME	ATTRIBUTE NAME	ATTRIBUTE DEFINITION
	estimated hardware cost amount	**Estimated hardware cost amount** is the planned cost of hardware acquisition in support of the implementation of this project.
	estimated internal expense amount	**Estimated internal expense amount** is the planned cost of internal enterprise resources in support of the implementation of this Project.
	estimated software cost amount	**Estimated software cost amount** is the planned cost of software acquisition in support of the implementation of this Project.
	estimated start date	**Estimated start date** denotes when the Project is planned to commence.
	project current phase id	**Project current phase id** specifies the Phase the Project is in at the present point in time. A **phase id** is a system-generated, nonintelligent designator that uniquely specifies the Project Phase. A Phase is a discrete segment of a Project.
	project description	**Project description** is definitional information about the Project. A Project is a distinct work undertaking or initiative.
	project group id	**Project group id** denotes the **project id** of the Project that is the parent of the Project in this record (for example, the Project in this record may be "Build Extranet Interface for Order Management System," which may be a subproject of the larger "Build and Deploy Order Global Management System." Both projects would be in the Project table. The **project id** of the latter would be found in the **project group id** (that is, parent Project) of the former.
	project id	**Project id** is a system-generated, nonintelligent designator that uniquely specifies the Project. A Project is a distinct work undertaking or initiative.

Table 6.8 *(continued)*

ENTITY NAME	ATTRIBUTE NAME	ATTRIBUTE DEFINITION
	project name	**Project name** is the alphanumeric descriptive term specific for the Project. A Project is a distinct work undertaking or initiative.
	project on time flag	**Project on time flag** indicates if the Project was completed on schedule. The Project is deemed on time when the Actual Completion Date is less than or equal to the Estimated Completion Date. If the Actual Completion Date exceeds the Estimated Completion Date then the Project is deemed late. Values include: O, L.
	project result code	**Project result code** denotes the outcome of a completed or canceled IT project in terms of its favorability and benefit to the business. This is done on a numerical rating scale (of course you can create your own rating scale): 5 = Business Sponsors' and Users' Expectations Exceeded 4 = Business Sponsors' and Users' Expectations Met 3 = Some Business Sponsors' and Users' Expectations Met 2 = Most Business Sponsors' and Users' Expectations Not Met 1 = Business Sponsors' and Users' Expectations Not Met
	project status code	**Project status code** represents a standard category of a Project by its standing in a project life cycle (for example, A = Active, P = Planned, X = Cancelled, C = Completed).

(continued)

Table 6.8 *(continued)*

ENTITY NAME	ATTRIBUTE NAME	ATTRIBUTE DEFINITION
	project within budget flag	**Project within budget flag** indicates if the Project was completed within budget. The Project is deemed on time when the sum of actual cost amounts (hardware, software, internal expense, and consulting expense) is less than or equal to the sum of estimated cost amounts. If the actual sum exceeds the estimated sum then the Project is over budget. Values include: W, O.
PROJECT DOCUMEN-TATION	**project document image**	**Project document image** is a document of some type (word-processing document, spreadsheet, PDF file, and so on) that provides pertinent information about the Project. It is stored as a binary object.
	project document name	**Project document name** is the descriptive designation of a file supporting or describing an aspect of the Project.
	project file location	**Project file location** is the location of the Project Document on a network file server.
	project file url	**Project file url** is the Internet or intranet address of the Project Document.
	project id	**Project id** specifies a Project for which Project Documentation is maintained in the meta data repository. A **project id** is a system-generated, nonintelligent designator that uniquely specifies the Project. A Project is a distinct work undertaking or initiative.
PROJECT PHASE	**actual completion date**	**Actual completion date** denotes when the Project Phase ended.
	actual start date	**Actual start date** denotes when the Project Phase commenced.
	estimated completion date	**Estimated completion date** denotes when the Project Phase is planned to end.

Table 6.8   *(continued)*

ENTITY NAME	ATTRIBUTE NAME	ATTRIBUTE DEFINITION
	estimated start date	**Estimated start date** denotes when the Project Phase is planned to commence.
	phase id	**Phase id** specifies a Phase for a particular Project. A **phase id** is a system-generated, nonintelligent designator that uniquely specifies the Phase. A Phase is a discrete segment of a Project.
	project id	**Project id** specifies a Project for which a Phase has been identified. A **project id** is a system-generated, nonintelligent designator that uniquely specifies the Project. A Project is a distinct work undertaking or initiative.
PROJECT RESOURCE ASSIGNMENT	person id	**Person id** identifies an individual who has been assigned to a Project in a particular role.
	project id	**Project id** identifies a Project to which a Person has been assigned in a particular role. A **project id** is a system-generated, nonintelligent designator that uniquely specifies the Project. A Project is a distinct work undertaking or initiative.
	project resource role id	**Project resource role id** specifies the position or function of a resource on the Project.
	resource allocated time percentage	**Resource allocated time percentage** is the proportion of time the resource(s) (Person) is reserved for the Project, expressed as a positive decimal less than or equal to one.
	resource employment category id	**Resource employment category id** is a unique, system-generated, nonintelligent designator that uniquely specifies the Resource Employment Category. A Resource Employment Category is the type of employment or contractual arrangement of a given project resource (Person).
	resource hourly cost amount	**Resource hourly cost amount** specifies the hourly expense incurred by the resource (Person) on the Project in his or her given role.

(continued)

Table 6.8 *(continued)*

ENTITY NAME	ATTRIBUTE NAME	ATTRIBUTE DEFINITION
	phase id	**Phase id** specifies a Phase for a particular Project. A **phase id** is a system-generated, nonintelligent designator that uniquely specifies the Phase. A Phase is a discrete segment of a Project.
	project id	**Project id** specifies a Project that requires a type of resource. A **project id** is a system-generated, nonintelligent designator that uniquely specifies the Project. A Project is a distinct work undertaking or initiative.
	project resource role id	**Project resource role id** specifies the position or function of a resource on the Project.
	resource required quantity	**Resource required quantity** is the number of this Resource type (Role) required by the Project.
	resource required time percentage	**Resource required time percentage** is the proportion of time the resource(s) (Person) is required on the project, expressed as a positive decimal less than or equal to one.
PROJECT RESOURCE ROLE	**project resource role id**	**Project resource role id** specifies the position or function of a resource on the Project.
	project resource role name	**Project resource role name** describes the functional position of a resource (Person) on a Project or Project Task. Examples include: Developer, Analyst, DBA, Project Manager, and so on.
PROJECT RESULT	**project result code**	**Project result code** denotes the outcome of a completed or canceled IT project in terms of its favorability and benefit to the business. This is done on a numerical rating scale: 5 = Business Sponsors' and Users' Expectations Exceeded 4 = Business Sponsors' and Users' Expectations Met

Table 6.8 *(continued)*

ENTITY NAME	ATTRIBUTE NAME	ATTRIBUTE DEFINITION
PROJECT RESULT	project result code	3 = Some Business Sponsors' and Users' Expectations Met 2 = Most Business Sponsors' and Users' Expectations Not Met 1 = Business Sponsors' and Users' Expectations Not Met
	project result name	**Project result name** is the alphanumeric descriptive term specific for a Project Result. A Project Result is the outcome of a completed or canceled IT project in terms of its favorability and benefit to the business.
PROJECT STATUS	project status code	**Project status code** denotes a standard category of a Project by its standing in a project life cycle (for example, A = Active, P = Planned, X = Cancelled, C = Completed).
	project status name	**Project status name** is the alphanumeric descriptive term specific for the Project Status. A Project Status denotes a standard category of a Project by its standing in a project life cycle (for example, Active, Planned, Cancelled, or Completed).
PROJECT TASK	actual completion date	**Actual completion date** denotes when the Project Task ended.
	actual start date	**Actual start date** denotes when the Project Task commenced.
	deliverable name	**Deliverable name** is the alphanumeric descriptive term specifying the outcome or product of the Project Task.
	estimated completion date	**Estimated completion date** denotes the planned end date of the Project Task.
	estimated start date	**Estimated start date** denotes the planned commencement date for the Project Task.
	milestone flag	**Milestone flag** indicates if the Task is a Task (with Estimated and Actual Start Dates) or a Milestone (a point in time with no Start Dates, only Estimated and Actual Completion Dates). Values are: Y, N

(continued)

Table 6.8 *(continued)*

ENTITY NAME	ATTRIBUTE NAME	ATTRIBUTE DEFINITION
	phase id	**Phase id** specifies a Phase for a particular Project. A **phase id** is a system-generated, nonintelligent designator that uniquely specifies the Phase. A Phase is a discrete segment of a Project.
	project id	**Project id** specifies a Project for which a Task has been identified. A **project id** is a system-generated, nonintelligent designator that uniquely specifies the Project. A Project is a distinct work undertaking or initiative.
	project task description	**Project task description** is definition information about the Task. A Project Task is a defined activity within a Project Phase to which specific resources (Persons) may be assigned for a specific purpose and duration.
	project task id	**Project task id** is a unique, system-generated, nonintelligent designator that uniquely specifies the Project Task. A Project Task is a defined activity within a Project Phase to which specific resources (Persons) may be assigned for a specific purpose and duration.
	project task name	**Project task name** is the alphanumeric descriptive term specific for the Task. A Project Task is a defined activity within a Project Phase to which specific resources (Persons) may be assigned for a specific purpose and duration.
RESOURCE EMPLOYMENT CATEGORY	**resource employment category description**	**Resource employment category description** is definitional information about the Resource Employment Category. A Resource Employment Category is the type of employment or contractual arrangement of a given project resource (Person). For example: Internal FTE, Consultant, or External Contractor.
	resource employment category id	**Resource employment category id** is a unique, system-generated, nonintelligent designator that uniquely specifies the Resource Employment Category. A Resource Employment Category is the type of employment or contractual arrangement of a given project resource (Person).

Table 6.8   *(continued)*

ENTITY NAME	ATTRIBUTE NAME	ATTRIBUTE DEFINITION
SYSTEM PROJECT	**project id**	**Project id** specifies a Project that is associated with a System. A **project id** is a system-generated, nonintelligent designator that uniquely specifies the Project. A Project is a distinct work undertaking or initiative.
	system id	**System id** specifies a System that is associated with a Project. A **system id** is a system-generated, nonintelligent designator that uniquely specifies the System. A System is an aggregate of Hardware, Software, Data Package, and/or Network components.
TASK RESOURCE ASSIGNMENT	**person id**	**Person id** specifies an individual assigned to a particular Task in a particular role in a Project.
	phase id	**Phase id** specifies the project Phase of a Task to which a resource has been assigned. A Phase ID is a system-generated, nonintelligent designator that uniquely specifies the Phase. A Phase is a discrete segment of a Project.
	project id	**Project id** specifies a Project Task to which a resource has been assigned. A **project id** is a system-generated, nonintelligent designator that uniquely specifies the Project. A Project is a distinct work undertaking or initiative.
	project resource role id	**Project resource role id** specifies the position or function of a resource assigned to a particular Task of a Project.
	project task id	**Project task id** specifies a Project Task to which a resource has been assigned. A Project Task is a defined activity within a Project Phase to which specific resources (Persons) may be assigned for a specific purpose and duration.

(continued)

Table 6.8   *(continued)*

ENTITY NAME	ATTRIBUTE NAME	ATTRIBUTE DEFINITION
	resource employment category id	**Resource employment category id** is a unique, system-generated, nonintelligent designator that uniquely specifies the Resource Employment Category. A Resource Employment Category is the type of employment or contractual arrangement of a given project resource (Person).
	resource hourly cost amount	**Resource hourly cost amount** specifies the hourly expense incurred by the resource (Person) on a Project Task in a given role.

Data Quality Management

Data quality management supports the definition of data quality metrics, the recording of specific measurements, and the reporting of data quality exceptions to the business. The data model for data quality management is shown in Figure 6.6. This data model is designed to support data quality measurement processes that use the quality criteria recorded here. The heart of the Data Quality subject area is DATA QUALITY METRIC, where specific, quantifiable criteria for measuring data quality are defined. DATA QUALITY METRIC has three optional foreign key relationships to the three levels of data representation:

- **data element id** to DATA ELEMENT
- **data group id** to DATA GROUP
- **data package id** to DATA PACKAGE

These relationships are generally mutually exclusive. They represent the fact that the data quality criterion to be measured applies either to a single DATA ELEMENT within a DATA GROUP (for example, to a column in a table) or to a whole DATA GROUP (for example, to rows in a table meeting criteria in more than one column), or to an entire DATA PACKAGE (for example, to conditions across multiple tables within a database). DATA ELEMENT, GROUP, and PACKAGE are described in detail in Chapter 4.

Most of the attributes of DATA QUALITY METRIC define the data quality criteria to be measured: **name**, **description**, and **comment**, and two quantitative fields: **minimum threshold quantity** and **maximum threshold quantity**. The latter two attributes define the lowermost and uppermost values considered acceptable: for example, if the data quality metric is "Percent of records in the Open Cases table where Case Worker ID is not null (that is, a case worker has been assigned)" then a minimum threshold quantity might be .90 (90 percent) and maximum 1 (100 percent), meaning it is unacceptable to have more than 10 percent of cases with no case worker assigned.

When a measurement is conducted (a DATA QUALITY MEASUREMENT, described below) and one of these thresholds is exceeded—over the max or under the min—the data being examined is assigned a **data quality exception code**. This code represents a predetermined numeric severity rating of the exception: "3" = Informational Error, "2" = Error Warning, or "1" = Critical Error. If neither threshold is exceeded in the measurement, then the default rating of "4" (Meets Data Quality Metric Criteria) is assigned. **Notification group id** identifies the group of individuals that are to be informed of data quality exceptions. **Measurement frequency code** specifies how often the measurement should be performed (for example, "A" = Ad Hoc, "Y" = Yearly, "Q" = Quarterly, "M" = Monthly, "W" = Weekly, "D" = Daily, "H" = Hourly, "R" = Real Time or Near Real Time). MEASUREMENT FREQUENCY is simply a reference table, providing a **description** for the **measurement frequency code**.

The metric criteria may involve acceptable field values or other element characteristics taken from DOMAIN or DOMAIN VALUE, or may be arithmetic functions performed on sets of data (see Chapter 4 for descriptions of DOMAIN and DOMAIN VALUE). It is important to note, that the DATA QUALITY METRIC may define much more than valid value range checks. For example, the metric may be specified to be a sum of a certain amount column in a particular table, where the minimum should never be less than $100,000 and the maximum never more than $100 billion. Or, the metric may specify that the result of the following should fall between 20 and 80: sum of column A from Table L where account type = X, divided by a count of column B from Table M, where customer type = Y. Because of the wide range of types and operands in metrics, such select statements are specified in pseudocode or SQL statements and recorded in data **quality metric description**. The processes that execute these calculations may use the fields in DATA QUALITY METRIC to drive the measurement, exception detection, and subsequent reporting.

DATA QUALITY MEASUREMENT represents the results of performing the DATA QUALITY METRIC (identified by **data quality metric id**) at a particular point in time (**data quality measurement date**)—hence the multiple instances of *measurement* allowed to a single instance of *metric*. Measurements that meet the quantitative criteria defined in DATA QUALITY METRIC are deemed acceptable and given an **assigned data quality level code** of "4" (Meets Data Quality Metric Criteria). If a given measurement exceeds one of the thresholds—over the max or under the min—then the measurement process assigns it a **data quality level code** that is less than acceptable ("3" or less), according to the predetermined data quality exception code specified for the DATA QUALITY METRIC (described previously).

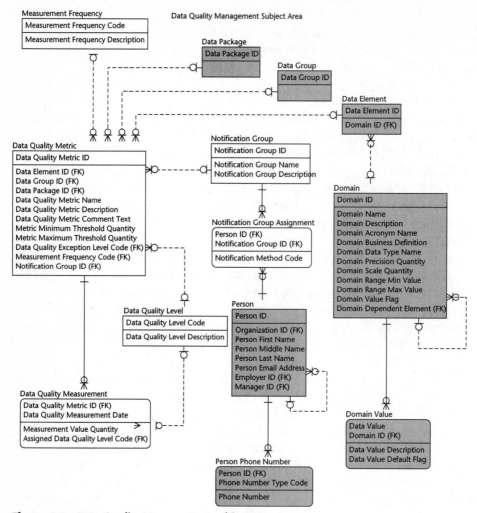

Figure 6.6 Data Quality Management subject area.

DATA QUALITY LEVEL is simply a reference table for **data quality level code**, showing its code values and their descriptions, used in both DATA QUALITY METRIC (as **data quality exception code**) and DATA QUALITY MEASUREMENT (as **assigned data quality level code**). Examples of the values and descriptions designated in the data model range from "4" = Meets Data Quality Measurement Criteria, down to "3" = Informational Error, "2" = Error Warning, and "1" = Critical Error.

When a DATA QUALITY MEASUREMENT detects exception conditions, certain individuals must be notified. These individuals are specified in a NOTIFICATION GROUP, which is a set of PERSONs identified as contacts in the event exception conditions are found on a particular metric. This NOTIFICATION GROUP is specified within DATA QUALITY METRIC (**notification** group id). The group has a **name** and an optional **description**. The information that is operationally used by the notification process is contained in NOTIFICATION GROUP ASSIGNMENT, an M:M associative entity between NOTIFICATION GROUP and PERSON, specifying exactly who is to be notified when an exception condition is found. More than one PERSON may wish to be notified when such a condition is recorded, and the same set of individuals may wish to be contacted when any of several different exception conditions occur in DATA QUALITY MEASUREMENTs. Finally, as described in other subject areas within the *IT Portfolio Management* section, certain contact information is used with respect to the PERSON, usually an **email address** (recorded in PERSON) or **fax number** (recorded in PERSON PHONE NUMBER) to which to deliver an automated data quality exception report. The individual's preferred delivery method is indicated by the **notification method code** in NOTIFICATION GROUP ASSIGNMENT.

Tables 6.9 and 6.10 describe the entities and attributes of the Data Quality Management subject area.

Table 6.9 Data Quality Management Entities

ENTITY NAME	ENTITY DEFINITION
DATA ELEMENT	Refer to Table 4.1 for this entity's definition.
DATA GROUP	Refer to Table 4.1 for this entity's definition.
DATA PACKAGE	Refer to Table 4.1 for this entity's definition.
DATA QUALITY LEVEL	Data Quality Level contains data quality ratings applied to data quality measurements. These can be used in the automated and ad hoc reporting of data quality conditions and events.
DATA QUALITY MEASUREMENT	Data Quality Measurement records the quantified results of performing the Data Quality Measure at a particular point in time.
DATA QUALITY METRIC	Data Quality Metric is a quantifiable audit criterion for quality assessment of a given Data Package, Data Group, or Data Element. The criterion for measurement may be at the level of: (1) a single Data Element—for example, record count of invalid or missing values for a given Element in a single Data Group, or a checksum of a given Element in a single Data Group; (2) a given Data Group—for example, record count where Element A = 0 and Element B <> 'X'; (3) a given Data Package—for example, a count of instances where a Customer is in tables X and Y but not in table Z.
DOMAIN	Refer to Table 4.1 for this entity's definition.

(continued)

Table 6.9 *(continued)*

ENTITY NAME	ENTITY DEFINITION
DOMAIN VALUE	Refer to Table 4.1 for this entity's definition.
MEASUREMENT FREQUENCY	Measurement Frequency denotes how often the Data Quality Measure is to be performed. Examples include: Ad Hoc, Quarterly, Monthly, Weekly, Daily, and Hourly.
NOTIFICATION GROUP	Notification Group is a collection of Persons to be contacted in connection with a Data Quality Measurement and its associated Data Quality Level (for example, when a particular Data Quality Measurement receives a Data Quality Level Code < 4, members of the Notification Group will receive email notification of the Measurement, with appropriate details garnered from the Data Quality Measure and Measurement tables).
NOTIFICATION GROUP ASSIGNMENT	Notification Group Assignment specifies the Persons who belong to a Notification Group, for use in automated reporting of data quality conditions and events.
PERSON	Refer to Table 7.4 for this entity's definition.
PERSON PHONE NUMBER	Refer to Table 7.4 for this entity's definition.

Table 6.10 Data Quality Management Attributes

ENTITY NAME	ATTRIBUTE NAME	ATTRIBUTE DEFINITION
DATA QUALITY LEVEL	**data quality level code**	**Data quality level code** designates the rating of a specific data quality measurement at a point in time. Examples include: a range from 4 ("Meets Data Quality Measurement Criteria") to 3 ("Informational Error") to 2 ("Error Warning") to 1 ("Critical Error").
	data quality level description	**Data quality level description** decodes the Data Quality Level Code, which is the rating of a specific data quality measurement at a point in time. Examples include: a range from "Meets Data Quality Metric Criteria" to "Informational Error" to "Error Warning" to "Critical Error."

Table 6.10   *(continued)*

ENTITY NAME	ATTRIBUTE NAME	ATTRIBUTE DEFINITION
DATA QUALITY MEASUREMENT	assigned data quality level code	**Assigned data quality level code** is the Data Quality Level Code designated to a Data Quality Measurement as a result of conducting the measurement at a particular point in time. The Data Quality Level Code designates the rating of a specific data quality measurement at a point in time. Examples include: a range from 4 ("Meets Data Quality Metric Criteria") to 3 ("Informational Error") to 2 ("Error Warning") to 1 ("Critical Error").
	data quality measurement date	**Data quality measurement date** denotes when the Data Quality Measurement was performed.
	data quality metric id	**Data quality measure id** is a system-generated, nonintelligent designator that uniquely specifies the Data Quality Measure. Data Quality Measurement records the quantified results of performing the Data Quality Measure at a particular point in time.
	measurement value quantity	**Measurement value quantity** is the numerical value of the quantified data quality measurement. Measurement Value Quantity may be a sum, count, percentage, or ratio.
DATA QUALITY METRIC	data element id	**Data element id** specifies, as applicable, the single Data Element that is the subject of the Data Quality Measure.
	data group id	**Data group id** specifies, as applicable, the single Data Group that is the subject of the Data Quality Measure.
	data package id	**Data package id** specifies, as applicable, the Data Package that is the subject of the Data Quality Measure.

(continued)

Table 6.10 *(continued)*

ENTITY NAME	ATTRIBUTE NAME	ATTRIBUTE DEFINITION
	data quality exception level code	**Data quality exception level code** is the **data quality level code** assigned when the Measure Minimum or Maximum Threshold Quantity is exceeded in a given measurement. **Data quality level code** designates the rating of a specific data quality measurement at a point in time. Examples include: a range from 4 ("Meets Data Quality Measurement Criteria") to 3 ("Informational Error") to 2 ("Error Warning") to 1 ("Critical Error").
	data quality metric comment text	**Data quality metric comment text** is free-form, supplemental information or remarks about the Data Quality Metric.
	data quality metric description	**Data quality metric description** is the definition of the specific data quality or audit criterion for which a measurement is recorded in Data Quality Measurement Value Quantity (within Data Quality Measurement). This may be a sum, count, percentage, or ratio. It will generally be conditional, a sum, count, or percentage of records or elements meeting (or not meeting) certain parameters—for example, the quantity of records in a Customer table where Customer Type Code is null or blank or invalid (per the valid values in Domain). The measure may be quantities of records or elements meeting or exceeding certain threshold quantities, as defined in Measurement n Minimum Threshold Quantity and Measurement n Maximum Threshold Quantity (for example, quantity of records in an Account tables where the Account Balance is < 0 or $> 100,000,000$).
	data quality metric id	**Data quality metric id** is a system-generated, nonintelligent designator that uniquely specifies the Data Quality Metric. A Data Quality Metric is a quantifiable audit criterion for quality assessment of a given Data Package, Data Group, or Data Element.

Table 6.10   *(continued)*

ENTITY NAME	ATTRIBUTE NAME	ATTRIBUTE DEFINITION
	data quality measure name	**Data quality measure name** is the alphanumeric descriptive term specific for the Data Quality Measure. A Data Quality Measure is a quantifiable audit criterion for quality assessment of a given Data Package, Data Group, or Data Element.
	measurement frequency code	**Measurement frequency code** denotes how often the Data Quality Metric is to be performed. Examples include: A = Ad Hoc, Y = Yearly, Q = Quarterly, M = Monthly, W = Weekly, D = Daily, H = Hourly, and R = Real Time or Near Real Time.
	metric maximum threshold quantity	**Metric maximum threshold quantity** specifies the greatest quantity, count, amount, or percentage for use in a range test, if any, in the Metric.
	metric minimum threshold quantity	**Metric minimum threshold quantity** specifies the lowest quantity, count, amount, or percentage for use in a range test, if any, in Metric.
	notification group id	**Notification group id** specifies the Notification Group to be contacted when an Exception condition is recorded in the Data Quality Measurement. A **notification group id** is a system-generated, nonintelligent designator that uniquely specifies the Notification Group. A Notification Group is a collection of Persons to be contacted in connection with a Data Quality Measurement and its associated Data Quality Level.
MEASUREMENT FREQUENCY	measurement frequency code	**Measurement frequency code** denotes how often the Data Quality Metric is to be performed. Examples include: A = Ad Hoc, Y = Yearly, Q = Quarterly, M = Monthly, W = Weekly, D = Daily, H = Hourly, R = Real Time or Near Real Time.
	measurement frequency description	**Measurement frequency description** decodes the Measurement Frequency Code. Examples include: A = Ad Hoc, Y = Yearly, Q = Quarterly, M = Monthly, W = Weekly, D = Daily, H = Hourly, R = Real Time or Near Real Time.

(continued)

Table 6.10 *(continued)*

ENTITY NAME	ATTRIBUTE NAME	ATTRIBUTE DEFINITION
NOTIFICATION GROUP	notification group description	**Notification group description** is definitional information about the Notification Group. A Notification Group is a collection of Persons to be contacted in connection with a Data Quality Measurement and its associated Data Quality Level.
	notification group id	**Notification group id** is a system-generated, nonintelligent designator that uniquely specifies the Notification Group. A Notification Group is a collection of Persons to be contacted in connection with a Data Quality Measurement and its associated Data Quality Level.
	notification group name	**Notification group name** is the alphanumeric descriptive term specific for the Notification Group. A Notification Group is a collection of Persons to be contacted in connection with a Data Quality Measurement and its associated Data Quality Level.
NOTIFICATION GROUP ASSIGNMENT	notification group id	**Notification group id** specifies the Notification Group to which a Person is assigned.
	notification method code	**Notification method code** specifies the medium by which the Person desires to be notified of data quality exceptions. Examples include: E = email and F = fax
	person id	**Person id** specifies the individual assigned to a Notification Group. A Notification Group is a collection of Persons to be contacted in connection with a Data Quality Measurement and its associated Data Quality Level.

Reports from the IT Portfolio Management Meta Model

At the beginning of the chapter, we posed a number of questions of interest to the business to be answered by the meta data in the IT Portfolio Management meta model. Let's take a look at how we can answer these questions from the IT Portfolio Management meta model.

Software Module CRUD Report

Which applications access which tables and files? And which applications update the data as opposed to only reading it?

One of the reliable tools of systems analysis and portfolio planning has been the classic CRUD matrix—which processes create, read, update, and delete (CRUD) information. In business analysis and design, such as business process reengineering, this typically occurs at a conceptual level. Ultimately, this has to translate to the physical level: software modules (processes) acting on database tables or file records. The MME maintains exactly such a cross-reference via the DEPLOYED SOFTWARE MODULE-DATA GROUP relationship. Figure 6.7 shows the CRUD report, sorted by Data Group and Action, revealing the diversity of accesses to these shared data structures.

Software Module –Data Group CRUD

Software Module –Data Group CRUD Report	Acme Materials Manufacturing	November 20, 2003
Software Module Name	Data Package Name	Data Group Name	Action
Account Update	Customer Account Management DB	Account	CUD
Order Entry	Customer Account Management DB	Account	R
Payment Processing	Customer Account Management DB	Account	U
Rebates	Customer Account Management DB	Account	U
Customer Update	Customer Account Management DB	Customer	CUD
Order Entry	Customer Account Management DB	Customer	R
Payment Processing	Customer Account Management DB	Customer	R
Telemarket Portal	Customer Account Management DB	Customer	R
Customer Update	Customer Account Management DB	Customer Address	CUD
Telemarket Portal	Customer Account Management DB	Customer Address	R
Order Entry	Customer Account Management DB	Customer Address	RU
Demographic Update	Customer Account Management DB	Customer Demographic	CU
Telemarket Portal	Customer Account Management DB	Customer Demographic	R
Customer Update	Customer Account Management DB	Customer-Account	CUD
Telemarket Portal	Customer Account Management DB	Customer-Account	R
Vendor Module	Procurement FS	Vendor	CRUD
Purchasing Module	Procurement FS	Purchase Order Header	CRU
Purchasing Module	Procurement FS	Purchase Order Item	CRU
Purchasing Module	Procurement FS	Vendor	R

Figure 6.7   Software module: data group CRUD report.

Hardware Obsolescent Report

Which systems operate on obsolescent hardware?

A key function of IT Portfolio Management subject area is to understand and examine the business exposure of running mission-critical systems on aging/obsolete hardware platforms. The MME report in Figure 6.8 identifies the enterprise systems operating on hardware where the technology maturity code has been rated "Obsolete/Unsupported." It also identifies where the hardware resides and how old it is; this information is derived from the acquisition date. This report is valuable to IT managers in identifying relative technology risk exposures by business system.

Data Storage Capacity Report

What is the total processing and data storage capacity of each computing site?

Another view of computing hardware by location is a summary of each site's computing and data storage capacity. This report, shown in Figure 6.9, would usually focus on dedicated data centers and departmental computing sites, excluding personal computers. Such an inventory may reveal, as in the example, that an office location collectively may have the equivalent of an entire data center squirreled away in various computing closets, which may drive a review into the costs and benefits of consolidating some operations.

System Obsolescent Technology Summary

System Obsolescent Technology Summary		Acme Materials Manufacturing		November 20, 2003
System	Vendor	Hardware	Age in Years	Location
Student Loan Collections	DEC	VAX 500	19.1	Boulder Data Center
Currency Transactions Clearing	IBM	System 370	20.2	Detroit Computing Ctr
Currency Transactions Clearing	IBM	3084 TCS	17.2	Detroit Computing Ctr
Legal Transcripts Processing	Wang	2000	22.8	Corporate HQ

Figure 6.8 System obsolescent technology summary report.

Computing and Data Storage Capacity by Site

Computing and Data Storage Capacity by Site	Acme Materials Manufacturing			November 20, 2003
Location	Organization	Operating Environment	Total Processing Capacity (GHz)	Total Data Storage Capacity (GB)
Atlanta Business Campus, Bldg A - 2nd Flr	Financial Management	Unix	36	13,000
Atlanta Business Campus, Bldg C - 1st Flr	Accounts Receivable	Unix	13	4,800
Atlanta Business Campus, Bldg C - 2nd Flr	Purchasing	Unix	21	7,700
Atlanta Business Campus, Bldg C - 3rd Flr	Corporate Accounting	AS400	50	18,000
Atlanta Business Campus, Bldg D - 1st Flr	Market Analysis	Unix	59	2,100
Atlanta Business Campus, Bldg F - 2nd Flr	Product Testing	Unix	89	3,200
Atlanta Business Campus, Bldg F - Lab	Product Research	Linux	28	1,000
Boulder Data Center	Information Technology Division	OS390	290	78,200
Detroit Computing Ctr	Information Technology Division	Unix	120	43,000

Figure 6.9 Computing and data storage capacity by site report.

Installed Software Patch Report

Which software patches have been installed on what systems and in which environments?

The mundane subject of vendor software patches rarely fascinates managers. But an occasional comparison of available software patches to applied software patches can provide some useful insights to IT and consequently benefits to the business. Figure 6.10 shows such a report. Notice that months ago one patch, ICv6.1o44, was tested and applied all deployments of a software module but one, Inventory MS – El Paso, identifiable by a null application date. A catch like that could prevent or pinpoint system reliability or data quality issues before the users feel the pain and let IT know their displeasure.

Installed Software Patch Summary

Installed Software Patch Summary		Acme Materials Manufacturing			November 20, 2003
System	Vendor	Environment	Software Module	Software Patch Number	Application Date
ERP	SAP	Production	General Ledger	UBF-6.1-20031579	5/4/2003
HRMS	PeopleSoft	Test	Payroll	3Q20RT5-00007-A	4/22/2003
HRMS	PeopleSoft	Production	Payroll	3Q20RT5-00007-A	4/26/2003
HRMS	PeopleSoft	Test	Payroll	3Q20RT5-00009-NB	4/29/2003
HRMS	PeopleSoft	Production	Payroll	3Q20RT5-00009-NB	5/3/2003
Inventory MS - Canton	MCS	Test	Inventory Control	ICv6.1o44	2/7/2003
Inventory MS - Canton	MCS	Production	Inventory Control	ICv6.1o44	2/16/2003
Inventory MS - El Paso	MCS	Production	Inventory Control	ICv6.1o44	
Inventory MS - Portland	MCS	Production	Inventory Control	ICv6.1o44	2/15/2003

Figure 6.10   Installed software patch summary report.

Annual Vendor Software Fee Liability Report

What is our annual software license and maintenance liability by vendor?

More often than IT managers want to analyze software patch applications, they want to get a handle on their ongoing financial exposure to vendors. Unlike most hardware, which can be purchased in a single year's capital budget and then have the responsibility for its numbers handed off to the bean counters in future years, most software is an expense that never fades away. License or maintenance fees can linger as long as the enterprise uses the vendor's software and, in some cases even after the organization has stopped using the software. Maintaining cost information with the software inventory enables IT management to readily summarize software expense liability by vendor. The report in Figure 6.11 can provide valuable insights concerning software fee trends, pricing comparisons, and sheer volumes, arming IT management with information to better negotiate license agreements.

Annual Vendor Software Fee Liability

Vendor	Annual Vendor Software Fee Liability			Acme Materials Manufacturing			November 20, 2003		
	2003 Software License Fees	2004 Software License Fees	% chg Software License Fees	2003 Software Maintenance Fees	2004 Software Maintenance Fees	% chg Software Maintenance Fees	2003 Total Vendor Software Fees	2004 Total Vendor Software Fees	% chg Total Vendor Software Fees
Oracle	1,234,500	1,419,675	15%	246,900	255,542	4%	1,481,400	1,675,217	13%
IBM	620,000	750,000	21%	93,000	115,000	24%	713,000	865,000	21%
SAP	550,000	615,000	12%	99,000	110,700	12%	649,000	725,700	12%
Microsoft	450,000	370,000	-18%	0	0	0%	450,000	370,000	-18%
Sun	319,000	420,000	32%	63,800	80,200	26%	382,800	500,200	31%
Informatica	252,900	168,600	-33%	63,225	84,300	33%	316,125	252,900	-20%
PeopleSoft	175,000	175,000	0%	24,500	28,000	14%	199,500	203,000	2%
TOTAL	$3,601,400	$3,918,275	9%	$590,425	$673,742	14%	$4,191,825	$4,592,017	10%

Figure 6.11   Annual vendor software fee liability report.

System Trouble Report Volume Report

Which organizations submit the most trouble reports?

In addition to analyzing suppliers and the inventory of systems components, IT management is also concerned with keeping clients and users satisfied. Frequently, IT departments look at trouble report metrics system by system. Figure 6.12 shows another way of looking at them: which organizations are having the most trouble? In the example, the overall trouble volume of the Order Management department is not high, but have we noticed that their trouble reports have recently doubled? And trouble report volume by the Comptroller's Office may be low for each of its five systems, but we would like to know that the aggregate volume of all the reports for that department as a whole is substantial.

Unscheduled Maintenance by Component Report

Which system components have the most unscheduled maintenance?

Related to trouble reports is unscheduled maintenance. Maintenance is a good thing because it prevents trouble reports. On the other hand, unscheduled maintenance is usually a reaction to a problem, often one that has already had an impact on service levels or is about to. Figure 6.13 is a report of all recent unscheduled maintenance by component. The components are individually identified and are categorized by type and subtype. This report can help pinpoint system vulnerabilities before they get out of hand.

Trouble Report Volume by Organization

Trouble Report Volume by Organization	Acme Materials Manufacturing					November 20, 2003		
Organization	Mar 03	Apr 03	May 03	Jun 03	Jul 03	Aug 03	Last 6 Months	Prior 6 Months	% Change
Accounts Receivable Dept.	3	5	6	4	2	2	22	19	16%
Customer Service Dept.		8		1	15	1	17	24	-29%
Comptroller's Office	9		7	5	11	9	49	21	133%
Order Entry Dept.	6		3	9			18	16	13%
Order Management Dept.			1	5			6	2	200%
Shipping Dept.		2	1			3	6	13	-54%
TOTALS	18	15	18	24	28	15	118	95	24%

Figure 6.12   System trouble report volume by organization report.

Unscheduled Maintenance by Component

Unscheduled Maintenance by Component		Acme Materials Manufacturing	November 20, 2003
System Component Type	Sub-Type	Description	Total Last 3 Months
Hardware	Server	IBM 7025/F80 1067-AXN-943	3
	Server	IBM X255 2686-JK2-001	1
	Storage	EMC Centera WTMV-178456999	1
	Network	Cisco 10720 5HA87325NK	7
Subtotal			12
Software Module	Vendor	SAP GL	2
	NonVendor	Facilities Management Control	3
Subtotal			5
Data Package	Flat File	Order Masterfile	2
	Relational Database	CRM Database	4
Subtotal			6
Network	TCP/IP	CorporateNet	19
	AppleTalk	Macnet 20	2
Subtotal			21
TOTAL			**44**

Figure 6.13 Unscheduled maintenance by component report.

IT Project Resource Projection Report

What types of staffing will be required—and how many staff members—by the portfolio of projects for the next 12 months?

Another area of interest to IT management is planning the skilled project personnel required for upcoming systems implementations. Figure 6.14 shows the distribution of required project resources by type for the next 12 months for all projects. This report is invaluable for determining when and how many contracted or consulting resources may be needed to augment IT staff on projects, or if additional IT staff need to be hired.

IT Project Resource Projection

IT Project Resource Projection				Acme Materials Manufacturing								November 20, 2003			
				Quantity Required by Month												
Resource Type	Jan	Feb	Mar	Apr	May	Jun	Jul	Aug	Sep	Oct	Nov	Dec	Low	High
BO Reports Developer	2.0	2.0	2.0				1.0	3.0	3.0	3.0	2.0	2.0	0.0	3.0
Business/Reqts Analyst	1.0	1.5	2.5	2.0	2.0	2.0	2.5	2.0	0.5				0.0	2.5
COBOL Developer			1.0	1.0	2.0	2.0	1.0	1.0					0.0	2.0
Conversion Analyst	1.0	1.0	0.5			0.5	1.0	1.0	1.0	1.5	1.5	1.0	0.0	1.5
Data Analyst/Modeler	3.0	3.0	2.5	4.0	4.5	4.0	3.0	3.5	3.5	2.5	1.0	1.0	1.0	4.5
DB2 DBA	0.5	1.0	1.0	0.5	0.5	0.5	1.0	1.0	1.0	1.0	1.5	0.5	1.0	1.5
ETL Developer	2.0	1.0	1.0		1.0	2.0	2.0	3.0	3.0	3.0	3.0	3.0	0.0	3.0
Java Developer			1.0	2.0	2.0	1.0		1.0	3.0	4.0	3.0	1.0	0.0	4.0
Oracle DBA			1.0	1.0	1.0	2.0	2.0	2.0	3.0	2.5	1.5	0.5	0.0	2.5
PL/SQL Developer			1.0	1.0	1.0	2.0	2.0	2.0	2.0	1.0			0.0	2.0
Project Manager	2.0	2.5	3.5	3.0	3.5	3.5	4.5	4.5	4.5	4.5	3.5	1.5	1.5	4.5
SIT/SAT Test Specialist		2.0	2.0			1.5	0.5		1.5	4.0	3.0	0.5	0.0	4.0
Technical Architect/Lead	3.0	3.5	4.5	3.5	4.5	4.5	6.0	5.5	5.0	4.5	3.0	1.0	1.0	6.0
ALL	14.5	17.5	23.5	18.0	22.0	25.5	26.5	29.5	31.0	31.5	23.0	12.0		

Figure 6.14 IT project resource projection report.

Project Success Rate Analysis Report

What is the business success rate of projects completed on time or within budget versus those that come in late or over budget? Who are the most successful project managers?

Once projects are completed, other reports and metrics come into play. The Project Portfolio Management submodel of the MME maintains a knowledge base of project vital statistics, including the project's performance to budget and schedule, plus its success, concisely represented in the Project Result Rating:

5 = Business Sponsors' and Users' Expectations Exceeded

4 = Business Sponsors' and Users' Expectations Met

3 = Some Business Sponsors' and Users' Expectations Met

2 = Most Business Sponsors' and Users' Expectations Not Met

1 = Business Sponsors' and Users' Expectations Not Met

This allows for any number of interesting reports, including a high-level summary of project success rates by scheduled and budget characteristics, shown in Figure 6.15, and a project managers scorecard, shown in Figure 6.16.

Project Success Rate Analysis

Project Success Rate Analysis	Acme Materials Manufacturing	November 20, 2003
Project Category	Project Success Rate	Average Result
Projects on time and within budget	74%	4.4
Projects on time and over budget	82%	4.1
Projects late and within budget	53%	3.4
Projects late and over budget	64%	3.7
All Projects (average)	68%	3.9

Figure 6.15   Project success rate analysis report.

Project Managers Scorecard

Project Managers Scorecard	Acme Materials Manufacturing				November 20, 2003
Project Manager	Projects Completed Count	Project Success Rate	Project On-Time Rate	Project Within Budget Rate	Average Project Size (resource-months)
Beck, Mary	2	50%	50%	100%	42
Duvall, Yvonne	4	100%	25%	0%	23
Ivory, James	3	33%	67%	67%	28
Perez, Carlos	6	67%	83%	83%	16
Smith, Harry	1	100%	0%	20%	15
Stromberg, Michelle	5	20%	100%	80%	20
Taylor, Keeshan	5	75%	50%	25%	17

Figure 6.16   Project managers scorecard report.

Data Quality Exception Summary Report

Which data is of questionable quality, and who needs to know about it?

Data quality management is often seen as the purview of the business rather than IT management, but proactive IT managers want to identify data quality problems early so they can be addressed before they adversely affect business operations or incorrectly influence management decision-making. The Data Quality Management submodel of the MME supports the definition and recording of a wide variety of data quality metrics. Figure 6.17 shows a summary of reported exceptions, each one resulting in specific email or pager notifications.

Data Quality Exception Summary

Data Quality Exception Summary			Acme Materials Manufacturing			November 20, 2003	
Data Quality Metric Name	Data Package Name	Data Group Name	Data Element Name	Measurement Data	Data Quality Level	Measurement Value Quantity	Notification Group
Composite reject ratio exceeds maximum threshold	Materials DB	(multiple)	(multiple)	5/1/2003	Critical Error	0.07	Manufacturing Quality Control
Negative Fulfillment Backlog	Materials DB	Backlog_Control	Backlog_Day_Ct	4/30/2003	Error Warning	-0.3	Inventory Planning
Corporate account type Q average balance below minimum threshold	General Ledger	Corporate_Accts	Account_Balance_Amt	5/1/2003	Informational Error	$9,245	Corporate Account Management
Standard deviation of Material length / material breaking strength exceeds maximum threshold	Materials DB	Finished_Material_Test	(multiple)	5/1/2003	Informational Error	18.2	Manufacturing Quality Control
Total deposits / total withdrawals ratio exceeds maximum threshold	General Ledger	Small_Business_Accts	(multiple)	5/1/2003	Informational Error	1.22	Small Business Account Management

Figure 6.17 Data quality exception summary report.

Summary

In this chapter, we looked at five subject areas within IT portfolio management. We have seen how IT portfolio management is really all about the interplay of people, places, and things in the complex world of IT, the central nervous system of the enterprise. We examined how systems are packaged and related to the spectrum of systems components: hardware, software, data stores, and networks. These components have details, subtypes, and interrelationships, all of which are planned, tracked, and managed by the IT business function. Management itself is a subject of meta data in the MME; the people (users and IT), places, suppliers, and work efforts are themselves planned, tracked, and managed by IT. Meta data is in place to help prevent things going wrong within IT's complicated world of people and systems. And when things do go awry, additional meta data is in place to help IT detect and communicate problems and manage corrective action.

This intricate constellation of IT Portfolio meta data does not exist simply for IT's internal benefit. The raison d'être of the MME is enabling IT to better process and deliver information to the business. It is imperative that information be not only a cacophony of bits and bytes, but also rich in business meaning, relevance, and, above all, value. In Chapter 7, we explore the meta data of business context and meaning.

Universal Meta Model for Business Rules, Business Meta Data, and Data Stewardship

In the previous chapter, we illustrated how to represent IT portfolio management in the MME meta model. It is fairly easy to think of this data in terms of physical entities and attributes; now we are going to look at business meta data. Business meta data provides the context to the content of the data and is necessary for transforming data into truly usable information. This chapter's meta model offers an intuitive method of navigating the data. It presents the data within a government agency or corporation that is important to business users, and (hopefully) IT, from a business perspective. With a solid MME, the business data that was previously locked in the heads of employees and dispersed haphazardly throughout the company is now readily available to the entire organization. This business meta data can be found in word-processing documents, electronic spreadsheets, binders, and the minds of key users. The goal of the Business Meta model is to make that critical information easily available to your enterprise.

Business Rules, Business Meta Data, and Data Stewardship are the three subject areas in the Business Meta model. Because the purpose of this meta data is to reflect the minds of the business users, the data found in these tables should reflect the way the users see the data. Consequently, the answers to both basic and complex questions about the data found in the data warehouse can be found here. Examples of the questions that can be answered are the following:

- What business rules are associated with a specific data element?
- Which business rules are related to other business rules?
- What are the source systems of the data in an application such as data warehousing or CRM?
- What business user approved a specific business rule?
- Who is the data steward that I should talk to if I have questions about a specific business rule?
- Which data groups are in a specific subject area?

Purpose of the Business Rules, Business Meta Data, and Data Stewardship Meta Model

The purpose of the Business Rules, Business Meta Data, and Data Stewardship meta model is to support the business user view of the business. Having a common repository for the storage and maintenance of business rules is critical to an organization. It provides one common source for documenting, maintaining, and approving the rules that run an organization. This common repository of information enables decisions to be made quickly. We have all wasted endless hours at meetings arguing over or trying to figure out why previous decisions were made or why data looks the way it does. Those arguments become a thing of the past with a business rules repository. We can now see that in January 2002 it was decided that late charges would be five dollars for every outstanding 100 dollars. Instead of searching the network drives, binders full of documents, and the brains of business users, we can simply pull the information from the repository.

Business Meta Data allows us to organize data according to the way the business sees the data. We can find the business relationships among pieces of data even if they live on technically incompatible platforms. Data stewards are people who act as conduits between information technology and the business portion of a company. Such people align the business needs with the IT systems supporting them. It is critical that we assign data stewards, for many reasons. They are the people who define, approve, and research the decisions needed to run a business. By assigning data stewards, we encourage the users to feel that they own their pieces of the meta data.

Assumptions in the Business Rules, Business Meta Data, and Data Stewardship Models

In Chapter 6, we listed the assumptions made when creating the meta model for IT portfolio management. Many of those assumptions also apply here; to review, they include the following.

The MME is an operational system, not a data warehouse. As such, it maintains information about the current state of its meta data subjects, not time-variant historical snapshots. For point-in-time reporting and analysis of meta data history, history tables of the entities of the MME may be implemented and include a representation of the time dimension.

Operational fields such as data effective dates and audit fields (for example. create and update dates and user IDs) are not included in the meta model.

Tables for industry-standard global reference data such as state codes, country codes, and the like are assumed to be available in the enterprise and to the MME, and they are not included in the meta model.

Now that we have reviewed the assumptions, let us look at the subject areas with business rules.

Business Rules, Business Meta Data, Data Stewardship Subject Areas

This section of the universal meta model contains three major subject areas:

Business Rules.   This subject area addresses the components that compose business rules. The major data subjects are BUSINESS RULE EXPRESSION, BUSINESS RULE TERM, MISCELLANEOUS BUSINESS RULE, BUSINESS RULE ISSUES, and BUSINESS RULE CATEGORIES.

Business Meta Data.   Refers to the meta data, which provides the context to the content of the data that a business user will access. In addition, the manner in which the user views the data structures is stored in the business meta data subject area. Major data subjects include SUBJECT AREA, ORGANIZATION, and PERSON. Most of the entities in the other sections of the MME contain very concrete entities. SUBJECT AREA, ORGANIZATION, and PERSON are a little more abstract. This was done intentionally to ensure that they covered all types of persons or organizations.

Data Stewardship.   The users who are responsible for the business directions, decisions, and approvals are documented in the data stewardship subject area (see the "Data Stewardship" section of Chapter 3 for a detailed discussion of data stewardship). Major data subjects are DATA STEWARD, BUSINESS RULE DATA STEWARD, SUBJECT AREA DATA STEWARD, DATA ELEMENT DATA STEWARD, DATA PACKAGE STEWARD, and DATA GROUP STEWARD.

These three subject areas are interrelated. Many business rules link directly to specific pieces of business meta data, and the business rules themselves are business meta data. The business rules may apply to the business meta data at a data group, data package, or data element level. Business meta data is also assigned by data stewards, who are responsible for the definition and maintenance of the meta data. The data stewards may be assigned at a higher level, such as subject area, or assigned for an individual data element. Business rules are also assigned a data steward and may in fact be assigned multiple data stewards to perform multiple roles. Along with relationships with each other, these subject areas also have many relationships with other subject areas.

Let's take a look at the first subject area, Business Rules.

Business Rules

Business rules represent the logic applied to calculate or derive a business-related value. They are the rules that document why data appears the way it does. It may contain a formula used to derive a value, or it may point to the source data element that a warehouse element value was moved directly from. The formula may range from the simple to the very complex. Formulas may also contain conditional (IF-THEN) logic (see Figure 7.1).

Table 7.1 describes the Business Rules subject area entities. The most important entity in the Business Rules subject area is, of course, the BUSINESS RULE. This entity contains the highest-level information about the rules developed and approved by data stewards. These are the rules that are used within an organization's decision-making process. An example of a business rule may be the formula used to calculate an account balance (base price + shipping and handling + late charges – discounts). This is the main focal point of the subject area. All of the other entities in this subject area are important because they further define the BUSINESS RULE.

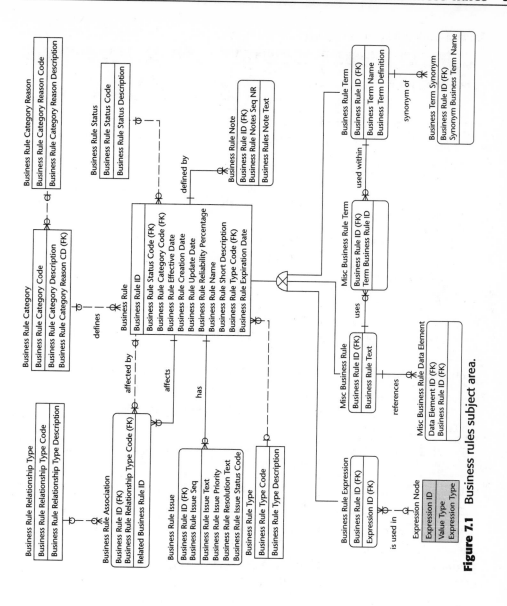

Figure 7.1   Business rules subject area.

Table 7.1   Business Rules Entities

ENTITY NAME	ENTITY DEFINITION
BUSINESS RULE	Rules developed and approved by business representatives that are used within an organization's decision-making processes.
BUSINESS RULE ASSOCIATION	Defines the relationships between business rules.
BUSINESS RULE CATEGORY	A high-level grouping of business rules. May be by department, subject area, or any classification that assists in the categorization of the rules.
BUSINESS RULE CATEGORY REASON	Contains descriptions for business rule category reasons. This is the reason for the business rule category.
BUSINESS RULE EXPRESSION	Connects a business rule with an expression node. The expression node may represent the business rule as a calculation, comparison, or direct move.
BUSINESS RULE ISSUE	Documents and tracks any ongoing issues with a business rule.
BUSINESS RULE NOTE	Any information that is important to keep that could not be easily derived from the business rule detail.
BUSINESS RULE RELATIONSHIP TYPE	Textual description of the relationship types.
BUSINESS RULE STATUS	Tracks the status of the business rule as viewed by the business.
BUSINESS RULE TERM	Stores a textual description of a business rule as approved and defined by the data steward.
BUSINESS RULE TYPE	Stores a textual description and valid values for a business rule type.
BUSINESS TERM SYNONYM	Relates business terms that have the same business definition.
EXPRESSION NODE	This represents a link to tables that can be used to set up expressions. The expressions could be direct moves, calculations, comparisons, or combinations of these.
MISCELLANEOUS BUSINESS RULE	Contains a textual description of a business rule that cannot be represented by the other available methods.
MISC. BUSINESS RULE DATA ELEMENT	Connects a miscellaneous business rule to a data element.
MISC. BUSINESS RULE TERM	Relates business terms to business rules.

A BUSINESS RULE CATEGORY is a high-level grouping of BUSINESS RULEs. The groupings may be made by department, subject area, or any other classification that may assist in the categorization and management of the rules. The rules may be related for the following reasons:

- Same business area
- Related source system
- Same project implementation
- Special approval criteria

There are three main subtypes of BUSINESS RULEs. They are BUSINESS RULE EXPRESSION, BUSINESS RULE TERM, and MISCELLANEOUS BUSINESS RULE. The BUSINESS RULE may be an EXPRESSION, a MISCELLANEOUS BUSINESS RULE, or a BUSINESS TERM, but not more than one. Each BUSINESS RULE must be one and only one of the subtypes.

A BUSINESS RULE EXPRESSION connects a BUSINESS RULE with an EXPRESSION NODE. The EXPRESSION NODE (described in Table 4.8) represents the BUSINESS RULE as a calculation, comparison, or direct move. It is the place where you can find the details behind the transformation of a downstream application (for example, CRM, ERP, data warehouse) data element from a source system. This is where you can tie a DATA ELEMENT in a data warehouse back to the columns that were used to derive its value.

The second type is a BUSINESS RULE TERM. This is where you can place a definition of a common word or phrase used by an organization with a BUSINESS TERM. Here, business users can find a common definition for a word or phrase commonly used throughout the corporation. For example, a direct mail company definition of a Customer may be "A unique individual or corporation who is solicited by, makes purchases from, or is the recipient of items mailed by the company." These definitions should be created and approved by business users. It is critical for a corporation to have an approved set of definitions. These definitions should be specific enough so that when everyone uses a term they are all talking about the same thing. A BUSINESS RULE TERM may have zero, one, or many BUSINESS TERM SYNONYMs. When there are multiple terms used by a business that are defined by the exact same definition, relate them within this attribute.

For example, most of us are familiar with the book and compact disc clubs that send you a postcard every month. Each month you must remember to quickly return the card, or else they will send you a book or compact disc. To ensure that you do not receive the Greatest Hits of Milli Vanilli, you must return that card telling the company that you do not want the merchandise automatically sent; this is called a *No-Book* or a *Refusal*. Both terms mean exactly the same thing (see Figure 7.2). The BUSINESS TERM SYNONYM is especially important to companies with multiple divisions or those that are going through mergers and acquisitions. Often, these separate companies or divisions will develop their own language or terms that, in reality, represent the exact same thing.

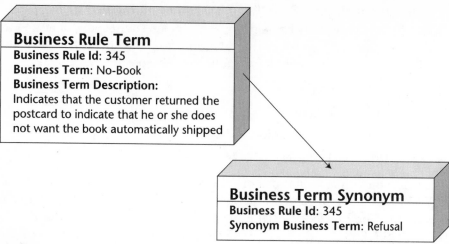

Figure 7.2   Business rule term example.

A MISCELLANEOUS BUSINESS RULE is the third type of BUSINESS RULE. It is a textual representation of a BUSINESS RULE that could not be represented as an expression or business term. If the rule requires manual intervention or special processing, it may not be possible to represent it with an expression. An example is "A customer's status will be changed to fraudulent only after the manual review by a credit specialist." This rule requires manual intervention and therefore cannot be represented by a calculation or conditional statement. When these or similar conditions occur, the MISCELLANEOUS BUSINESS RULE is created. Even though a MISCELLANEOUS BUSINESS RULE could not be defined as an expression, it still contains data elements and business terms. MISCELLANEOUS BUSINESS RULE DATA ELEMENT is used to attach one or many DATA ELEMENTs to a MISCELLANEOUS BUSINESS RULE. A MISCELLANEOUS BUSINESS RULE TERM is used to link a MISCELLANEOUS BUSINESS RULE to one or many BUSINESS RULE TERMs.

A BUSINESS RULE may have zero, one, or many BUSINESS RULE ISSUEs. BUSINESS RULE ISSUE documents and tracks any ongoing issues with a BUSINESS RULE. The table is set up to hold any type of issues that may arise. It may record the fact that an outstanding conflict between business users is holding up the approval of a BUSINESS RULE.

An entity similar to BUSINESS RULE ISSUE is BUSINESS RULE NOTE. This is where we would store any information about the BUSINESS RULE that we think may be valuable but does not fit into any of the other, more specific tables. The main difference between a BUSINESS RULE NOTE and a BUSINESS RULE ISSUE is that a BUSINESS RULE ISSUE requires some action to resolve. A BUSINESS RULE NOTE is permanent documentation that requires no further action.

A BUSINESS RULE ASSOCIATION documents the relationship between BUSINESS RULEs. This entity points a business user to other rules that may provide additional information related to the BUSINESS RULE they are researching. A BUSINESS RULE may affect, support, contradict, or replace a related BUSINESS RULE. For example, a BUSINESS RULE that calculates a customer's total lifetime purchases may be related to a BUSINESS RULE that contains the address-matching rules that would be used to determine if an order is for a new or existing customer.

The remaining tables in the Business Rule subject area—BUSINESS RULE CATEGORY REASON, BUSINESS RULE RELATIONSHIP TYPE, BUSINESS RULE STATUS, and BUSINESS RULE TYPE CODE—are decode tables. They contain the list of valid values for a code and a textual description of each value. These entities are used to find a description to display to the user or validate the values being entered. Each value may appear on many data rows.

The **business rule id** is the unique identifier for a BUSINESS RULE. It is the key that is used to relate other attributes to a BUSINESS RULE. It will appear in many other entities in many other subject areas as a foreign key. You can tell if a BUSINESS RULE is active, obsolete, or pending by looking at the **business rule status code**. The **business rule status code** may change over time and indicates the BUSINESS RULE's most current status.

The **business rule category** represents which high-level grouping a particular BUSINESS RULE belongs in. BUSINESS RULEs may be categorized by business area, related source system, or project implementation, or according to some special approval criteria. This allows you to group BUSINESS RULEs together to quickly locate them for reporting, validation, or updating. For example, if you are starting a new project and want all the BUSINESS RULEs that are created from this project to be easily identifiable, each will be assigned a **business rule category** for that specific project.

Business rule effective date, business rule creation date, business rule expiration date, and **business rule update date** are used to document when certain events happen to a BUSINESS RULE. When a rule is first entered into the system, that date is captured in the **business rule creation date**. The **business rule effective date** represents the date that the rule was approved and used by the corporation. When any changes are made to a BUSINESS RULE or its definition, you capture that with the **business rule update date**. If a previously effective rule is no longer valid, the date that the BUSINESS RULE became no longer effective is stored in **business rule expiration date**. Often these dates are automatically updated by creating database triggers. A trigger automatically runs when certain events occur. When a BUSINESS RULE is first inserted, a trigger may run that puts the current date in **business rule creation date**.

The **business rule reliability percentage** defines the percentage of confidence in the BUSINESS RULE. By confidence we mean how sure you are that the data found in the source system is up to date and accurate. The information used to create a BUSINESS RULE may be old or unreliable, but the rule was still created and approved. That BUSINESS RULE may have a reliability percentage of 45 percent. A BUSINESS RULE that represents a calculation involving data that has been scrubbed and validated may have a reliability of 95 percent.

The business user needs an easy way to select a rule. The **business rule name** is used to store a short name, not a full description, that business users can use to quickly find a rule they are looking for. Examples of **business rule names** are "Account Balance Calculation" and "Order Status Assignment." A **business rule short description** provides more detail then the **business rule name** but does not need to fully define the BUSINESS RULE. The full context of the BUSINESS RULE will be contained in one of the subtypes. The subtype contains enough information to differentiate between BUSINESS RULEs with similar **business rule names**.

There are three subtypes of BUSINESS RULEs:

EXPRESSION

MISC. BUSINESS RULE

BUSINESS TERM

These entities contain information that provides further detail about a BUSINESS RULE. **business rule type code** tells us which of these subtypes a particular BUSINESS RULE uses to contain the rule details.

Figure 7.3 shows a sample entry and maintenance screen for a BUSINESS RULE. The next Rule ID is assigned automatically to each new BUSINESS RULE. This screen would allow the data stewards to update meta data directly in the MME. The Rule Name is a free-form text area where the business user gives the rule a name. Category should be chosen from a predefined list of categories. A percentage from 0 percent to 100 percent is entered into Reliability percentage. Description is another free-form text area; here the business user enters a more detailed description of the rule. The Audit Dates—Creation, Effective and Last Updates—are automatically updated based upon the user's actions. When the rule is first entered, the creation date is updated. When the status is changed to effective, the effective date is updated, and every time a change is made to a rule the last update date is incremented. The business rule Type and Status must be chosen from the three options given for each.

The next group of buttons directs the user to more detail about the rule. Notes, Related Rules, Subject Areas, Issues, and Data Steward direct the users to screens where they will enter additional rule data. The three subtypes of a business rule are represented by the next three buttons:

Expression

Miscellaneous

Business Term

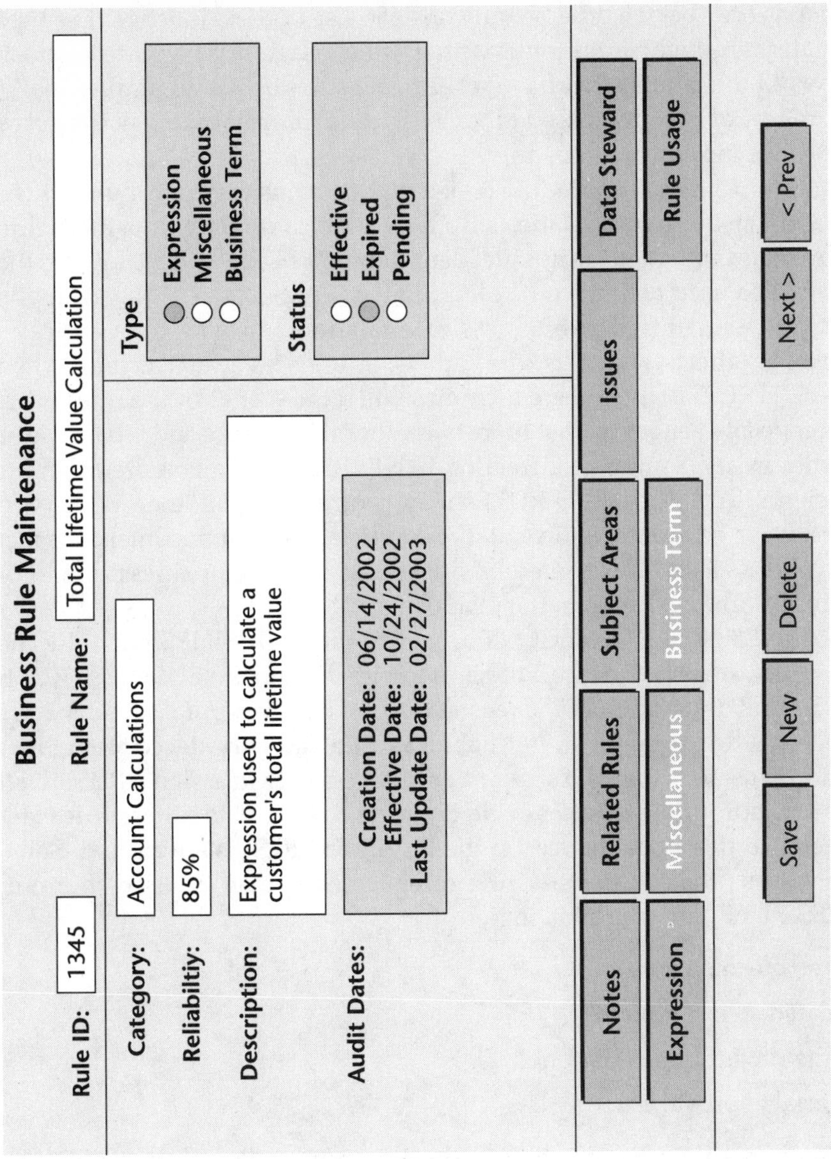

Business Rule Maintenance

Rule ID: 1345   Rule Name: Total Lifetime Value Calculation

Category: Account Calculations

Reliabiltiy: 85%

Description: Expression used to calculate a customer's total lifetime value

Audit Dates:
Creation Date: 06/14/2002
Effective Date: 10/24/2002
Last Update Date: 02/27/2003

Type
○ Expression
○ Miscellaneous
○ Business Term

Status
○ Effective
○ Expired
○ Pending

Notes   Related Rules   Subject Areas   Issues   Data Steward

Expression   Miscellaneous   Business Term   Rule Usage

Save   New   Delete   Next >   < Prev

Figure 7.3   Business rule entry screen.

A rule may only be one type, so only one of these buttons is active. The type chosen determines which button is active. Rule Usage takes you to a screen that shows all the entities that have relationships to thisbusiness rule. Finally, the bottom row of buttons is used to save or delete this rule, add a new rule, or navigate to the next or previous rule.

The BUSINESS RULE ASSOCIATION entity contains three attributes, **business rule id, business rule relationship type code,** and **related business rule id**. The **business rule id** is the unique identifier for a BUSINESS RULE. It is the key that will be used to relate a BUSINESS RULE ASSOCIATION back to the BUSINESS RULE entity. The **business rule relationship type code** indicates whether a rule affects, supports, contradicts, or replaces a related rule. When creating BUSINESS RULEs, there are times when the scopes of the rules overlap. This code lets you know that there is another related rule and what type of relationship exists. Sometimes, creating BUSINESS RULEs is more of an art than a science, and BUSINESS RULEs may contradict each other. While you may not always be able to resolve all the conflicts, you can document the fact that the conflicts exist. The **related business rule id** is the **business rule id** of the second BUSINESS RULE in the relationship.

The BUSINESS RULE CATEGORY is used to group BUSINESS RULEs. The **business rule category code** is found as a foreign key on the BUSINESS RULE entity. A textual description of the reason that the **business rule category code** was created is documented in the **business rule category description**. This description is used by the data steward or business user to assign a BUSINESS RULE to an appropriate **business rule category code**. The **business rule category reason cd** describes the reason the BUSINESS RULEs are related. Some possible reasons that a **business rule category code** may be used to group BUSINESS RULEs are the following:

- Same business area
- Related source system
- Same project implementation
- Special approval criteria

The **business rule category reason cd** is the primary key of the BUSINESS RULE CATEGORY REASON. It exists as a foreign key on the BUSINESS RULE CATEGORY. A textual description of attribute value is stored in the attribute **business rule category reason description**.

Because BUSINESS RULE EXPRESSION is a subtype of BUSINESS RULE, the **business rule id** is the primary key to this entity. A subtype must have the same primary key as the supertype. **Expression id** is a link to the EXPRESSION NODE explained in an earlier chapter. The expression could consist of a direct move, a calculation, or conditional logic.

Business rule id and **business rule issue sequence** are the primary keys for this entity. **Business rule issue sequence** allows multiple issues to be associated with a single BUSINESS RULE. The first issue for a BUSINESS RULE is assigned **business rule issue sequence** of 1. Each new issue is assigned the next number in sequential order. The **business rule issue sequence** starts at 1 for each BUSINESS RULE. The description of the BUSINESS RULE ISSUE is found in **business rule issue text**. Here, the businessperson who enters the issue explains the problem in business language. At the time the issue is entered, a priority must also be selected. This enables you to prioritize the issues in order to attack the highest-priority issues first. When an issue is resolved, two things most occur. First, the resolution must be entered into the **business rule resolution text.** Second, the **business rule issue status** must be changed from open to closed.

Figure 7.4 shows a sample entry screen for a BUSINESS RULE ISSUE. The business user enters the **business rule id** he or she wants to query. The Rule Text and Business Steward are automatically populated from the BUSINESS RULE. They appear gray because they are not updatable. The next and previous buttons can be used to navigate through the BUSINESS RULE ISSUEs. Selecting another choice can change Status and Priority. When a status is selected, the current status is unselected. The Issue and Resolution are free-form text. Save and Delete update the changes or remove the issue from the database. New opens a screen with the next available sequence number calculated and the text fields emptied.

Business rule id and **business rule note sequence** are the primary keys for this entity. Multiple notes may be attached to a BUSINESS RULE using the **business rule notes sequence**. Like the **business rule issue sequence**, each new issue is assigned the next number in sequential order. The **business rule note text** is a free-form text area for adding notes to further document or explain the business rule. The data stored here does not represent issues but includes any further documentation that may be important.

Business rule relationship type code is used within the BUSINESS RULE ASSOCIATION to describe a relationship between two BUSINESS RULEs. The textual description of the **business rule relationship type code** is documented in the **business rule relationship type description**. The BUSINESS RULE ASSOCIATION only contains the code value. All valid **business rule relationship type codes** and the corresponding descriptions are stored in this entity.

BUSINESS RULE STATUS is a code table like BUSINESS RULE RELATIONSHIP TYPE. **Business rule status code** is used within the BUSINESS RULE to describe the approval status of a BUSINESS RULE. The textual description of the **business rule status** is documented in the **business rule status description**. Like other code tables, the BUSINESS RULE STATUS only contains the code value and the corresponding descriptions.

BUSINESS RULE TERM is one of the three subtypes of BUSINESS RULEs; therefore, it has the same primary key as a BUSINESS RULE. The **business term name** is simply a word or phrase used by the business that has a definition unique to the business. Most industries and organizations have their own

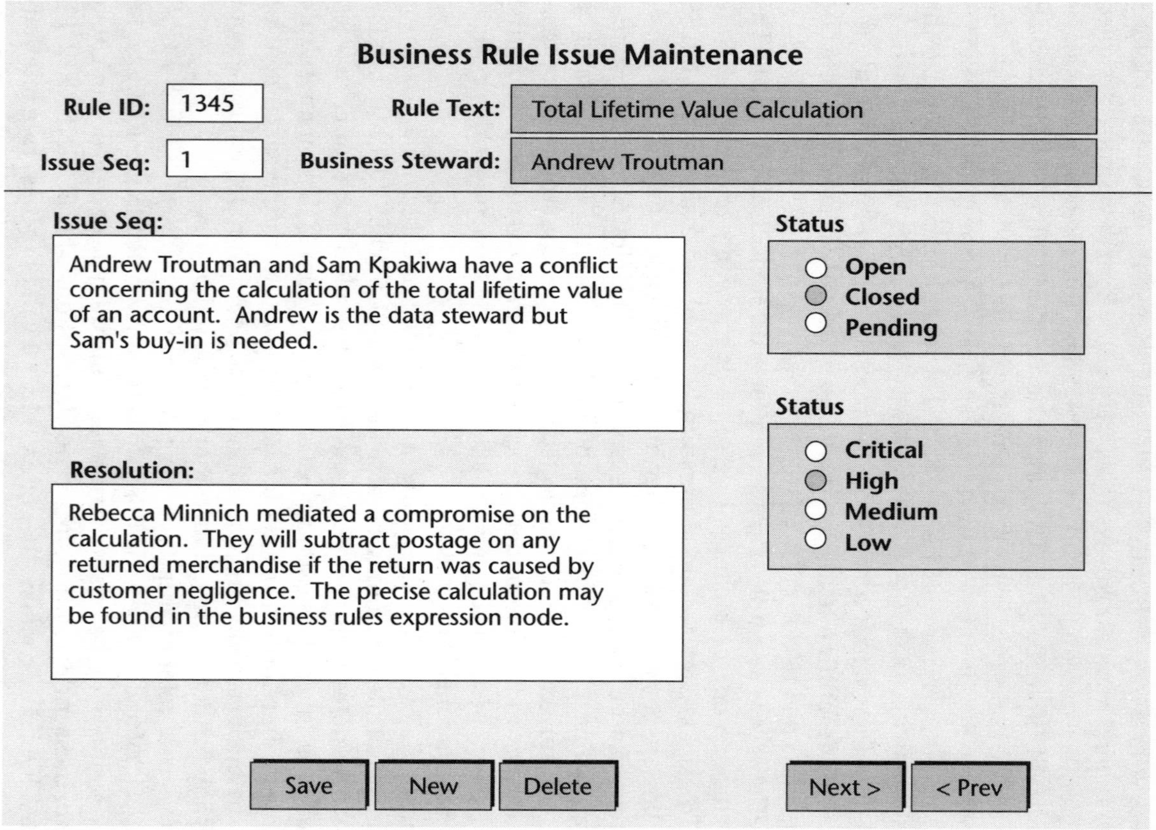

Business Rule Issue Maintenance

Rule ID: 1345

Issue Seq: 1

Rule Text: Total Lifetime Value Calculation

Business Steward: Andrew Troutman

Status
- ○ Open
- ○ Closed
- ○ Pending

Status
- ○ Critical
- ○ High
- ○ Medium
- ○ Low

Issue Seq:

Andrew Troutman and Sam Kpakiwa have a conflict concerning the calculation of the total lifetime value of an account. Andrew is the data steward but Sam's buy-in is needed.

Resolution:

Rebecca Minnich mediated a compromise on the calculation. They will subtract postage on any returned merchandise if the return was caused by customer negligence. The precise calculation may be found in the business rules expression node.

Save	New	Delete

Next >	< Prev

Figure 7.4 Business rule issue entry screen.

definitions for certain terms. An announcement to a direct marketing company may mean a monthly catalog mailing, but it could mean something entirely different to an insurance company. The precise agreed-upon definition that is used throughout the organization is stored in the **business term definition**. In the best scenario, the business user creates all definitions. If the business users cannot or will not create the definitions, they should, at the very least, approve all definitions.

Like the previously described code tables, BUSINESS RULE TYPE provides a description and list of valid values for the **business rule type code**. The **Business rule type code** can be found on the BUSINESS RULE. The **business rule type code** is used to indicate which table contains additional information about the BUSINESS RULE. The valid values are as follows:

1. *Expression*: For example, a customer's lifetime value equals the total purchased amount minus the total returned amount plus the total adjustment credits minus delinquency charges.

2. *Miscellaneous Rule*: For example, "an account is cancelled after a manual review by an account credit specialist."

3. *Business Term*: Where an account is a unique relationship between a customer and a specific line of business. One customer may have many accounts if he or she has a relationship with many lines of business.

BUSINESS TERM SYNONYM simply relates one BUSINESS TERM to another BUSINESS TERM. The **business rule id** is the identifier for the BUSINESS TERM. The **synonym business term name** contains a **business term name** with the same definition as the related BUSINESS TERM. Refer back to Figure 7.2 for an example.

MISCELLANEOUS BUSINESS RULE, BUSINESS RULE EXPRESSION, and BUSINESS RULE TERM are the three subtypes of BUSINESS RULEs. A subtype is a further classification of a supertype, so it has the same primary key as a BUSINESS RULE. The textual description of the BUSINESS RULE is stored in **business rule text**. If the BUSINESS RULE cannot be expressed with an expression or is not a business term, the rule is captured here.

MISCELLANEOUS BUSINESS RULE DATA ELEMENT is an associative entity. That means that it exists to resolve a M:M relationship between BUSINESS RULE and DATA ELEMENT. A MISCELLANEOUS BUSINESS RULE may be associated with many DATA ELEMENTs, and a DATA ELEMENT may be associated with many BUSINESS RULEs. This entity contains **business rule id** and **data element id,** which are the primary keys of the two tables with an M:M relationship.

MISCELLANEOUS BUSINESS RULE TERM, like MISCELLANEOUS BUSINESS RULE DATA ELEMENT, is an associative entity. It resolves a M:M relationship between a MISCELLANEOUS BUSINESS RULE and a BUSINESS RULE TERM. **Business rule id** contains the primary key of a MISCELLANEOUS BUSINESS RULE, and **term business rule id** contains the **business rule id** of a BUSINESS RULE TERM.

Table 7.2 shows more details about the attributes of the business rule subject area.

Table 7.2 Business Rule Attributes

ENTITY NAME	ATTRIBUTE NAME	ATTRIBUTE DEFINITION
BUSINESS RULE	business rule id	**business rule id** is a unique Identifier for a set of statements or expressions that documents the rules that govern a business.
	business rule status code	**business rule status code** is the current status of the business rule.
	business rule category code	**business rule category code** is a high-level grouping of business rules.
	business rule effective date	**business rule effective date** is the date the business rule became effective.
	business rule creation date	**business rule creation date** is the date the business rule was first created.
	business rule update date	**business rule update date** is the date of the last update to the business rule.
	business rule reliability percentage	**business rule reliability percentage** is a percentage representing the degree of confidence in the accuracy of this rule.
	business rule name	**business rule name** is the textual description of the rule (in noun form).
	business rule short description	**business rule short description** is the textual description of the rule in English.
	business rule type code	**business rule type code** describes the type of business rule. This indicates which supporting tables contain further information to describe the business rule.
	business rule expiration date	**business rule expiration date** is the date the business rule became no longer valid to the business.
BUSINESS RULE ASSOCIATIONS	business rule id	**business rule id** is a unique identifier for a set of statements or expressions that documents the rules that govern a business.
	business rule relationship type code	**business rule relationship type code** describes the relationship between two business rules.

Table 7.2   *(continued)*

ENTITY NAME	ATTRIBUTE NAME	ATTRIBUTE DEFINITION
	related business rule id	**related business rule id** is a business rule ID of a business rule that has a relationship with another rule.
BUSINESS RULE CATEGORY	business rule category code	**business rule category code** is a value for a high-level grouping of business rules.
	business rule category description	**business rule category description** is a textual description of a business rule category.
	business rule category reason cd	**business rule category reason cd** describes the reason that business rules are related.
BUSINESS RULE CATEGORY REASON	business rule category reason cd	**business rule category reason cd** describes the reason that business rules are related.
	business rule category reason description	**business rule category reason description** is a textual description of a vusiness rule category reason.
BUSINESS RULE EXPRESSION	business rule id	**business rule id** is a unique identifier for a set of statements or expressions that documents the rules that govern a business.
	expression id	Refer to Table 4.8 for this attribute's definition.
BUSINESS RULE ISSUE	business rule id	**business rule id** is a unique identifier for a set of statements or expressions that documents the rules that govern a business.
	business rule issue sequence	**business rule issue sequence** is a unique sequence number assigned to an issue within a rule.
	business rule issue text	**business rule issue text** is a textual representation of an issue associated with a business rule.
	business rule issue priority	**business rule issue priority** indicates the priority that needs to be applied to a specific issue.
	business rule resolution text	**business rule resolution text** is a textual explanation of how a business rule issue was resolved.

(continued)

Table 7.2 *(continued)*

ENTITY NAME	ATTRIBUTE NAME	ATTRIBUTE DEFINITION
	business rule issue status code	**business rule issue status code** is the status of the business rule issue.
BUSINESS RULE NOTE	**business rule id**	**business rule id** is a unique identifier for a set of statements or expressions that documents the rules that govern a business.
	business rule note sequence nr	**business rule note sequence nr** is a sequential number used to order notes as they are added to the transformation process.
	business rule note text	**business rule note text** is a free-form text area used to add notes to further document or explain the business rule.
BUSINESS RULE RELATIONSHIP TYPE	**business rule relationship type code**	**business rule relationship type code** describes the relationship between two business rules.
	business rule relationship type description	**business rule relationship type description** is a textual description of a business rule relationship type.
BUSINESS RULE STATUS	**business rule status code**	**Business rule status code** describes the approval status of a business rule.
	business rule status description	**business rule status description** is a textual description of a business rule status.
BUSINESS RULE TERM	**business rule id**	**business rule id** is a unique identifier for a set of statements or expressions that documents the rules that govern a business.
	business term name	**business term name** is a name of a word or phrase uniquely defined by a business user to define how the term is used within an organization.
	business term definition	**business term definition** is an approved definition for a business term.
BUSINESS RULE TYPE	**business rule type code**	**business rule type code** describes the type of business rule. This indicates which supporting tables contain further information to describe the business rule.

Table 7.2 *(continued)*

ENTITY NAME	ATTRIBUTE NAME	ATTRIBUTE DEFINITION
	business rule type description	**business rule type description** is a textual description of a business rule type.
BUSINESS TERM SYNONYM	**business rule id**	**business rule id** is a unique Identifier for a set of statements or expressions that documents the rules that govern a business.
	synonym business term name	**synonym business term name** is a business term that is a synonym for another business term.
MISC. BUSINESS RULE	**business rule id**	**business rule id** is a unique Identifier for a set of statements or expressions that documents the rules that govern a business.
	business rule text	**business rule text** is a textual description of a business rule that does not fit into the other business rule types.
MISC. BUSINESS RULE DATA ELEMENT	**business rule id**	**business rule id** is a unique identifier for a set of statements or expressions that documents the rules that govern a business.
	data element id	Refer to Table 4.2 for this attribute's definition.
MISC. BUSINESS RULE TERM	**business rule id**	**business rule id** is a unique identifier for a set of statements or expressions that documents the rules that govern a business.
	term business rule id	**term business rule id** is a business rule for a term that is related to a miscellaneous business rule.

Business Meta Data

Business meta data defines the information we use to organize the data found in the data enterprise into subject areas and to describe the people who perform actions on or are affected by the data. We create groupings of data that represent the way the data is viewed by the business. DATA GROUPs, DATA PACKAGEs, and DATA ELEMENTs may be organized into subject areas to aid in the management of the data. SUBJECT AREAs allow the data to be organized the way the business uses the data and are not limited to a single database or hardware platform. Even if there are technical constraints that do not permit data to be linked within a particular database, that data can still be related through a SUBJECT AREA.

For example, an employee database table may contain information such as name, address, and hiring date. The Human Resources department may maintain a file that contains previous employment information. The employee database does not have a place to store the previous employment data. The employee database is stored in an Oracle database, and the previous employment information is stored in a sequential flat file. This data is related only by the fact that both sets of data contain information about an employee. Both of these DATA GROUPs would be in the Employee subject area (see Figure 7.5).

Table 7.3 describes the Business Meta Data subject area entities.

Table 7.3   Business Meta Data Entities

ENTITY	ENTITY DEFINITION
DATA ELEMENT	Refer to Table 4.1 for this entity's definition.
DATA ELEMENT BUSINESS RULE	Relates a business rule to a data element.
DATA ELEMENT SUBJECT AREA	Relates a business rule to a subject area.
DATA GROUP	Refer to Table 4.1 for the entity definition.
DATA GROUP BUSINESS RULE	Relates a business rule to a data group.
DATA GROUP SUBJECT AREA	Relates a data group to a subject area.
ORGANIZATION	A structure through which individuals cooperate systematically to conduct business. An organization may represent a corporation, a specific company, a department, or a work group.
PERSON	Represents a unique individual. A person will typically perform a role within an organization.
PERSON PHONE NUMBER	Contains phone numbers as a person uses them. Individual people may use different types of phones.
SUBJECT AREA	A high-level grouping of a business used to classify business rules and business tables. A subject area may represent a department, business application, or other grouping relevant to a particular business.
SUBJECT AREA BUSINESS RULE	Relates a business rule to a subject area.

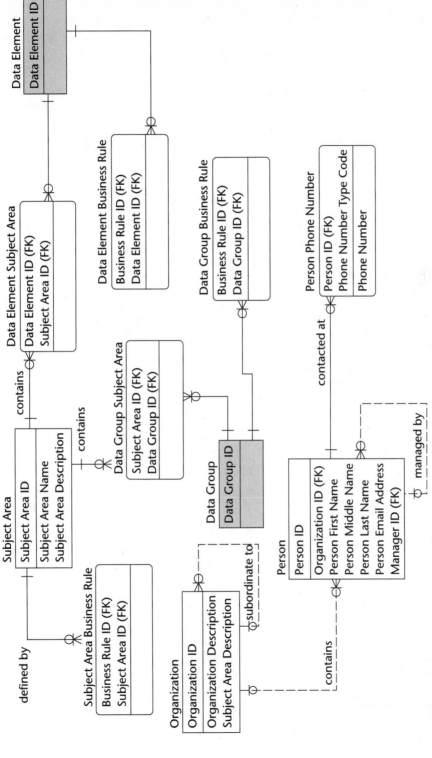

Figure 7.5   Business meta data subject area.

SUBJECT AREA represents a high-level grouping of a business. It is used to classify business rules and business tables. SUBJECT AREAs typically represent departments or organizations within a corporation. They represent the way the business views the data. The data in the groupings may cross hardware types and software platforms.

BUSINESS GROUPs and BUSINESS ELEMENTs may be assigned to a SUBJECT AREA. The entities DATA ELEMENT SUBJECT AREA and DATA GROUP SUBJECT AREA are used to show this association. SUBJECT AREA BUSINESS RULE links a SUBJECT AREA to one or many BUSINESS RULEs. The same BUSINESS RULE may also be attached to one or many SUBJECT AREAs.

BUSINESS RULEs may apply to a specific DATA ELEMENT or DATA GROUP. Two entities, DATA GROUP BUSINESS RULE and DATA ELEMENT BUSINESS RULE, are used to associate them with a BUSINESS RULE. A DATA GROUP or DATA ELEMENT can be associated with many BUSINESS RULEs, and a BUSINESS RULE may be associated with many DATA GROUPs and/or DATA ELEMENTs.

The PERSON ENTITY contains information about the people that play roles within the organization. The PERSON ENTITY is used throughout the Universal Meta Model. This entity allows us to ensure that an individual person is defined only once. It provides a common place to link to a person to find out contact and other information. The PERSON entity has a recursive relationship for a manager. A PERSON is managed by another PERSON; therefore, the PERSON entity has a recursive relationship with itself.

PERSON PHONE NUMBER and ORGANIZATION are used to further define a PERSON. The PERSON PHONE NUMBER contains any phone numbers that we have for a PERSON. That may include their home, work, and cell phone. ORGANIZATION is used to organize people in a way that reflects their roles and assignments within an ORGANIZATION.

Now let us look at the detail behinds the entities.

- DATA ELEMENT BUSINESS RULE relates a BUSINESS RULE to a DATA ELEMENT. Because a BUSINESS RULE can be associated with many DATA ELEMENTs and a DATA ELEMENT may be associated with many BUSINESS RULEs, both attributes must be part of the primary key. The only attributes needed on this table are **business rule id** and **data element id,** the primary keys of the two tables.

- DATA ELEMENT SUBJECT AREA is another associative entity. It is used to resolve the M:M relationship between a DATA ELEMENT and a SUBJECT AREA. The **subject area id** is a unique identifier for high-level classifications for areas of a business. This attribute is used to group DATA ELEMENTs into specific business groupings.

- DATA GROUP BUSINESS RULE and DATA GROUP SUBJECT AREA serve the same purpose for a DATA GROUP that DATA ELEMENT BUSINESS RULE and DATA ELEMENT SUBJECT AREA serve for a DATA ELEMENT. They are associative entities between a DATA GROUP and a BUSINESS RULE and SUBJECT AREA. They each contain the primary keys of the two tables for which they are resolving the M:M relationship.

organization id is the unique identifier for the ORGANIZATION. It may represent a company, line of business, division, or department within an organization. Different levels of a corporation's structure are represented here. The name or short description of the ORGANIZATION is stored in **organization description**. The **parent organization id** relates an ORGANIZATION to another ORGANIZATION. The **parent organization** is the identifier for the organization that is one level up in the corporation's reporting structure. Figure 7.6 is a partial organization structure showing how the **organization id** and **parent organization id** might be assigned within a typical insurance corporation.

The unique identifier for a person playing a role within an organization is found in **person id**. This may indicate an employee, consultant, customer, or any other individual that an ORGANIZATION may need to store information about. The link to the ORGANIZATION to which the PERSON belongs is stored in **organization id**. If the PERSON is not part of the corporation, **organization id** is set to null (no value). Person First Name, Person Middle Name, and Person Last Name contain the given name for the person. If a middle name is not available, the field is left empty. Because of the explosion of communication via the Internet, it is now standard to carry an email address that is used to contact the PERSON. This address is stored in **person email address. manager id** creates a recursive relationship within PERSON. A recursive relationship occurs when an entity relates to itself. The **manager id** contains the **person id** of the Manager of the Person.

person id is the unique identifier for a person that you store a phone number for. **phone number type code** describes the type of PERSON PHONE NUMBER you are storing. Some possible values are:

- Home
- Work
- Cell
- Fax

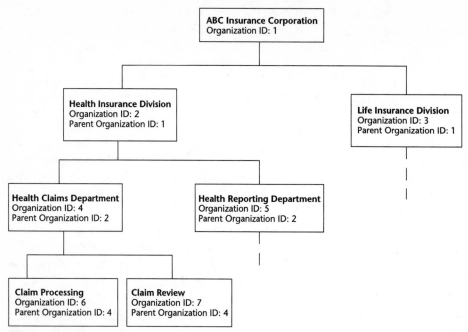

Figure 7.6 Organization example.

phone number contains the actual number to be dialed to reach a PERSON at the Phone Type.

The **subject area id** is the unique identifier for a SUBJECT AREA. It represents a high-level classification of the areas of a business. This classification is used to place attributes into specific business groupings. **subject area id** is a sequentially defined number so that the **subject area name** contains the name by which the SUBJECT AREA is known to the business. A more detailed description of a SUBJECT AREA may be found in the **subject area description**.

The SUBJECT AREA BUSINESS RULE contains the primary keys to BUSINESS RULE and SUBJECT AREA. The keys resolve many relationships between a SUBJECT AREA and a BUSINESS RULE.

Table 7.4 shows more details about the attributes of the Business Meta Data subject area.

Table 7.4   Business Meta Data Attributes

ENTITY NAME	ATTRIBUTE NAME	ATTRIBUTE DEFINITION
DATA ELEMENT BUSINESS RULE	**business rule id**	**business rule id** is a unique identifier for a set of statements or expressions that documents the rules that govern a business.
	data element id	Refer to Table 4.2 for this attribute's definition.
DATA ELEMENT SUBJECT AREA	**data element id**	Refer to Table 4.2 for this attribute's definition.
	subject area id	**subject area id** is a high-level classification of the areas of a business. This is used to group data attributes into specific business groupings.
DATA GROUP BUSINESS RULE	**business rule id**	**business rule id** is a unique identifier for a set of statements or expressions that documents the rules that govern a business.
	data group id	Refer to Table 4.2 for this attribute's definition.
DATA GROUP SUBJECT AREA	**data group id**	Refer to Table 4.2 for this attribute's definition.
	subject area id	**subject area id** is a high-level classification of the areas of a business. This is used to group data attributes into specific business groupings.
ORGANIZATION	**organization id**	**organization id** is a unique identifier for a department or section of a business.
	organization description	**organization description** is a textual description of an organization.

(continued)

Table 7.4 *(continued)*

ENTITY NAME	ATTRIBUTE NAME	ATTRIBUTE DEFINITION
	parent organization id	**parent organization id** is a pointer to the organization id one level up in the corporation's reporting structure.
PERSON	person id	**person id** is a unique identifier for an individual playing a role within a corporation.
	organization id	**organization id** is a unique identifier for a department or section of a business.
	person first name	**person first name** is the given name for a person.
	person middle name	**person middle name** is the middle name of a person.
	person last name	**person last name** is the surname of a person.
	person email address	**person email address** is the preferred email address used to contact an individual.
	manager id	**manager id** is the identifier of a person's manager. This is another person ID.
PERSON PHONE NUMBER	person id	**person id** is a unique identifier for an individual playing a role within a corporation.
	phone number type code	**phone number type code** describes the usage of a phone by a person.
	phone number	**phone number** is the number used to reach a person at the phone number type.
SUBJECT AREA	subject area id	**subject area id** is a high-level classification of areas of a business. This is used to group data attributes into specific business groupings.
	subject area name	**subject area name** is the business name assigned to a subject area.
	subject area description	**subject area description** is a textual description of a subject area.

Table 7.4   *(continued)*

ENTITY NAME	ATTRIBUTE NAME	ATTRIBUTE DEFINITION
SUBJECT AREA BUSINESS RULE	**business rule id**	**business rule id** is a unique identifier for a set of statements or expressions that documents the rules that govern a business.
	subject area id	**subject area id** is a high-level classification of areas of a business. This is used to group data attributes into specific business groupings.

Data Stewardship

Data is the most important asset of a company. Data stewardship assigns users to the management, approval, and maintenance of the data definitions and the corresponding business rules (see Figure 7.7). A data steward acts as a conduit between IT and the business users. He or she assists in aligning the business needs with the IT systems that support them. It is the data stewards' responsibility to make sure that the business can make the optimum use of its data resources. Multiple data stewards may be assigned to the same business attribute. The different stewards perform different roles, ranging from an executive sponsor to the programmer who maintains the repository information.

Table 7.5 describes the Business Rule subject area entities.

Table 7.5   Business Rule Entities

ENTITY	ENTITY DEFINITION
BUSINESS RULE DATA STEWARD	Relates a business rule to a data steward.
DATA ELEMENT STEWARD	Relates a data element to a data steward.
DATA GROUP STEWARD	Relates a data group to a data steward.
DATA PACKAGE STEWARD	Relates a data package to a data steward.
DATA STEWARD	Defines a person who is a conduit between IT and the business areas of a company. Such as person aligns the business needs with the IT systems supporting them.
SUBJECT AREA DATA STEWARD	Relates a subject area to a data steward.

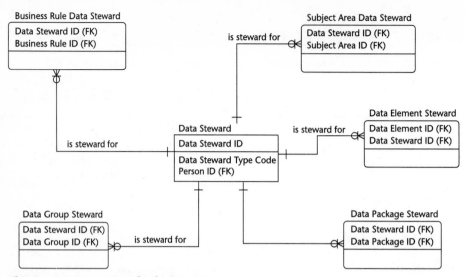

Figure 7.7 Data steward subject area.

A DATA STEWARD defines a PERSON who is a conduit between IT and the business areas of a company. Such a person aligns the business needs with the IT systems supporting them. A DATA STEWARD is a general term for a person who may fill one of many roles. These roles may include executive sponsor, chief steward, business steward, and technical steward. The details about the PERSON performing the role of DATA STEWARD can be found via the relationship between DATA STEWARD and PERSON.

A DATA STEWARD may be assigned to many other entities. The entities in this chapter that have a relationship with DATA STEWARD are DATA ELEMENT, DATA GROUP, DATA PACKAGE, SUBJECT AREA, and BUSINESS RULE. Each of these entities may have one or many DATA STEWARDS, and each DATA STEWARD may be associated with one or many of these entities. An associative entity exists to resolve each of these relationships. These entities are: BUSINESS RULE DATA STEWARD, DATA ELEMENT STEWARD, DATA GROUP STEWARD, DATA PACKAGE STEWARD, and SUBJECT AREA STEWARD.

- DATA GROUP STEWARD and DATA ELEMENT STEWARD are both associative entities for the relationship between DATA STEWARD and

DATA GROUP and DATA ELEMENT. The **data element id** is the primary key of DATA ELEMENT, and the **data steward id** is the primary key of DATA STEWARD. **Data steward id** may point to one of many types of DATA STEWARDs. The DATA STEWARD being referenced may be an executive sponsor, chief steward, business steward, or technical steward. A more detailed description of the DATA STEWARD types may be found in the description for DATA STEWARD.

The **data steward id** and the **business rule id** are the primary keys of this entity and the foreign keys to the DATA STEWARD and BUSINESS RULE. A single BUSINESS RULE may have many DATA STEWARDS providing different functions.

- A DATA PACKAGE is a grouping of DATA GROUPs (see Chapter 4 for more details). DATA PACKAGE STEWARD provides a junction between a DATA PACKAGE and a DATA STEWARD. A DATA STEWARD may be responsible for many DATA PACKAGEs, and a DATA PACKAGE may have many DATA STEWARDs performing different roles.

- A DATA STEWARD helps maintain a company's business resources. The **data steward id** is a unique identifier for this entity. The **data steward id** appears as a foreign key in any entity that needs to have a DATA STEWARD assigned. The **data steward type code** defines the data stewardship role the PERSON is playing. These types may be executive sponsor, chief steward, business steward, or technical steward.

An executive sponsor is a member of executive management who helps resolve issues that cut across a company's line of business. It is very important to have executive management support to help break down any roadblocks that may arise. At the beginning of a project it is easy to underestimate the obstacles the political environment may create.

The chief steward is responsible for the day-to-day management and organization of a data initiative. He or she should be a senior-level person who can act as a project manager, should be well respected within the organization, and should have knowledge of the technical and business issues of the company.

The business steward performs most of the day-to-day business processes. The business steward defines procedures, policies, and definitions. He or she should have a strong knowledge of the business rules that apply to the particular area being worked on.

A representative from the organization's IT department should be assigned as the DATA STEWARD. He or she is responsible for the technical resources, technical meta data, and other data needed to support the effort.

The unique identifier for a PERSON who provides a rule as a DATA STEWARD is stored in **person id**. The individual is further described in PERSON.

SUBJECT AREA DATA STEWARD resolves an M:M relationship. It contains the primary keys to BUSINESS RULE and SUBJECT AREA.

Table 7.6 shows more details about the attributes of the business rule subject area.

Table 7.6 Business Rule Attributes

ENTITY NAME	ATTRIBUTE NAME	ATTRIBUTE DEFINITION
DATA ELEMENT STEWARD	**data element id**	Refer to Table 4.2 for this attribute's definition.
	data steward id	**data steward id** identifies a person assigned by the company to perform a role in defining, maintaining, or approving business meta data.
DATA GROUP STEWARD	**data group id**	Refer to Table 4.2 for this attribute's definition.
	data steward id	**data steward id** identifies a person assigned by the company to perform a role in defining, maintaining, or approving business meta data.
BUSINESS RULE DATA STEWARD	**data steward id**	**data steward id** is a person assigned by the company to perform a role in defining, maintaining, or approving business meta data.
	business rule id	**business rule id** identifies a unique identifier for a set of statements or expressions that documents the rules that govern a business.
DATA PACKAGE STEWARD	**data package id**	Refer to Table 4.2 for this attribute's definition.
	data steward id	**data steward id** is a person assigned by the company to perform a role in defining, maintaining, or approving business meta data.

Table 7.6 *(continued)*

ENTITY NAME	ATTRIBUTE NAME	ATTRIBUTE DEFINITION
DATA STEWARD	**data steward id**	**data steward id** is a person assigned by the company to perform a role in defining, maintaining, or approving business meta data.
	data steward type code	**data steward type code** defines the data stewardship role that the person is playing.
	person id	**person id** identifies a unique identifier for an individual playing a role within an organization.
SUBJECT AREA DATA STEWARD	**data steward id**	**data steward id** identifies a person assigned by the company to perform a role in defining, maintaining, or approving business meta data.
	subject area id	**subject area id** is a high-level classification of areas of a business. This is used to group data attributes into specific business groupings.

Reports from the Business Rules, Business Meta Data, and Data Stewardship Meta Models

Now that we have reviewed all the subject areas, entities, and attributes in detail, let us look at some of the reports you can generate from this data. You are beginning to understand the data that is stored, but what useful information can you obtain from that?

All Business Rules Report

The All Business Rules report is a simple report that gives the user an overall view of all the business rules (see Figure 7.8). You may have been tasked with obtaining an understanding of the company's data assets. You need to get an overview of the company. This report is a good start. It shows what kinds of rules are recorded and which ones are active. This report's main purpose is to evaluate how the company is using the business rules. Other reports are required to find out more detailed or specific information. We show the most important information, including the ID, type, status category, reliability percentage, and name.

All Business Rules					ABC Corporation August 15, 2003
Category	Rule ID	Type	Status	Reliability	Rule Name
Account Calculations	234	Expression	Effective	85%	Lifetime Value Calculation
	235	Expression	Effective	95%	Total Balance Due Calculation
Data Warehouse Feed	236	Miscellaneous	Effective	50%	Account Status Derivation
	238	Expression	Effective	75%	Account Number Transformation
Financial Information	237	Business Term	Expired	100%	Account Dunning Statement
Mailing Address	239	Business Term	Pending	99%	Customer Address Standardization

Figure 7.8 All business rules report.

The SQL needed to create this report is pretty straightforward. The only complicated part is that you must use a join to the decode tables to get the description for the **business rule category code** and **business rule type code**. The steps to create the SQL are as follows:

1. Use **business rule category code** to join BUSINESS RULE to BUSINESS RULE CATEGORY CODE.

2. Use **business rule type code** to join BUSINESS RULE to BUSINESS RULE TYPE CODE.

3. Order by **business rule category code**.

You may also want to make the following adjustments to this report:

- Add a filter for the **business rule category code** (and **business rule category code** = 5).

- See the data ordered differently than just by the **business rule id**.

- Select only active rules (and **business rule status code** = 1).

Depending upon your specific focus, this query could be altered to present the data in the most usable way.

Business Rules by Business Rule Category Report

After reviewing the All Business Rule report, you may need more detailed information. When starting a large project on a particular system, you will need to know what rules apply to the system you are about to modify. At the beginning of analysis and design, you want to ensure that you have reviewed all of the current information about that system.

The first step in creating this report is deciding what information is most important to display. After discussing this with the data user, we decided that this report would group data by business rule category but only show the **business rule category description** (see Figure 7.9). Users also need to see the actual **business rule id** so that they can use that to find out more information if needed. The status of the BUSINESS RULE is also critical, so we displayed the description associated with the BUSINESS RULE. The business steward's name is also given in case a user needs additional information.

In many ways, this report's SQL is similar to the All Business Rules report SQL. The different and the most complicated part of this SQL is the determination of the business steward. In order to do that, we must perform the following steps:

1. Use the **business rule id** to join BUSINESS RULE to BUSINESS RULE DATA STEWARD.

2. Use the **data steward id** to join BUSINESS RULE DATA STEWARD to DATA STEWARD.

3. Use the **person id** to join DATA STEWARD to PERSON.

| Business Rules by Business Rules Category | | | | | August 15, 2003 |
| ABC Corporation | | | | | |
Business Rules Category	Rule ID	Status	Rule Name	Business Steward	Business Rule Type
Sales Reporting	321	Effective	Total Amount Paid Calculation	Michelle Fink	Expression
	354	Effective	Order Status Derivation	Mark Ferguson	Miscellaneous
	386	Effective	Sales Region Assignment	Mark Ferguson	Business Term
	392	Expired	Return Reason Assignment	Michelle Fink	Expression
Customer Summary Reporting	318	Effective	Lifetime Value Calculation	Peter Seiler	Expression
	722	Pending	Address Standardization	Catherine Baker	Miscellaneous

Figure 7.9 Business rules by business rule category.

Data Warehouse Customer Business Rules

Now that you have seen the information available at the business rule category level, you may need to find more specific information about a specific table or file (see Figure 7.10). Perhaps you decide that you need to see the details behind the Data Warehouse Customer table. The DATA GROUP represents the database table or computer file, so we will use the **data group id** to find all the data for the Data Warehouse Customer Table. In order to get the **data group name**, we must create a join to the DATA GROUP using the DATA GROUP BUSINESS RULE.

As with the previous two reports, we need to join two tables to get the description for business rule status. In order to do that, we must perform the following steps:

1. Select from BUSINESS RULE where the business rule status is effective or pending.

2. Use **business rule id** to join BUSINESS RULE to DATA GROUP BUSINESS RULE.

3. Use **data group id** to join DATA GROUP BUSINESS RULE to DATA GROUP to find the **data group id** for the Data Warehouse Customer table.

4. Use **business rule status code** to join BUSINESS RULE to BUSINESS RULE STATUS CODE.

5. Order by **data group id** and **business rule id**.

Data Groups by Subject Area

We saw how data is physically structured by reviewing the DATA PACKAGE, DATA GROUP, and DATA ELEMENT structures in Chapter 6, but now we want to know how the data is related from a business user's perspective. SUBJECT AREAS are used to group the data from this business perspective. DATA GROUPs by SUBJECT AREA displays the DATA GROUPs and corresponding DATA STEWARDs organized by SUBJECT AREA (see Figure 7.11). For example, the Customer Subject Area contains Account and Address relational tables and a Customer History sequential file. This would probably be the only place where we could see the relationship between these data.

Data Warehouse Customer Business Rules ABC Corporation				August 15, 2003
Data Group Name	Rule ID	Status	Rule Name	Rule Details
Data Warehouse Customer	412	Effective	Customer Match Routine	The address attached to a new order will be matched against the existing address table. If a complete match of name and address is found, the order will be assigned to the matching customer.
	543	Effective	Customer Address Standardization	All addresses will be run through address standardization software. In order to obtain postal savings, any changes the standardization software makes will be retained.
	567	Effective	Customer Lifetime Value	Total Amount Paid –Total Refund Amount –Return Postage Amount + Total Customer Credits
	603	Pending	Customer Status	Direct move from Cust-Stat-Cd from operational Cust-Acct table.

Figure 7.10 Data warehouse customer business rules.

Data Groups by Subject Area				
	ABC Corporation			August 15, 2003
Subject Area	Data Group	Executive Sponsor	Business Steward	Technical Steward
Customer	Account Table	Benjamin Druck	Andrew Roscoe	Timothy Stewart
	Address Table	Elizabeth Roscoe	Donald Culpepper	Richard Mullins
	Customer History File	Robert Aller	Stephen Warner	Scott Dawson
Product	Product Price Table	Harold Chapin	Andrew Roscoe	Timothy Stewart
	Product Type Codes	Robert Aller	Andrew Roscoe	Matthew Powell
	Obsolete Product File	Robert Aller	Jacob Allen	Sara Harper

Figure 7.11   Data groups by subject area.

The report also shows the different types of DATA STEWARDs that are related to a DATA GROUP. We found the data to display in the executive sponsor, business steward, and technical steward areas in the DATA GROUP STEWARD, DATA STEWARD, and PERSON entities. The pointers to the DATA STEWARDs are found in the DATA GROUP STEWARD entity. The DATA STEWARD entity tells us what role the data steward is playing, and the name and contact information is found in the PERSON entity. The steps needed obtain this data are as follows:

1. Use **subject area id** to join DATA GROUP SUBJECT AREA to SUBJECT AREA.

2. Use **data group id** to join DATA GROUP SUBJECT AREA to DATA GROUP.

3. Use **data group id** to join DATA GROUP to DATA GROUP DATA STEWARD.

4. Use **data steward id** to join DATA GROUP STEWARD to DATA STEWARD, where **data steward type code** = Executive Sponsor.

5. Use **person id** to join DATA STEWARD to PERSON.

6. Repeat the previous two steps, with **data steward type code** = Business Steward.

7. Repeat those steps again, with **data steward type code** = Technical Steward.

8. Order the data by **subject area id** and **data group id.**

Open and Pending Business Rule Issues

This report shows all issues that are still open or pending across the IT department (see Figure 7.12). The issues are organized by **business rule id** in order to see the issues for the same BUSINESS RULE together. Issue Sequence number will be used to point us back to a specific issue if we need to find out more information. The Issue Text is used to provide some detail. The Issue Status tells us if the issue is open and requires more immediate attention or is pending and is waiting for something before it can be resolved. Issue Priority is displayed so we can determine which issues to address first.

Open and Pending Business Rule Issues		ABC Corporation		August 15, 2003
Business Rule ID	Issue Sequence	Issue Text	Issue Status	Issue Priority
234	1	Should Account Lifetime Value calculation be decremented for return postage?	Open	High
342	3	Should a purchase be added to account lifetime value when the purchase is ordered, shipped, or paid for?	Open	Medium
342	5	Where is the authoritative source for a product's price?	Pending	Low
352	23	Who will map product types from the recently acquired company?	Open	High
	27	How will we resolve conflicts in product type from multiple sources?	Pending	Low
362	2	When determining if an address is an existing customer, do we match on name and address or just address?	Open	Critical

Figure 7.12 Open and pending business rule issues.

There are some other variations of this report. If you are working on a particular project, you may want to see all the issues associated with BUSINESS RULEs for a particular SUBJECT AREA. If you are a data steward, you will want to see all the issues related to BUSINESS RULEs that you are a steward for. Each of these variations would only involve minor changes to the report.

The SQL steps to create this report are very straightforward:

1. Select all rows from BUSINESS RULE ISSUE where the **business rule status code** is open or pending.

2. Order the data by **business rule id** and **business rule issue sequence**.

Person by Organization and Manager

People are another asset of the company that you may need to report on. The report in Figure 7.13 represents an organizational structure for a company. It lists all the managers and the people employed by the organization. An organization may represent a division, department, or work group. The manager represents all employees within the organization with other people directly reporting to him or her. The Person Name column will contain the names of the employees working for a particular manager. A person may appear in the Person Name column and in the Manager column. He or she will appear in the Person Name column after the manager that person reports to. A manager will then be listed again in the Manager column followed by the employees that report to him or her.

The steps to create the SQL for this report are as follows:

1. Select all rows from PERSON ordered by **organization id** and **manager id**.

2. Use **organization id** to join PERSON to ORGANIZATION.

3. Use **manager id** to join PERSON to itself, where **manager id** = **person id**.

| Person by Organization and Manager | | | | August 15, 2003 |
| ABC Corporation | | | | |
Organization	Manager	Person Name	Work Phone	Email Address
Outside Sales	Sara Harper	Virginia Houser	(732) 555-3432	Vhouser@WidgetCorp.com
		Johnathan Morgan	(732) 555-4322	JohnMorgan@WidgetCorp.com
	Virginia Houser	Jay Riggins	(732) 555-1364	JayRiggins@WidgetCorp.com
		Donald Webb	(717) 555-8212	DonWebb@WidgetCorp.com
	Johnathan Morgan	David Beimborn	(717) 555-8654	Dave.Beimborn@WidgetCorp.com
		Timothy Maddox	(544) 555-8773	Timothy.Maddox@WidgetCorp.com

Figure 7.13   Person by organization and manager.

Summary

This chapter defined the structures that hold business rules, business meta data, and data stewardship information. We discussed how these subject areas are all interrelated and contain different types of business meta data. You also saw how this data benefits the business by reviewing sample reports.

In the previous chapters, we discussed enterprise systems, XML, messaging and business transactions, IT portfolio management, and data quality in detail. We walked through all the entities and attributes in those areas and looked at sample reports. In the next chapter, we look at all these subject areas as a whole to see how all these pieces work together.

CHAPTER 8

The Complete Universal Meta Model

As you can see from the previous chapters, meta data models can become quite complex. Chapters 4 to 7 presented the meta models and subject areas that compose the universal meta model (UMM). In this last chapter, we examine a consolidated and summarized view of meta models from the previous technical chapters. This model provides a holistic view of all of the components that compose the entire universal meta model. We look at the primary integration points between the model areas, as well as factors that you should take into account before actually implementing the model. This includes considerations around logical-to-physical modeling conversion. Finally, we will look at one example of an implementation design for a data quality meta data mart.

Typically, the meta data mart design is derived from the Enterprise Systems and Business Meta Data models. The meta data mart design will be physically implemented in an OLAP cube product with sample analysis views around data quality measurement. The OLAP cube and data files used in its creation are available on the accompanying CD for you to continue your own analysis. This chapter is organized differently from the previous four chapters in Part Two. The assumption is made that you have reviewed the previous chapters and are familiar with the entity package components of the complete model, since this represents a summary level view. The remainder of the chapter focuses on how to implement the UMM. This includes a physical implementation design example.

The key topics covered in this chapter are:

- A complete high-level meta model
- Implementation considerations
- Data quality meta data mart
- OLAP implementation of the meta data mart

This chapter ends with the summary section included with every model in Part Two, followed by some concluding thoughts on the importance of the MME in any successful enterprise.

A Complete High-Level Meta Model

The meta data models presented thus far in the book are critical components in the successful construction of an MME and serve as a foundation for this chapter. Understanding how each of the models interrelates is key to completing this journey. We begin by examining a high-level, logical view of the model that illustrates the major interaction areas of the model. Not every entity or relationship is shown in the complete meta data model. The entities have been summarized into primary entity package groupings. These particular entity package groupings were chosen because they represent the most important concepts and content of the universal meta models.

Figure 8.1 shows the key model interaction areas. The figure shows a top-down view of the major areas composing the universal model, including project, systems, organization, data and structure, data movement and transformation, business rules, and business process and transaction. The nineteen subject areas from the previous chapters are now represented as subsystems in the UMM. This diagram provides an uncluttered view of the relationships among the subsystems. For example, *Business Process and Transaction* are connected to *Data Movement and Transformation* because the subsystem is in a sense just an extension of the functionality that the module provides to the environment. Interactions with the *Organization* subsystem are kept to a minimum to simplify understanding of the structural relationships in the environment. Otherwise, *Organization* would connect extensively throughout the model, because of the person component, which would not aid in understanding the model. The relationship between *Organization* and *Person* is required to capture details of the resource in the enterprise. The interaction of an enterprise to its information technology assets is encapsulated in the relationship between *Organization* and *System*. These two relationships denote the primary purpose of the *Organization* entity package to the meta data environment.

Key Model Interaction Areas

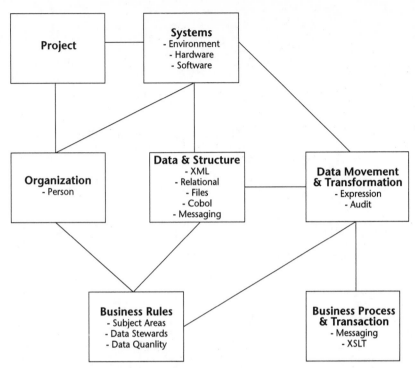

Figure 8.1 Key model interaction areas.

Going to the next level of detail in our analysis leads us to the complete logical model view shown in Figure 8.2. The complete model shows a composite view of the universal meta data, providing information that is more navigational in nature and detailed than that in the key interaction diagram. The model is a derived logical data model. The complete model illustrates UMM components at an entity package level of abstraction as opposed to the previous entity and attribute level. The model provides a concise view of the entity concepts and relationships, which are more important from a comprehension perspective, rather than individual attributes. Let's look further at the detail of the entity packages and their interactions with other components.

We begin by focusing in on the center of the model, *Data Package and Structure*, which provides the meta data foundation for the rest of the components. The *Data Package and Structure* entity package represents the many physical forms data may take in an organization. Enterprise applications move data to

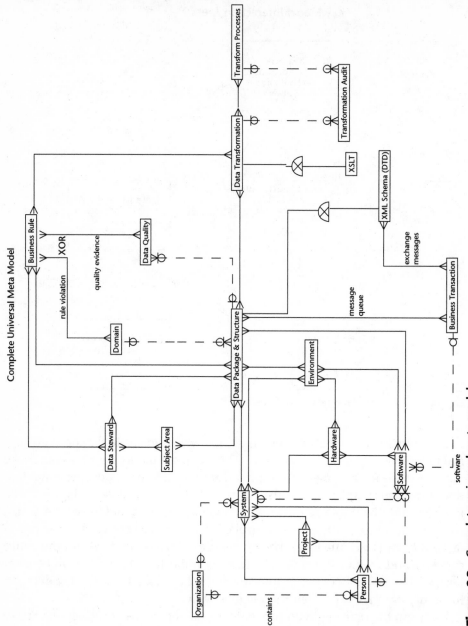

Figure 8.2 Complete universal meta model.

and from any of these data forms through the direct relationship with the *Data Transformation* and the indirect relationship with *Transform Process* entity packages. The movement of data is the central concept for the enterprise and for the MME models. This concept for modeling data movement among various forms is handled simply and efficiently through the realization that different sets of data have a common base structure. A specific form of data transformation through for XML types is depicted through the subtype relationship between *Data Transformation* and the subtype *XSLT*. A specific form of data package for XML Schema (DTD) types is depicted through the subtype relationship between *Data Package and Structure* and the subtype *XML Schema (DTD)*. XSLT and XML Schema (DTD) are highlighted on the complete model simply because of the focus on these transformation and data package types in Chapter 5.

Additionally, a record of data movement activity occurring in the enterprise is captured through the relationship between *Transformation Audit* and both *Data Transformation* and *Transform Processes*. The *Data Transformation* entity package area consolidates such entities as TRANSFORMATION GROUP, SOURCE TO TARGET MAP, and EXPRESSION NODE. The *Transform Processes* entity package area represents entities such as TRANSFORMATION STEP, TRANSFORMATION PROCESS, and TRANSFORMATION PACKAGE.

Next, we look at the relationship between real-world objects and data that is depicted in the relationships between *System* and *Environment*, and *Data Package and Structure*. The relationship of these two entity packages business analysis from an implementation management outlook plus see the data lineage and analyze impact throughout the firm. How data is associated to an application, whether purchased or developed in-house, is shown through the connection between *Software* and *Data Package and Structure*. This area also shows which data structure provider is being used—either a relational database, Enterprise JavaBeans (EJB), or message queue. The specific case of how message queues are processed and controlled through application components is depicted in the link from *Data Package and Structure* to *Business Transaction* to *Software*. The explicit use of messaging as a data package type for a business transaction is illustrated through the connection of *XML Schema (DTD)* and *Business Transaction*. This representation in the complete model results from the detail shown in the Business Transaction subject area in Chapter 5. Key associated entities include SYSTEM PERFORMS, INTERACTIONS, PROCESS, TRANSITIONS, and TRANSACTION CONTROL.

The abstraction of software, installed and running software, and data structure users is depicted in the relationships between *System, Hardware, Environment, Software,* and *Organization*. The association of these entity packages allows technology and architecture to be described and tracked. For example, business applications and databases are associated with deployment environments (for example, development, quality assurance, user acceptance testing quality control, production, stress testing, and training). The detail of the association of the hardware to the network has been distilled, since a network comprises many interconnected hardware components. Service level agreement–related entities have been summarized in the relationship between *Organization* and *Hardware*. Recursive types found originally on entities such as ORGANIZATION, PERSON, PROJECT, NETWORK, and HARDWARE have been removed from this generalization. Further discussion of these reflexive types can be found in the next section of this chapter. A project can be accomplished and tracked for a system by a person in an organization. A person belongs to an organization. These associations are depicted through the relationship of *Project* to *System* and *Person* as well as those of *Organization* to *System* and *Person*. Key associated entities include TASK RESOURCE ASSIGN-MENT, VENDOR, and SYSTEM PROJECT.

The relationship of the business to information is shown through the links between *Data Steward* and the *Subject Area, Data Package and Structure*, and *Business Rule* entity packages. The link between a data steward and person is removed for simplicity in the model view. The business view of accessing information is represented through the use of subject areas that provide the connection to the more detailed data perspective. Data stewards also define the business meaning of data, hierarchies, calculations, and interdata dependencies through this area of the model. The responsibility for defining the usage of data in the enterprise falls on the data steward, who defines the data's purpose and the rules for its usage. The detailed processing of data through expression-base business rules is depicted in the relationship between *Business Rule* and *Data Transformation*. Key associated entities for this portion of the complete model include BUSINESS RULE EXPRESSION, DATA GROUP and DATA ELEMENT BUSINESS RULE, DATA GROUP SUBJECT AREA, BUSINESS RULE DATA STEWARD, and SUBJECT AREA DATA STEWARD.

The final area of focus in the complete model is data quality measurement. This is depicted in the model through the dual relationships between *Data Package and Structure* through *Domain* to *Business Rule*, and *Data Package and Structure* through *Data Quality* to *Business Rule*. This will be an area of implementation focus later in this chapter, when we review a design for a meta data mart and an OLAP cube. If data domain violations are encountered during detailed transformation or data profiling, the resultant domain or business rule violation can be tracked for further analysis. Depending on how this area is implemented, there could be a different rule for each data element or a single rule for all single element violations. Domain value violations could be single values, a range specification, or a pattern mismatch. The Data Quality Measurement subject area found in Chapter 6 has been summarized into this area of the model. Key associated entities for this portion of the complete model include DATA QUALITY METRIC, BUSINESS RULE, DOMAIN, DOMAIN VALUE, and BUSINESS RULE EXPRESSION.

Now, let's continue our examination of the complete meta model by addressing some of the challenges involved in its implementation.

Implementation Considerations

In large organizations, many standards exist to make enterprise architectures work effectively. Meta data should be an enterprise-level system and thus should be integrated into the enterprise architecture. That architecture often has techniques and technology for handling the complexity of some standard problems and issues that arise from the functional and nonfunctional requirements. There are special techniques that are helpful in keeping the system maintainable and extensible. Some of these are covered here to help you integrate the supplied models into your established architectures and practices.

First, we will review some important nonfunctional issues that can strongly influence model design and physical implementations.

Scalability.   The system's ability to handle many users and a lot of data.

Extensibility.   The ability for adding new functionality without modifying other parts. We know that change will occur, and some designs are more extensible than others.

Maintainability.   Maintainability is similar to extensibility but relates to smaller functional changes.

Performance.   Performance relates to the system's response time and throughput.

There are some other factors to consider for the models and designs. The volume of meta data should be small relative to many other applications. In fact, in most cases it should be able to reside in an in-memory database, which can greatly relieve performance difficulties. Using an in-memory database changes the way that some physical elements are designed, so be aware of that. When the volume of data is small, data requests are generally not very large either, which makes it is possible to have many users, depending on the applications that are supposed to utilize the meta data. Scalability for the number of users may be important. This has a larger impact on the design of the meta data applications, but depending on the technologies used, it will also have an impact on the physical designs of the MME. For example, using EJB in the meta data applications should have an impact on the physical design of the meta data. These are issues that someone needs to be aware of if the previously mentioned nonfunctional issues are important.

Extensibility and maintainability are perhaps the most important issues for good design in both the base meta models discussed here and in the physical translation of their design. It is often a design complexity trade-off. Making a design easier to extend and maintain entails adding a base level of complexity up front to make other things uniform and easier to manage. The meta models in this book employ a moderate level of extensibility, leaving adaptation and improvement to the reader. The model structures touch on the complexities of the various subject areas but remain relatively flexible. For example, our models use a great deal of subtyping to make some treatments uniform. Subtyping is not commonly used by many data modelers because it makes the physical implementation more complex. It is a trade-off that we will discuss in more detail in the following sections.

Levels of Data Models

Conceptual data models (CDM), logical data models (LDM), and physical data models (PDM) are the general levels of data models, and their relationship is a major element of the system design. The eventual result of a design is a PDM, and the PDM's construction requires some design decisions. In CDM and LDM, some of the modeling elements are entities, attributes, and relationships, while in PDMs they correspond to tables, columns, and foreign keys. However, there are other modeling elements and relationships in each model type that do not exist directly in the others. The models presented in this book are LDMs, and we assume that you will make changes to reflect your needs and modeling standards, using the LDMs as a starting point.

We will discuss the following design topics: the use of database unique identifiers, the implementation of code tables, and the translation of more abstract LDMs into a physical implementation model, which includes M:M relationships, entity subtyping, multiple inheritance, and meta-level information loss.

Database Unique IDs

If all entities, and thus related tables, excluding associative entities, have a single integer key, it is possible to make that ID unique in the database. Then, an additional table can be used to map a particular ID to its given table or entity. Another table is then used to provide ID ranges to applications that will be creating entries in the database. There are some techniques to prevent an input/output (I/O) bottleneck on the main tables for ID assignment and table typing, but they are implementation techniques and outside our scope. This approach has some advantages and disadvantages. The strongest advantages are that it can be used for making common associations to any table, and it provides a good solution for several LDM-to-PDM translation difficulties. The latter will be discussed in the "Translating LDM to PDM" section. Implementing this from a data-modeling perspective only requires making sure that the primary key of the entities is a single generated integer and that the autogeneration of IDs that many databases can do is not done. The applications will be responsible for generating IDs. This restriction greatly aids the use of Enterprise JavaBeans and similar technology in these applications.

Common associations can now be made to other tables using the database unique IDs (DBUID). For example, by using DBUIDs in the meta data models, nearly all major entities of interest could take as attachments other entities representing Responsible Party, Documentation, Descriptions, and Notes. This set of entities has information and additional structure that is applicable to nearly all other entities in the model. They would all be M:M relationships. For example, a business process could have several notes and responsible parties, and each of those could also be attached to other entries. Using the common attachment technique of a DBUID and a mapping table allows the overall simplification of the application. The programs dealing with Responsible Party, Documentation, Descriptions, and Notes are the same for all uses. In addition, for example, having all descriptions in one table greatly simplifies the searching of descriptions for certain terms.

Like all design issues, using DBUIDs has trade-offs. This technique adds complexity in some areas but also greatly simplifies other areas. You need to understand more of how your meta data solution will be used and how it will grow over time in order to decide what the design decisions should be.

Code Tables

Code table use is limited explicitly in our models. Many entities use codes, for example *Software Use Mode* in the SOFTWARE MODULE USAGE entity, and good modeling practice for third normal form requires codes to be in a different table. However, they may be collected into one table or be separate tables for each code category. Generally, a more advanced design uses one table for all codes, since this allows a uniform treatment for manipulating and maintaining them. This single-table design also provides greater flexibility and maintainability. For instance, often code tables will have a mnemonic, a short name, a long name, and possibly a description for each code. In addition, they may support multiple languages, and this type of structure simplifies the translation process. Instead of repeating this structure for each code table, having one table for all codes allows the use of a single procedure to manipulate this complex structure for all areas. Since this structure is variable and depends on each site's basic design protocol, code tables are not shown in our designs, but attributes that should refer to a code structure are clearly indicated.

A single common code table implementation example is shown in Figure 8.3. The structure is set up to handle multiple languages and parts of a code. The bottom half of the figure shows the structure to support how they are used. Since all the codes are in a single table, additional data is needed to indicate which tables and columns a particular code element pertains to. This is needed for both data consistency on entries and for generating a pick list of choices for a particular column. Note that the TABLE COLUMN and TABLE REFERENCE tables are at a meta-meta level, since they refer to tables and columns in the model for meta data.

Translating LDM to PDM

Translating an LDM to a PDM can be such a complex task that it requires a whole book in itself to cover completely. However, we will cover a few important elements of the translation here so that the meaning of the supplied models is not lost in the final use of the physical models. Most of the translation process is very straightforward. Usually an entity becomes a table, and attributes become columns with a type that matches. However, there are two major abstractions that are in LDMs that are not in PDMs. They are entity subtypes and many-to-many relationships. Both of these abstractions are widely used in our models.

Many-to-Many Relationships

Many-to-many relationships indicate exactly what they say. Each entity instance on either side of the relationship may be related or linked to many entity instances on the other side of the relationship. This M:M relationship is usually translated to the PDM as a linking table, and we refer to them here as associative entities or associative tables in the PDM. Usually, the linking entity or table just carries the primary keys of each table it connects, but sometimes additional attributes are added that specify the nature of the relationship more clearly. For example, the relationship may be sequenced, and the associative entity would then carry a sequence attribute.

In general, the M:M relationships in a CDM/LDM are easy to convert in a PDM. However, there is a meta-level information loss in the model. The PDM does not have a way of indicating that a particular table is used only as a linking table or that an attribute is for sequencing, and this is a loss of information that makes later maintenance a bit more troublesome. There could be a naming standard in place that indicates associative tables for a particular company, but there is no generally accepted standard.

Physical Code Table Implementation Example

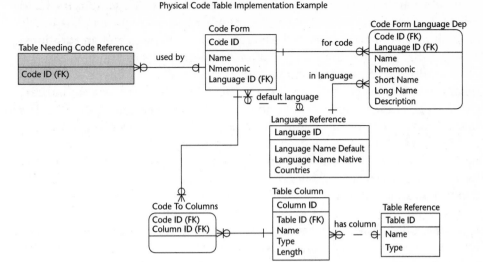

Figure 8.3   Physical code table implementation example.

Entity Subtyping

Translating the entity subtyping in an LDM to a PDM representation is the more problematic of the two abstractions presented here and thus will get much more attention. The subtyping of an entity means that two entities have an inheritance relationship, or a generalization-specialization relationship. One is the supertype and the other is the subtype. The subtyped entity has all the structure of the supertype and is in a 0 or 1 relationship to the supertype entity. The subtypes are usually exclusive, that is, an instance may be of only one subtype of the supertype (also known as non-overlapping or disjoint). In addition, the supertype may or may not be complete. It is complete if an instance must be of one of its subtypes. An additional complication is multiple-inheritance (MI), whereby a subtype can have multiple supertypes or inheritance parents. MI is covered in its own section later in this chapter.

The common transformations for entity subtyping from an LDM to a PDM have three variants:

- Separate tables for each entity
- Rolled up to one table
- Rolled down

In the separate tables version, the PDM structure looks the same as the LDM model. Its main drawback is the higher number of joins required to assemble all the information belonging to the entity. The supertype carries an additional attribute that indicates the subtype of an instance.

The rolled-up representation takes all attributes of the subtype and places them in the supertype, and the supertype carries a type attribute to indicate the subtype of the instance. The subtype is then removed from the PDM. The main disadvantage of the roll-up approach is that the extraneous attributes and foreign keys that are not used for each type appear in the final table. Roll-up is technically a denormalization operation. However, it does not usually have any of the create, update, or delete anomalies that usually come with denormalization. An exception is the case where a relationship at a subtype level was mandatory but at the supertype level is optional except for one subtype. The rolled-down representation places all the attributes of the supertype into the subtype and removes the supertype. The main disadvantage of the roll-down approach is the complexity of resolving foreign keys in other tables that referenced the original supertype. That is, There can be a reference via a foreign key to any of the subtypes, and additional structure is needed to resolve which type it is. The DBUID technique can help solve this problem, however.

Each representation has advantages and disadvantages. The complicating factors are foreign key references to the supertype, the difficulty encoding the meta-level information of subtyping in the PDM, and the complexity of joins. The resolution of an LDM to a PDM can use a combination of the common methods or even more general abstract mappings. The design choices greatly affect performance, meta information representation, and ease of maintenance. Table 8.1 has a summary of the trade-offs.

Meta-Level Information Loss

Each form of translating subtyping in an LDM to a PDM translation involves some meta-level information loss. The loss can be completely compensated for by having mapping information of what corresponds to what and the type of transformation used for both the LDM and the PDM. To record the mapping, a language is required that is appropriate for both model types and for the transformations used. With formal languages and representations, tools can be used to generate the needed outputs and manage the inherent complexity. This, in fact, is the essence of the Model Driven Architecture (MDA) from the Object Management Group (OMG, www.omg.org). Some tool vendors are currently working in this direction to address exactly this problem with LDMs and PDMs. However, in the absence of vendor support, you are faced with making a system that supports this approach to some degree, implementing it

Table 8.1   Trade-offs of LDM-to-PDM Designs

REPRESENTATION	FOREIGN KEY TO	FOREIGN KEY FROM	SINGLE ENTITY JOIN COMPLEXITY	META-LEVEL INFORMATION LOSS	MULTIPLE INHERITANCE HANDLING
Separate Tables	Good	Good	Poor	Fair	Good
Rolled Up	Fair	Fair	Good	Poor	Very Poor
Rolled Down	Poor	Good	Good	Poor	Fair

manually, modifying a tool to help, or perhaps using a different technology. LDMs have much in common with object-oriented models, and there are tools that do object-to-relational mapping that may add value in these tasks.

Extensibility is related somewhat to the meta-level information loss in that without maintaining both models and the transformations used, changes can be become very confusing. The LDM is the master plan for how things work together, and not maintaining it as changes and extensions occur can result in difficulties, because the intent of a structure in the PDM can be lost. Going from the LDM to the PDM is a process of taking certain abstractions and making them concrete, and thus the reverse—trying to make an LDM from a PDM—is not really possible.

Of the three translation forms, using separate tables—which clearly maintains a 1:1 relationship between entities and tables—has the least loss of meta-level information. The discriminator attributes need to be indicated, but that is true for all the forms of transformation.

On the roll-up translation form, views can be used to separate the attributes and foreign keys into the actual subtype groupings, but knowledge of what columns are grouped for each type is not shown directly there.

Multiple Inheritance

Multiple inheritance (MI) is not often needed, but when it is needed and used, it is very powerful. MI is used in two places in our models, and more of it would be expected as you extend the models for your needs. It is used for the XML SCHEMA entity and for the XSLT entity. XML SCHEMA is a subtype of XML DOC and of DATA PACKAGE. XSLT is a subtype of XML DOC and of TRANSFORMATION GROUP.

The problem is that the common subtype will use only one of the inherited keys as its primary key and will use the other as an alternate key. Problems arise when there are foreign key references to each of the supertypes in a MI group (see Figure 8.4). The key for the join to one of the references must be the alternate key and not the primary key. However, the use of DBUID allows the same key to be used for both parent joins, since the alternate key would then be exactly equal to the primary key. Without the use of a DBUID, the join condition must sometimes be modified to use the alternate key.

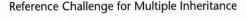

Reference Challenge for Multiple Inheritance

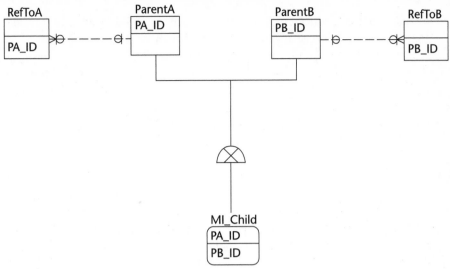

Figure 8.4   Reference challenge for multiple inheritance.

Design Issues Revisited

The design at a logical level can also really differ greatly from the physical level in a manner independent from the abstractions mentioned above. For example, in the code tables talked about earlier, the code entities could be represented in the logical model as independent tables, but in the PDM, all codes may be kept in one table or a few tables, depending on other design requirements. Further still, the PDM may differ even more drastically from the LDM. Some tables may not exist as independent tables at all, but as entries in another table, and attribute values may be generalized into one or a just a few tables. In fact, some relational database systems organize the physical structure in the disk this way since it optimizes some types of operations.

In addition, some common structures such as a classification scheme to support multiple hierarchies may be physically implemented only once but reused on many types to add that detailed hierarchy control. This level of design uses a high level of abstraction and requires a detailed meta-information level to use it. Many complex designs become a combination of all these techniques, since each technique has traits that make it desirable in different design requirements.

Data Quality Meta Data Mart

A meta data mart is a database structure, usually sourced from a meta data repository for the purpose of supporting a specific meta data user. The need to build a meta data mart occurs in response to a particular business requirement. A particular meta data user group may require meta data available in a form different from what is in the meta data repository. Large meta data environments may experience performance problems due to the third normal form–based approach sometimes used to model the meta data repository for data capture. The meta data mart can be spawned from the repository to optimize analysis and reporting.

Figure 8.5 illustrates one possible design for a meta data mart derived from the entire complete meta model. In this example, we have the business requirement to report on data quality issues by measuring business rule and domain violations in the MME. For this example, we will be using entities from Chapter 4, Chapter 6, and Chapter 7. The meta data mart utilizes a star schema design. The star schema is a modeling technique that typically uses a single table (an element quality fact table) in the middle of the schema connected to a number of tables (data element, data group, data package time, business rule, domain, error, and error type dimension tables) surrounding it. The star schema design is used in this case because it provides optimized performance for end-user business query and reporting access. The table in the center of the star is called the fact table, and the tables that are connected to it in the border are called the dimension tables.

We can take some steps in the design of the model in order to facilitate query performance and reduce complexity. DATA GROUP and DATA PACKAGE dimension tables are denormalized with attributes from the *Software, System, Hardware,* and *Environment* entity areas to reduce the number of joins required in the analysis of the mart. This allows additional analysis regarding what technology and/or architecture was involved in an issue. The Error dimension combines attributes from the Data Profiling subject area of the Enterprise Systems model. The ERROR TYPE dimension table contains derived values obtained through the examination of business rules and domains during the transformation processing of data sent to the mart. The TIME dimension is added as our first real physical artifact to a model and provides the added temporal aspect needed for further analysis of data quality issues.

Now let's go a bit further and actually physically implement and produce reports from the meta data mart.

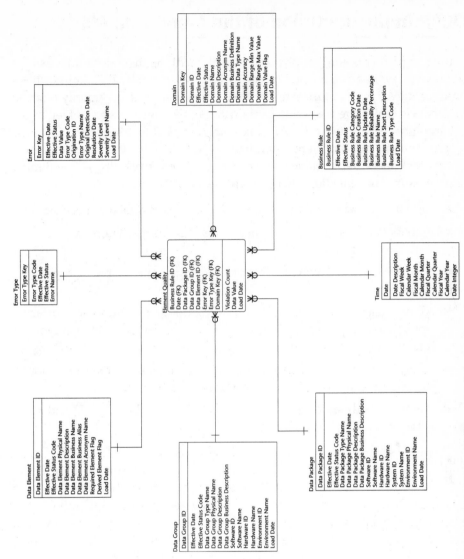

Figure 8.5   Data quality meta data mart.

OLAP Implementation of the Meta Data Mart

During implementation, we physically implement the meta data cube using a commercial Online Analytical Processing (OLAP, coined by E.F. Codd in 1993) product. OLAP type products use precalculated data files, commonly referred to as cubes, which are created to contain all possible answers to a given range (dimensions) of questions. OLAP cubes are best used for predictable analysis where the same questions are reiterated. The OLAP cube offers the advantage of very fast query performance but can have limited scalability as the number of dimensions and the data volume increase. OLAP cubes also:

- Are an analysis technique based on multidimensional architecture
- View data as being multidimensional (a fact has many dimensions) visualized in grids
- Are used for trend analysis, forecasting, aggregations, and statistical analysis
- Allow a user to manage business information in any number of dimensions (for example, sales, expense, profit (facts) by product by region by time (dimensions))
- Allow both comparative and projective calculations across dimensions (for example, trends, ratios, consolidation, variances)
- Were originally used in financial analysis, financial modeling, and marketing research

There are several issues to consider when deploying OLAP cubes to a user population. What is the volume of data that needs to be available in the cube? Transformation processing time to create and update the cube starts to increase substantially once the size of the cube goes above 5 GB. You need to examine if the data refresh frequency (daily, weekly, monthly, and so on) and data transformation processing window size are sufficient to meet business needs. Depending on your infrastructure, the cube may be built on one server and have to be distributed to multiple servers for user access.

Next, consider what type of security needs to be applied to the cube. Role-level security requires very little implementation effort in order to apply it to the cube. The incorporation of row-level security for each user accessing the cube can increase transformation processing time by 200 percent to 500 percent, making it even harder to meet processing window schedules. Next, what is the size and composition of the user population receiving access to the cube? The skills needed to successfully navigate, analyze, and drill into a cube typically require additional training and support for end users because this is a new paradigm. Some of this complexity can be reduced through the use of *view access to the cube*, which provides a method similar to that used by query reporting products.

In our sample implementation of an OLAP meta cube, we do not have any of these implementation issues to contend with due to focus on data quality measurement and limited test data. The OLAP cube files and test data files are available on the CD accompanying this book for your further review.

Let's look at the physical design that is going to be used to generate the meta data cube. Figure 8.6 shows the cube design as it exists in the OLAP design product. Typically OLAP products provide for the design of dimensions, facts, dimension hierarchies, filtering, calculations, and other characteristics of the cube. For the sample cube, we have taken further liberties with the design as compared to the meta data mart in an effort to promote understanding rather than aiming for completeness. You will notice that we have taken a subset of the data mart dimensions for the cube design, using only the applicable data columns for our example. Additionally, the DOMAIN and Business Rule dimension tables have been combined to facilitate obtaining straightforward reporting examples from the cube. Our data sources are comma-delimited flat files representing each of the dimensions illustrated in Figure 8.6. Once the design is completed the OLAP cube can be created for review and analysis.

Now with the cube generated, we can begin our analysis of data quality violation measurement. In the first analysis view (see Figure 8.7), we look at where our data quality issues originate, from a data column perspective. Using a pie chart display, we can see which data elements were involved in violating either a business rule or domain value validation.

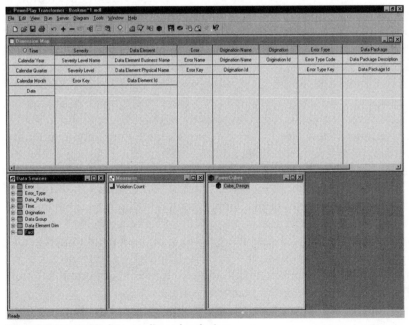

Figure 8.6 OLAP data quality cube design.

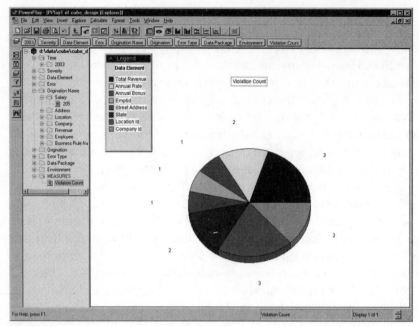

Figure 8.7 Cube view – Violation Count by Data Element.

At this point, you should be asking yourself questions about how this type of analysis could be accomplished today in your firm. How does your organization report on this type of data quality issue? What level of effort would it take in your firm to produce this type of data quality view? How much of the effort would require manual steps? The violation count by data element gives the user an initial alert as to data quality issues in a particular subject area. Violation hits may be indications of data transformation rule changes or source application modifications. In this particular case, the Location and Total Revenue columns had the most violations, with three each. Further analysis is needed to determine the underlying cause of these data discrepancies.

In the next analysis view (see Figure 8.8), we look at where the data quality issues originate, from a severity level and time perspective. Using a 3-D column chart display, we can see the number of violations in particular months over the past year, broken down by severity level. In this example, April had the highest number of high-severity violations, and March had the highest level of medium-severity occurrences. Technology users can utilize this type of analysis to assess the impact of data integration with new or modified applications on the enterprise (for example, ERP, CRM, and SFA applications). Business users can use this type of analysis to look for trends in data quality levels possibly due in part to variations in business volumes. Retailers may expect an upsurge in data anomalies due to increased volume during seasonal or holiday periods. Firms running marketing campaigns may experience a similar upsurge at those times.

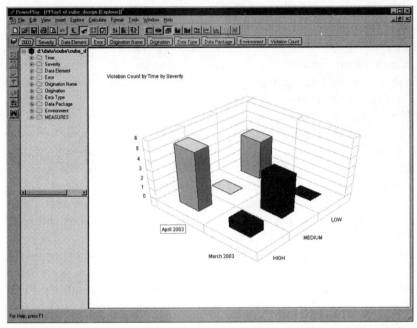

Figure 8.8 Cube view – Violation Count by Time by Period by Severity Level.

Our third analysis view (see Figure 8.9) looks at violations as they relate to Data Packages and Severity Levels. Using a stacked column chart, we can see the ratio of violations per data package, categorized by severity level. In this case, the greatest number of violations originates from the Internal HR and Internal Financial production systems. This type of analysis view can allow technology users to determine which application or system is eroding overall data quality in the enterprise. From this initial high level analysis view, users can drill down into the detail to isolate and determine the root cause of the data anomaly. Determination can be made as to which specific data integration process or business transaction is at fault. Examples include an EAI message routing from a telecom application, financial or HR XML business transactions, data warehouse ETL processing, and database replication. Threshold level alerts can be assigned and automated to proactively warn both business and technology users of out-of-range data quality volumes.

Our next analysis view (see Figure 8.10) looks at violations at a greater level of detail as they relate to Data Packages, Data Elements, Error Type, and Severity Levels. Using a nested tabular column display, we begin drilling into the granular detail of how severity and error type violations are distributed at an application and column level. In this example, the domain value violations appear to be more of an issue than business rule error types across all data structures. This insight provides the user of the report with an important clue that was not evident in the other higher level analysis views to help determine the underlying cause of the data discrepancies. Since the majority of the violations are domain-based the user can focus his or her analysis on this area. Higher domain violation counts occurring against a particular application or subsystem may be an indication of a recent system change or modification. Widely dispersed violations against the same transaction area or column may indicate a recent change in content definition.

The fifth analysis view (see Figure 8.11) drills down further to look at violation detail focused at the data element level. Using a 3-D column graph, we get a more centered look at to how severity and error type break down at a data element level. By drilling down to a data element level of detail, the user can look for trends in similar business functional areas (human resources, financial, payroll, benefits) or data groupings (customer, product, locations). Users can use the severity type level as a means to prioritize their analysis and resolution activity. High and medium level violations may require immediate resolution plus possible roll back and restarting of the data integration process. A low level of severity may simply be an indication of an infrequently used domain or business rule. In this case, spikes can be seen in relation to the Total Revenue data element for Domain-type errors. State data element has a higher ratio of business rule violations.

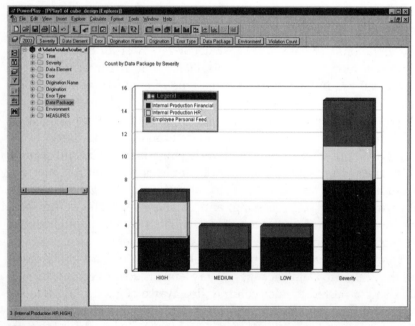

Figure 8.9   Cube view – Violation Count by Data Package by Severity.

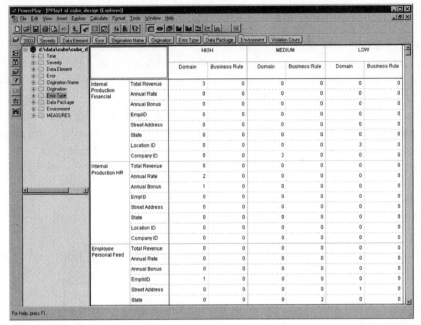

Figure 8.10   Cube view – Count by Data Package\Element by Severity\Error Type.

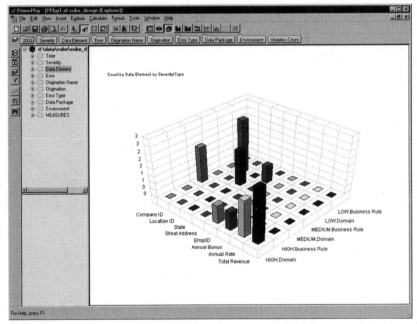

Figure 8.11   Cube view – Count by Data Element by Severity\Error Type

In our final analysis view (see Figure 8.12), we combine most of the dimensions from our previous analysis to take a more multifaceted view of our data quality issues. Using a nested 3-D column graph, we get the most holistic view of the violation areas. Medium severity level violations can now be easily attributed to the Company and State ID data elements during March. This view allows users to focus their analysis on these two specific columns in order to resolve the discrepancy more efficiently. High and Low severity level violations are more apparent during April for multiple data elements. Unusual business activity or the introduction of new production applications may have occurred during this period. The granular detail available in this type of report should provide the user with sufficient information to pinpoint and act on the origin of the discrepancy.

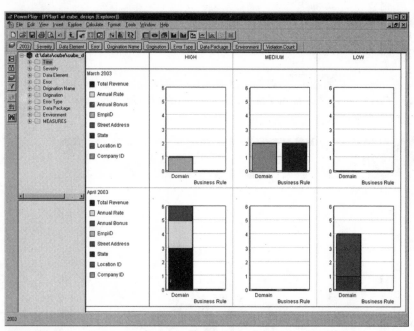

Figure 8.12   Cube view – Count by Data Element by Severity\Error Type by Time.

Summary

We now have a consolidated view of all meta models that compose the MME. This model cans be used as a basis for an internal meta data design project or as part of a checklist for purchasing a commercial product. Although many companies understand the importance of MME, few have the experience to construct the underlying data models from scratch. This is where the complete meta data model can be used to get a head start on a project by providing a foundation that can be customized for the specific business needs of the enterprise.

Conclusions

Faced with the challenges of data and application integration, regulatory compliance, CRM, ERP, EAI, data warehousing, and a host of other hurdles, organizations must truly understand their data and applications from an enterprise perspective. The MME and related topics, such as enterprise architecture, are vital to making the transition to an information-driven enterprise.

As with any other major IT undertaking, building an MME will not be a trivial endeavor. However, the MME will be a necessity if your organization is going to effectively manage your IT applications at an enterprise level. As we have seen, those companies with the vision and commitment to implement a world-class MME have provided their organizations with a significant advantage. Keep in mind that there are corporations and government agencies that are developing even larger MME applications than those that we have presented. Maybe your MME initiative could become one of them.

Model Diagrams

This appendix provides you with illustrations all of the logical data models presented in Part Two of the book. Here is what you will find:

Chapter 4 - Enterprise Systems
Chapter 5 - XML Schema Subject Area
Chapter 5 - XML DTD Subject Area
Chapter 5 - XSLT Subject Area
Chapter 5 - Business Transactions Subject Area
Chapter 5 - XML Document Classification
Chapter 6 - Service Management Subject Area
Chapter 6 - Software Management Subject Area
Chapter 6 - Hardware and Network Management Subject Area
Chapter 6 - Project Portfolio Management Subject Area
Chapter 6 - Data Quality Management Subject Area
Chapter 7 - Business Rule Subject Area
Chapter 7 - Business Data Subject Area
Chapter 7 - Data Steward Subject Area
Chapter 8 - Complete Universal Meta Model
Chapter 8 – Data Quality Meta Data Mart

The CD-ROM accompanying the book contains the these same data models and meta data mart files described in Part Two of the book. The data model files are available on the CD-ROM in both Adobe Portable Document Format (PDF), for easy review and printing, and in Computer Associate's Erwin file format for analysis and modification. The files used to design and create the data quality meta data mart presented in Chapter 8 are also on the CD-ROM.

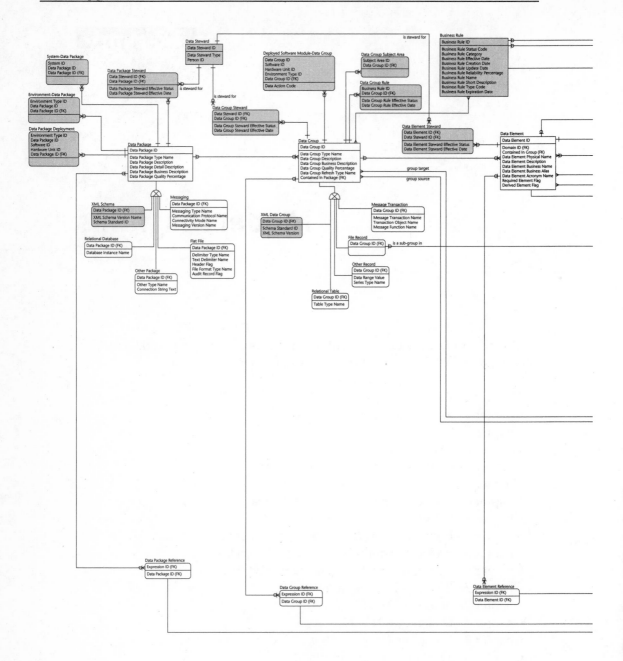

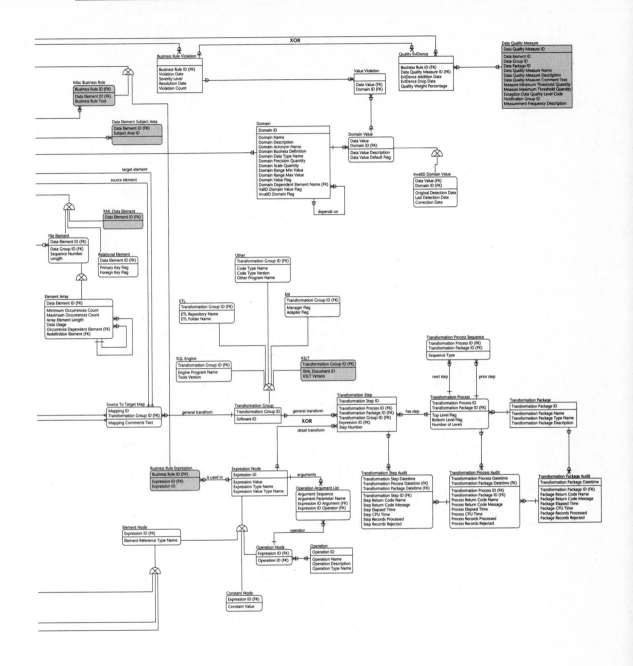

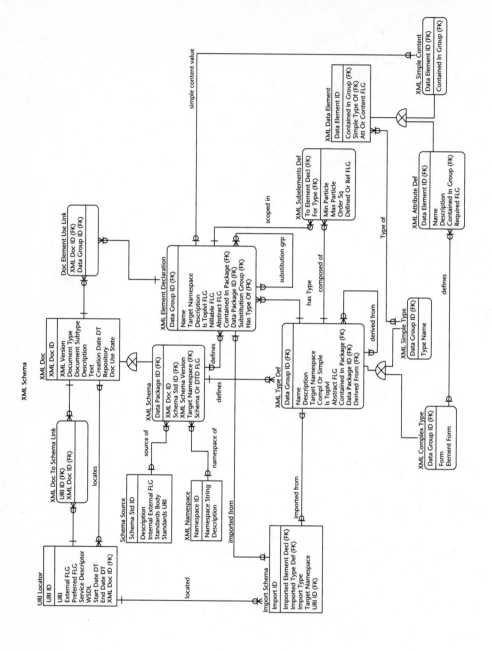

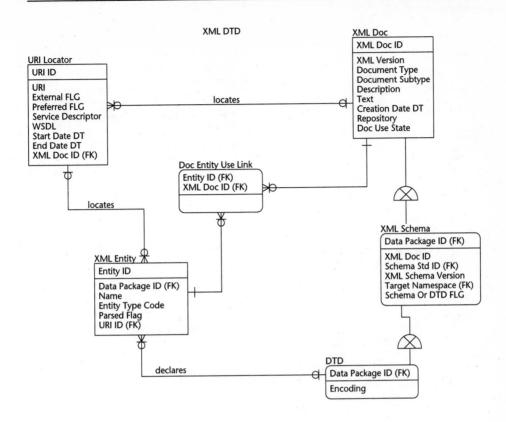

XML DTD

URI Locator

URI ID
URI
External FLG
Preferred FLG
Service Descriptor
WSDL
Start Date DT
End Date DT
XML Doc ID (FK)

XML Doc

XML Doc ID
XML Version
Document Type
Document Subtype
Description
Text
Creation Date DT
Repository
Doc Use State

locates

Doc Entity Use Link

Entity ID (FK)
XML Doc ID (FK)

locates

XML Entity

Entity ID
Data Package ID (FK)
Name
Entity Type Code
Parsed Flag
URI ID (FK)

XML Schema

Data Package ID (FK)
XML Doc ID
Schema Std ID (FK)
XML Schema Version
Target Namespace (FK)
Schema Or DTD FLG

DTD

Data Package ID (FK)
Encoding

declares

XML XSLT

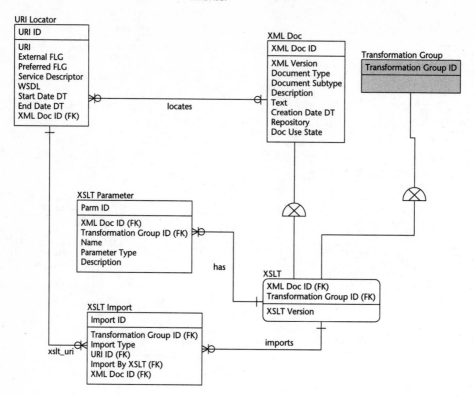

Business Transactions

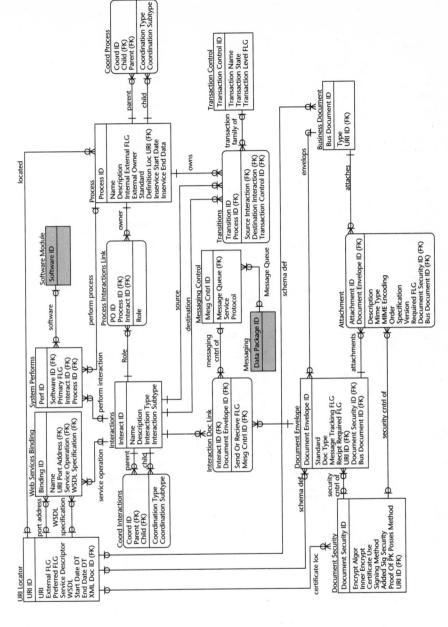

Document Classification

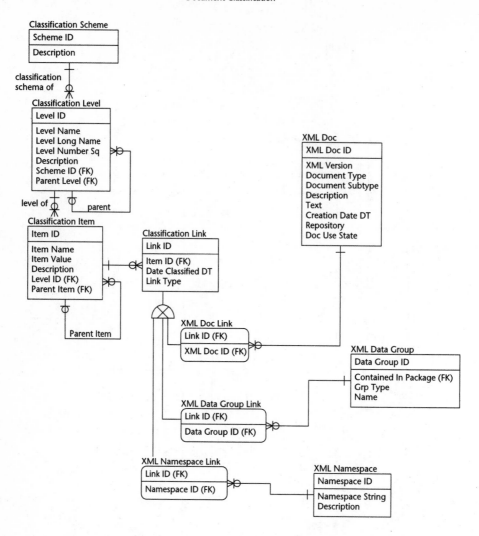

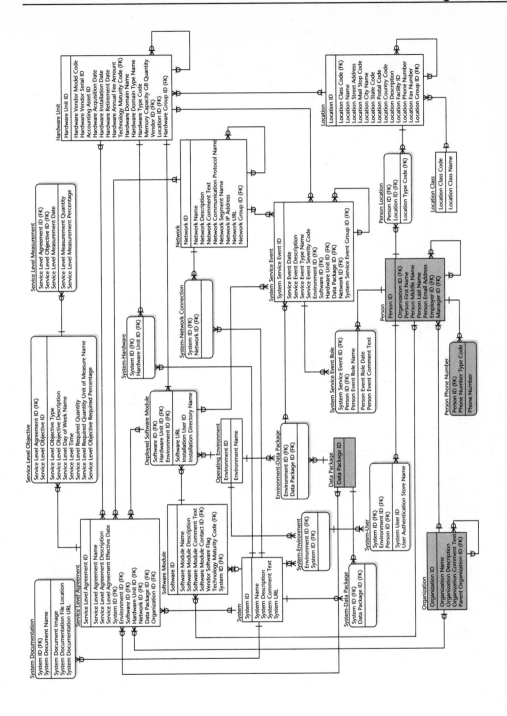

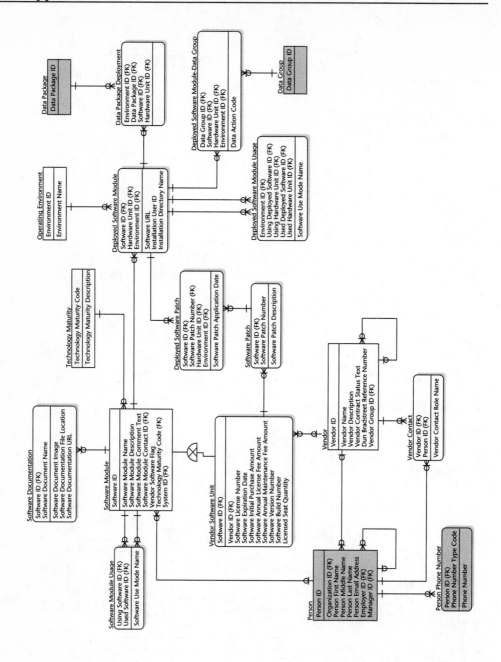

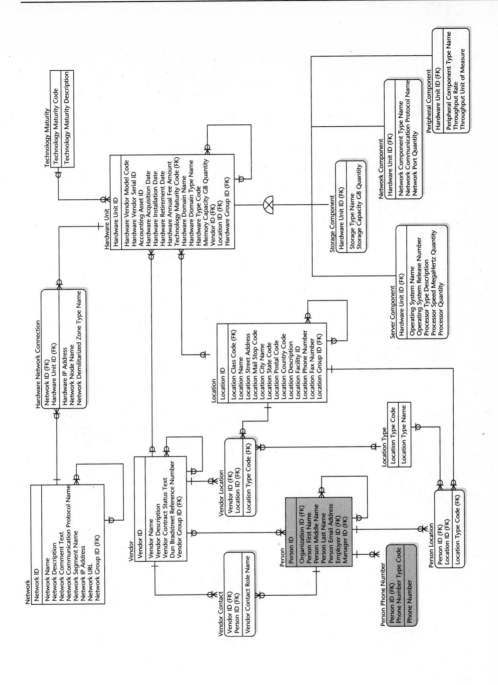

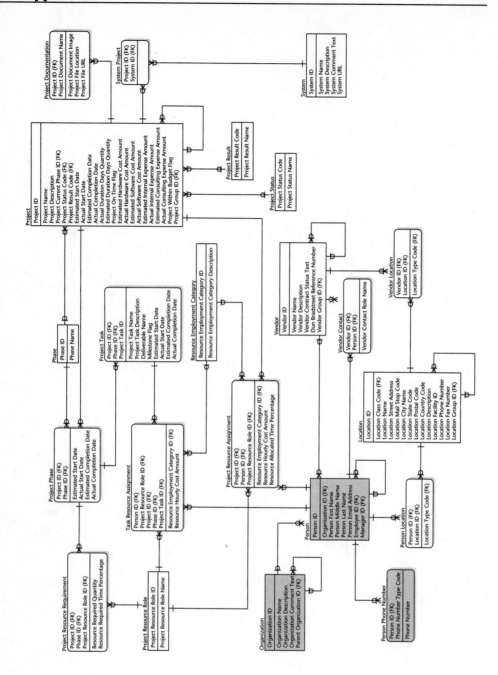

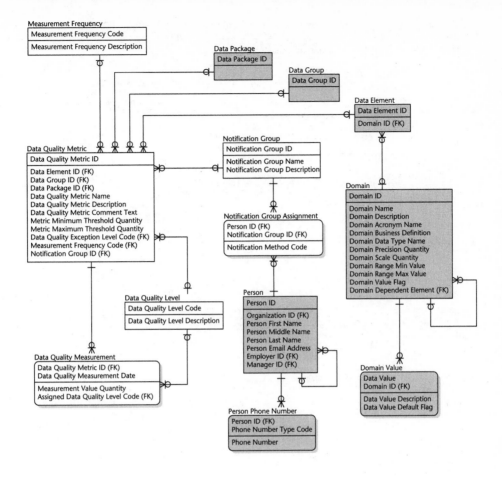

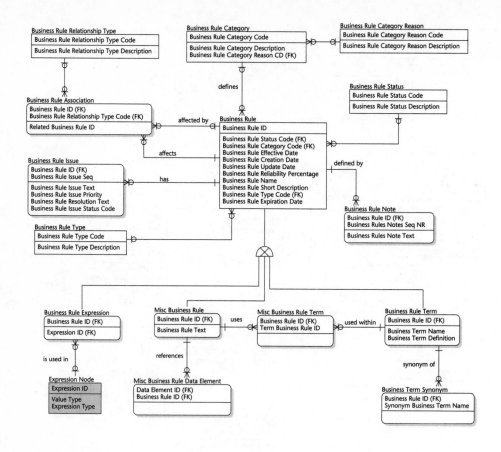

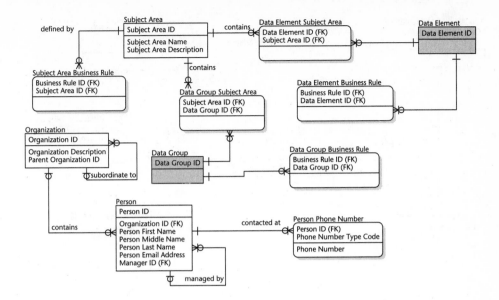

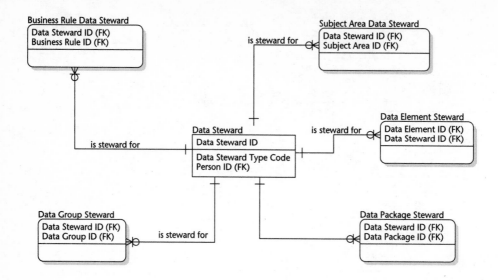

Business Rule Data Steward
Data Steward ID (FK)
Business Rule ID (FK)

Subject Area Data Steward
Data Steward ID (FK)
Subject Area ID (FK)

is steward for

Data Element Steward
Data Element ID (FK)
Data Steward ID (FK)

is steward for

is steward for

Data Steward
Data Steward ID
Data Steward Type Code
Person ID (FK)

is steward for

Data Group Steward
Data Steward ID (FK)
Data Group ID (FK)

is steward for

Data Package Steward
Data Steward ID (FK)
Data Package ID (FK)

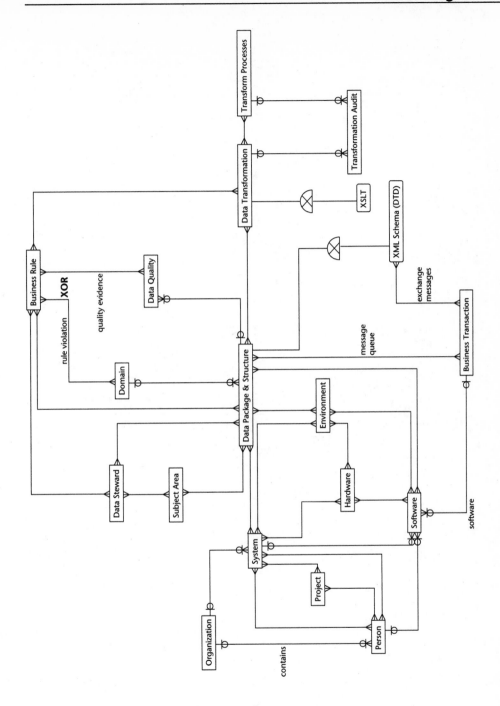

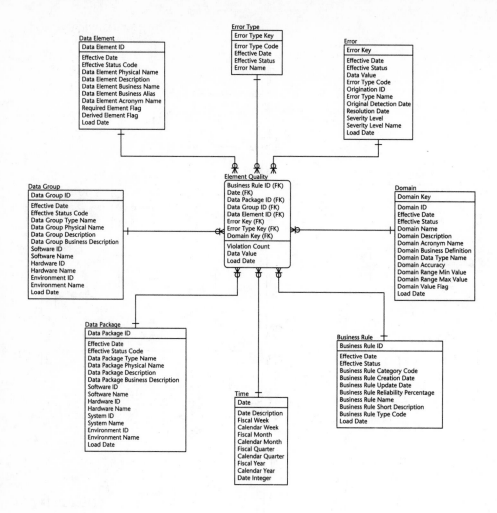

Error Type

Error Type Key

Error Type Code
Effective Date
Effective Status
Error Name

Data Element

Data Element ID

Effective Date
Effective Status Code
Data Element Physical Name
Data Element Description
Data Element Business Name
Data Element Business Alias
Data Element Acronym Name
Required Element Flag
Derived Element Flag
Load Date

Error

Error Key

Effective Date
Effective Status
Data Value
Error Type Code
Origination ID
Error Type Name
Original Detection Date
Resolution Date
Severity Level
Severity Level Name
Load Date

Data Group

Data Group ID

Effective Date
Effective Status Code
Data Group Type Name
Data Group Physical Name
Data Group Description
Data Group Business Description
Software ID
Software Name
Hardware ID
Hardware Name
Environment ID
Environment Name
Load Date

Element Quality

Business Rule ID (FK)
Date (FK)
Data Package ID (FK)
Data Group ID (FK)
Data Element ID (FK)
Error Key (FK)
Error Type Key (FK)
Domain Key (FK)

Violation Count
Data Value
Load Date

Domain

Domain Key

Domain ID
Effective Date
Effective Status
Domain Name
Domain Description
Domain Acronym Name
Domain Business Definition
Domain Data Type Name
Domain Accuracy
Domain Range Min Value
Domain Range Max Value
Domain Value Flag
Load Date

Data Package

Data Package ID

Effective Date
Effective Status Code
Data Package Type Name
Data Package Physical Name
Data Package Description
Data Package Business Description
Software ID
Software Name
Hardware ID
Hardware Name
System ID
System Name
Environment ID
Environment Name
Load Date

Business Rule

Business Rule ID

Effective Date
Effective Status
Business Rule Category Code
Business Rule Creation Date
Business Rule Update Date
Business Rule Reliability Percentage
Business Rule Name
Business Rule Short Description
Business Rule Type Code
Load Date

Time

Date

Date Description
Fiscal Week
Calendar Week
Fiscal Month
Calendar Month
Fiscal Quarter
Calendar Quarter
Fiscal Year
Calendar Year
Date Integer

What's on the CD-ROM?

This appendix provides you with information on the contents of the CD that accompanies this book. For the latest and greatest information, please refer to the ReadMe file located at the root of the CD. Here is what you will find:

- System requirements
- Using the CD with Windows
- What's on the CD
- Troubleshooting

System Requirements

Make sure that your computer meets the minimum system requirements listed in this section. If your computer doesn't match up to most of these requirements, you may have a problem using the contents of the CD.

For Windows 9x, Windows 2000, Windows NT4 (with SP 4 or later), Windows Me, or Windows XP:

- PC with a Pentium processor running at 300 MHz or faster
- At least 64 MB of total RAM installed on your computer; for best performance, we recommend at least 128 MB

- Ethernet network interface card (NIC) or modem with a speed of at least 56 Kbps
- A CD-ROM drive
- Computer Associates Erwin Data Modeler version 3.5.2 or higher (optional to open/read .ER1 files)
- Cognos Powerplay version 7.*x* or higher (optional to open/read .MDC, .MDL, & .PPR files)

Using the CD with Windows

To install the items from the CD to your hard drive, follow these steps:

1. Insert the CD into your computer's CD-ROM drive.
2. A window will appear with the following options:

   Install: Gives you the option to install the supplied software and/or the author-created samples on the CD-ROM.

   Explore: Allows you to view the contents of the CD-ROM in its directory structure.

   Exit: Closes the autorun window.

If you do not have autorun enabled or if the autorun window does not appear, follow these steps to access the CD:

1. Click Start ➪ Run.
2. In the dialog box that appears, type *d:***\setup.exe**, where *d* is the letter of your CD-ROM drive. This will bring up the autorun window described in the previous list of steps.
3. Choose the desired option from the menu. (See Step 2 in the preceding list for a description of these options.)

What's on the CD

The following sections provide a summary of the software and other materials you'll find on the CD.

Author-created Materials

All author-created material from the book, including code listings and samples, are on the CD in the folder named "Author."

Author

  Data Models

    PDF format

      Chapter 4 - Enterprise Systems.pdf

      Chapter 5 - Business Transactions Subject Area.pdf

      Chapter 5 - XML Document Classification.pdf

      Chapter 5 - XML DTD Subject Area.pdf

      Chapter 5 - XML Schema Subject Area.pdf

      Chapter 5 - XSLT Subject Area.pdf

      Chapter 6 - Data Quality Management Subject Area.pdf

      Chapter 6 - Hardware and Network Management Subject Area.pdf

      Chapter 6 - Project Portfolio Management Subject Area.pdf

      Chapter 6 - Service Management Subject Area.pdf

      Chapter 6 - Software Management Subject Area.pdf

      Chapter 7 - Business Data Subject Area.pdf

      Chapter 7 - Business Rule Subject Area.pdf

      Chapter 7 - Data Steward Subject Area.pdf

      Chapter 8 - Complete Universal Meta Model.pdf

      Chapter 8 - Meta Data Mart Model.pdf

  ERwin format

      Chapter 4 - Enterprise Systems.ER1

      Chapter 5 - Business Transactions Subject Area.ER1

      Chapter 5 - XML Document Classification.ER1

      Chapter 5 - XML DTD Subject Area.ER1

      Chapter 5 - XML Schema Subject Area.ER1

      Chapter 5 - XSLT Subject Area.ER1

      Chapter 6 - Data Quality Management Subject Area.ER1

      Chapter 6 - Hardware and Network Management Subject Area.ER1

      Chapter 6 - Project Portfolio Management Subject Area.ER1

      Chapter 6 - Service Management Subject Area.ER1

      Chapter 6 - Software Management Subject Area.ER1

      Chapter 7 - Business Data Subject Area.ER1

      Chapter 7 - Business Rule Subject Area.ER1

Chapter 7 - Data Steward Subject Area.ER1

Chapter 8 - Complete Universal Meta Model.ER1

Chapter 8 - Meta Data Mart Model.ER1

Meta Data Mart

BookModel.mdl - (Cognos Powerplay model of Meta Data Mart from Chapter 8)

BookReport.ppr - (Cognos Powerplay model view of Meta Data Mart from Chapter 8)

Business_Rule.csv - (Data file of Business Rule dimension)

cube_design.mdc - (Cognos Powerplay cube of Meta Data Mart from Chapter 8)

Data Element Dim.csv - (Data file of Data Element dimension)

Data Group.csv - (Data file of Data Group dimension)

Data_Package.csv - (Data file of Data Package dimension)

Domain.csv - (Data file of Domain dimension)

Error.csv - (Data file of Error dimension)

Error_Type.csv - (Data file of Error Type dimension)

Fact.csv - (Data file of Fact table)

Origination.csv - (Data file of Origination dimension)

Time.csv - (Data file of Time dimension)

Applications

The following applications are included on the CD:

- **Adobe® Reader®.** Free software for viewing and printing (PDF) files. Created from applications like Adobe Acrobat, Adobe Photoshop® Album and more, Adobe PDF files can be viewed on most major operating systems. For more information, check out www.acrobat.com

- **AllFusion ERwin Data Modeler.** AllFusion ™ ERwin® Data Modeler, the industry-leading data modeling solution, enables organizations to effectively design, implement, and maintain high-quality databases, data warehouses, and enterprise data models. For more information, check out www.ca.com.

Shareware programs are fully functional, trial versions of copyrighted programs. If you like particular programs, register with their authors for a nominal fee and receive licenses, enhanced versions, and technical support. *Freeware programs* are copyrighted games, applications, and utilities that are free for personal use. Unlike shareware, these programs do not require a fee or provide technical support. *GNU software* is governed by its own license, which is included inside the folder of the GNU product. See the GNU license for more details.

Trial, demo, or evaluation versions are usually limited by either time or functionality (for example you may be unable to save projects). Some trial versions are very sensitive to system date changes. If you alter your computer's date, the programs will "time out" and will no longer be functional.

Troubleshooting

If you have difficulty installing or using any of the materials on the companion CD, try the following solutions:

- **Turn off any antivirus software that you may have running.** Installers sometimes mimic virus activity and can make your computer incorrectly believe that it is being infected by a virus. (Be sure to turn the antivirus software back on later.)

- **Close all running programs.** The more programs you're running, the less memory is available to other programs. Installers also typically update files and programs; if you keep other programs running, installation may not work properly.

- **Refer to the ReadMe.** Please refer to the ReadMe file located at the root of the CD-ROM for the latest product information at the time of publication.

If you still have trouble with the CD-ROM, please call the Wiley Product Technical Support phone number: (800) 762-2974. Outside the United States, call 1(317) 572-3994. You can also contact Wiley Product Technical Support at http://www.wiley.com/techsupport. Wiley Publishing will provide technical support only for installation and other general quality control items; for technical support on the applications themselves, consult the program's vendor or author.

To place additional orders or to request information about other Wiley products, please call (800) 225-5945.

Glossary

24x7 operation   This refers to an application that is always operational: 24 hours a day, 7 days a week.

Acronym   A word formed from the initial letters of a name; a combination of letters used to represent a series of words.

ActiveX   A Microsoft standard for computer application components.

Ad hoc   A query or analysis that is nonrecurring or random.

ADE (application development environment)   A programming language or environment used to develop applications to solve business problems.

Agent Technology   Event-driven software that is structurally invisible to the business user and is always active.

Aggregate   The summing of data from one or more data sources or dimensions to create a new fact table.

Aggregation   An aggregation (or summary) is usually a sum, count, or average of underlying detailed transactions or data from one or more tables. Aggregations tend to be calculated along logical business dimensions for example, sales by product by region).

Analytics   All programming that analyzes data about an enterprise and presents it so that better and quicker business decisions can be made. Analytics can be considered a form of online analytical processing (OLAP) and may employ data mining.

API (application programming interface)   A reference provided by software developers to facilitate other computer applications in communicating with their application.

Artificial intelligence (AI)   The process of programming a computer to mimic human intelligence.

ASCII (American Standard for Computer Information Interchange) A format for data storage and transmission commonly referred to as *text* format.

ATM (Asynchronous Transfer Mode)   A packet-based switched point-to-point data transmission protocol capable of transmitting data, voice, video, and audio simultaneously at very high speeds.

Atomic data   Data elements that represent the lowest level of detail. For example, in a daily sales report, the individual items sold would be atomic data, while rollups such as invoice and summary totals from invoices would be aggregate data.

Attribute   Contributes to the description of the entity of which they are associated. They are classified as identifiers or descriptors. Identifiers, usually named keys, uniquely identify an instance of an entity. A descriptor describes a nonunique characteristic of an entity.

Backbone   A high-speed network used to connect servers, mainframes, storage devices, and network routing and switching equipment.

Bandwidth   A measurement of throughput rates. Usually used in conjunction with measuring network transmission speed.

Batch   A computer application that runs in a sequential series of processing steps that does require interaction with a user.

Bit   One unit of binary information. A bit represents a one or a zero.

Bitmap indexing   An efficient method for data indexing whereby almost all of the operations on database records can be performed on the indices without resorting to looking at the actual data underneath. By performing operations primarily on indices, the number of database reads is reduced significantly.

Bottom up   A data warehouse strategy based on first building incremental architected data marts to test products, methodologies and designs, then using those data marts to justify the construction of an enterprise data warehouse.

BPR (business process reengineering   The process for analyzing and redesigning business processes and associated application systems.

Browsers   Browsers are *thin* client applications that are used to navigate and access the World Wide Web (WWW) and/or intranets. In addition, these are the tools of choice for data warehouse/data mart users for accessing and navigating the decision support information and meta data.

Business case (or business driver)   The business problem, situation, or opportunity that justifies the pursuit of a technology project.

Business intelligence (BI)   A broad category of applications and technologies for gathering, storing, analyzing, and providing access to data to help enterprise users make better business decisions. BI applications include decision support systems, query and reporting, Online Analytical Processing (OLAP), statistical analysis, forecasting, and data mining.

Business rules   The logic applied to calculate or otherwise derive a business-related value.

Byte   A byte is 8 bits of information.

Cardinality   The notation used to describe the connection between modeled entities that indicates how many of one type of business object can be related to the other business object.

CASE (computer-aided software engineering)   A software application that automates the process of designing databases, designing applications, and implementing software.

CDC (change data capture)   The process of identifying and segmenting the changed incremental data generated from an OLTP system for a defined time period.

CDIF (CASE data interchange format)   A standards effort that attempted to tackle the problem of defining meta models for specific CASE tool subject areas by means of an object-oriented entity relationship modeling technique.

CGI (Common Gateway Interface)   A standard protocol for communication between a Web server and a database server.

Change data capture   The process of identifying and/or segmenting the incremental data generated from an OLTP system over a given time period.

Client/server system   A software application where the processing of the application is provided jointly by components that are separated: the client and the server. A client computer communicates over a network to exchange data with a server computer that accesses a database.

COBOL (Common Business Oriented Language)   A high-level, third generation programming language based on English, that is used primarily for business applications.

Clustering   The act of requiring physical database tables to reside physically next to each other on a storage media. This allows sequential prefetching to produce significant performance gains when accessing a large number of rows.

Clusters   A grouping of interconnected SMP machines with the work partitioned across them.

Conceptual schema   A descriptive representation of data and data requirements that supports the *logical* view or data administrator's view of the data requirement. This view is represented as a semantic model of the information that is stored about objects of interest to the functional area. This view is an integrated definition of the data that is unbiased toward any single application of data and is independent of how the data is physically stored or accessed.

CPU (central processing unit)   A processor that contains the sequencing and processing facilities for instruction execution, interruption action, timing functions, initial program loading, and other machine-related functions.

DASD (direct access storage device)   Disk drives, which are data storage devices that record information.

Data A representation of facts, concepts, or instructions in a formalized manner suitable for communication, interpretation, or processing by humans or by automatic means.

Data architecture The framework for organizing and defining the inter-relationships of data in support of an organization's missions, functions, goals, objectives, and strategies.

Data cleansing or scrubbing The correction of errors and omissions in data extracted from a source system. This typically involves removing errors in source data before attempting to load it into the data ware-house.

Data cube A proprietary data structure used to store data for an OLAP end-user data access and analysis tool.

Data dictionary A cross-reference of definitions and specifications for data categories and their relationships. A subset of an MME.

Data element A specific item of information. The smallest unit of information.

Data group A combination of data elements that represents a complete set of information or business transaction.

Data integrity The condition that exists as long as accidental or inten-tional destruction, alteration, or loss of data does not occur.

Data mapping The process of assigning a source data element to a target data element.

Data marts A set of data designed and constructed for optimal decision support end-user access. Data marts can be sourced from a data ware-house (dependent or architected data marts) or sourced directly from legacy systems (independent data marts).

Data mining The process of examining large sets of detail data to arrive at unknown relationships, trends, and projections of future outcomes.

Data model In a database, the user's logical view of the data in contrast to the physically stored data, or storage structure. A description of the organization of data in a manner that reflects the information structure of an enterprise.

Data modeling   The activity of representing data and its relationships in diagram form.

Data package   A collection of information organized to accomplish a business function in the enterprise. The data package defines the data groups, data elements, and relationships between these items.

Data pivot   A process of rotating the view of data.

Data propagation/replication   The process of transmitting a copy of the data inside tables in a database to another remotely connected database. This process keeps the two databases synchronized when data changes.

Data quality   The correctness, timeliness, accuracy, completeness, relevance, and accessibility that make data appropriate for use.

Data refreshing   The process of continuously updating the data warehouse's contents from its data sources. In addition, depending on the archive criteria, the current data warehouse data will be archived for historical purposes.

Data scrubbing   The process of filtering, merging, decoding, and translating source data to create validated data for the data warehouse.

Data security   The protection of data from accidental or intentional modification or destruction and from accidental or intentional disclosure to unauthorized personnel.

Data warehouse architecture   An integrated set of products that enable the extraction and transformation of operational data to be loaded into a database for end-user analysis and reporting.

Data warehouse infrastructure   A combination of technologies and the interaction of technologies that support a data warehousing environment.

Data visualization   The process of displaying data in a graphical form (that is, pie charts, scatter charts, bar graphs, and so on) to ease analysis.

Data warehouse   An enterprise-wide collection of data that is subject-oriented, integrated, nonvolatile, and time variant. This data is organized for end-user access and use.

Database   A collection of interrelated data stored together with controlled redundancy according to a schema to serve one or more applications.

Database administrator (DBA)   An individual responsible for the design, development, operation, safeguarding, maintenance, and use of a database.

Database schema   The logical and physical definition of a database structure.

Decision support system (DSS)   A computer application that contains data sets used to help business users with strategic planning and business-related decisions.

Delta   The difference between two values.

Denormalized   A data storage design that merges all related data into as few tables as possible.

Derived data   Data that results from calculations or processing applied by the data warehouse to incoming source data.

Detail fact table   A table used in a star schema used to store the detailed transaction-level data.

Dimension tables   A table used in a star schema to store descriptive, hierarchical, and metric information about an aspect of the business that is used for an analytical perspective (for example, time, product, and customer).

Disaster recovery   The policies and plans used to restore a computer system after system failure.

Domain   A method of identifying and grouping types of data for the standardization and maintenance of business and technical meta data.

Drill-down   The activity of exposing progressively more detail by making selections of items in a report or query, usually by navigating a dimensional hierarchy.

DSS   See *Decision support system.*

EAI   Describes specifics about the enterprise application integration (EAI)-based utility used to perform data transformations, carry out message routing, and provide adapters, usually associated with e-business, application integration, or Web services.

EDI (electronic data interchange)   A standard for exchanging information electronically between computer systems. Commonly used to exchange order, billing, and shipping information between corporations.

Enterprise   A complete business consisting of functions, divisions, or other components used to accomplish specific objectives and defined goals.

Enterprise architecture   High-level enterprise-wide data warehouse framework that describes the subject areas, sources, business dimensions, metrics, business rules, and semantics of an organization. It is used to identify shared sources, dimensions, metrics, and semantics in an iterative data mart or iterative subject area development methodology.

Enterprise data   Data that is defined for use across a corporate environment.

Enterprise informational portal (EIP)   A single gateway to a company's information and knowledge base for employees and possibly for customers, business partners, and the public, as well.

Enterprise resource planning (ERP)   ERP systems comprise software programs that tie together all of an enterprise's various functions—such as finance, manufacturing, sales, and human resources. This software also provides for the analysis of the data from these areas to plan production, forecast sales, and analyze quality.

Entity   A data type in the high-level overview is modeled as an entity in an entity-relationship diagram (E/RD) to represent a real-world data type.

ER (entity-relationship) model   A type of database design used to identify the topics of interest (entities) and their connections to each other (relationships).

Executive information systems (EIS)   Tools programmed to provide canned reports or briefing books to top-level executives. They offer strong reporting and drill-down capabilities. Today these tools allow ad hoc querying against a multidimensional database, and most offer analytical applications along functional lines such as sales or financial analysis.

Extensible Markup Language   See XML.

Extract frequency   The latency of data extracts, such as daily, weekly, monthly, quarterly, and so on. The frequency with which data extracts are needed in the data warehouse is determined by the shortest frequency requested through an order, or by the frequency required to maintain the consistency of the other associated data types in the source data warehouse.

ETL (extraction, transformation, and load)   Three separate functions that are typically combined into a single programming tool. First, the extract function reads data from a specified source database and extracts a desired subset of data. Next, the transform function works with the acquired data—using rules or lookup tables, or creating combinations with other data to convert the data to the desired state. Finally, the load function is used to write the resulting data (either all of the subset or just the changes) to a target database, which may or may not previously exist.

Fact table   A table used in a star schema to store the detailed measure data (usually numerical) that can be summed according to one or more dimensions or dimensional combinations.

Fat client   The client workstation manages the informational processing (business logic) as well as the graphical user interface in a client/server architecture.

FDDI (Fiber Distributed Data Interface)   A standard for light wave network physical topology devices using fiber-optic connections for high-speed data transmission.

Filters   Saved sets of chosen criteria that specify a subset of information in a data warehouse.

Firewall   A set of related programs, located at a network gateway server that protects the resources of a private network from users from other networks.

Flat file   A text document (EBCDIC on a mainframe or ASCII on non-mainframe platforms) without a structured interrelationship between its data groups and data elements.

FOCUS A reporting and system development computer application sold by Information Builders, Inc. (IBI). Focus is a popular system for the development of end-user-driven reporting systems on mainframe computer systems.

Foreign key A unique identifier used to connect a table in a relational database to another external or *foreign* table.

Fragmentation A condition in which there are many scattered areas of storage that are too small to be used productively.

Frequency The timing characteristics of the data.

Frequency of update The time period between updates of data sets in a data mart or data warehouse (for example, daily, weekly, monthly, and so on).

FTP (File Transfer Protocol) A protocol for the transfer of data files across TCP/IP networks, including the Internet and intranets.

Granularity Granularity expresses the level of detail in a data warehouse. The higher the granularity, the more detailed the data is (the higher level of abstraction).

GUI (graphical user interface) A computer system interface that uses visual pictures, graphics, controls, and icons to provide control and interaction with users.

Hardware The mechanical components of a computer or network system.

History table A table used to capture changing relationships in a decision support system. Usually used to capture slowly changing elements of a dimension table.

HTML (Hypertext Markup Language) A text-tagging protocol used to provide a uniform display of fonts, tables, and other WWW (World Wide Web) page elements on any compatible WWW browser computer application.

HTTP (Hypertext Transfer Protocol) A standard for transmitting and exchanging HTML pages.

Indexing A technique for improving database performance by improving the access method for finding and retrieving database records.

Integration   The process of combining data from multiple, nonintegrated OLTP systems to populate a data warehouse or data mart.

Internet   A worldwide system of interconnected computer networks. The Internet is built on a series of low-level protocols (HTTP, HTML, FTP) and provides easy and powerful exchange of data and information.

Intranet   A company's internal system of connected networks built on Internet standard protocols, usually connected to the Internet via a firewall.

ISDN (Integrated Services Digital Network)   An unleased digital phone line. ISDN is provided by RBOCs (regional Bell operating companies) in the United States and various phone services in other areas of the world. It is a digital standard that allows data transmission of up to 128 Kbs (kilobits per second) over standard copper twisted-pair wiring using BRI (Basic Rate Interface) service. ISDN is currently the primary way to deliver relatively high-speed data service to remote offices and homes, although it will most likely be surpassed by various quickly emerging XDSL (Digital Subscriber Line) services that offer much higher transmission rates over the same copper wire transmission medium.

JCL (Job Control Language)   A mainframe programming language used to control the execution of applications (programs).

Key attribute   An entity attribute or collection of attributes whose values uniquely identify objects belonging to the set of objects in the entity or entity set.

LAN (local area network)   A group of connected client computers and servers usually targeted to providing shared print and file storage services.

Legacy systems   Sources of historical data (the existing OLTP systems) for the data warehouse.

Logical data model   A model of data that represents the inherent structure of the data and is independent of individual applications for the data and also of the software or hardware mechanisms that are employed in representing and using the data.

Magnetic tape   A strip of plastic that has been coated with metal oxide, allowing the recording of patterns of magnetic flux, which are interpreted as the 1s and 0s that form the bits used in the computing world.

Mainframe   A large-capacity computer that offers high levels of processing power, security, and stability.

Managed meta data environment (MME)   The managed meta data environment represents the architectural components, people, and processes that are required to properly and systematically gather, retain, and disseminate meta data throughout the enterprise.

Massively parallel processor (MPP)   An interconnected group of processors with work spread over them.

Mbs (megabits per second)   One thousand kilobits per second, usually used to measure network bandwidth, or throughput rates.

MDDBMS (Multi-Dimensional Database Management System)   A database system that optimizes the storage, retrieval, and recalculation of multiple-dimension data sets. MDDBMS are commonly used to support MOLAP applications. They provide lightning fast response at the price of limited scalability and significant management overhead.

Message   An assemblage of data groups and/or data elements sent or received together between applications. Messaging uses messages to communicate with different applications to perform an operation or set of operations.

Meta data   All physical data (contained in software and other media) and knowledge (contained in employees' heads and on various media) from within and outside an organization, containing information about a company's physical data, industry, technical processes, and business processes.

Meta data repository   The physical database tables used to store meta data.

Meta model   A physical schema design engineered to store meta data.

Methodology   A procedural documentation of the steps required for the successful design, implementation, and maintenance of a data warehouse or data mart system.

Middleware   The layer that exists between the application and the underlying complexities of the network, the host operating system, and any resource servers (such as database servers). Middleware makes vastly different platforms appear the same to an application. Middleware places an easy-to-use API between the application and the resource that the application needs.

MIPS (millions of instructions per second)   A measurement of computing power. It is the measurement of the number of instructions executed by a CPU within one second.

Mission-critical system   Describes software applications that are essential to the continued operation of the enterprise. If these systems experience failure, the very viability of the enterprise is in jeopardy.

MOLAP (Multi-dimensional Online Analytical Processing)   OLAP analysis provided by a system relying on dedicated, uncalculated data sets.

MME (managed meta data environment)   See *Managed meta data environment*.

MPP (massively parallel processing)   A computing architecture that combines many CPUs with dedicated RAM and DASD resources.

Multidimensional aggregation tables   An aggregation that contains metrics calculated along multiple business dimensions (for example, sales by product by customer, over regions).

Network computer   A thin client computer platform that relies on server-resident computation, resources, data, and applications to provide computing services to users.

Network   System of interconnected computing resources (computers, servers, printers, and so on).

Network bandwidth   A measurement of the transmission speed of the interconnection medium of a network. Usually expressed in Mbs (megabits per second) (for example, 10 bms, 100 Mbs).

Normalization   The process of reducing a complex data structure to its simplest, most stable structure. In general, the process entails the removal of redundant attributes, keys, and relationships from a conceptual data model.

OLAP (Online Analytical Processing)   A computer application that allows multiple dimensional manipulation, display, and visualization of data for reporting purposes.

OLTP (Online Transaction Processing)   A computer application that automates one or more business processes (for example, order entry).

OODBs (object-oriented databases)   A database that allows the storage and retrieval of multiple data types (for example, text, video, audio, and tabular data).

Operational data store (ODS)   A set of integrated data, without history or summarization, provided for tactical decision support.

Optimizer   An element of database systems that seeks to optimize the use of the database resources and speed the retrieval of data by controlling the order of processing and the use of internal resources.

Parallel query execution   A method for improving database performance. It accomplishes this by splitting the database query into components and executing all components that can be simultaneously executed, in parallel through concurrent processes. The performance of the query is executed at the optimum speed given the data dependencies within the query.

Partition   The breaking up of data into multiple physical units. Partitioning is used to break a single table from the source into two or more tables inside the data warehouse. This is commonly done on the basis of time (for example, year-by-year partitions).

PERL (Practical Extraction and Report Language)   An interpreted programming language common in the UNIX environment.

Primary key   A portion of the first block of each record in an indexed data set that can be used to find the record in the data set.

Query   A clearly specified formal request for information from the data warehouse posed by a user.

Query tools   Software that allows a user to create and direct specific questions to a database. These tools provide the means for pulling the desired information from a database. They are typically SQL-based tools and allow a user to define data in end-user language.

RAID (redundant array of inexpensive disks)   A DASD hardware/software system that uses a series of interconnected disk drives to provide storage. RAID 1 and RAID 5 are the two most common RAID implementations in data warehousing and data marts. RAID 1 is a mirroring standard, whereby data is written to two identical disk arrays, providing full backup of information. RAID 5 involves at least one parity disk drive, which facilitates the recreation of data if a primary data storage disk fails. RAID 1 is quick, but more expensive; RAID 5 requires fewer drives, but is much slower to write information to.

RAM (random access memory)   An electronic component of computers that allows the storage of data in a very fast, read/write environment. Operating systems and applications are loaded into memory from disk, and the CPU sequentially executes them.

RDBMS (relational database management system)   A data storage system built around the relational model based on tables, columns, and views. Relational databases store data in a series of joined tables.

Recursive relationship   A relationship between data objects of a single entity.

Regression analysis   Statistical operations that help to predict the value of the dependent variable from the values of one or more independent variables.

Referential integrity   A feature of database systems that ensures that any record recorded into the database will be supported by accurate primary and foreign keys.

Relationship   A connection between two entities that mutually associates them. Relationships are denoted by their degree, connectivity, cardinality, direction, type, and existence.

Replication server   A dedicated computer system that executes a replication application.

RISC (reduced instruction set computer)   A CPU that is designed to execute a very limited set of instructions at very high speeds.

ROLAP (relational online analytical processing)   A computer application that provides OLAP functionality from data stored in a relational database.

Roll up   The process of creating higher levels of summarization or aggregation for reports and queries.

Rollout   The activity of distributing the same data warehouse solution to a larger audience than the one initially served by the first implementation. A rollout involves such concerns as how to scale the decision support system to accommodate many additional users and standardization.

Scalability   The capability of hardware and software systems to expand to accommodate future requirements.

Schema   A description or global model of the structure of a database.

Semantic layer (SL)   A GUI abstraction layer placed between the user and the technical structure of the database.

Server   A computer system connected to one or more client computers that provides file storage, printer sharing, data storage, and application execution.

Slice 'n dice   The activity of data analysis along many dimensions and across many subsets. This includes analysis of the data warehouse from the perspective of fact tables and related dimensions.

SMP (symmetrical multiprocessing)   A computer system design that utilizes multiple CPUs that share memory and DASD resources. This hardware architecture breaks up the work among multiple processors on one CPU.

Snowflake schema   An extension of the star schema design where each of the points of the star further radiates out into more points. In this form of schema, the star schema dimension tables are more normalized. The advantages provided by the snowflake schema are improvements in query performance due to minimizing disk storage for the data and improved performance as a result of joining smaller normalized tables rather than large denormalized ones. The snowflake schema also increases the flexibility of applications because of the normalization, which produces a lower granularity of the dimensions.

Software   Computer code that provides instructions to computer hardware.

Spiral development methodology   An iterative software development methodology in which software functionality is delivered in incremental stages, and improvements are identified by successful deployments of the software with tight controls but increasing functionality.

SQL (Structured Query Language)   A computer programming language used to communicate with database systems.

Staging area   A collection of data extracted from OLTP systems and provided for populating DSS systems.

Standard data element   A data element that has been approved formally in accordance with the organization's data element standardization procedures.

Star schema   A modeling technique that has a single table (fact table) in the middle of the schema connected to a number of tables (dimension tables) encircling it. The star schema design is optimized for end-user business query and reporting access. This design will contain a fact table (such as, sales, compensation, payment, or invoices) qualified by one or more dimension tables (month, product, time, and/or geographical region). The table in the center of the star is called the fact table, and the tables connecting to it in the periphery are called the dimension tables.

Subject areas   Controllable set of entities that support the overall mission of the enterprise from the perspective of a specific organizational view.

Subtype   See *Supertype*.

Supertype   A form of abstraction that denotes that two or more entities that share common attributes can be generalized into a higher level entity type called a supertype. The lower level or dependent entities are called subtypes to the supertype.

Syndicated data sources   Commercially available databases containing representative data for specific vertical markets. This information is used for market assessment and simulation of proposed business strategies. Syndicated data sources are available either as one-time database samples or as subscription services for more accurately tracking changes in the marketing environment.

System of record   An OLTP system that has been identified as the sole or primary source for a target data warehousing or data mart field.

T1/DS1   A dedicated, leased digital phone line capable of speeds of 1.544 Mbs (megabits per second).

T3/DS3   A dedicated, leased digital phone line capable of speeds of 45 Mbs (megabits per second).

TCP/IP (Transmission Control Protocol/Internet Protocol)   A networking standard that forms the basis for the Internet.

Thick client   The client workstation manages the informational processing (business logic), as well as providing the graphical user interface, in a client/server architecture.

Thin client   The client workstation principally manages the graphical user interface, while the server handles the informational processing (business logic), in a client/server architecture.

Top down   A data warehouse and data mart development method in which the enterprise data warehouse is constructed first, then all dependent data marts are sourced off it.

Topology   A description or representation of the physical devices and connections in a computer or network system.

Transaction   A unit of work acted upon by a data application to create, modify, or delete business data. Each transaction represents a single-valued fact describing a single business event.

Transformation engine   A computer application that transforms data dynamically via a direct connection to the source system and a direct load of the target system.

UNIX   A multiuser, multitasking operating system.

URL (Uniform Resource Locator)   An Internet standard for providing addressing information for WWW (World Wide Web) pages.

Value   An instance of an attribute.

Verification mode   A data analysis technique whereby a hypothesis is created and then the contents of the data warehouse are used to verify its accuracy.

VLDB (very large database)   A database containing a very large amount of data.

WAN (wide area network)   A network system that connects LANs.

Waterfall development methodology   A methodology that mandates that every step of the development process be fully completed before moving on to the subsequent step. A waterfall methodology is not appropriate for data warehouses or data marts because this approach is very slow.

WWW (World Wide Web)   A global selection of HTML pages made available by the Internet.

XML (Extensible Markup Language)   XML is a specification developed by the W3C for defining, transmitting, validating, and interpreting document formats used by various applications and organizations.

Recommended Reading

Adelman, Sid. 2002. *Impossible Data Warehouse Situations* (2002). Boston, MA: Addison-Wesley Professional.

Adelman, Sid and Moss, Larissa T. 2000. *Data Warehouse Project Management*. Boston, MA: Addison-Wesley Publishing Company.

Hoberman, Steve. 2002. *Data Modeler's Workbench*. New York, NY: Wiley Publishing, Inc.

Imhoff, Claudia; Loftis, Lisa and Geiger, Jonathan G. 2001. *Building the Customer-Centric Enterprise: Data Warehousing Techniques for Supporting Customer Relationship Management*. New York, NY: Wiley Publishing, Inc.

Inmon, W. H. 2002. *Building the Data Warehouse, Third Edition*. New York, NY: Wiley Publishing, Inc.

Kimball, Ralph and Ross, Margy. 2002. *The Data Warehouse Toolkit: The Complete Guide to Dimensional Modeling*, Second Edition. New York, NY: Wiley Publishing, Inc.

Marco, David. 2000. *Building and Managing the Meta Data Repository*. New York, NY: Wiley Publishing, Inc.

Poole, John; Chang, Dan; Tolbert, Douglas and Mellor, David. 2002. *Common Warehouse Metamodel: An Introduction to the Standard for Data Warehouse Integration*. New York, NY: John Wiley & Sons.

Poole, John; Chang, Dan; Tolbert, Douglas and Mellor, David. 2003. *Common Warehouse Metamodel Developer's Guide*. Indianapolis, IN: Wiley Publishing, Inc.

von Halle, Barbara. 2001. *Business Rules Applied: Building Better Systems Using the Business Rules Approach*. New York, NY: Wiley Publishing, Inc.

www.EWSolutions.com features *Real-World Decision Support*, which is a free, quarterly electronic newsletter dedicated to business intelligence and data warehousing. The site also contains a large number of metadata-related articles. The archives are available.

Index

Wiley Publishing, Inc.
End-User License Agreement

READ THIS. You should carefully read these terms and conditions before opening the software packet(s) included with this book "Book". This is a license agreement "Agreement" between you and Wiley Publishing, Inc."WPI". By opening the accompanying software packet(s), you acknowledge that you have read and accept the following terms and conditions. If you do not agree and do not want to be bound by such terms and conditions, promptly return the Book and the unopened software packet(s) to the place you obtained them for a full refund.

1. **License Grant.** WPI grants to you (either an individual or entity) a nonexclusive license to use one copy of the enclosed software program(s) (collectively, the "Software" solely for your own personal or business purposes on a single computer (whether a standard computer or a workstation component of a multi-user network). The Software is in use on a computer when it is loaded into temporary memory (RAM) or installed into permanent memory (hard disk, CD-ROM, or other storage device). WPI reserves all rights not expressly granted herein.

2. **Ownership.** WPI is the owner of all right, title, and interest, including copyright, in and to the compilation of the Software recorded on the disk(s) or CD-ROM "Software Media". Copyright to the individual programs recorded on the Software Media is owned by the author or other authorized copyright owner of each program. Ownership of the Software and all proprietary rights relating thereto remain with WPI and its licensers.

3. **Restrictions On Use and Transfer.**

   (a) You may only (i) make one copy of the Software for backup or archival purposes, or (ii) transfer the Software to a single hard disk, provided that you keep the original for backup or archival purposes. You may not (i) rent or lease the Software, (ii) copy or reproduce the Software through a LAN or other network system or through any computer subscriber system or bulletin- board system, or (iii) modify, adapt, or create derivative works based on the Software.

   (b) You may not reverse engineer, decompile, or disassemble the Software. You may transfer the Software and user documentation on a permanent basis, provided that the transferee agrees to accept the terms and conditions of this Agreement and you retain no copies. If the Software is an update or has been updated, any transfer must include the most recent update and all prior versions.

4. **Restrictions on Use of Individual Programs.** You must follow the individual requirements and restrictions detailed for each individual program in the About the CD-ROM appendix of this Book. These limitations are also contained in the individual license agreements recorded on the Software Media. These limitations may include a requirement that after using the program for a specified period of time, the user must pay a registration fee or discontinue use. By opening the Software packet(s), you will be agreeing to abide by the licenses and restrictions for these individual programs that are detailed in the About the CD-ROM appendix and on the Software Media. None of the material on this Software Media or listed in this Book may ever be redistributed, in original or modified form, for commercial purposes.

5. **Limited Warranty.**

   (a) WPI warrants that the Software and Software Media are free from defects in materials and workmanship under normal use for a period of sixty (60) days from the date of purchase of this Book. If WPI receives notification within the warranty period of defects in materials or workmanship, WPI will replace the defective Software Media.

(b) WPI AND THE AUTHOR OF THE BOOK DISCLAIM ALL OTHER WARRANTIES, EXPRESS OR IMPLIED, INCLUDING WITHOUT LIMITATION IMPLIED WARRANTIES OF MERCHANTABILITY AND FITNESS FOR A PARTICULAR PURPOSE, WITH RESPECT TO THE SOFTWARE, THE PROGRAMS, THE SOURCE CODE CONTAINED THEREIN, AND/OR THE TECHNIQUES DESCRIBED IN THIS BOOK. WPI DOES NOT WARRANT THAT THE FUNCTIONS CONTAINED IN THE SOFTWARE WILL MEET YOUR REQUIREMENTS OR THAT THE OPERATION OF THE SOFTWARE WILL BE ERROR FREE.

(c) This limited warranty gives you specific legal rights, and you may have other rights that vary from jurisdiction to jurisdiction.

6. **Remedies.**

    (a) WPI's entire liability and your exclusive remedy for defects in materials and workmanship shall be limited to replacement of the Software Media, which may be returned to WPI with a copy of your receipt at the following address: Software Media Fulfillment Department, Attn.: Universal Meta Data Models. Wiley Publishing, Inc., 10475 Crosspoint Blvd., Indianapolis, IN 46256, or call 1-800-762-2974. Please allow four to six weeks for delivery. This Limited Warranty is void if failure of the Software Media has resulted from accident, abuse, or misapplication. Any replacement Software Media will be warranted for the remainder of the original warranty period or thirty (30) days, whichever is longer.

    (b) In no event shall WPI or the author be liable for any damages whatsoever (including without limitation damages for loss of business profits, business interruption, loss of business information, or any other pecuniary loss) arising from the use of or inability to use the Book or the Software, even if WPI has been advised of the possibility of such damages.

    (c) Because some jurisdictions do not allow the exclusion or limitation of liability for consequential or incidental damages, the above limitation or exclusion may not apply to you.

7. **U.S. Government Restricted Rights.** Use, duplication, or disclosure of the Software for or on behalf of the United States of America, its agencies and/or instrumentalities "U.S. Government" is subject to restrictions as stated in paragraph (c)(1)(ii) of the Rights in Technical Data and Computer Software clause of DFARS 252.227-7013, or subparagraphs (c) (1) and (2) of the Commercial Computer Software - Restricted Rights clause at FAR 52.227-19, and in similar clauses in the NASA FAR supplement, as applicable.

8. **General.** This Agreement constitutes the entire understanding of the parties and revokes and supersedes all prior agreements, oral or written, between them and may not be modified or amended except in a writing signed by both parties hereto that specifically refers to this Agreement. This Agreement shall take precedence over any other documents that may be in conflict herewith. If any one or more provisions contained in this Agreement are held by any court or tribunal to be invalid, illegal, or otherwise unenforceable, each and every other provision shall remain in full force and effect.